Praise for *At the Bridge*

"At first blush this is a biography of James Teit, whose life has been overshadowed by others in American anthropology. But it is so much more. It is a political history of the Pacific Northwest, an account of organizing against the iron fist of Canadian statecraft and settler colonialism, and a rigorous account of anthropological relationships in the late nineteenth and early twentieth centuries – consensual, strategic, sometimes clearly parasitic – that made for the fields of cultural theory, museology, and social science. This book is a must-read."

AUDRA SIMPSON, professor of anthropology, Columbia University, and author of *Mohawk Interruptus: Political Life across the Borders of Settler States*

"With the verve of a gifted storyteller, the passion of a lifetime's work in the region, and immaculate research, Wickwire traces Teit's journeys between Shetland and Spences Bridge, Boasian anthropology and Indigenous forms of knowledge, northern Scots socialism and Indigenous community. This book is a timely and intimate study of the painstaking work of building cultural bridges."

ELIZABETH VIBERT, associate professor of history, University of Victoria, and author of *Traders' Tales: Narratives of Cultural Encounters in the Columbia Plateau*

"An enthralling exploration of the undervalued life and legacy of Shetland-born anthropologist James Teit. Wendy Wickwire's comprehensive biography rescues from obscurity a remarkable man whose ethnographic studies and informed political activism for Indigenous rights continue to shape British Columbia's history."

MARJORY HARPER, chair in history, University of Aberdeen, and author of *Scotland No More? The Scots Who Left Scotland in the Twentieth Century*

"Wendy Wickwire's book about James Teit has been eagerly awaited in Shetland, his place of birth. The story of the modest young man who began a new life overseas and became a helpmate to the Indigenous people in his new home is inspiring and engrossing ... a tale told well."

BRIAN SMITH, archivist at the Shetland Museum and Archives and author of *Toons and Tenants: Settlement and Society in Shetland, 1299–1899*

"This is a remarkable book about a remarkable man. A must-read for anyone interested in BC's history. No one has understood what we now call truth and reconciliation better than James Teit. And Wendy Wickwire has done a magnificent job of bringing the man, his anthropology, and his dedication to Indigenous rights alive. A *tour de force.*"

HAMAR FOSTER, professor emeritus of law, University of Victoria, and author of *Let Right Be Done: Aboriginal Title, the Calder Case, and the Future of Indigenous Rights*

"As a Secwepemc, I knew of James Teit and his work, but I did not know his background or why he felt the urge to work with Indigenous people in what is now British Columbia. In *At the Bridge*, Wendy Wickwire brings Teit to life and gives him the credit he is due by vividly recounting the early history of the Indigenous struggle and of the man who became one of us. I LOVE THIS BOOK."

BEV SELLARS, former chief of the Xat'sull (Soda Creek) First Nation and author of *They Called Me Number One: Secrets and Survival at an Indian Residential School*

"James Teit spoke three Interior Salish languages, wrote several superb ethnographies, and devoted himself to Indigenous rights. Wendy Wickwire's splendid book reveals this great man – his politics, his situated anthropology, his difficult relationship with Franz Boas – as never before."

COLE HARRIS, professor emeritus of geography, University of British Columbia, and author of *Making Native Space: Colonialism, Resistance, and Reserves in British Columbia*

"Wendy Wickwire's biography of James Teit is the first comprehensive and authoritative account of this important ethnographer and political activist. This compelling book should become a classic addition to our knowledge of Indigenous-settler relations in early British Columbia."

IRA JACKNIS, senior research anthropologist, Phoebe A. Hearst Museum of Anthropology, and author of *The Storage Box of Tradition: Kwakiutl Art, Anthropologists, and Museums, 1881–1981*

At the Bridge

At the Bridge

James Teit and an Anthropology of Belonging

WENDY WICKWIRE

UBC Press • Vancouver • Toronto

28 27 26 25 24 23 22 21 20 5 4

Printed in Canada on FSC-certified ancient-forest-free paper (100% post-consumer recycled) that is processed chlorine- and acid-free.

Library and Archives Canada Cataloguing in Publication

Title: At the bridge : James Teit and an anthropology of belonging / Wendy Wickwire.

Names: Wickwire, Wendy C., author.

Description: Includes bibliographical references and index.

Identifiers: Canadiana (print) 2019008393X | Canadiana (ebook) 20190083980 | ISBN 9780774861519 (hardcover) | ISBN 9780774861526 (softcover) | ISBN 9780774861533 (PDF) | ISBN 9780774861540 (EPUB) | ISBN 9780774861557 (Kindle)

Subjects: LCSH: Teit, James Alexander, 1864-1922. | LCSH: Ethnologists – British Columbia – Biography. | LCSH: Anthropologists – British Columbia – Biography. | LCSH: Indigenous peoples – British Columbia – Social life and customs – 19th century. | CSH: Native peoples – British Columbia – Social life and customs – 19th century.

Classification: LCC GN21.T45 W53 2019 | DDC 305.80092—dc23

Canadä

UBC Press gratefully acknowledges the financial support for our publishing program of the Government of Canada (through the Canada Book Fund), the Canada Council for the Arts, and the British Columbia Arts Council.

This book has been published with the help of a grant from the Canadian Federation for the Humanities and Social Sciences, through the Awards to Scholarly Publications Program, using funds provided by the Social Sciences and Humanities Research Council of Canada.

UBC Press
The University of British Columbia
2029 West Mall
Vancouver, BC V6T 1Z2
www.ubcpress.ca

To Sigurd Teit

(1915–2002)

Contents

Illustrations

Maps

Photographs

Preface

I am here before you to-day not only as Special Agent for the Allied Tribes but also as special representative of the leading chief of the Interior Tribes. This chief for the purpose of proving that I represent him gave me one of his own names at a public meeting and gave me his medals to wear ... These medals he considers very precious. One of them is a King George the Third Medal given to his grand uncle, Chief Nicola for special services rendered to the Hudson's Bay Company, when this Company first came into the Southern Interior of British Columbia, over 100 years ago. His father in the years between 1870 and 1876 restrained the Interior Tribes from attacking the whites on account of this land trouble. Commissioner Sproat gave him credit for averting war at this time and thus saving many lives. Notwithstanding the record of this Chief and his immediate ancestors in numerous faithful acts to the British Crown and in the interests of peace in British Columbia, he and his brother are in sorrow to-day on account of what they consider to be acts of oppression against them by the Dominion Government ... Over a year ago, the Allied Tribes appointed me their special agent ... I am doing this [work] to meet the desire of the chiefs that I help them in trying to bring about a fair settlement of this long outstanding trouble.

– James Teit, Statement on behalf of the Allied Indian Tribes of British Columbia, to the Senate Standing Committee on Banking and Commerce, Ottawa, June 16, 1920

Every once in a while an important historical figure makes an appearance, makes a difference, and then disappears. This book is the story of such a figure, James Teit (1864–1922), a Shetland-born Canadian who lived and worked in Canada during a transformative time in the country's history. Arriving in British Columbia just over a decade after its entry into Confederation, Teit spent forty years as a student of the Indigenous peoples of BC, Washington, Idaho, Oregon, and Montana. This led to eleven ethnographic monographs and large collections of artifacts, field notes, plant and wildlife inventories, maps, wax-cylinder recordings, and photographs. He spent the last fifteen years of his life at the centre of an Indigenous rights campaign aimed at resolving BC's contentious land-title issue. As only a tiny fraction of the province was under treaty, the leaders of this campaign argued that, until the sovereignty issue was resolved, the settler-colonial project stood on stolen land. Despite his remarkable life and legacy, Teit was, like most "friends of the Indians" at the time, quickly blacklisted and dismissed as a "white agitator."

On June 16, 1920, Teit presented a statement on behalf of the Allied Indian Tribes of British Columbia, to the Senate Standing Committee on Banking and Commerce, which was meeting in Ottawa. He told the committee he was doing this work "to meet the desire of the chiefs that I help them in trying to bring about a fair settlement of this long outstanding trouble." In its sympathies and its contents, the statement stands as a testament to Teit's "intimate relations" with chiefs from across the province. These were tense times for the chiefs as two contentious bills were winding their way through the House of Commons and the Senate, and few of the chiefs could speak English well enough to challenge their contents. Bill 14 would allow the Department of Indian Affairs to enfranchise individual Indians by removing their status as "Indians" under the Indian Act; according to a report by an appointee of the Superintendent General of Indian Affairs, it could do so against the individual's will. Bill 13 would empower the federal government to alter the boundaries of reserve lands in British Columbia without the consent of those reserves' members. Teit, an eloquent speaker of English and a fluent speaker of three southern Interior languages, was in Ottawa with the chiefs as their "special agent" to oppose these bills.

So what is the full story of this long-standing friend of the Indians, and what were his motives for serving as a "special agent" on Parliament Hill?

I started on the trail of James Teit in the fall of 1977, and after more than three decades I have only begun to scratch the surface. Indeed, his extensive handwritten notes – on ethnobotany, linguistics, basketry, songs, storytelling, traditional clothing, hunting and fishing traditions, housing, and spiritual traditions – warrant books of their own. By the end of his life, Teit had amassed some six hundred pages of ethnobotanical notes, only a fraction of which made it into his posthumous publication on the topic. His extensive field notes on songs, all carefully linked to the singers' names, community affiliations, and photographic portraits, have never been published. His maps of Indigenous territorial boundaries and place names have yet to be fully collated and analyzed. His copious notes on the hundreds of handmade items – buckskin dresses, baskets, fishing nets, bows, arrows, snowshoes – in museums across the continent have never been systematically analyzed. Indeed, the western designation "renaissance man" (apart from its obvious colonial connotations) does not begin to do justice to the scope of James Teit's creativity, productivity, and insight.

On Terminology

Some of the terms used in this book, most notably the term "Indian," require an explanation. As British historian Catherine Hall points out in her study of "metropole and colony in the English imagination, 1830–1867," it is important, when drawing from nineteenth-century settler-colonial discourse, to consider all racialized labels as social constructs with "historically located and discursively specific meanings."[1] In the North American context, the term "Indian" has a long settler-colonial lineage that covers a wide geographical expanse.

During the time frame of this study – 1880s to 1920s – the Indigenous peoples across British Columbia had many collective names for themselves and their neighbours. Having endured decades of life under settler colonialism, they also had multiple names for newcomers. Due to linguistic and cultural barriers, these two sets of names remained largely in-house. Such was not the case within the settler society. Over the course of the nineteenth century, its members blanketed the region with a series of racialized terms such as "Indian," "Siwash," "Squaw," and "Klootchman" as they asserted sovereignty over a new land base. Some of these terms were descriptive; others were derogatory. Through the "Indian Act" of 1876, the settler society gave its most robust label, "Indian," high legal and administrative status by making it a staple of the Department of "Indian Affairs," complete with "Indian agents" and "Indian commissioners" charged with managing the affairs of "Indian reserves," "Indian tribes," and "Indian bands."

Anthropologists, linguists, archaeologists, museologists, and others added a new twist to the settler-colonial naming project when they introduced – via monograph titles, photograph captions, film scripts, and museum displays – a string of anglicized and regionally focused terms such as "Nootka" Indians, "Shuswap" Indians, "Lillooet" Indians, "Kootenay" Indians, "Beaver" Indians, "Carrier" Indians, and "Kwakiutl" Indians. These terms dominated until the 1980s, when a new generation of Indigenous leaders, scholars, and artists replaced them with their own original names. Among the first to make this change were the "Thompson Indians" of south central British Columbia, who argued that their assigned name, "Thompson," was not only wrong ("Thompson" was an anglicized name introduced by the fur traders) but misleading, as their territory included the Fraser River, Coldwater River, and Nicola River watersheds as well as the Thompson River watershed. They promptly replaced "Thompson" with Nlaka'pamux (roughly pronounced "In-kla-KAP-muh"). Within a decade, the name-reclamation project grew into a full-scale decolonization project: "Nootka" became Nuu-chah-nulth, "Nishga" became Nisga'a, "Beaver" became Dunne-za, "Carrier" became Dakelh, "Kootenay" became Ktunaxa, "Bella Coola" became Nuxalk, "Shuswap" became Secwépemc, "Chilcotin" became Tsilhqot'in, "Bella Bella" became Heiltsuk, and so on.

In urban settings – especially university settings – the naming project took a different turn. From the 1980s on, academics, Indigenous activists, political activists, and various international Indigenous organizations replaced the term "Indian" with an array of more inclusive terms. It began with the shift to "Native Peoples" and gradually moved on to "Aboriginal Peoples" and "First Nations." Today the accepted term is "Indigenous peoples," and it includes, in addition to "Indians," First Nation, Inuit, Innu, and Metis peoples. With the federal government's 2016 decision to replace the term "Aboriginal" with "Indigenous" in government communications, the term has gained currency across the country.[2]

In reserve communities today, "Indian" lives on as a common *self*-designation, especially among the older generations. As Ruby Dunstan, former chief of the Lytton First Nation, told me a few months ago, "As far back as I can remember, we were always called 'Indians' and today we still call ourselves 'Indians.'" She added that she and her colleagues often use the phrases "Nlaka'pamux peoples" and "First Nations" but rarely the phrase "Indigenous peoples." She also uses the old in-house term "SHA-ma" when referring to visitors like myself. It reminds me that as much as I am a friend, I am always an outsider.

My approach to such terminology is, wherever possible, to call each group by its own preferred name – i.e., Nlaka'pamux, St'at'imc, Secwépemc, and Syilx. Because the term "Indian" and the old anthropological terms (i.e., "Thompson," "Shuswap," "Lillooet," and "Okanagan") were the common terms in the documents for my time period (1880s to 1920s), I have no choice but to use them. Initially, I looked for ways to avoid the term "Indian." However, encouraged by friends in reserve communities who regularly refer to themselves as "Indians" and make no apologies for it, and others such as Grand Chief Stewart Phillip (of the Union of BC Indian Chiefs), and Thomas King (author of *The Inconvenient Indian* and *A Short History of Indians in Canada*), who make liberal use of the term in public settings, I had a change of heart. Ruby Dunstan helped me through this by urging me to think about how she and her Nlaka'pamux colleagues use the term and not to worry about it: "I see no problem with you using the term 'Indians' in your book," she explained.

Like the territorial names, many of the old family and personal names began to fade in the early decades of the twentieth century as missionaries, residential school personnel, and government agents replaced them with new anglicized names (Mary, Jane, Lucy, John, George, etc). One of Teit's first ethnographic projects at Spences Bridge was a written inventory of the Nlaka'pamux names in and around the village. Starting with Wheestim-neetsa, the chief of the Cooks Ferry Band, his final list, dated January 1893, included over one hundred names.[3] He transcribed each name according to his own phonetic system – for example, Whal-eenik, Silka-peskit, and Tsilla-gheskit. Under instruction from Franz Boas, he later applied a phonetic orthography that was more focused on grammar and lexicon. The problem was that while the new system provided more reliable data for linguistic analysis, its diacritics added a layer of incomprehensible visual clutter to the transcriptions. In some cases, the new iteration of a name was so altered that the two versions looked like different names. Wheestim-neetsa became X̲wistEmnīt′sa, Whal-eenik became X̲wElī′inEk, Silka-peskit became nsElkapês′kEt, and Tsilla-gheskit became TsElEqê′skEt. In the pages that follow, I have used Teit's 1893 transcriptions wherever possible because they allow for quick and easy access to the names. As Teit was fluent in the Nlaka'pamux language when he recorded the names, they are as close to the spoken originals as he could make them. I encourage readers to try to pronounce the names as a way to draw attention to the men and women behind them.[4] Over time, some of these people learned to write their names in English so that they could sign documents with their names rather than with X's. This was the case with Chief John Tetlanetza (roughly pronounced "Tet-lan-EET-sa"),[5] so I have used Tetlanetza's own spelling rather than the more common linguistic transcription, Tetlᴇnī′tsa.

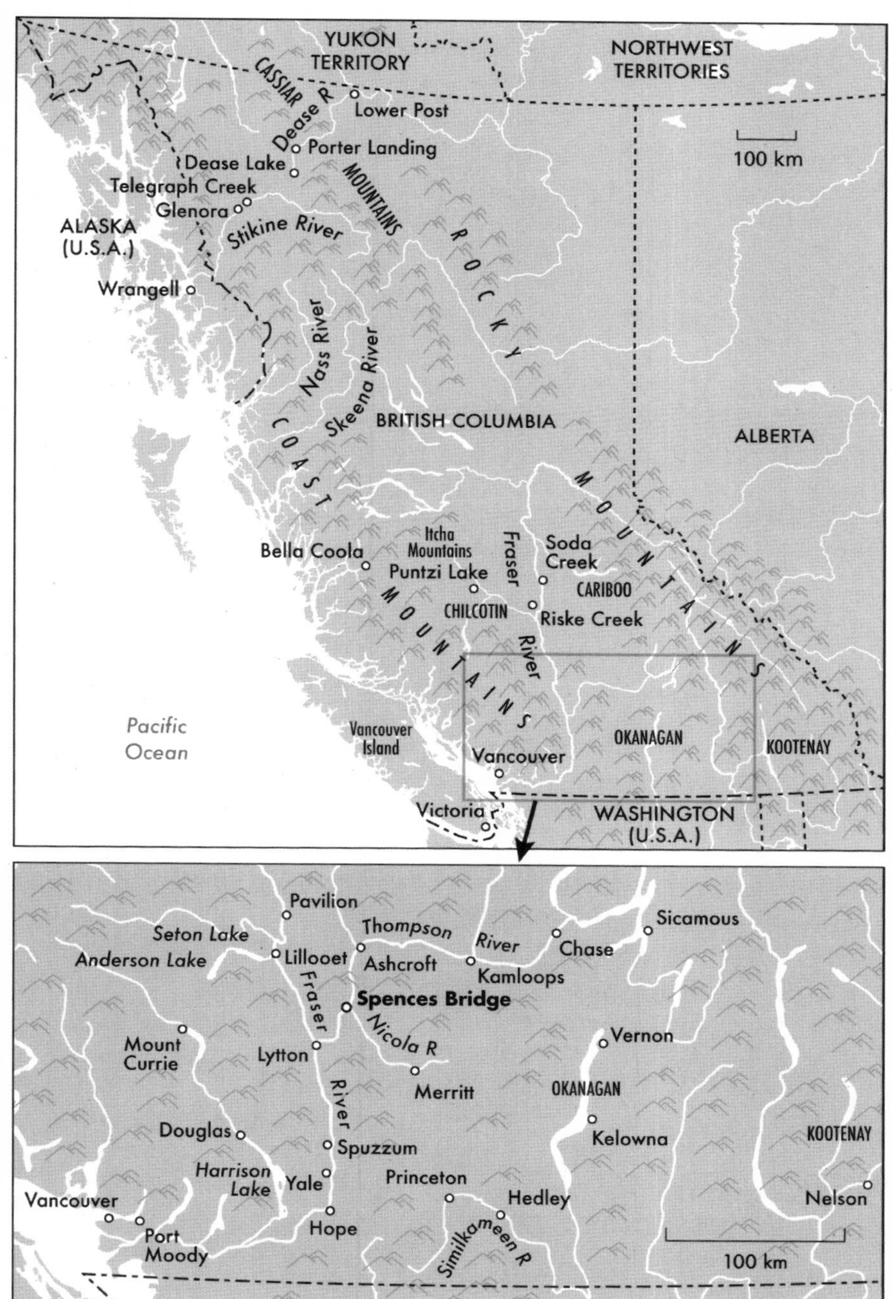

Map 1 British Columbia, with south central Interior inset. | Cartography by Eric Leinberger.

Current name (selected)	Approximate pronunciation	Name formerly used
Ktunaxa	Too-NA-ha	Kootenai, Tona'xa
Kwakwaka'wakw	Kwak-wak-ya-wak	Kwakiutl
Nisga'a	Nis-gaa	Nishga
Nlaka'pamux	In-kla-KAP-muh	Thompson
Secwépemc	She-whep-m	Shuswap
St'at'imc	Stat-liem	Lillooet
Syilx	Seelk	Okanagan
Tsek'ene	Sik-AN-ee	Sekani
Tsilhqot'in	Chil-co-teen	Chilcotin

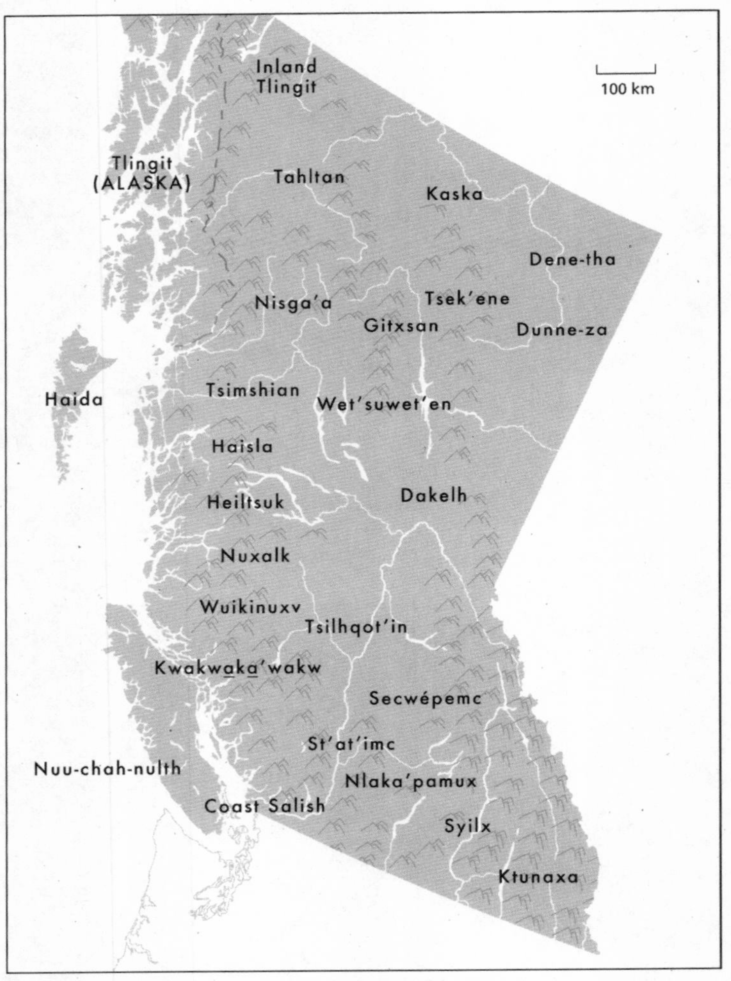

Map 2 Indigenous peoples of British Columbia. | Cartography by Eric Leinberger.

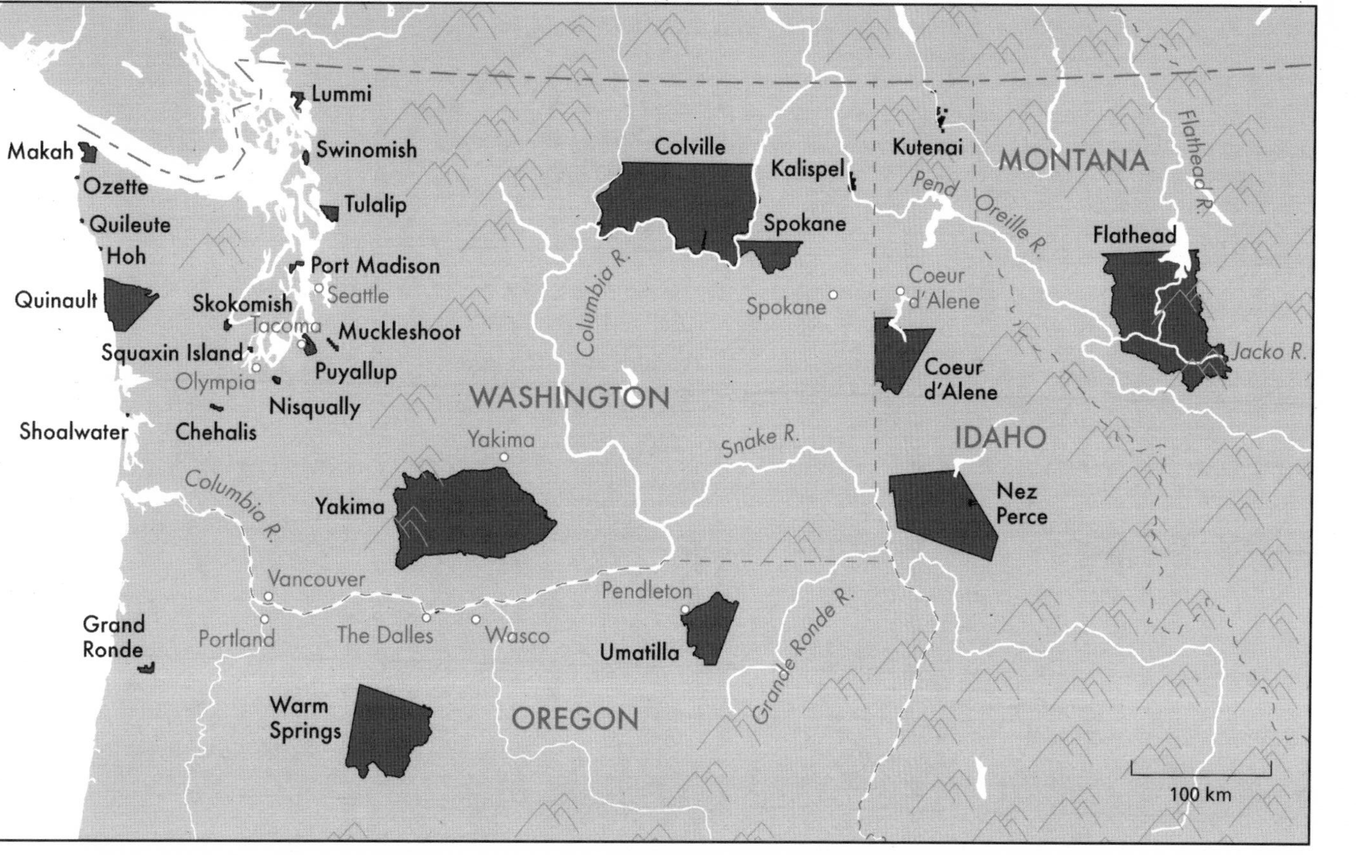

Map 3 Indian reservations in Washington, Idaho, Montana, and northern Oregon, c. 1900. | Cartography by Eric Leinberger.

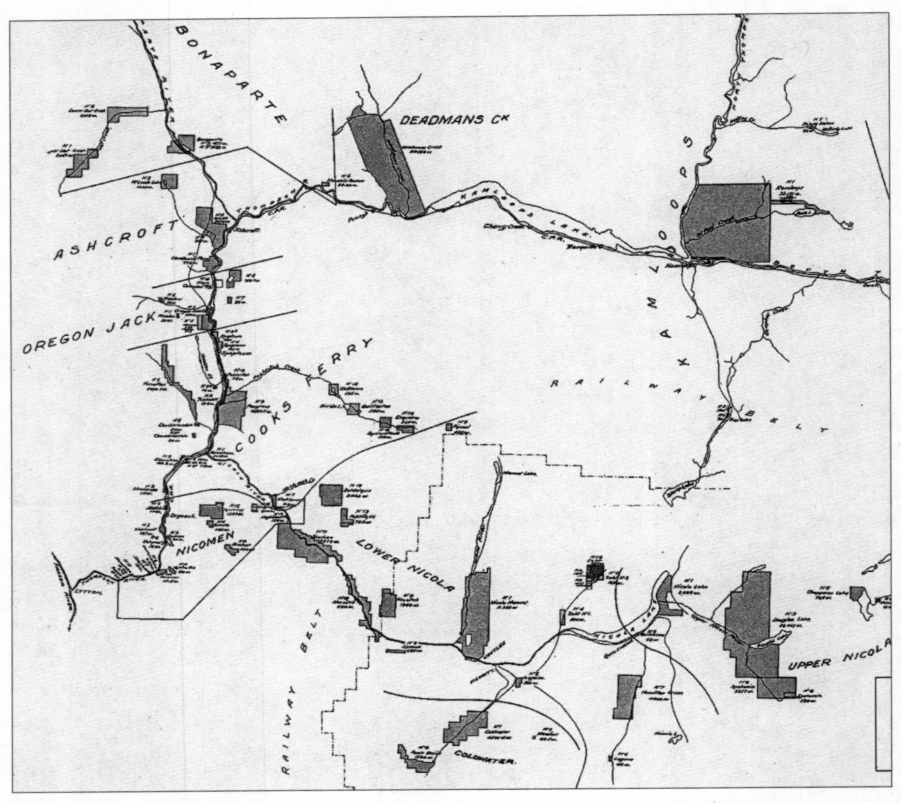

Map 4 A section of the Kamloops Indian Agency map, 1916. | "Kamloops Agency Map," in *Final Report of the Royal Commission on Indian Affairs for the Province of British Columbia* (Victoria: Acme Press, 1916), 305.

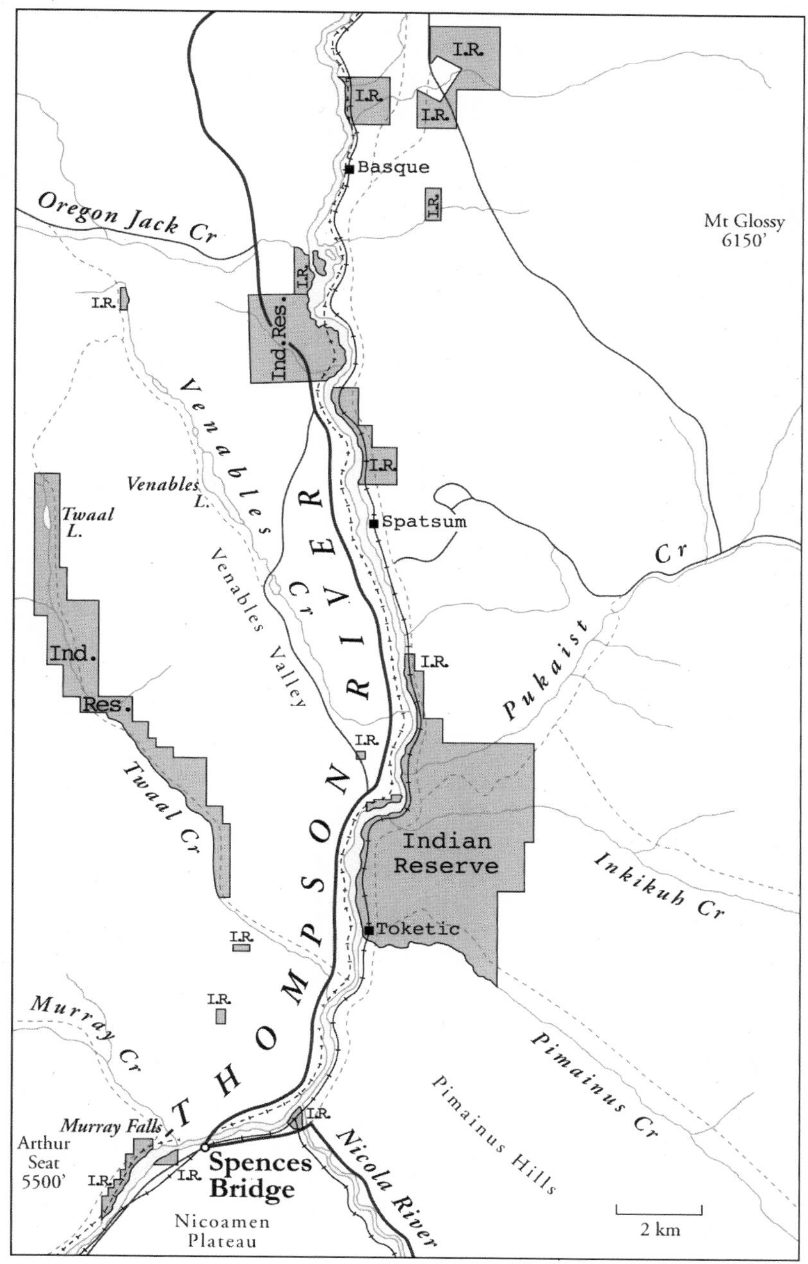

Map 5 Spences Bridge and vicinity, 1914. | Based on the map "New Westminster and Yale District," Fonds AM1594, Map 82, City of Vancouver Archives. Cartography by Eric Leinberger.

Map 1 British Columbia, with south central Interior inset.
From his home at Spences Bridge, James Teit spent close to four decades travelling, often by horse and pack train, through all of the regions noted on this map.

Map 2 Indigenous peoples of British Columbia.
Indigenous peoples are identified largely by their broadly inclusive names and within their home territories. Most of these groups now use the specific names of their nations, but due to limited space those names are not included here. For example, "Coast Salish" has been largely replaced by many localized names such as Quw'utsun' (Cowichan), Lekwungen (including Esquimalt and Songhees), W̱SÁNEĆ, Squamish, Stó:lō, Tsawwassen, and T'Sou-ke. The Kwakwa̱ka̱'wakw, Nuu-chah-nulth, and Tsimshian also have many localized names.

Map 3 Indian reservations in Washington, Idaho, Montana, and northern Oregon, c. 1900.
Between 1908 and 1910, James Teit made three two-month trips by train and stagecoach through the regions shown here. His notes and letters suggest that he relied largely on four well-travelled, well-informed, and multilingual men: Michel Revais (Pend d'Oreille/Kalispel/French Canadian) of the Flathead reservation in Montana; Peter Kalama (Nisqually/Kanaka) of the Nisqually reservation in western Washington (Kalama had also lived on the Warm Springs reservation in northern Oregon); Korotus Nicodemus (Coeur d'Alene) of the Coeur d'Alene reservation in Idaho; and Thomas McCrossan, a government agent with links to both the Colville reservation (in central Washington) and the Quinault reservation (on the coast). In his edits of Teit's reports on these groups, Franz Boas made only scant reference to these men's names and their specific contributions.

Map 4 A section of the Kamloops Indian Agency map, 1916.
The McKenna-McBride Royal Commission included a full map of the Kamloops Agency in its final report to show its recommendations for reserve cut-offs and additions. The divisions on the map – "Cooks Ferry," "Oregon Jack," "Bonaparte," and so on – were designations given by the Department of Indian Affairs. The chiefs of the divisions were John Whistemnitsa, John Tetlanetza, and Basil David, respectively. This map offers a visual representation of the land issues that the chiefs challenged at this time – their restriction to tiny reserves scattered across the territorial land base.

Map 5 Spences Bridge, 1914.
This is a redrawing of a small section of a large map published by British Columbia's Department of Lands in 1914. James Teit and his wife Antko lived on a ranch in the valley located between Twaal Creek and Venables Creek. The trail leading to the reserve in the Twaal Valley (the long, pencil-thin reserve at the far left) is indicated. Murray Creek, Arthur's Seat, and Murray Falls (named by Teit's uncle) are in the lower left corner.

At the Bridge

1
Missing in History

Only those few whites who help us ... uphold the honor of their race.

– Chiefs of the Shuswap, Couteau or Thompson, Okanagan, Lillooet, Stalo or Lower Fraser, Chilcotin, Carrier, and Tahltan Tribes in the interior of British Columbia, assembled at Spences Bridge, May 10, 1911[1]

If there is any truth to the saying that a man finishes his house and then he dies, I should worry. The house that is this book has been so all-consuming for so long that when I picture life beyond it I draw a blank. It stretches back to the summer of 1977, when I accepted a contract to transcribe audio-recordings of Syilx (Okanagan)[2] songs for the Victoria-based BC Indian Language Project.[3] With an ethnomusicology degree in progress and a new, portable Uher reel-to-reel tape recorder in hand, it seemed a good fit for my summer on the West Coast. After several weeks of trying to transfer the ever-shifting sound waves to paper, I was not so sure. The job had turned into a cumbersome task that taxed my musical ear and my patience. Many pencils and erasers later, I finished the assignment, tentatively satisfied with my sketches but frustrated with their lack of human connection.

Sensing my discomfort, my employers organized a road trip to introduce me to some singers. We left Vancouver on a hot August afternoon – a party of four that included my partner, Michael – and drove east through the lush Fraser Valley to Hope, and east again through the mountainous Allison Pass to Princeton. After a brief stop there it was on to the old gold-mining town of Hedley in the heart of the Similkameen Valley. The plan was to spend the evening with Harry Robinson, a member of the Lower Similkameen Band, and then to accompany him the next day to the Omak Stampede in central Washington State. As a Nova Scotian raised on flat, white-sand beaches and spindly pine forests, everything about the

Similkameen's topography – its big rivers and steep rock canyons, sage-covered hills and Ponderosa pine forests – looked foreign.

We pulled into Harry's driveway in the dead heat of the afternoon and found him waiting for us at the back of his house. He had spent the morning, he said, preparing various sleeping arrangements so there was no need for a motel. The scene by the back door – brooms, shovels, rakes, and carpentry tools arranged like artwork along the outside wall – spoke to his precision and preparedness. Inside, it was more of the same: photographs, calendars, and sundry items pinned to the walls, and pads of paper and writing utensils sitting neatly on an arborite table in the middle of an otherwise sparse front room. Completing this picture of orderliness was a wall-mounted Regulator clock that chimed at every quarter hour.

With our itinerary settled and our bags in their assigned spots, we chatted our way through dinner and dishes. As dusk turned to dark, the chit-chat gave way to storytelling. It started with a question as to why there were no salmon in the Similkameen River. "It's all Coyote's fault," Harry replied, and just like that, he was off – his answer an hour-long monologue about Coyote's travels along rivers, peddling salmon in exchange for wives. When the locals (Harry's distant forebears) refused to submit to Coyote's terms, Coyote retaliated by creating a dam to block the fish from passing through. Unlike the freeze-dried, sanitized, and mythologized Coyote I had encountered in published folklore collections,[4] Harry's Coyote was a rowdy, sly, and raunchy fellow. Harry called him "a bad bad boy" and chuckled like one describing a rogue relative. On our drive to Omak the next morning, he told us more stories about Coyote's antics that were etched in the unusual rock formations along our route.

The Omak Stampede was a true Wild West show, complete with a terrifying "suicide race." The race began with a shotgun blast atop Suicide Hill on the north bank of the Okanagan River. Seconds later a large cluster of horses and riders charged into view and, en masse, leapt off the cliff and dashed headlong down the steep, 100-foot slope to the river below. After splashing through the river they galloped to the finish line in the adjacent rodeo grounds, leaving one horse and its rider splayed corpse-like on the sidehill. With the race's reputation for killing many a horse and occasionally a rider, I was relieved to hear that in this case both horse and rider had survived. At the end of the day we piled into our vehicle and headed back to Hedley, with Harry regaling us with yet more Coyote stories.

The visit with Harry was more than a short diversion. As I would soon discover, the Vancouver transcription project had transported me into a new (old) world. Over the next thirteen years, I returned regularly to Harry's small bungalow, where I would sit night after night listening to a stream of stories about Coyote and the large cast of characters who inhabited his landscape. It led us to publish three volumes of his stories.[5] The transcription project also introduced me to a wide circle of Harry's contemporaries, who animated my pencil-sketches of songs in ways that I could not have imagined. As I learned months after my first encounter with Harry, another man, James Teit, had drawn these new-found friends – and their songs and stories – together with their forebears.

But back to that first road trip in 1977. After dropping off Harry, we continued on to the Head of the Lake reserve near Vernon to visit Mary Abel. I was keen to meet Mary, as she was one of the singers whose songs I had just transcribed. We intercepted her on her way to feed her cows. A short, stout woman in her mid-sixties, she greeted us with hugs and a boisterous laugh that hinted at mischief. We stayed only long enough for a cup of tea because she was busy with chores that day. On hearing that I was working on a song project, however, she invited me to come back another time.

The next morning, we drove two hours north through lush farming and ranch country into the Shuswap Valley. Our destination was the Neskonlith reserve on the north bank of the South Thompson River, opposite the town of Chase, to visit two Secwépemc sisters,[6] Adeline Willard and Aimee August. Older than Mary by a decade, they were under the care of several doting daughters and nieces. Except for their matching braids, the two sisters were mirror opposites – Aimee, tall and upright with sharp features and an aura of quiet contemplation, and Adeline, short and stooped with soft, round features and a sprightly demeanour. On hearing that I had spent much of the summer transcribing songs, Aimee announced that she and Adeline wanted to sing a song for us. It was one of their father's songs, she said, that he had sung to them many times when they were children. There was a sadness in their eyes that I later learned was associated with their father's demise. He had enlisted in the First World War and returned with severe headaches that eventually killed him. The two sisters followed this with their Aunt Maggie Moore's berry-picking song, several dance songs, and a stick-game song. They ended with a bear song, which Aimee described as a special song that she and Adeline hadn't sung in years. It's about "the bear ... before he dies ... [when] he knows he's being hunted."[7]

She then started beating her drum and singing, Adeline following along with soft, staccato-like translations: "Wonder what's the matter with me, the world is so lonely ... why am I stumbling?" Five or so minutes into this and Aimee stopped to explain that there was a second part to the song that the hunters of the bear sing while "they are skinning the bear." Again, she started beating her drum and singing with Adeline translating: "Let them be like you ... every animal like the deer ... They'll be the only ones alive where you used to play."[8] They ended their singing with a song that they grew up hearing at gatherings.

Two weeks later, I returned to the Interior on my own. My first stop was Mary Abel's ranch. Again she was busy with farm chores and grandchildren. Nevertheless, she welcomed me in. I hesitated even to mention songs because I knew she had no time, but things changed on the third day when we climbed into Mary's pickup with her daughter, Rosie, her foster daughter, Cathy, and three grandchildren and headed up Silver Star Mountain to pick huckleberries. Mary was barely in the bushes when she started humming and singing, and she didn't stop until her baskets were full. Back at her house I had hoped for more singing, but she was so preoccupied with visitors and chores that I didn't ask. It was more than enough that she had incorporated me into her household for the week. But she hadn't forgotten.

After dinner on my last evening, Mary picked up her drum, sank into her sofa, and started singing. It was a "good-time[s] song," she said, that had belonged to her Douglas Lake grandparents. (Douglas Lake was one valley to the west.) Mary's father, Joe, who was fast asleep in his recliner in the corner of the room, suddenly sat up and joined in. He followed Mary with one of his songs. It was a doctoring song, Mary said, that made people cry at winter dances. Joe prefaced his song with a long, meandering, free-form musical improvisation. I realized then why my transcription project had caused me such grief. I had encountered many such improvisations on the tapes and, with great effort, had managed to transfer rough facsimiles into western musical notation. On hearing Joe's live performance, however, I realized the futility of such a task. Joe's songs were complex improvisations that changed slightly with each performance. My transcriptions had caught crude outlines of single performances. This became more apparent when Mary took over from her father and sang a string of dance songs with similar improvisatory segments. She attributed the songs to the old singers of her youth: Jack Buffalo, Narcisse Jack, Isaac Harris, and others.[9]

Mary ended our session with a tiger-lily song. It was a song, she said, that she sang to keep herself and her family safe. "You sing that tiger-lily's song," she said, "and no one will ever get ahead of you." On sensing danger or trouble within the family, she explained, she would climb up the hills behind her house before sunrise to talk to the tiger lilies through her song. With eyes closed, she started beating her drum and singing. "That's a short and sweet song," she explained. "And that's all I'm going to sing for you."[10]

The next day, I drove to the Neskonlith reserve, where Aimee and Adeline sang more songs. In the discussion that ensued, I asked about mourning songs for humans. "Yes," Aimee replied, "we have a song like that but we can't just sing it. We have to *feel* sad to sing that song." To put themselves in the mood, the two sisters sang a Roman Catholic funeral hymn. They followed with their mourning song. Seconds into the song, both sisters started to sob – and so did I. It's "the way the Indians cry when they lost a loved one," Aimee explained on regaining her composure. "It's not really a song," she added. "It's a sighing ... that comes from the bottoms of our hearts."[11]

This was the beginning of a journey for which this book is a conclusion.

Deeper and Deeper

On my return to Toronto, I headed to a library to check the sources on BC's plateau peoples, and I emerged with an enticing lead. A journal article listed an ethnographer, James Teit, as having recorded some two hundred "plateau Indian songs" from south central British Columbia on wax cylinders between 1912 and 1920.[12] It located the collection at the National Museum of Man in Hull, Quebec (recently renamed the Canadian Museum of History), so I quickly booked a train ticket to Ottawa and an appointment at the museum's archives. On my first morning at the museum, a curator led me to a table in a back corner of its Ethnology wing and handed me a pair of headphones attached to a large reel-to-reel tape recorder. The reel on the machine, she said, was a 1960s copy of Teit's wax-cylinder originals. I figured I must have been the first in years to set it in motion because the tape cracked and snapped all the way through its cycle. Along with the reel, the archivist handed me a collection of Teit's photographs and a stack of his original, handwritten field notes.

For three days I lost myself in this assemblage of songs, notes, and photographs. With the singers' names and community affiliations meticulously cross-referenced to their photographs and their stories of dreams and visions, it offered a full multimedia experience. By following the chronology of Teit's notes, I could even track who turned up with whom on specific days. Three women, Yiôpā'tko ("Yee-oh-PAT-ko"), Whal-eenik

("Hwa-LEE-nek"), and Koint'ko ("KOINT-ko") were obviously regulars because their names appeared all through his notes – and often together.[13] Yiôpā'tko's granddaughter, Rosie Joe of the Shackan reserve (near Spences Bridge), confirmed this when I interviewed her a few years later: "Whenever my grandmother had time to spare, she'd go over to Jimmy Teit's house."[14] Of the thirty singers listed in his notes, approximately half were women.

Teit opened each cylinder recording by announcing the name of the song and the name of the singer (for example, "bear song sung by Whaleenik"). He followed this with a sharp blow of a pitch pipe to allow for later speed adjustments if required. There were numerous extraneous sounds on the recordings, such as drumming, whistling, blowing and inhaling, tongue trills, and laughter. In his notes, Teit explained the significance of everything but the laughter. I wondered if it was triggered by the singers having to stick their heads – sometimes two at a time – deep into the recording machine's prolonged metal horn, and then sing for two minutes straight.[15]

It did not take long to see connections between the singers and songs on Teit's recordings and those of my recent trip. For example, Yiôpā'tko sang the same lullaby, with the same trill of the tongue, to Teit that Aimee and Adeline had sung for me; she also sang the hunters' "bear song" to Teit that Aimee and Adeline had sung for me. In fact, Yiôpā'tko had described it to Teit in almost identical terms, as

> a kind of mourning song sung by all present when a bear (of any kind) is killed ... The singer (slayer of the animal) always put words in the song addressing the bear ... praising him for his generosity in pitying the hunter and allowing himself to be killed, excusing himself (the hunter) for having killed his friend (the bear), and asking that he (the hunter) will have continued success in hunting.[16]

Koint'ko sang the mourning song for Teit that Aimee and Adeline had sung for me. She also explained, as they had, "nearly all the women ... sang [it] in unison ... to show sympathy with the bereaved."[17]

It was uncanny to think of these women, seventy years and several valleys removed, yet intimately connected by their stories and songs. It was also uncanny to think of their songs as connecting them all to a much deeper past. Yiôpā'tko had described the "bear song" to Teit as an "ancient song" that had "originated in very remote times" through a bear who told a man "to sing this kind of song when he killed a bear."[18] She told Teit that her lullaby was as "old as the tribe."[19] Whal-eenik sang a twin song that she said was given to the people by the grizzly bear at the beginning of time,[20] and a "sweathouse song" that she said "Old Coyote" had taught the people "in mythological times."[21]

This was very old material from peoples who, for millennia, had inhabited the hills and valleys that I had just encountered for the first time.

Koint'ko sang Teit a song with links to Mary Abel's tiger-lily song. She described it as originating on a trip she took alone into the mountains to gather huckleberries. All was well until it started snowing:

> It continued to storm fiercely and to snow for four days. She determined to see the storm out and go home with a quantity of berries so she stayed there. The fourth day of the storm, in the evening, she felt tired, lonely and hungry. [Teit noted at the start of the story that she had taken only two days' worth of food for two nights of camping.] She had a small fire burning and, feeling drowsy, she fell in a half sleep alongside the fire. She suddenly was awakened by someone speaking to her. The fire had burned rather low and it was becoming dusk. She looked and saw a woman standing some distance off and looking at her. The woman said "My friend you have stayed here a long time seeking me and you have experienced hunger, and fatigue and cold. However, you will be rewarded on the morrow for the wealth will be good and you will find what you seek. I welcome those who come to see me. All people are attracted by me. I wield power over all. The best people think of me and they come here to see me. I draw them here and they cannot resist." The woman then commenced to sing this song and said "when you seek me sing this song." Kointko then followed her in the singing and thus learned the song. The woman disappeared in the darkness and after a while the singing ceased in the distance. The woman was in her prime and very good looking. She was the Tsaltsā'la [huckleberry].[22]

By the end of this archival immersion, I was smitten with the songs and notes and entranced by the man behind it all. What, I wondered, had motivated him to undertake such a project? I returned to British Columbia the following December, eager to share my discovery with Mary, Aimee, and Adeline. My first stop was once again Mary's home at the head of Okanagan Lake. As news of the old Jimmy Teit recordings spread through her community, people turned up in droves, many with cassette recorders in hand, to hear them. Mary's daughters, Rosie and Hilda, and her son,

The scene in Mary Abel's kitchen on the evening of July 25, 1979, when her neighbour Eva Lawrence and her old friend Nellie Guitterrez (from the Nicola Valley) dropped by to listen to the Teit cylinder recordings. From left to right, Nellie, Mary, and Eva. | Photograph by Wendy Wickwire.

Victor, were the first to arrive. Mary Paul, Eva Lawrence, Annie Swallwell, and Mary Louise Powers from down the road soon followed. Their excitement was palpable, especially when the oldest members of the group recognized some of the voices on the recordings. Mary Louise Powers described Alex Kwikweitês'ket ("Kwee-kway-TES-ket") as her uncle; others remembered Therese Kei.mat'ko ("Kai-MAT-ko") as a Douglas Lake woman who had visited their reserve often. Some even knew the stories of lost loves and heartbreaks behind Kei.mat'ko's "lyric songs."

After a week at Mary's, I headed to the Neskonlith reserve to play the old recordings for Aimee and Adeline. Like Mary and her friends, the two sisters reminisced at length about their many connections to the singers and songs. Teit's collections took me the next summer to Lytton, Merritt, Spuzzum, and Coldwater – communities closer to Teit's base at Spences Bridge. Many at Lytton recognized one young singer, Silka-peskit as Tommy Lick, a noted Indian doctor ("shaman") who had lived most of his adult life at Lytton.[23]

Old Tommy was the closest I came to meeting one of the singers on Teit's wax-cylinder recordings. On my first drive through Lytton, I stopped beside a small shed advertising "Baskets for Sale." On finding it closed, I headed to the house across the street to ask about it. I knocked on the front door and a faint, eggshell voice beckoned me in. The scene inside was almost as colourful as the basketry sign. An elderly woman sat in an armchair at the far end of the front room with a partly made basket in her

Hilda Austin with her mother, Tcei.a, c. 1913. | Photograph by J.A. Teit, #23206, James A. Teit Collection, courtesy of the Canadian Museum of History.

lap and a bundle of roots soaking in a pan of water by her feet. As she spoke no English, I had to use other means to ask my question. Her quizzical smile turned into full laughter as she tried to decipher my facial contortions and hand-wagging. I later learned that she was Dora Lick, Tommy Lick's widow, and that I had missed meeting Tommy by only five years. Tommy had died in the spring of 1974 at age ninety-nine.[24] Tommy also had a close connection to Teit through marriage: he was the son of Whaleenik (another singer), who was the sister of Teit's wife, Antko.[25]

Teit continued to open a world of connection for me. During a visit with Nlaka'pamux elder Hilda Austin, I surprised her with a copy of a photograph that Teit had taken of her when she was about a year and a half old and sitting in the lap of her mother, Tcei.a ("CHAY-yah"), whom Teit listed as a twenty-one-year-old member of the "Potatoe Garden Band" near Spences Bridge. As it happened, this was Hilda's first image of her mother. The photo brought her to tears as she had lost both parents in the 1918 flu epidemic.[26] After their deaths, Hilda and her younger sister, Millie, lived with their grandmother, Cha-pell, in the back hills of the Okanagan.[27] Like Tommy Lick, Cha-pell was an Indian doctor. She had bucked the residential school scoop by hiding her two grandchildren from the annual fall roundup of school-aged children. As a result, Hilda grew up speaking the Nlaka'pamux and Syilx languages but little English. Through her grandmother, she knew not only the old songs and the singers but also intimate details of the traditions behind them. She sang her versions of Yiôpā'tko's cradle song, Whal-eenik's twin song, and many others.[28]

It was now clear that I was on the trail of a most remarkable ethnographer. My bibliographic survey had uncovered eleven major monographs in Teit's name. Six were full ethnographic surveys of individual groups (based in British Columbia, Washington State, Idaho, Oregon, and Montana) and five were specialized studies of basketry, ethnobotany, oral narratives, body-painting, tattooing, and rock art.[29] I also tracked down references to hundreds of pages of field notes and large artifact collections housed in museums in New York City, Chicago, Boston, Washington, DC, Victoria, and Ottawa, along with links to ethnobotanical collections and wildlife reports in Vancouver, Ottawa, and New York City.[30] Yet Teit, it seemed, was unknown. How could this be?

These discoveries sent me back to my Uher recorder with renewed enthusiasm. When I later enrolled in a doctoral program in ethnomusicology, I mapped out a dissertation that integrated Teit's early recordings and notes with the living song traditions. This blend of old and new enabled me to spend half of my time at my own desk, working through Teit's cylinder recordings and notes, and the other half at the kitchen tables of Mary Abel, Aimee August, Hilda Austin, Annie York, Nellie Guitterrez, Harry Robinson, and others discussing songs.[31] My portable Uher served an important role at both ends. I lugged all ten pounds of it (along with heavy boxes of reels, microphones, and microphone stands) into households throughout the Interior. As word of the old recordings and photographs spread, people materialized from everywhere to hear them. I was unprepared for some of the responses. For many, the old songs and singers evoked painful memories of childhoods stifled by residential schools.

A New Context

A few years later, I encountered Teit in a new context. Unlike my first encounter, which had centred on elders' (mostly women's) reflections on songs and singing, this one centred on a large river valley that had given many songs and stories to the Nlaka'pamux peoples over the centuries. The Stein River watershed was still a living whole, unroaded and unlogged – the last of its kind in Nlaka'pamux territory. My acquaintance with it began with one of my regular trips to the Interior to visit Nlaka'pamux elders Hilda Austin and Louie Phillips at Lytton. Michael, who often accompanied me on these trips, had set up a campsite across the Fraser River from Lytton. One day, as he read by our tent, a local Forest Service employee stopped by to chat. When Michael asked about the status of the valley, the forester told him that road-building was imminent as the valley was slated for logging.

An environmentalist with experience in protest movements, Michael headed up the river the next day to see for himself what was at stake. He returned from his hike determined to find out more. This led him to a small group of Vancouver-based Stein advocates who, under the auspices of the BC Mountaineering Club, the Federation of Mountain Clubs of BC, and other outdoors groups, had spent close to a decade writing reports and organizing meetings to challenge the government's plans for logging the area.[32] On hearing that there was little local resistance and no public campaign to preserve the river and the valley, he and I chewed it over and then made a life-changing decision: we would move to Lytton to start building a local resistance movement. In collaboration with Chief Byron Spinks of the Lytton Band and Chief Leonard Andrew of the Mount Currie Band, Michael set up a hiking program the following summer to take local kids into the far reaches of the Stein. The project took Michael and me (with our baby Leithen on our backs) on extended hikes along the lower reaches of the river, up its many side-creeks, and high into the alpine meadows and ridges.

In the decade-long campaign that ensued, Teit's monographs and notes became indispensable as we interviewed elders who had spent their lives in and around the river.[33] In preparation for his 1900 monograph on the Nlaka'pamux *(The Thompson Indians of British Columbia),* he too had interviewed people at Lytton and around the mouth of the Stein about their knowledge of the valley. He had also travelled upriver to sketch the

Stein's rock art panels and then tracked down elders to explain their meanings.[34]

Teit's depiction of the Stein trail as a quick, three-day route to the Coast gave our campaign a boost as it allowed us to cast it as a heritage trail and a heritage valley that, along with its cedar, fir, and pine forests – and the river itself – would be destroyed by logging. Teit's interviews with local Nlaka'pamux people about the rock art panels along the route and in the caves above the river provided hard evidence of the valley's long-standing role as a spiritual refuge. His monographs and song notes gave us a glimpse of the life that had revolved around the many large winter house depressions at the Stein's mouth. His detailed sketches of pit-houses helped explain how such depressions shielded people during the frigid months of winter. His discussions of the human use and occupation of the lower and upper reaches of the valley in the summer and fall for hunting, fishing, and cedar root gathering, and all through the year for puberty training, were valuable sources on the valley's important role in sustaining the peoples who lived adjacent to it. His interviews with elders included stories that grandparents had passed on about seeing Simon Fraser and his crew stop at the mouth of the Stein and Lytton in June 1808. Those stories spoke to the fears and anxieties that arose as people tried to figure out who these strangers were and where they were headed. Teit also recorded the fears that ensued fifty years later as the Nlaka'pamux witnessed huge numbers of newcomers pass through their territory, eyes gleaming at the sight of gold deposits and open rangeland (and whose descendants were now intent on "developing" the community's last "wild" refuge). His detailed depiction of the Nlaka'pamux annual subsistence cycle allowed us to see what had been consciously and systematically dismantled by settler colonialism.

In 1983, all that remained of the once-vibrant Stein village on the grassy flat above the river's mouth was the shell of St. David's Anglican church, a network of dried-up irrigation ditches, and a small, still-functioning cemetery. In his 1917 monograph *Folk-Tales of Salishan and Sahaptin Tribes,* Teit mentioned two rocks adjacent to the footpath to the little church that bore the footprints of two ancient transformers.[35] Our Nlaka'pamux friends, Louie Phillips and Hilda Austin, corroborated Teit's documentation by taking us to see the rocks.

Two research contracts – one in the winter of 1986 with Chief Ruby Dunstan of the Lytton Band and Chief Leonard Andrew of the Mount Currie Band to review all ethnographic and archaeological sources on the Stein, and the other in the summer of 1988 with Chief Bob Pasco of the

Nlaka'pamux Tribal Council to interview elders about their knowledge and use of the Stein – sent me back into Teit's ethnographic monographs and field notes with a new purpose: to find more connections between the 1980s Nlaka'pamux use and occupation of the Stein Valley and those of a century earlier. As I worked my way through the 1988 field project, I could not help but wonder if Teit had had future land-use conflicts in view, given his detailed documentation of the place names, maps, plants, and seasonal cycles of the valley.[36] After all, his life at Spences Bridge had been filled with similar campaigns. It turned out he was an expert on that too.

Sadly, my old German Uher did not accompany me on this trip. I now travelled with the latest innovation in portable recording technology – a tiny Japanese Sony Walkman Professional. A little clip-on device replaced my two large stand-up microphones, and a small box of cassette tapes replaced my suitcase of reel-to-reel tapes. Again, an old world made way for a new.

American Giant

By the late 1980s, I had most of Teit's publications and field notes in hand, but I was shy on biographical material. Beyond a master's thesis and a few short magazine and journal articles, there were few secondary sources on Teit.[37] Given his twenty-eight-year research collaboration with Franz Boas (1858–1942), the famous Columbia University professor and the founding "father of American Anthropology," I assumed that I would find some of the missing pieces of the Teit story in the large literature on Boas and Boasian anthropology. Boas met Teit at Spences Bridge in the fall of 1894 and, within two days, hired him to write a major report on the Nlaka'pamux. He was so pleased with the finished product that he kept Teit writing reports until his death in 1922. It filled an important gap for Boas as his own fieldwork in the region had not gone well.

My search for Teit in the history of Boasian anthropology unleashed a story of its own. It quickly became apparent that if Teit appeared at all in that literature, it was as a passing footnote or as an "informant," "sheep-herder," "technician," or "squaw man" (depending on the source), who had provided the esteemed Franz Boas with the field data that allowed him to write a series of "splendid" monographs on the plateau peoples.[38] After reading Teit's correspondence with Boas, I knew that this was wrong. Those splendid plateau monographs were fully the work of Teit, compiled through years of field research, often on horseback, in some of the remotest regions of the province. Boas had indeed edited and shepherded them through the publication process, but he had not written them. Because there was little in the texts of these monographs about the author behind the texts, they were similarly unhelpful. Initially, I thought this might have been a conscious decision on Teit's part to keep himself – and his local sources – out of his texts.

The more I learned about Franz Boas's agenda for anthropology and his editorial practices, however, the more I saw other reasons for such gaps and silences. As a highly educated scientist trained in mathematics, physics, and geography, Boas's goal for his new university-based anthropology was to purge it of the subjective personal "bias" instilled by amateur ethnographers, especially missionaries and government agents who saw the world of Indians through a Christian, colonial lens.[39] Boas advocated for a "studied neutrality" in anthropological reporting with the narrator posing as "an impersonal conduit" who "passes on more-or-less objective data in a measured intellectual style that is uncontaminated by personal bias, political goals, or moral judgments."[40] The diversity of personal names and stories only interfered with his search for scientific truths.

All this helped explain the absence of Teit in his monographs. It did not, however, explain his absence in the histories of Americanist anthropology. I soon discovered that I was not the only one with this concern. Teit's son Sigurd, in Merritt, British Columbia, was on the same path. Sigurd and I had met in the early 1980s when I contacted him for help with my song project. In 1989, he reversed roles and contacted me for help with the "missing Teit" problem. Having recently retired from a life as a logger, Sigurd had turned the search for his father – who had died in Merritt when Sigurd was seven – into a full-time hobby. His review of the literature on Boas and American anthropology had left him with an uneasy feeling about his father's place in history. Knowing of my interest in his father, he proposed that I write a book aimed at raising Teit out of obscurity. I agreed on the spot without realizing the implications of what I had promised or how long it would take to complete. It was one thing to bite off small chunks of Teit's massive legacy; it was another thing to digest his story whole.

Ex-pats

In our initial discussions, Sigurd tried to draw me into Teit's early life in Shetland – but I was so fixed on Teit's full life in British Columbia that I did not pay much attention. What seemed significant was not that Teit was born and raised on Shetland, but rather that he had left in 1884 at age nineteen to work for an uncle at Spences Bridge, British Columbia, and, except for one short trip eighteen years later to visit his parents, he had not returned. An island archipelago located 321 kilometres north of Aberdeen, Scotland, and 354 kilometres west of Bergen, Norway, Shetland is known for its treeless rolling heather-and-grass moorlands, its many lochs and streams, dramatic cliffs and rock outcroppings, long white sand beaches, and distinctive mammals, birds, fish, and flora, not to mention its remoteness. Other than its connection to the United Kingdom (as Scotland's most northerly island), it was about as far removed from British Columbia as one could get.

Raised on his mother's stories of his father's reminiscences of the "Old Rock," Sigurd knew that Shetland was an important piece of the Teit story. He organized a research trip to Lerwick, his father's hometown and Shetland's main commercial centre, in May 1992 to find out more. From start to finish, the trip felt like a homecoming.[41] It had been more than a century since his father had left his family home, but unlike the biographical void in North America, two generations of community historians in Lerwick had kept his father's name and legacy alive. Sigurd's surname drew him straight into this sphere. During a visit with Mona Dalziel, an elderly Lerwegian, she recalled that her friend John Graham, a retired schoolteacher and local historian, had stories about a "Tait" who had changed his name to "Teit." A short telephone call to Graham, and Sigurd headed off to the Shetland Archives to meet him.

The scene at the archives unleashed a flood of stories about Teit. Brian Smith, the head archivist, greeted Sigurd with numerous letters and documents related to his father. Like Mrs. Dalziel, Smith was curious about Teit's decision to change his name from "Tait" to "Teit." Sigurd explained that his father had made the change on arriving in British Columbia, to which Smith replied that it was most unusual "for a person of [his] age to have known about and to have wanted to change his name in 1884." Another Shetland historian, Roy Grønneberg, turned up for the occasion. He had a special interest in meeting Sigurd as he had published an article on James Teit in 1978.[42] Graham took one look at Sigurd and announced that "had it not been for your accent, I could believe that I was talking to another Shetlander!" Graham was keen to tell Sigurd about his recent visit to British Columbia, as it had included a road trip from the Coast to the Rockies. He was excited about the trip as he knew it would pass through Spences Bridge, the home of a famous Shetland expatriate. His friends stopped in the village, whereupon Graham hopped out of the car and asked a resident if there was a "memorial" in the town to "Jimmie Teit." The response was "No, the only memorial to Jimmie Teit that you will find around here is in the hearts of those old Indians down by the river," and he pointed toward the reserve.[43]

Much of the conversation on that spring day in the Shetland Archives centred on the efforts of an earlier Shetland history buff, Peter Jamieson (1898–1976), to preserve the memory of Teit. Among Jamieson's papers, now housed at the archives, was a set of files that showed him stumbling on Teit in 1930 while working on a research project on Shetland's pioneer socialists. Jamieson had struck up a correspondence with Sam Anderson, a Shetland expat who had lived for a while in Vancouver before emigrating to New Zealand in 1921. In a letter in November 1930, Anderson had highlighted "Jeemie Teit" of Lerwick as a prominent member of Vancouver's socialist community and "one of the most wonderful men I have ever met." He wrote that in British Columbia Teit was known as not only "the best guide in the Northwest" but also "a great linguist and an anthropologist of distinction." His "book on the Thompson River Indians" was "the authoritative work on the subject" and a staple of "American college" curricula.[44] In subsequent letters about the socialist movement, Anderson continued to mention Teit. "Of all the men I have met so far," he wrote in 1942, "the two who impressed me most were Haldane Burgess and Jamie Teit. Jamie Teit was a name to conjure with in British Columbia both among the Whites and among the Indians ... The Indians loved him." Anderson wrote that just before departing for New Zealand, he paid a visit to Teit at a Vancouver hotel to say goodbye to his friend. "I was amazed at the sight," wrote Anderson. "All around the hotel ... on the pavement were Indians sitting crunched with their backs against the building patiently waiting for news of their best friend. Jamie was dying of cancer."[45] Anderson ended with a comment that was clearly aimed at enticing Jamieson into a larger project: "What a companion [Teit] was! What a storyteller! What a Scholar and Scientist! ... I hope that someday someone will write his life."[46]

Jamieson took the bait. In the summer of 1946, he sent out written calls to Shetland ex-pats, Tait/Teit family members, and government officials, requesting information on Teit. He then spent the next ten years crafting their responses into a coherent and colourful story. He published the first instalment, "James Teit of Spence's Bridge, B.C.: A Remarkable Shetlander," in the April 1957 issue of the local newspaper, the *Shetland News,* and he published a second instalment, "Jimmy Teit of Spence's Bridge, British

Columbia" in the January 1960 issue of *New Shetlander* magazine.[47] In both articles he presented James Teit to his Shetland readership as one of the island's "most distinguished sons."[48]

In his BC respondents' descriptions of Teit's physique – a "broad-shouldered, muscular and hardy" man with "fair, freckled" (or "fern-tickled," as Shetlanders would say) skin, blue eyes, and brownish hair – Jamieson saw "a true Norseman." In their character descriptions – his "twinkling eyes," his "fine, hearty ... humour,"[49] his "soft ... slow movements," his "great patience," and most of all, his intense modesty,[50] Jamieson saw a "true Shetlander." Sam Anderson was Jamieson's best source. He described Teit as "a legend" and "one of the most unassuming men [he had] ever met."[51] Add a fiddle to the mix, wrote one respondent, and Teit was the first to kick up his heels and the last to stop. Another letter described Teit as "a champion dancer of the Shetland reel."[52] William Irvine, a Shetland expat who, in 1946, was the federal MP for British Columbia's Cariboo District, recalled Teit as a "great character and a philosopher."[53] All of Teit's former Shetland friends noted his passion for his Shetland dialect. Some said he spoke it better than anyone they knew.

Jamieson made good use of all of this information in his two articles on Teit. He also incorporated some stories he found at the Shetland end – for example, that Teit's many friends in Lerwick had been sad to see him leave as he was the life of any social event or jaunt "da Sooth End boys got up" – in his articles. He also learned that Teit had sent a copy of his 1900 monograph, *The Thompson Indians of British Columbia,* to his "boyhood friend" Alexander Ratter, who had promptly placed it in "the Reading Room at the South Esplanade," where it gained the reputation of "the work of a Lerwick man, Jeemie Teit o' da Sooth End; aald John Tait's son 'at good awa to Canada.'"[54]

Sigurd knew about Jamieson's 1940s efforts to reconstruct the story of Teit, as Jamieson had contacted his mother, Josie, for information. He had also contacted Sigurd.[55] Seeing it all replayed in the Shetland Archives in 1992, however, was another experience altogether.

And Back to British Columbia

In addition to the Shetland side of the story, Sigurd opened a large window on the family side of the Teit story. A letter to a Tait relative in New Zealand turned up a lengthy correspondence that Teit had carried on with his uncle Robert Tait (his father's brother, then based in Wellington, New Zealand) on family history.[56] Sigurd had also pursued his uncles and aunts, cousins, and siblings for more information and photographs. Memories within Sigurd's circle of siblings were slim, however, as only three – Erik (born in 1905), Inga (born in 1907), and Magnus (born in 1909) – were old enough in 1922 to retain tangible memories of their father. As mentioned earlier, Sigurd was only seven years old when his father died, and his little brother, Thor, was only three.

Through Sigurd, I arranged several interviews with Inga at her home in Aldergrove (on the outskirts of Vancouver) in May 1991. She remembered her father as an absent "Papa" who died before his time. She also remembered that, during the short periods when he was at home, he had been an attentive "Papa." She recalled their trips together into the woods and meadows, where he would collect plant specimens and carefully stick them in his backpack. Back at his "office," he labelled them and packaged them up in boxes for shipment to colleagues in Victoria and Ottawa for further identification.[57] Inga had vivid memories of the small cottage adjacent to the family house at Spences Bridge that her father called his "office":

> You came in the door there [to] one room, a big room. [Papa] had Mr. Murray's big desk over on the side ... and a big table in the centre with books all over the shelves all along. From there down it was storage bins and stuff from a counter and below the counter were bins of storage, baskets of stuff, Indian stuff hanging there ... There was a kitchen and a bedroom there too in that building ... in case people came who had no place to stay.[58]

Everyone loved Papa, said Inga. His office was always filled with people, she said, many of whom kept him up all night long.

Inga took me to see an old friend, Joe Karaus, who had moved with his family to Spences Bridge from Austria in 1915. Joe's father worked for Joe Martel on the latter's ranch. Karaus was only fifteen when he arrived there, but he had crystal clear memories of his first image of Teit:

> Jimmy, the first time I seen him we were at Martel's [ranch] in the winter of 15/16 and he had a big St. Bernard dog and he had a pack on [to transport some] pieces of venison ... That's where I first met him walking, you know. I met him lots of times after that. He worked with me on the ranch sometimes.[59]

I was hoping for some negative impressions – some balance perhaps – but it never materialized. Karaus responded like everyone else: "I love Jimmy," he said. "He's sure a good man." The Indians "adored him," he said. "They worshipped him," he added. "Anytime you go by there, horses were tied up – saddle horses – or democrats." Like Inga, he had vivid memories of Teit's "office." "Do you remember the big doors?" he asked Inga, "and the cast iron full of quicksilver that [your father] used for a doorstop?"

At Spences Bridge, I found only one old-timer who knew Teit. He was Tom Curnow and he lived down the road from the Teit family residence. He recalled Teit as an easygoing, likeable neighbour who stuck mostly to himself. Curnow noted that Teit always wore moccasins and a fringed buckskin jacket, and he seemed permanently glued to his "office." "He looked after the Indians," said Curnow.[60]

In the late 1970s, two local historians, Katharine Howes and Pat Lean of Merritt, interviewed Robert Taylor, who had lived next door to the Teit family when the family relocated to Merritt in 1919. Taylor recalled Teit as "not a tall man, rather heavy-set with a ruddy complexion" and "the looks of an outdoorsman." He also recalled that Teit was always on the road. He regretted not paying more attention. "I feel badly now," he said. "Here was this man living next door to us carrying on very important work and I was not even interested."[61]

Among the documents that Sigurd Teit passed on to me were petitions, declarations, and correspondence that showed his father working closely with four political organizations – the Indian Rights Association, the Interior Tribes of British Columbia, the Nishga Land Committee, and the Allied Indian Tribes of British Columbia – from 1909 until his death in 1922 to help settle their outstanding land-title problem (95 percent of British Columbia's land base at the time was untreatied). For thirteen years, Teit organized major trips with the chiefs to Victoria to lobby Premier Richard McBride and his successors, and to Ottawa to lobby Prime Minister Robert Borden and Duncan Campbell Scott (head of Indian Affairs) on the chiefs' right to have their land-title question settled in the British high courts. Because only a handful of the leaders of these four organizations could speak English, he acted as their translator. As I soon discovered, Sigurd was one of the few people who knew anything about Teit's involvement in the campaign. There were only a few scattered references in the Canadian historiography about Teit's political activism.[62] To find out more, Sigurd had tracked down the Haida leader Peter Kelly in November 1953. Kelly had worked closely with Teit on the political campaign. His response was like all the others: the Interior chiefs "had infinite trust in Jimmy Teit ... I have never seen anything like it before, or to this day."[63]

It was a sad day when Sigurd died in the fall of 2002, because he had provided much of the momentum that kept me going. It was even sadder a few years later when word arrived from the Shetland Archives that a large, three-volume letterbook kept by John Tait (Teit's father) had surfaced in Lerwick. The letterbook shed new light on Teit's youth as it contained copies of multiple letters the senior Tait had sent to his young son in British Columbia. After years of trying to piece together details of his father's youth in Shetland and his transition to British Columbia, Sigurd would have relished his own grandfather's comments to his brother-in-law (Sigurd's great-uncle), John Murray, in British Columbia on the eve of young James's departure to Canada in December 1883. John Tait expressed his sorrow at seeing his eldest child leave the family fold and his worry that because James was such a "truthful and gentle" lad with an "easy and mild disposition," he was "apt ... to be misled."[64] Sigurd would also have enjoyed some of the family secrets that came to light through his grandfather's letterbook.

Sigurd also missed out on a book project that would have pleased him. In 2007, Judy Thompson, curator of the Canadian Museum of Civilization's subarctic collections, published *Recording Their Story: James Teit and the Tahltan* under the auspices of the museum. A beautiful 205-page coffee-table book featuring Teit's life story set against a rich collage of stunning colour images of Tahltan artifacts and photographs, the book provided a first step in bringing Teit's legacy to public attention.[65] Two of Thompson's museum colleagues, Leslie Tepper and Andrea Laforet, had also curated exhibits and published catalogues and book chapters highlighting Teit's prominence as an ethnographic collector.[66] Given the place of Teit's collections – of song recordings, baskets, artifacts, textiles, photographs, and field notes – in Ottawa's national museum, it was not surprising to see its curatorial staff take the lead in bringing his story forward.

The Revered and the Forgotten

It was a different story in the North American anthropological community, where Teit was all but forgotten.[67] Such silence raises questions about the authority of mainstream history and historiography – who is celebrated and who is not and why. Anthropology, like all disciplines, has a long list of eminent ancestors. Franz Boas, the anthropologist at the centre of the Teit story, is one of its most celebrated, and for good reason. From his academic base at Columbia University in New York City, he set the still-infant field of anthropology on a new course by unseating its early scientific claims of social evolutionism.[68] His critique of racism later inspired the American civil rights movement and the campaign to end racial segregation. Boas's student Margaret Mead is another eminent ancestor. From her base at the American Museum of Natural History in New York City, she gained a high public profile through her pursuit of a research agenda and a public platform in the 1960s that challenged American sexual norms and helped pave the way for an insurgent feminist movement and the 1970s "sexual revolution." Frank Cushing's five-year sojourn with the Zuni peoples of New Mexico in the 1880s earned him the title of the discipline's first participant-observer. Edward Curtis's name soared into the spotlight in the 1970s when North Americans rediscovered his twenty-volume *North American Indian* with hundreds of sepia-toned photographs of his subjects in "traditional" attire set against backdrops of canoes and bulrushes, teepees and open plains.[69] My own hometown's Royal British Columbia Museum, in Victoria, attests to Curtis's continuing allure. Its First Peoples Gallery features floor-to-ceiling reproductions of Curtis photographs – portraits of men wearing his imported wigs and air-brushed nose-rings, and women wearing his stock cedar-bark cape and silver earrings.

Canada has its own pantheon of anthropological heroes. From his institutional base at Canada's Victoria Memorial Museum in Ottawa from 1911 until his death in 1969, anthropologist Marius Barbeau became the nation's authority on "folk" and "Indian" traditions.[70] Like Edward Curtis, he made documentary films about "Canada's Indians" and published books on "Indian life and legends." He took liberties that burnished his reputation, arguing, for example, that the Haida and Tsimshian peoples of the British Columbia coast were descendants of Genghis Khan and that totem poles were postcontact inventions rather than ancient, cultural creations.[71] Barbeau often gave stage performances of the songs and stories culled from his field notes and recordings. Although his theories have long been debunked, his hand-hewn reputation lives on.[72] Edward Sapir, a former student of Boas and a prominent figure in the Teit story, is a highly respected anthropological ancestor in Canada whose theoretical work, unlike that of Barbeau, has stood the test of time. In his capacity as head of the federal government's Anthropology Division from 1911 to 1925, he appointed the country's first team of ethnographers and archaeologists (Harlan Smith, Marius Barbeau, and Diamond Jenness, as well as Teit) and, through them, issued some of the first serious reports on the country's Indians.[73]

Two notorious imposters had ties to this group. Archibald Belaney ("Grey Owl") and Sylvester Clark Long ("Long Lance") spent much of their adult lives studying and marketing Indian culture through stage performances and books. An Englishman by birth, Belaney emigrated to rural Canada, changed his name to "Grey Owl," and assumed a new identity as a transplanted Indian of part-Scottish, part-Apache descent. With his unique man-of-the-woods persona in place, he toured Canada and England in "authentic" Indian dress to perform the story of Canadian Indians. His *Pilgrims of the Wild* sold in the 1930s at the rate of five thousand copies per month. Sylvester Clark Long enjoyed similar literary success. Born in Winston-Salem, North Carolina, in 1890, he entered Canada as "Chief Buffalo Child Long Lance," a full-blooded Blackfoot Indian. Like Grey Owl, he gained a huge following in 1928 through the publication of his autobiography, *Long Lance,* chronicling his life as the son of a great Indian chief. People flocked to hear his stage performances. His star plummeted in 1929 while working on a film about traditional Ojibwe life when one of his fellow crew-members challenged him on his identity. It turned out that he had no Indian heritage at all.[74]

My family has a small place in the Grey Owl story. In 1937, Michael's uncle, Mort Fellman, a young reporter for the *North Bay Nugget,* unearthed a detail about Grey Owl that hinted at trouble. Grey Owl was now using the surname McNeil, and Fellman had found evidence that his real name was Archie Belaney. In an interview with Grey Owl at a hotel in North Bay on March 4, Fellman asked him to explain this discrepancy. According to Fellman's photographer, who accompanied him to the interview, Grey Owl quickly ended the interview and left. Fellman returned to the *Nugget* office hoping to release the story of Grey Owl's fraudulence to the world. Instead, his editor insisted that he keep the story under wraps because Grey Owl was too positive a Canadian icon to dethrone, especially in the trough of the Great Depression. Fellman dutifully waited until Grey Owl's death the next year to release his story. It caused a sensation, but did little damage to Grey Owl's standing.

Pauline Johnson (1861–1913) was a highly respected authority on Indian life and legends during Teit's time. The daughter of a prosperous Mohawk chief and an English mother, she grew up in a stately house, "Chiefswood," near Brantford, Ontario. Educated by governesses, she read all the classics and at an early age began writing and reciting poetry. She carried on to a career as writer and stage performer. Through costume changes – buckskin dresses for performances of Indian poems and Victorian attire for Tennyson et al. – she highlighted the different sides of her background. Her stage persona, combined with her published books of poems and stories, gained a huge following in North America and England. One of her poems, "The Song My Paddle Sings," became a Canadian classic. Her funeral in Vancouver in 1913 was the largest in the city's history.

In any celebration of heroes, there will always be some who are invited into the pantheon and others, just as deserving, who are left at the door. To gain entry, one must know the rules of the game and be willing to play by them. A century ago, one had to accept both the foundational premise that modernization was inevitable and good, and its corollary that Indian cultures were destined to disappear. As British cultural historian Catherine Hall explains, between 1880 and 1914, "most of the world outside Europe and the Americas was formally partitioned into territories controlled by major European states, the United States and Japan," with "approximately a third of the world ... dominated by the British."[75] For settler societies to possess lands in their new territories, "they needed to map them, to name them in their own language, to describe and define them, to anatomize the land and its fruits, for themselves and the mother country, to classify their inhabitants, to differentiate them from other 'natives', to fictionalize them, to represent them visually, to civilize and cure them."[76] In Canada as in other parts of the so-called civilized world, imperialism was the new nationalism; the "colonial theatre" was its "laboratory" in waiting. Imperialism needed a new science with a new script. It found that in the new discipline of anthropology.[77]

Western imperialism and its ideology of social evolution and racial superiority justified the treatment of Indians as less than human. Its string of racialized labels – "klootchmen," "siwashes," and "squaws" – entrenched this position.[78] Unlike the fur traders, miners, and missionaries, anthropologists benefitted from the physical and cultural demise of the original inhabitants. Their goal was to "salvage" information about "the natives" before their disappearance; it was not to advocate for their survival or oppose the forces driving their demise. It was no coincidence that the museum became anthropology's first institutional home. From London's British Museum to New York's American Museum of Natural History, the display of Indian life and artifacts gave city dwellers a concrete view of the strange and fascinating worlds beyond their "civilized" reach. On one floor were exhibits of dinosaur bones and ancient rocks; on the next, spears, baskets, and arrowheads. Like fossil displays, dioramas of hunters chasing buffalo or miniature villages of teepees depicted a bygone world where life was untamed, spare, and short. Anthropologists played a leading role in the imperial mission by capturing the precontact purity of the North American

Indian, preserving it in camphor-filled glass containers, and putting it on artful display for a curious public.[79] It explains why the Coyote of the old storytellers like Harry Robinson represented, in Franz Boas's eyes, an archetype of precontact purity.

James Teit saw himself as neither a hero nor a mortician. It took me a long time, and a trip to Shetland, to appreciate why.

A People's History

Today we understand the limits of the scientific pursuit of disembodied knowledge. We acknowledge the value of the "phenomenological knowledge" that comes with living in (and with) the world. We recognize history as rising not only from the conquests of empires and armies but also from the efforts of peasants, barefoot doctors, Indigenous peoples, and activists to resist such conquest. We see the planetary consequences of a modernist narrative of progress that has long been taken for granted. In Teit's time, the Nlaka'pamux and their neighbours fought hard for the survival of their territories and cultures. Because of the remoteness of their struggles, few in the cities understood what was at stake. Even fewer felt the pain of their losses. Struggles continue over the impacts of logging, transmission lines, oil and gas exploration/extraction, and mining; inquiries such as the Indian Residential Schools' Truth and Reconciliation Commission and the National Inquiry on Missing and Murdered Indigenous Women mark some progress for Indigenous survivors and grieving families. History is still being made. The stakes now are higher, with a wider impact. The lessons of history should be clear: a society that erodes the health of its territories will not long survive their passing.

Teit's exclusion from anthropology's pantheon of heroes is offset by his hallowed place in local Indigenous communities. His monographs and field notes are staples of band offices, band schools, and home libraries; his works on basketry, clothing, subsistence cycles, ceremonialism, place names, storytelling, pictography, songs, and ethnobotany have inspired many theses and dissertations;[80] his maps, place names, and subsistence studies have provided the grist for environmental battles, land-claims cases, and "land-use and occupation" reports.[81]

I witnessed some of this fervour in the spring of 1991 when I co-organized three "Trail of Songs" workshops with Nlaka'pamux colleagues Mandy Jimmie, Darwin Hanna, and Carol Holmes at Lytton, Quilchena, and Vernon. Our goal was to bring the old Teit song recordings, notes, and

Teit in his hunting attire, c. 1890s. Sigurd Teit donated his father's L'Assomption sash, his buckskin rifle sheath, and his buckskin shirt to the Nicola Valley Museum and Archives. | Photographer unknown. Courtesy of Sigurd Teit and James M. Teit.

photographs to the attention of schoolteachers and language instructors so they could incorporate them into their curricula. People gathered from miles away to hear the old recordings.

With themes of "place" and "belonging" now at the forefront of many Indigenous projects, both academic and non-academic, Teit's legacy is attracting attention beyond the local communities. In the spring of 2016, his research on rock art was the focus of an international rock art symposium co-hosted by the Nlaka'pamux Nation Tribal Council (Lytton), UBC's Museum of Anthropology (Vancouver), and the National Centre of Prehistory (France). Teit's collections of stories, songs, and petitions have recently inspired three new theatrical works by two prominent Indigenous playwrights. They have also been the focus of several week-long music/theatre workshops at Lytton.[82] Nlaka'pamux playwright Kevin Loring, the current artistic director of the National Arts Centre's Indigenous Theatre Department, organized the Lytton workshops under the auspicies of his Vancouver-based theatre group, the Savage Society. And interest in Teit continues to build. The University of Nebraska Press has a new book in progress that will highlight Teit's unpublished field notes, letters, maps, songs, and museum collections. Of the five contributors to this book, two (John Haugen and Angie Bain) are of Nlaka'pamux heritage.[83]

Local historians in and around the small towns where Teit lived – Spences Bridge, Merritt, Telegraph Creek – continue to keep Teit's life and legacy alive.[84] The Nicola Valley Museum and Archives in Merritt now markets itself as a James Teit research centre. In addition to a large collection of print material on Teit, it displays some of his signature belongings: his multicoloured wool L'Assomption sash and embroidered buckskin shirt that he wore on his hunting trips, his Bible (bearing his two signatures – "James A. Tait, Lerwick, Shetland" and "James A. Teit, Spences Bridge, BC"), his gold pocket-watch given to him by his father as he left Shetland, his hunting knives, his buckskin rifle sheath, his 1910 diary, his photographs of hunting trips.

Spences Bridge does not have a museum but perhaps it doesn't need one. From the "James Teit" sign nailed to the fence in front of his old family bungalow, to a federal government plaque down by the river commemorating his legacy, to a gravestone in the local Anglican church cemetery dedicated "to Antko, Beloved wife of J.A. Teit," to a beautiful meadow in the Twaal Valley above the village, to the gravesite at "Hilltop Gardens Farm" (his in-laws' family farm) up the highway, there are Teit markers all through the town. As Shetlander John Graham found several decades ago, Teit is firmly lodged in the "hearts" of the local peoples. This is their story, as I hope Teit himself would want it.

2
Boats, Trains, Horses

I think they are the ugliest & laziest creatures I ever saw, & we shod. as soon think of being afraid of our dogs as of them.

– Joseph Trutch (Lieutenant Governor of British Columbia, 1871–1876) commenting on the Indians of Oregon Territory in 1850[1]

A weary traveller stepped tentatively off the Canadian Pacific Railway's westbound train at Spences Bridge at 4 a.m. on September 19, 1894.[2] Later to gain renown as the father of American anthropology, here in the desolate darkness of yet another dusty town, Franz Boas was unknown and far from his New York City home. He had spent the previous days trudging through the towns of Enderby, Sicamous, and Kamloops trying to kick-start some fieldwork on local reserves, but things had not gone well. "My trip to the Okanagan valley was a great failure," he wrote to his parents. "The Indians were very contrary ... and I could do nothing."[3] As Spences Bridge was one of his last stops before heading to the Coast, time was running out.

Desperate for some sleep before sunrise, Boas made his way to the hotel adjacent to the tracks, banged on the door, and in a thick German accent asked for a room. On being told that the hotel was full and his only option was a shared bed with a "drunken workman," he "would have run away right then if it had made any sense," he wrote to his wife, Marie.[4] After strenuous "object[ions]," he got a second offer: a single room with unwashed linens in the lady's quarters. He took the lady's room but he wasn't happy about it. He described the bedsheets to Marie as so soiled that he had to sleep with his clothes on, and the whole establishment as "dirtier" than "an Indian house."[5] The scene by daylight was little better. The village is a "little dump of three or four houses," he wrote Marie. Everything about the place looked quite "hopeless."[6]

Boas's goal at Spences Bridge was to collect data on the local Nlaka'pamux peoples. On hearing of a "big farmer" across the river who knew the Indians well, he ferried over to find him. The farmer surprised him by suggesting that he carry on to see his nephew, Jimmy Teit, a young man, he said, who was far more knowledgeable about the Indians than he. He pointed to a trail on a steep side slope as the route to his nephew's ranch. Fighting exhaustion, Boas "started up the mountain in the great heat."[7]

With Michael, I retraced Boas's mountain trek on a warm October afternoon in 2011. After obtaining permission from the local Walkem family to park on their property near the trailhead, we hiked up a series of steep, well-worn switchbacks, stopping several times to enjoy the panorama unfolding below us: the Thompson River surging westward through a steep-sided rock canyon; the smaller Nicola River flowing in from a softer landscape to the south; the Trans-Canada Highway and the Canadian National Railway (CNR) tracks skirting the Thompson's north bank, and the Canadian Pacific Railway (CPR) tracks skirting its south bank. With two bridges across the Thompson, the town more than lived up to its name. In fact, for many, its true name was the abbreviated "Bridge," which came with the 1860s bridge. On the day that Boas looked down on the scene, the town was without a bridge. A massive flood the previous spring had washed it out.

After a last look, Michael and I followed the path upward to a large notch in the canyon wall. On passing through it, we emerged onto a gentler trail beside a small creek that bubbled through a verdant landscape of grasses, shrubs, rose bushes, and aspen trees. This trail took us to a wide grass range dotted with Ponderosa pines and Douglas firs. Other than an abandoned cattle pen, there were few signs of life.[8] There would have been lots of life on the range the day Boas trekked across it in September 1894, because it was home to a Nlaka'pamux community (the Nicoelton reserve #6) and it was haying time. A German botanist who made the same trek close to the time Boas did reported seeing Nlaka'pamux farmers baling hay with horse-drawn wooden presses, and women cooking and bathing at local campsites. He also noted willow-twig sweathouses ("upside-down baskets" he called them) by the creeks, a group of women digging thistle roots, and a party of men riding along on horseback, singing in unison as they hauled hay down to the village.[9]

Michael and I meandered slowly to Teit's old homestead at the far end of the range. For Boas, however, there was no time for meandering. He was on an assignment with a tight deadline, and things were not going well. This was a pattern that seemed to define his life. He had just missed out on a curatorship at Chicago's new Field Columbian Museum that he had fully expected to get.[10] Only a handful of institutions employed anthropologists, and the Chicago job was one of the best. He was also reeling from the death of his eight-month-old daughter, Hedwig. She had died the previous January of a lung infection. Such losses and disappointments had dampened his enthusiasm for fieldwork. "It is so repulsive to me that I have to start work now or rather have to start coaxing the Indians. I don't even want to think of it," he wrote to Marie shortly after arriving in British Columbia in September 1894.[11] Boas disliked the small talk required of fieldwork. Such talk had never come easily, especially with strangers. It had been that way since childhood. "I try very hard in society to be courteous," he wrote to his parents in a letter from university, "but you know that is very hard for me."[12]

As Boas moved across British Columbia's southern Interior, he had encountered one obstacle after another.[13] In the Okanagan, a prominent chief politely brushed him off, and a French missionary announced loudly in front of a group of Indian bystanders that his research was "foolish."[14] Such exchanges left him so discouraged that by the time he reached Spences Bridge he questioned his ability to "get along with the Indians" at all.[15] With obligations to five organizations, Boas was weighted down with responsibilities and deadlines.[16] His field supervisor, Horatio Hale, added to the pressure. A retired American philologist and veteran of the 1838–1842 Wilkes United States Exploring Expedition, Hale had been delegated by Edward Tylor, a leading British evolutionary theorist at Oxford University, to oversee the production of a macro-survey of British Columbia for the British Association for the Advancement of Science.[17] From his home in Clinton, Ontario, Hale had laid out impossible research objectives for Boas. He then monitored Boas's work like a hawk. "What is especially desired from you," he wrote, "is not a minute account of two or three tribes or languages. We wish to learn from you a general synopsis of the ethnology of the whole of British Columbia ... from north to south, without omitting any stock."[18] In addition to documenting and mapping the region's languages, Hale also wanted Boas to collect stories, artifacts, and crafts and compile detailed head and body measurements – all this across a mountainous landscape twice the size of France. To convince people to participate in these exercises, especially the body measurements, required long hours of dexterous negotiation. A team of researchers fanning out in all directions could not have fulfilled such demands in a decade, and here was Boas doing it all on his own over a few summers.

Teit at work in his Twaal Valley cabin, c. 1890s. | Photographer unknown, courtesy of James M. Teit and Sigurd Teit.

Given his cool reception in the Okanagan, Boas did not expect much of his Twaal Valley trek, especially when he arrived at his destination and found that Teit was not there. Antko was there, however, and she invited him to stay as she expected her husband back shortly.[19] In a letter to Marie the next day, Boas wrote that Antko and "an old man ... entertained" him for an hour while he waited.[20] His comment evokes a colourful image of Boas and Antko struggling through a miscellany of Chinook Jargon words and phrases to make themselves understood.[21] If Antko greeted him with "klahowya" (hello), "mitlite tenas" (stay a little while), Boas might have responded with "mahsie" (thank you). If she offered him a cup of tea, he might have responded with "hyas kloshe" (very good).[22] One can also picture Boas eyeing with curiosity the couple's sparsely furnished one-room cabin, its shelves lined with books on folklore, history, and language, and a "case" in the back corner filled with "notebooks."[23] Antko and her

Franz Boas in New York City, c. 1884–86. | Photograph by noted German-American portrait specialist Albert Naegeli, Franz Boas Papers, PS B/B61/No. 22/N.B. #74. American Philosophical Society Library.

companion undoubtedly eyed their anxious visitor with similar curiosity. According to one of Boas's close colleagues, what most people noticed first about Boas were his "coal black and piercing" eyes.[24]

Boas realized within minutes of Teit's return that his afternoon trek was worthwhile. The young man he had come to visit was able to converse with Antko and her companion in their Nlaka'pamux language and was on close terms with their relatives from the adjacent reserve. The best part was that Teit had heard of the anthropological work Boas had been doing in British Columbia over the last few years.[25] Buoyed by the prospect of help with his fieldwork, Boas hastened back down the mountain to retrieve his tools and returned a couple of hours later to spend the rest of the afternoon and evening measuring "all the Indians" in the Valley. In a letter to Marie the next day he wrote of landing a "treasure," though he didn't stay long enough to take his full measure.[26] By day three he was back on the train, bound for his next destination.

Pioneer's Progress

Teit was now a full decade into his life at Spences Bridge. He had left his home in Lerwick, Shetland, on January 29, 1884, at the bidding of his uncle John Murray, who offered him a clerkship in his Spences Bridge trade store. He completed the trip in a record six weeks, courtesy of the new travel infrastructure that now spanned the globe. He took a steamship from Shetland to mainland Scotland and a train from Scotland to northwest England. At Liverpool, he caught a new coal-fired transatlantic steamer across the Atlantic to New York City. From there, he sailed by steamship up the eastern seaboard to Boston, where he boarded a train that connected to the new Northern Pacific Railway bound for Tacoma, Washington. Other than one short stop at Chicago to visit some old Shetland friends, it was a seamless coast-to-coast trip. At Tacoma, he caught a steamer to Victoria, where he spent twelve days waiting for another steamer to the mainland.[27]

The stopover gave the young traveller a chance to absorb the culture of his new home. Victoria in the spring of 1884 was a bustling metropolis of approximately ten thousand inhabitants, many of whom were recent arrivals from Britain, eastern Canada, the United States, and China. With few buildings over two decades old, it was a solidly colonial city with an atmosphere of "Hudson's Bay Company gentility" tinged with "frontier roughness."[28] The Hudson's Bay Company (HBC) had established Fort Victoria on Victoria's inner harbour in 1843 as a way to consolidate its hold on the Columbia Department, the vast region that stretched from present-day British Columbia in the north to the Columbia River basin in the south. With the creation of an international border at the forty-ninth parallel (through the signing of the Oregon Boundary Treaty in 1846), Fort Victoria became the HBC's official western headquarters (replacing Fort Vancouver, at the mouth of the Columbia River, which was now in American hands). The Fort gained official status in 1849 when it was designated the capital of the newly established colony of "Vancouver Island."[29] It maintained its capital status in 1866 when Britain amalgamated the colonies of "British Columbia" (the mainland) and "Vancouver Island" into the single colony of "British Columbia." With Confederation in 1871, Victoria became the capital of Canada's sixth province.[30]

A promotional article published in Portland, Oregon, in 1884 described Victoria as "the most pleasing and delightful city on the Pacific Coast."[31] In addition to government buildings, custom house, post office, and marine hospital, it had four banks, two express companies, several large churches, a public library, a large public park on Beacon Hill, a thriving business sector, three newspapers, and a collection of comfortable neighbourhoods, some with ornate Victorian mansions, manicured lawns, and well-tended gardens. There was great excitement over a soon-to-open opera house and the installation of "several powerful electrical lights ... suspended upon high masts in different parts of the city."[32] A busy industrial quarter on the city's outskirts housed iron and brass works, planing mills, soap works, boot and shoe factories, and cigar and match shops.[33]

"The air is always refreshingly cool," observed one visitor to the city in 1881, who noted that "the people look quiet and respectable and everything is intensely English."[34] This was the legacy of the first wave of colonists, writes historian Adele Perry. They put great effort into turning a "racially plural, rough and turbulent" town into "an orderly, respectable, white settler" town. In 1884, the city's new upscale neighbourhoods, churches, and parks were indeed "pleasing," "delightful," and "intensely English," but all it took was a quick stroll along Victoria's inner harbour and through its commercial core to see that the gentrification project had a long way to go.[35] In addition to the stench from the raw sewage running alongside the streets,[36] there was a Chinatown that housed some three thousand "Celestials" (as the colonists called the Chinese) in the downtown core, and an Indian reserve on the west shore of Victoria's inner harbour that housed the local Songhees peoples ("siwashes" as the colonists called Indians). During Teit's 1884 stopover, the reserve was the source of controversy because of the provincial government's desire to move it to an alternative site to make way for the Esquimalt to Nanaimo (the E & N) Railway terminus. Relocating the reserve was a complicated process in the 1880s because in 1850, James Douglas, chief factor of the HBC fort, had made land-purchase "agreements" with the Songhees peoples that stripped them of their land base "entirely and forever" but gave them "village sites" and adjacent "enclosed fields" to use in perpetuity. The deal had been sealed by payments of blankets worth seventeen shillings a piece to the male heads of 122 families.[37]

The Songhees were part of a permanent Indian population in British Columbia that, prior to the arrival of the first European ships along the coast in the 1770s, numbered approximately 200,000.[38] A series of deadly diseases and epidemics had reduced them to a mere 26,000 by the mid-1870s.[39] With a Songhees reserve on the inner harbour and large numbers of visiting Haida, Heiltsuk, Nuxalk, Kwakwa̱ka̱'wakw, Nuu-chah-nulth, and others on the wharves and city streets, however, there was little visible evidence of this population decline in Victoria.[40] Indeed, one of Franz

Boas's first impressions of Victoria in 1886 was the large visible presence of "Indians" everywhere. He also noted large numbers of "Chinese" and "Negroes."[41] Although the ratio of women to men was significantly higher in Victoria than elsewhere throughout the province, the city's infrastructure catered largely to men.[42] An 1880 report listed fifty-six saloons in the city's downtown core,[43] and an 1886 report listed seven brothels on Broad Street alone.[44]

After twelve days in the capital, Teit caught a steamer to Port Moody on the mainland. The trip took him across the Strait of Georgia into Burrard Inlet and past the small mill-town of Granville on the eve of its explosion into the booming city of Vancouver. According to a fellow passenger, Jessie Smith, Port Moody was a mess "of construction and confusion" on the day of their arrival. As the designated terminus of the nearly completed CPR rail line, it was home to an army of engineers and labourers who worked around the clock to meet the CPR's deadline.[45]

Jessie, like Teit, was seeing it all for the first time. Her journey had started a few months earlier in Aberdeen, Scotland, after her marriage to a fellow Scot, John Smith. She and John were also bound for Spences Bridge to work for John Murray. Smith had met Murray a few years earlier while working on a crew installing a telegraph line from Yale to Spences Bridge. Murray needed a farm manager, and because Smith had farm skills, Murray had offered him the job. He accepted on condition that, before starting, he could make a quick trip to Scotland to retrieve his bride. The timing of the newlyweds' return to Spences Bridge provided the nineteen-year-old Teit with travelling companions for the entire trip.[46]

River of Tears

Knowing that much of the new transcontinental rail line was now in place, Smith tracked down the CPR's chief engineer to ask if he and his two companions might catch one of its working trains to Yale. The engineer agreed to let them go, as long as they acknowledged they were travelling "at their own risk."[47] A few hours later, they were on their way – gliding along the gentle, hundred-kilometre stretch of track through the flat and wide-open Fraser Valley. Things changed dramatically at Hope, when the train made a sharp, ninety-degree turn to the north and began snaking slowly along the steep, twenty-four-kilometre section to Yale.

The Fraser River had a faint connection to both Teit and the Smiths through its namesake, Simon Fraser. The son of Scottish parents who had emigrated to the United States in 1773 and later relocated to Canada, Fraser had joined the Montreal-based Northwest Company (NWC) as a clerk in 1792. By 1805, he was a partner in the company, charged with exploring the region west of the Rockies. Inspired by stories that his Scottish mother had told him about her Highland home, he named it "New Caledonia."[48] With three inland trading posts – Fort McLeod, Fort St. James, and Fort George – in operation by 1807, the NWC desperately needed a navigable route west to the Coast. An earlier Nor'Wester, Alexander Mackenzie, had offered some promise of success in July 1793, when he crossed the Rockies and reached the Pacific via the Bella Coola River, but the river was so rough in places that he declared it unfit for regular brigade travel. Fraser's goal was to find an easier river route to the Pacific in the more southern regions. In May 1808, he and his crew of twenty-three men set out from Fort George on the river that would bear his name and reached the Pacific by canoe in early July. Echoing Mackenzie's assessment of the Bella Coola River, however, Fraser concluded at the end of his trip that this river was also unsuited to regular brigade travel. The rapids in some parts of the lower canyon sections were so fierce that he and his crew had to resort to dangerous portages and even more dangerous climbs along "a spider-web of [rope] ladders" hanging from steep rock faces.[49] A third Nor'Wester, David Thompson, finally reported success when he paddled the full length of the Columbia River and arrived at the Pacific in the spring of 1811.[50] There were subsequent efforts to navigate the waters of the Fraser River but none could master the challenges of the lower canyon. Travelling the same route some eighty years after Fraser's attempt, Teit and the Smiths could easily see why as they cruised along the newly installed steel track, necks craned to view the swirling river rapids below and the sheer rock faces above.

The train dropped Teit and the Smiths at Yale, where they spent a day awaiting a second working train to take them farther upriver. Yale, like Victoria, had roots in the fur trade. Concerned about interference along its old Columbia River route, the HBC established Fort Yale in 1848 as a way to strengthen its hold on the northern regions. At the time of Teit's stopover in 1884, Yale was at the end of a four-year economic boom triggered by construction of the CPR. At its peak, the town had housed a population of seven thousand, but in 1884 its numbers had fallen to three hundred. Most of its residents were either CPR labourers and engineers working on the rail line or businessmen and entrepreneurs running hotels, boarding houses, banks, saloons, brothels, and restaurants.[51]

Andrew Onderdonk, a prominent Chicago contractor, was in charge of the CPR construction. To speed things up and cut costs, he had imported six thousand labourers from mainland China. He stirred up trouble in the town's Chinese quarters when he denied his Chinese employees access to the CPR hospital. During the winter of 1883, many of these men desperately needed hospital care as they were suffering from beri-beri, a debilitating, often deadly, illness. Triggered by a vitamin-B deficiency, beri-beri causes numbness in the hands and feet, muscle loss in the lower body, mental confusion, and vomiting. As vitamin B exists only in the husks of the rice, the men's heavy diet of polished rice (rice with its husks removed as a preservation measure), made them highly susceptible to the disease. In addition to beri-beri, some of the Chinese residents were still dealing with a smallpox outbreak that had struck their community the previous winter. Things were so bad in the Chinese quarters by the spring of 1884 that many of its young men had resorted to "huddl[ing] ... at the back doors of hotels and restaurants [hoping] for hand-outs from whites."[52] Onderdonk was insulated from their suffering as he and his family resided in a grand house, Brookside, that sat in a serene setting on the outskirts of town. The estate included, in addition to ornate manicured gardens, a croquet lawn and tennis court.

This was Yale's second boom. The first had occurred twenty-five years earlier when word leaked out of gold discoveries on the Fraser River.[53] The news sent twenty-five thousand miners "rushing" into the Fraser Canyon in the spring and summer of 1858 in search of the motherlode. Although some travelled by the old HBC Columbia River brigade route, most sailed up the Pacific Coast to Victoria and then caught riverboats to Yale. From Yale on, all travellers used the old foot trails.

With riverboats dropping off thousands of would-be miners weekly, Yale exploded into a chaotic boom town almost overnight. As one eyewitness reported:

> Every other store was a gambling den with liquor attachments. Ruffians of the blackest dye, fugitives from justice, deserters from the United States troops who strutted about in army overcoats which they had stolen when they deserted ... vigilance committee refugees who had been driven from San Francisco under sentences of life banishment, ex-convicts, pugilists, highwaymen, petty thieves, murderers and painted women, all were jumbled together in that town and were free to follow their sinful purposes so far as any restraint from the officers of law were concerned.[54]

A flood of human greed and desire swept up the Fraser Canyon with the miners, invading the hitherto quiet, isolated river terrace homes of the

Nlaka'pamux. Women and girls were quick and easy targets. The rape of a Nlaka'pamux woman is reputed to have been behind the murder of two French miners by a group of local Nlaka'pamux men.[55] When news of the murders reached miner Ned Stout and his crew at Nicomen (on the Thompson River above Lytton), along with word that the Nlaka'pamux men were heading upriver for further retribution, Stout and his crew headed back to Yale to take refuge, attacking and burning Nlaka'pamux villages along the way. The Nlaka'pamux fought back. In the end, the death toll was high on both sides: Stout reported a loss of thirty-six men and the Nlaka'pamux reported a loss of thirty-one men and five chiefs.[56] When the headless corpses of nine miners drifted into an eddy in the river near Yale, the rest of the miners organized a volunteer militia and headed up the Fraser to retaliate. Governor Douglas raced from Victoria to Yale to head it off.[57] He arrived to good news: Captain H.M. Snyder, leader of one of the militia groups, and Shigh-pentlam ("Sha-PEENT-lum"), the Nlaka'pamux head chief, had negotiated peace treaties with twenty-seven local chiefs.[58]

Given the scale of the miners' invasion in 1858 and the lack of first-hand accounts – little on either side was documented in writing – the full extent of the thefts, rapes, disappearances, and murders will never be known. Language barriers, racial prejudice, and the absence of law enforcement shielded many a crime. On his trip up the Fraser in 1860, George Hills, bishop of the Columbia Diocese, documented some of the trauma on the Indian side. He wrote in his journal in July 1860 that "two women" had visited his tent "to complain ... of the treatment they receive from Americans. They say the evil men come & steal away even the wives in the face of their husbands, for evil purposes. They struggle & they cry but frequently it is to no avail."[59] The bishop offered the women the only advice available: that they take their grievances to the local "English Magistrate." Magistrates were few and far between, however, and most had little time or sympathy for the plight of Indians. On his second trip along the Fraser two years later, the bishop documented more stories of trauma. One involved a man who pleaded with him to help find his daughter, who had been abducted by a white man. "I have had complaints frequently from husbands & fathers of the forcible abduct[ion] of their wives & children by the white savage," Hills wrote in his journal on June 25, 1862.[60]

Rape, murder, and plunder were undoubtedly widespread but they were but a prelude to an even more horrific fate. At the peak of the gold rush, a massive smallpox epidemic struck British Columbia. It arrived in

Victoria in mid-March 1862 with an infected passenger aboard a ship from San Francisco, and it raced with a vengeance across the province. By the time smallpox ran its course, it had claimed some twenty thousand Indian lives,[61] with the central and northern coastal peoples suffering the most losses – an estimated fourteen thousand dead.[62] Given the knowledge at the time of the efficacy of quarantine, inoculation, and vaccination, the scale of the losses could have been much less.[63] Due to a "lack of governmental authority, fear, and a regrettable degree of bias,"[64] the colonial police in Victoria ordered all visiting Indians out of the city. The eviction notice sent hundreds of "northern peoples" fleeing to their home communities. Because many were infected with the disease when they took flight, they carried the disease with them. The Victoria-based Songhees suffered fewer losses than their northern counterparts because many spent the duration of the epidemic on Discovery Island. Some had double protection as they were vaccinated by a local doctor. The Nlaka'pamux peoples along the lower Fraser River between Boston Bar and Lytton, and along the south Thompson River (around Fort Kamloops), also received vaccinations. Because there was no systematic record-keeping at the time, the full story of the losses will never be known.

On their second day at Yale, Teit and the Smiths caught a working train to Cisco, just below Lytton. The trip took them through the notorious "valley of death," a section of track so-named because of the many deaths caused by blasting thirteen tunnels through thick rock. While shimmying down the towering cliffs to set dynamite charges, many a young Chinese labourer plunged onto rock faces or into the river. As their working train crept along the narrow precipices above the rapids, the Port Moody engineer's warning to "ride at your own risk" became real. According to Jessie, a loose piece of rock rolled down the hillside and smashed through a window of their train. No one was injured.[65]

Cisco was as far as the train could take them as a railway bridge was under construction at that point. On exiting the train, they faced yet another frightening mode of transport: a river crossing by a large basket hanging from an improvised zipline. From the river's edge, they watched the basket speed along the line and land on the bank in front of them. A man jumped out of the basket and promptly introduced himself as Joseph Burr, sent at the behest of Murray to chauffeur them to Spences Bridge.[66] Because Burr's horse and buggy were on the opposite bank, the three travellers had no choice but to zipline back across the river. In her memoir, Jessie Smith described the basket ride as one of the most hair-raising experiences of her life:

> When I was seated [in the basket], the operator came and asked me to close my eyes when he let go of the rope. I remember looking up at him and smiling bravely to hide my fear. I said, "No! If that rope breaks I would like to see where I am going." The man let go of the rope, and the basket with Mr. Teit, Mr. Burr, John and me in it, slid down a cable and landed us safely in a pile of hay on the other side of the raging Fraser River.[67]

After breakfast with the bridge construction crew, the group set off on the final leg of their journey. Little did they realize that it would be just as hair-raising as the previous leg. Burr's buggy bounced along the heavily cribbed, potholed Cariboo wagon road, often over cantilevered sections that extended far out into the void above the river. Extreme changes in terrain created a veritable roller-coaster ride: one minute switchbacking up sheer, narrow cliffs and the next minute pounding downhill over rough rock rubble. Jessie later recalled squeezing her husband's arm until it was black and blue as the buggy "clung to the rocky mountain ledges and wound and twisted along high above the rushing river."[68]

The road had a history as colourful as John Smith's arm. Bishop George Hills, who hiked along the route in 1860 when it was still a foot trail, described some of the challenges he faced along its rough sections:

> The footing in some places was certainly no more than half an inch, in one spot a mere indentation for a naked Indian heel. A slip from this would precipitate a fall down into the abyss of the whirling torrent. It is said many miners lost their lives in forcing their way here ... [In one spot] the only way of passing [was] ... to bend the back in a particular manner to preserve the balance ... Over two chasms twenty or thirty feet across, a plank was placed in one case; in another, two slender rounded poles tied together. Beneath these bending, slender pathways nothing intervenes to the roaring waters below.[69]

Hills was surprised to pass Indian packers on this terrifying trail who were carrying hundred-pound packs on their backs.[70]

With the sudden surge of travellers heading up and down the Fraser River, James Douglas decided in 1862 to replace the foot trails with a proper wagon road. He imported the Royal Engineers ("sappers") and a private construction crew to undertake the task. Two years later, the "Cariboo Road" between Yale and "Cook's Ferry" at the junction of the Thompson and Nicola Rivers opened to wagon and stagecoach travel.[71] Entrepreneurs flooded in, especially after Frank Barnard inaugurated a biweekly service with his Barnard Express and Stage Lines. Roadhouses soon popped up at thirteen-mile intervals to cater to travellers and their horses during stopovers.[72]

For newcomers, the Cariboo Road heralded promise; for the local Indians, it heralded betrayal. With the highway came the settlers' law and culture. Indeed, Britain's Colonial Office was now welcoming all British subjects and others to settle its "wild and unoccupied Territories." The idea of "unoccupied" land was a potent concept that gave colonists a legal right to land ownership based on the stage of civilization considered to have existed on that land at the time of acquisition. If a territory looked, in the eyes of the colonizers, to be devoid of people and/or civilized governments, they were free to take possession by settlement. Citing the 1693 English case *Blankard v. Gaddy*, legal scholar Mark Walters explains that where a colonial possession was acquired through *discovery* rather than *conquest*, "judges assumed that English law flowed across the legally empty terrain automatically to provide the newly arrived settlers with their law."[73] These laws established a government-sanctioned narrative that helped legitimize the English settler claims to "empty" lands.

As historical geographer Cole Harris writes, such views were "as old as the European connection with the New World."[74] Two centuries before Teit's trip, they were "powerfully and influentially elaborated" in the writings of John Locke (1632–1704), the English philosopher and colonial administrator. Locke had embarked on his own voyage of intellectual discovery to enshrine new ideas of land improvement, property, and trade that justified European settlement and development in the Americas. His *Two Treatises of Government*, published in 1690,[75] still serves as a foundational document for liberal democracy.[76] He characterized the Indian tribes of North America as "wild savage beasts with whom men can have no society nor security" and who "therefore may be destroyed as a lion or tiger."[77] As Harris writes, "Those who did not labor on the land wandered over what Locke called unassisted nature, land that yielded little and lay in common." Indeed, the land itself was "a wild common of Nature."[78]

Similar views emanated from other European centres. The renowned Dutch philosopher and lawyer Hugo Grotius (1583–1645) espoused a Christian duty for a "natural" war against those "who are still lost in the thick clouds of Paganism." These were "rather Beasts than men."[79] The French scholar Alexis de Tocqueville (1805–1859), whose book *Democracy in America* is seen as a classic in cultural subtlety and understanding, wrote of the Indians' "deep depravity which can only derive from a long abuse of civilization ... On first contact, one would be tempted to regard them as nothing but a beast of the forest, on which education has been able to confer a semblance of humanity, but which has nevertheless remained an animal."[80] De Tocqueville foresaw extermination as a pre-condition for settlement and nationhood.

By the mid-nineteenth century, these ideas, as Harris notes, were "powerfully reinforced by an increasingly strident racism and the achievements of the industrial revolution."[81] The colonists of British Columbia, especially those with political power, such as Joseph Trutch, put these cultural attitudes to work. There was no "room for alternative understandings of civilized modernity," writes Harris. Everything operated according to the simple "civilized" vs. "savage" binary with "little of consequence between."[82] Neither Locke nor de Tocqueville informed Teit's "colonial" mission, however.

Several hours into the buggy ride, Burr pulled into the town of Lytton and announced that his horses needed a rest. His passengers also needed a rest. Named in honour of Sir Edward Bulwer-Lytton, British Secretary of State for the Colonies, the frontier town sat on a high bench overlooking the dramatic confluence of the Fraser and Thompson Rivers. It was a site that Teit, in his later ethnographic role, would describe as the centre of Nlaka'pamux territory and the place where the world began. He would also discover that Simon Fraser had stopped there on his exploratory trip down the river in June 1808 to shake hands with the twelve hundred Nlaka'pamux men and women who had gathered to see him. In 1884, Lytton was a popular stagecoach stop and a soon-to-become-popular CPR stop. It boasted "several large stores, hotels, shops, livery stables and warehouses, a sawmill, grist mill, post office, telegraph office, railway station, public school, court house and many neat residences."[83]

The new St. Mary's and St. Paul's Anglican Church with its Gothic revival edifice announced the new settler religion that had infiltrated the region.[84] The church was a legacy of Bishop George Hills, the clergyman who had braved the Fraser River's foot trails in 1860 and 1862 to assess the region for Anglican mission churches and schools. In 1866, Hills dispatched the Reverend John B. Good to Yale to minister to the local miners and Indians. An ambitious missionary with lofty aspirations, Good moved upriver to Lytton the following year to establish a large Anglican mission centre.[85] He envisaged "a parsonage of convenient size, a commodious native church, and a training institution for boys and girls." He also had plans for a separate community complete with western-style houses to insulate his Anglican converts from the rest of the community.[86]

Good confronted major obstacles in his efforts to convert the local Nlaka'pamux peoples to Anglicanism. To be eligible for baptism in Good's church, a married person had to be in a monogamous relationship. Because many Nlaka'pamux marriages were polygamous, baptism required husbands to reject all but their first wives and their children. Even Good appreciated the pain of forcing people to make such unfamiliar choices.[87] His building plans for Lytton were expensive, and as his debts mounted they drew disapproval from his church superiors. When a new bishop arrived on the scene in 1876 and criticized him for overspending, Good began to withdraw from his project. Six years later he abandoned Lytton altogether and accepted a new post at Nanaimo on Vancouver Island.[88] When Teit and the Smiths lunched at Lytton in March 1884, the community was awaiting the arrival of Good's replacement.

With his horses and passengers refreshed, Burr embarked on the final leg of the trip: the thirty-six-kilometre stretch along the Thompson River from Lytton to Spences Bridge. The Thompson, like the Fraser, had tangible connections to Simon Fraser. On stopping at Lytton in June 1808, Fraser took note of another large river that flowed in from the east and promptly named it in honour of his Nor'West colleague David Thompson. Thompson, who had mapped much of western Canada, was then exploring the Columbia River basin in search of another route to the Pacific. He had hoped to be the first to reach the Pacific, but upon arriving at the Columbia's mouth, he discovered that the Pacific Fur Company (PFC) had beaten him to the task. In addition to erecting Fort Astoria on the site, the PFC was already surveying northerly points for additional trading posts. In May 1812, Alexander Ross established a post for the PFC at the junction of the North and South Thompson Rivers. He named it Fort Cumcloops after a large Secwépemc village in the vicinity. A few weeks later, a Nor'Wester, Joseph La Rocque, arrived at the same spot and built Fort Shuswap across the river from the PFC post, initiating a rivalry that continued until the NWC bought out the PFC a year later. A merger in 1821 between the HBC and NWC turned the junction of the rivers into a major HBC trade centre known variously as Thompsons' River Post, Fort Kamloops, and Fort Thompson.[89]

In 1884, the Cariboo Road between Lytton and Spences Bridge was lined with Indian "rancheries" – clusters of log cabins with adjacent barns, cow and horse pastures, and fenced-in vegetable gardens. Interspersed with these were strings of new settler farms, some of which doubled as roadhouses. Most had fenced gardens, and horse and cow pastures. The

Spences Bridge, c. 1886. John Murray's residence is the small white cottage on the north bank of the river directly in line with the bridge. His trade store is the large, eight-dormered building to the right of the bridge; and his hotel, Morton House, is the smaller five-dormered building to the right of the trade store. The horse trail leading up to the Twaal Valley follows the crevice in the mountain behind the hotel. The bridge disappeared in a major flood in the spring of 1894. | Photograph by William McFarlane Notman, McCord Museum, McGill University, Montreal, Quebec.

seas of stumps behind both sets of homesteads spoke to the clearing projects required to prepare the wild landscapes for agriculture.[90] All along the highway were visible reminders of the gold rush – creeks flanked by wooden flumes and ditches, some derelict and others still worked by small groups of Chinese miners.

The journey ended at dusk when Burr pulled his buggy up in front of the Morton House hotel and handed his passengers over to John Murray, who had raised a special flag in their honour.[91]

In a Frontier Town

After settling the Smiths into his "cottage" and his nephew into a room in the Morton House hotel, Murray invited the trio to dine with him at the hotel. He could extend such invitations as he was the hotel's new proprietor, having purchased it a year earlier from Charles Morton. This was the base for Teit's new life.

Murray, a mid-fifties bachelor, was Teit's mother's older brother. A native of Aberdeen, Scotland, he was lured to British Columbia in 1859 by the Fraser River gold rush. After working in New Westminster as a grocer and a newspaper reporter, he moved upriver to Spences Bridge in 1870 to work as a bridge toll-keeper. Like many ex-gold rushers, Murray saw more lucrative business opportunities in land development, especially when news arrived that the Canadian Pacific Railway line was slated to pass through the village.

Murray did well at Spences Bridge. By the spring of 1884, he was the most prosperous man in town. In addition to Morton House and the local trade store, he owned a large tract of agricultural land, Sunnyside Farm, that he planned to turn into a commercial orchard and seed-farm business. After securing the water rights to an adjacent mountain stream, he began blasting a tunnel through the rock and constructing a wooden flume across the hillside to deliver water to Sunnyside. On her first morning in the village, Jessie Smith expressed surprise at seeing crews of Indian women, "with tump-line straps across their foreheads," carrying water and flume boards "up the side of the mountain" to the workmen.[92]

Morton House hotel in 1884 was one of the premier establishments on the Cariboo Road. Its main floor had a large kitchen, a parlour, two dining rooms, a tavern, and several bedrooms, and its second floor had sixteen guest rooms.[93] The British Columbia Directory for 1882–83 described it as a fine place "that might grace a city." In addition to an adjacent garden featuring "every variety of annual flowers" and "all kinds of fruit and vegetables," it had a vineyard laden with "grapes of finest quality."[94] A German botanist who stayed at Morton House in the summer of 1887 described Murray's gardens as "magnificent."[95]

A testament to Murray's stature in the region was his place on the new "provincial" government maps. In 1884, he had three local landmarks named after himself – "Murray Mountain," "Murray Falls," and "Murray Creek." He had named a fourth landmark – a prominent rock outcropping on the edge of the village – "Arthur's Seat," in honour of a famous bluff

Teit (left) on the south bank of the Thompson River, just below Spences Bridge, with his Nlaka'pamux friend George Ta-magh-kyn. Two sets of wooden flumes extend to the right from Murray Falls. Those were the flumes that were under construction when Teit and the Smiths arrived at Spences Bridge in March 1884. | Photographer unknown, MA54-54-1SGN 1516, City of Vancouver Archives.

in Edinburgh, Scotland. He might have named the village after himself had a previous entrepreneur, Thomas Spence, not beaten him to it.[96]

In 1860, as the gold rush pushed northward into the Cariboo, a few enterprising newcomers capitalized on the need for fixed river crossings at certain strategic locations. One such location was the junction of the Nicola and Thompson Rivers, where travellers had to ford the Thompson River to continue upcountry. In 1861, two former HBC freighters, Mortimer Cook and Charles Kimball, set up a ferry service (and a toll booth) at that junction to facilitate an easier river crossing. They then built a hotel to service the many travellers passing through the region. Gradually, the junction became known as "Cook's Ferry."[97] As pressure on this and other ferries mounted, a new wave of entrepreneurs argued that bridges should replace the ferries. Joseph Trutch, Member of the Vancouver Island House of Assembly, led the way by securing a contract to build the

Alexandra suspension bridge, an impressive 268-foot span with 90 feet of clearance across the Fraser just north of Yale. It opened in 1862 and served Trutch well as he had negotiated a "five-year charter" to charge tolls on the bridge.[98] Based on Trutch's success, Thomas Spence, a veteran of the California and British Columbia gold rushes, convinced the colonial government of the need for a bridge to replace the ferry at the junction of the Thompson and Nicola Rivers ("Cook's Ferry"). With financial backing from Captain William Irving, a wealthy partner in the Victoria Steam Navigation Company, Spence built the bridge in 1864. Shortly after he opened it, a massive spring flood wiped it out. Spence rebuilt it within a year, and Irving recovered his costs by collecting tolls at the bridge. With the new bridge, "Cook's Ferry" gradually became known as "Spences Bridge."[99]

The completion of the Cisco railway bridge in 1885 gave Spences Bridge a major boost because it shifted the CPR base of operations from Yale to Spences Bridge. The CPR's goal now was to install rail lines along the 122-kilometre stretch between Lytton and Savona. Through this transition, the town gained a post office, a telegraph station, a blacksmith shop, two general stores, a drug store, railway buildings, and a tinsmith shop. Joseph Burr (who had chauffeured Teit and the Smiths from Cisco to Spences Bridge) opened a saddle shop. New homes were also built for Andrew Onderdonk and his two chief engineers, J.W. Heckman and H.A.F. McLeod.[100] There was great excitement over the Spences Bridge boom, but it was tempered by the situation at Yale. That town moved from boom to bust when the CPR pulled out.

On hearing of the situation at Yale, a group of Anglican nuns from Ditchingham, England, swooped in and bought up the town's newly vacated buildings wholesale. Yale's easy rail access from all points east and west, and its collection of abandoned buildings, offered the nuns the prospect of creating an upscale Anglican boarding school. In the fall of 1884, they designated the Anglican vicarage as a temporary school for Indian children while they renovated Onderdonk's Brookside estate (specifically the parlour, dining room, and bedrooms of the main house) into school classrooms and dormitories, and the stable into a school chapel. The nuns rented the abandoned CPR hospital and various other town residences for other school uses. They used Brookside's manicured gardens, lawns, tennis court, and croquet grounds to market their school as an upper-class educational establishment. They launched All Hallows school in 1890 with white girls in one section and Indian girls in another.[101] It was one of two Indian residential schools on the CPR route between Hope and Kamloops. The other was a Roman Catholic residential school at Kamloops run by Oblate missionaries.

In June 1886, two years after Teit's arrival in the village, the CPR's first official passenger train, No. 371 from Montreal, carrying seventy passengers, passed through Spences Bridge on its way to the Coast. This was a landmark day for Canada. The launch of coast-to-coast travel ended the slow and cumbersome stagecoach routes along the Cariboo wagon road. It was also monumental news for the commercial and political sectors of the country because it "opened" the region to big business, both domestic and international.

This linear transportation unleashed a new gold rush and, along the CPR's route, a wide panorama of displacement and development. Jessie Smith's description of Nlaka'pamux women packing wooden flumes and water jugs up the hillside above Murray's estate in 1884 spoke to that displacement. A mere twenty years separated these strong, young women from the deadly smallpox epidemic that had ravaged their village in the 1860s. Walter Moberly, who supervised the construction of the Cariboo Road between Lytton and Cook's Ferry at the peak of the smallpox epidemic, reflected later in life on the terror he felt when he saw an infected Indian on horseback pass through his work site just east of Lytton. The man wore a veil to hide his "badly smitten" face. A second man accompanied him on horseback. Moberly advised the two men to turn back to Lytton where there was a doctor administering vaccinations. Instead they carried on. On his own trip along the same trail later that day, Moberly saw first-hand why their decision to ride east instead of west was wrong. The first sign of trouble came a few miles east of his work site when he heard the sound of "dismal wailing of Indian women" near a local mountainside. It was "a certain indication of death having visited their community." He then encountered a pack of horses grazing around a cluster of tents. On noticing that there were "no signs of human life" around the tents, Moberly decided to dismount and investigate the situation. Inside the tents were "putrefying bodies" that had been dead for several days. At his next stop – the "Indian village" at the mouth of the Nicola River – it was "the same melancholy and disgusting sight."[102]

In the midst of this terrifying epidemic, the parents and grandparents of the women on the hillside faced another crisis: a new geopolitical regime aimed at removing them from their large land base. The removals had started in the early 1860s with the colonial administration's survey of dozens of "reserves" along the Fraser River between Yale and Soda Creek. By 1870, the Thompson River surveys included a number of small reserves in and around the mouth of the Nicola River. With the imperial parliament's passage of an Order in Council in 1871 admitting British Columbia into the confederation, the 1867 British North America (BNA) Act now applied to the new province. Section 91 (24) of the BNA Act gave Ottawa jurisdiction over Indians. The province was to provide "tracts of land" for the "use and benefit" of the Indians. Tensions between the two governments escalated as they argued over the size of the land allotments for reserves.[103] While Ottawa pushed for larger land allotments for reserves – and even at one stage contemplated forcing British Columbia to make treaties – the province pushed for smaller land allotments.[104]

With local Indians coming and going from their state-administered "reserves" on the north and south banks of the river, and large work gangs grading track on the south bank, the development side of the colonial project was in full view. Unlike the engineers and surveyors who used Murray's upscale hotel on the north bank of the river as a base, the labourers lived in primitive tent camps and bunkhouses on the river's south bank. A lucky few found food and lodging at the south bank's Nelson Hotel. The labourers were further divided along racialized lines: white workers lived at one end of the road and the Chinese workers lived at the other end. Unlike the Nlaka'pamux residents, the itinerant labourers had broken their ties with their mother countries, and in their New World settings, many were homeless. Knowing that their employment with the CPR was short-lived, many lived in a permanent state of anxiety over their futures.[105]

Spences Bridge was a working man's town. In her memoir, Jessie Smith recalled the loneliness and isolation she felt when she discovered that she was one of only two white women living on Murray's side of the river. The situation was worse on the other side of the river because there was only one settler woman in the mix, "Mrs. Nelson," wife of S.M. Nelson, the proprietor of the Nelson Hotel. The Nelsons had purchased the property adjacent to the bridge in 1876. Joseph Burr added to Jessie's female circle when he married Rosie Loring of Lytton and set up a home with her on the Thompson's north bank. The local blacksmith, Aaron Johnson, added to it again when he brought his new bride, a young woman from Victoria, back to live with him on the river's south bank. The CPR gave Jessie her first close female friend when it moved its chief engineer, Andew Onderdonk, upriver from Yale to Spences Bridge with his wife, Delia, and their children. According to Jessie, she and Delia formed an instant bond. Jessie made no mention of forming any bonds with the numerous Nlaka'pamux women living in and around Spences Bridge, not even those such as Marie Audap and Hannah Martel who had married into the settler community.[106]

Murray's trade store was the social and economic hub of the village. According to the store ledger book that Teit started soon after his arrival, it was a multipurpose shop that served as a grocery and dry goods store, a post office, a bank, and a mail-order centre.[107] Many Morton House guests and freight company employees maintained permanent accounts with Murray, and various CPR and government agents used it as a bank. Murray employed a collection of Chinese and European labourers to work at the hotel and on his farm. According to Jessie Smith, he stocked his shelves with specialty food items and colourful fabrics and scarves because of their appeal to the Nlaka'pamux women.[108] As the store's clerk, Teit interacted daily with these shoppers. In October 1887, one local woman's name appeared in the store's ledger book as purchasing goods on his personal account. She was a nineteen-year-old Nlaka'pamux woman, Lucy Antko from Nkaitu'sus (the "Nicoelton 6" reserve as it was designated by the Department of Indian Affairs) in the Twaal Valley.[109]

An Unreserved Life

By now, all of southern British Columbia was enmeshed in the tumult of colonial intrusion and extraction. With the completion of the CPR, new villages, towns, and cities popped up everywhere. Christian missionaries fanned out in all directions, leaving a network of churches and schools in their wake. New rail spurs, steamboats, and roads connected the remote nooks and crannies to the central rail lines. It was "an era of settling the frontier and province building to the accompaniment of almost unbridled optimism," writes historian Robert Galois.[110]

As a new member of the Canadian federation, British Columbia was subject to federal jurisdiction in Ottawa. Building on the stringent policies of earlier colonial governments, the federal government in 1876 created the Indian Act, which placed further restrictions on the lives and territories of the Nlaka'pamux and their neighbours.[111] The act disenfranchised Indians from the political community and reduced them to "a distinct legal category," to be treated as "minors" and "special wards of the government" without the rights of citizenship.[112] To implement the act, the federal government created the Department of Indian Affairs under the federal Minister of the Interior. It then appointed "Indian agents" across the country to administer the affairs of the Indians and their reserves.[113]

Two years after Teit's arrival at Spences Bridge, the Supreme Court of Canada (SCC) issued a judgment, *St. Catherine's Milling and Lumber Company v. The Queen,* that would become the foundational narrative for land "surrenders" for most of the next century. Depriving Indians of a legal right to the land, the judges agreed that any Indian claim to land depended on the "humanity and benevolence" of the government, for which "the state must be free from judicial control." To decide otherwise meant that "all progress of civilization and development in the country" would be "at the mercy of the Indian race."[114] On appeal from Canada, the judgment by the Judicial Committee of the Privy Council (JCPC) in London in 1888 upheld the SCC's decision, but with different reasoning that should have rendered this narrative inaccurate. However, it survived for another century because of the doctrine of sovereign immunity by which legal action could only be taken against the provincial government with its consent, thus protecting it from accountability.[115]

For British Columbia, the legal decisions entrenched the deterritorialization and reterritorialization of the region that had been underway since the 1860s, and effectively gave the new culture free rein to implement resettlement, resource exploitation, development, and legal oversight, along with a centralized state to ensure its success. As in the rest of Canada, British Columbia retained jurisdiction and ownership of its land base while the federal government assumed constitutional responsibility for "Indians and lands reserved for the Indians." Such assertions of state ownership soon became a national problem, as Indian leaders charged repeatedly that because there had been no treaties beyond fourteen land-purchase agreements (the so-called Douglas Treaties of the 1850s) on Vancouver Island and one treaty (Treaty No. 8) in northeastern British Columbia, settler society was sitting on stolen land.[116]

As Cole Harris writes, only a few benefitted from the "ensuing scramble for position [as] white legislative and coercive power, coupled with a simple categorization of people, eliminated much of the competition."[117] Everywhere newcomers staked out large landholdings for farms and ranches. They then capitalized on the large itinerant – and cheap – labour force for ranch hands, cooks, and domestics. With the new government legislation and its subsequent land clearances, writes Harris, "the line between the reserves and the rest became the primary line on the map of British Columbia."[118] And yet, these boundaries were a mixed curse. On the one hand they were "isolated enclaves" of segregation under strict government surveillance, where "missionaries and agents of the state could indoctrinate Indigenous populations in economic behavior, political activity, religious practices and social conduct acceptable to liberal Canada."[119] On the other hand, they were "safe havens" that offered escape from the "staggering isolation" of adjacent settler communities.[120] In their reserve communities, writes historian Keith Smith, Indians could remove themselves from "the disapproving eyes and discriminatory actions of Canadian citizens, even as they remained under the liberal gaze of the state and the church."[121] Today, reserves retain this ironic double edge because, in many cases, they are all that remain of the old communal land and social base, however inadequate and fractured.

As predicted, Spences Bridge went the way of Yale when the CPR construction crews and engineers pulled out in 1886. Local businesses folded, and Murray's hotel and store lost business. When Murray could no longer afford to cover Teit's salary, Teit had to seek work elsewhere. In the early fall of 1887, he loaded up a pack-horse team and headed seven hundred kilometres north to Stuart Lake in the Cariboo district to trap and sell furs. He did the same in the fall of 1888. In a letter to a fellow Shetlander during this second season of trapping, he wrote that he was "knocking around ... in a very out-of-the-way ... part of [the] country, where there were no post-offices, and white people were few and far between." When his friend responded that it must be a lonely life, Teit responded that sometimes it was a "little lonely" but it didn't bother him:

> You say you think I must be somewhat venturesome, and very lonely, the life I lead. Well, I believe it is venturesome crossing some of these rivers, making rafts and swimming horses, etc. etc. Some of them are pretty rapid. It is sometimes a little lonely, but I don't mind it much. I have not talked any Shetland for a long time, and all last summer I hardly ever talked any English.[122]

Teit seems to have thrived on such isolation, because over the next two decades it defined his life. According to Shetland historian Ian Tait, he would have acquired some of his backcountry survival skills prior to arriving in BC as hunting geese, ducks, rabbits, birds, and seals for home consumption was prevalent in Shetland in the mid- to late nineteenth century. Many islanders also participated in the sealskin trade. Given that Teit's father had joined the Zetland Rifles in the 1850s and won numerous prizes for his marksmanship, it is likely that the Tait children, especially the boys, were exposed to guns and target shooting at an early age.[123]

Teit stayed in Spences Bridge in the fall and winter of 1888–89 to manage the hotel on the Thompson's south bank while its new owner, Archie

Clemes, was away. To supplement his income, he sold firewood and worked part-time in a local mine. He had another reason for spending the year there. After two years of living together on the reserve adjacent to the village, he and Antko had decided to establish a ranch together. Because land development was a prerequisite to acquiring land title, and such development required cash flow, Teit moved to Nanaimo in the summer of 1890 to earn some quick cash in the coal mines to help pay for the land. He returned to Spences Bridge in the spring of 1891, where he and Antko staked out a seventy-acre parcel in the Twaal Valley, adjacent to Antko's home village, as an ideal place for their new ranch.[124] They moved onto the land in June and began fencing it for horses and cattle and clearing it for an orchard and garden. To help pay for it, Teit returned to Nanaimo at the end of the summer to work in the powderwork division of the collieries. By spring, he was off to the Nechako Valley (north of what would soon become the city of Prince George) to trade furs. On his return, he and Antko retained Reverend Richard Small (Good's replacement) to officiate their marriage at the Twaal Valley ranch on September 12 (1892). They invited William Kulla-mas-choot (Antko's uncle) and Johnnie Wheestimneetsa (the chief of her band) to serve as their witnesses.[125] Together, the couple built themselves a forty-by-twenty-square-foot log cabin on the property and planted an orchard and a vegetable garden. Their plan now was to use the ranch to launch Teit's new career as a hunting guide.

Through her marriage to Teit, Antko entered into a new relationship with her home community. According to the terms of the Indian Act, the marriage stripped her of both her Indian status and her right to live on her home reserve. The couple's calculated purchase of land in the Twaal Valley compensated partly for this by allowing Antko to live adjacent to her reserve community. The location of the ranch – a stunning plateau in the Twaal Valley set amongst the forests and high hills above the Thompson River Valley – suited both. It allowed Teit to move into the sphere of guiding and it gave Antko a permanent home in the valley in which she had been raised. As Michael and I discovered on our hike into Twaal Valley, their homestead offered a quiet, tucked-away refuge well above the bustle and noise of Spences Bridge.

Siwash Man

Just as Teit and Antko's marriage redefined Antko's relationship to her home community, it also redefined Teit's relationship to his home communities (both in British Columbia and in Shetland). It was one thing to witness from the outside the segregation and racism associated with interracial heterosexual relations between Indian women and white men; it was another thing to experience that segregation and racism as an insider. Sensing that his relationship with Antko would be difficult for his parents to grasp, he had waited four years before informing them of it, and he did so only after he and Antko had sanctioned it with an Anglican church marriage certificate.[126] He was right to worry. His father, who had previously expressed hope that his son would return to Shetland, informed Teit that his marital situation made such a return impossible: "You cannot bring her here if you wished," he wrote. "She would naturally find herself out of place."[127] This was the tenor of the times and as the senior Tait revealed through his letters to his son, it was just as strong in the outer reaches of the United Kingdom as it was on the West Coast of Canada.

Teit's twelve-year relationship with Antko transported him into what he would later describe as a "siwash" world. In her study of gender and race in colonial British Columbia, historian Adele Perry writes that "within colonial settlements" there was a "general disgust" at "the simple presence of Aboriginal people."[128] The idea of marriage between a white man and an Indian woman was abhorrent. To keep Indian women away from the respectable spheres of white settler women, and to keep white settler men away from unions with such women, settler society invented a string of racialized labels for Indian women (i.e., "klootchmen" and "squaws"), which they reinforced with a string of descriptors, such as "overly sexual, physical and base," as well as "lascivious, shameless, unmaternal," and "incapable of high sentiment or manners."[129] White men who aligned themselves with Indian "squaws" were "seen as dangerously flirting with relinquishing their place among the responsible gender and, more profoundly, the civilized race."[130] Some cast such men as akin to "savages," who "ceased to be white and became nearly and sometimes entirely Aboriginal."[131] In her recent study of "crossracial encounters" in British Columbia, social historian Renisa Mawani extends Perry's mid-century analysis into the late nineteenth and early twentieth century.[132] She writes that white men who aligned themselves with Indian women were seen as "race-traitors and thus undesirables who were to be reprimanded for abandoning whiteness and all the privileges that accompanied it."[133] The mixed-race progeny of such unions – "breeds" and "half-breeds" as they were called – heightened such anxiety by "complicat[ing] racial taxonomies and orders of rule that were invested in maintaining distinctions between Indians and whites." The major concern was the threat that such hybridity imposed on the "imperial visions of permanent European settlement."[134]

Toward the end of his life, Teit listed the racialized labels that white settler males faced when they aligned themselves with Indian women. "Squaw man" and "siwash man" were the two major ones. "Siwash," he explained, was a derivation of the French word "sauvage" that had entered the English language via Chinook Jargon. As if to underscore the negativity associated with the term, he offered several examples of its usage. A white man "who lives like an Indian or lives and acts below the common standard of the whites," he wrote, was commonly described as a man who had been "siwashed." To depict a man as such, he added, "put [that] white man in the same class as Indians by not being allowed to get liquor."[135] In her memoir, Jessie Smith alluded to its application to Teit: "People could not understand [Teit's] great interest in the Indians," she wrote. "In fact, when the stage bringing gold down from the mines of the Cariboo was robbed near Scottie Creek in 1890, the police picked up James Teit" as a suspect.[136] Teit's daughter, Inga, recalled her childhood playmates taunting her as the daughter of a "klootchman" because of her father's relationship with Antko. "Before Father died," she explained, "people had said to us children, 'You know your father was a Klootchman,' meaning that he had lived with an Indian woman."[137]

Michael and I experienced the visceral severity of the term "siwash" on a hot day in August 2012 while visiting two old friends, Bert Seymour and Jimmy Toodlican, members of the Shackan Band, near Spences Bridge. In line with past visits, we suggested a car ride along the old gravel road on the south side of the Thompson River between Spences Bridge and Ashcroft. The road passed through a series of old farms with many tangible connections to Teit. The main connection was the old John Tetlanetza ("Tet-lan-EET-sa") homestead on the Pekaist reserve.[138] Tetlanetza, who died in 1918, had been one of Teit's closest friends. Jimmy and Bert had their own connections to Teit. Bert's grandmother, Olip'tsa ("Oh-LEEP-tsa"), an Indian doctor, had been one of the large circle of women at the Shackan reserve who contributed to Teit's basketry project. Jimmy's grandmother, Josephine George, another well-known Indian doctor, was also part of this circle of women. As Josephine spoke no English, Jimmy became her translator at an early age. The experience turned him into one of the region's most knowledgeable language instructors. We headed off, Bert and Michael in the front seats and Jimmy and me in the back.

Prior to picking up our friends, Michael and I had been mulling over the term "siwash." Our travels through the province had taken us past many landmarks and creeks bearing this name. Siwash Rock off Stanley Park in Vancouver and Siwash Creek in the Similkameen Valley were well-known place names. We wondered how this could be, given the word's racialized associations. In contrast to the term "Indian," which had no negative connections in their reserve communities, we wondered how Bert and Jimmy felt about the term. After an hour or so of bumping along the old, potholed road, Michael put the question to them: "There is a word for Indians that used to be common. We are wondering what you think of it, you know, what sort of things it means to people." Summoning up the courage, Michael then blurted out "siwash." An uneasy silence filled the car. "That is *not* a good word," Bert said sternly. Jimmy nodded in agreement from the back seat. Michael quickly changed the subject. The word seemed to have stuck with Jimmy, however. At lunch at a café in Ashcroft a couple of hours later, he repeatedly turned our conversation to the discrimination he had experienced as a boy in the Spences Bridge elementary school.

What Boas Saw

Boas could not help but see a side of "siwash" in the Twaal Valley on that first visit in September 1894. If he paid it any heed, however, he mentioned nothing of it in his letters to Marie and his parents. He was too busy taking measurements for that. Teit and Antko's help served him well. By the end of his first day with the couple, he had measured most of the Nlaka'pamux people resident in the Twaal Valley.[139] The second day in the village was even more successful than the first. Teit turned up at his hotel at 5 a.m. with two horses to take him on a tour of the local "Indian camps." Boas described the day's highlights in letters to Marie and his parents – at one stop seeing an elderly, long-haired "medicine man" with a painted face finishing up a doctoring session. He wrote that he was finally getting "good results" and he felt like a new man. That "disagreeable feeling I had that I don't get along with the Indians is slowly wearing off now."[140] Best of all, he had a firm commitment for more work from the Shetlander he had encountered in the Twaal Valley two days earlier: "James Teit knows a great deal about the tribes. I engaged him right off."[141] He was happy to report to Marie that he was "slowly getting into the mood for 'fieldwork' again."[142]

The gratitude was mutual. For Teit, those two days with Boas came with a contract to write a full report on the Nlaka'pamux. It was work that he could easily integrate into his ranch work and his guiding work. It was also a continuation of work that he had already been doing on his own with Antko and her elderly relatives and friends. Indeed, this was work for which Teit, without intention, had long prepared, even before coming to Canada.

3
Dear Auld Rock

Ever ready to adapt himself to his environment, the Shetlander soon takes root in the new soil; and new associations and ties are formed which are not easily shaken off. But, if he be a true son of the isles, he never forgets the "Old Rock,"[1] *and the kindred he has left behind; and if circumstances permit, he will revisit the scenes of his childhood again and yet again. [He might pay Shetland a visit; but in the end] he returns to the country of his adoption; and thenceforth his native isles are to him as isles of dream, seen through a golden haze of memory.*

– W.F. Clark, *The Story of Shetland* (1906)[2]

We are not Scotch. We have never been Scotch. And ... we never will be Scotch.

– J.J. Haldane Burgess, Shetland poet and novelist, *Lowra Biglan's Mutch* (1896)[3]

Early in the Teit project, Sigurd Teit arrived on my Vancouver doorstep with a box of old books. I should have these, he said; they were staples of his father's library. There were several Shetland novels and books of poetry, a history of the parish of Lerwick, a nineteenth-century Shetland travelogue, an old photo album of Shetland scenes, a water-stained copy of *Oppressions in the Islands of Orkney and Zetland,* a couple of books on the Shetland dialect, several books on Shetland history and folklore, and an 1873 collection of Orkney sagas. At first glance, it looked like the sort of antique book collection that might have graced the shelves of many settler Canadian homes. Michael and I had such a collection – classics by nineteenth-century Old World writers such as Tennyson, Thackeray, Zola, and Dickens – on our own shelves, passed on to us by an elderly Ontario aunt. I skimmed through Teit's books and promptly placed them on a shelf reserved for old photographs and other bits of Teit memorabilia. They were a tangible link to my biographical subject. Just as Teit had touched their pages, so could I, and I left it at that. So attached was he to Canada's westernmost province that I took it to be his one "true" home, and the books mere mementoes. Aside from one trip to Shetland in 1902 to visit his aging parents, Teit had spent his full adult life in British Columbia.

I would soon learn that I was wrong, very wrong. The first clue turned up in the pages of an obscure Chicago-based newspaper, the *Orkney and Shetland American* (OSA), that Sigurd had given me. Magnus Flaws, a young Shetland expat based in Chicago, had founded the newspaper in 1887 to serve his fellow expats in the city and beyond.[4] Almost as soon as I started leafing through its pages, I spotted Teit ardently cheering on Flaws for his Shetland initiative.[5] Several issues later, I found Teit submitting stories about his life in British Columbia and lists of expat Shetlanders in the Pacific Northwest.[6] An article by Flaws in the February 1890 OSA turned my BC-centred story of Teit on its head. Under the headline "A Young Shetlander," it portrayed Teit as a die-hard Shetlander with a devotion to his island home that had intensified with absence.[7] "Love for the 'Dear Old Rock,'" wrote Flaws, "is a large portion of [Teit's] make-up, and this is the principal reason he gives for this great interest in his countrymen:"

> In publishing the following (without doubt much against the wishes of Mr. Tait), a little explanation may be necessary. The writer is a young man who hails from Lerwick, and who some years ago went to British Columbia, where he has been engaged principally in trapping and trading with the Indians, many times being located where he never hears the English language spoken the entire season.[8] Yet withal this, he was probably previous to the issuing of the *Orkney & Shetland American,* the best posted man in America as to the doings and whereabouts of Shetlanders on this continent.[9]

One of Flaws's comments spoke to Teit's "politics of being" in ways that I had not seen in his own writings:

> In all his lonely travels he has companions, in the company of which he reveled. Whiles he was with the ancient sea kings in their victorious exploits, and anon at Stewart's "Auld Wife's Fireside," or an eager listener to the tales of Burgess, or perhaps enthused by the poetic lines of Saxby or Anderson, or perhaps delving into the musty lore of Goudie.[10]

This short passage sent me back to Teit's book collection, looking for details that I might have missed on my first pass through. A quick internet search revealed that the five names that Flaws had listed as Teit's travelling "companions" – Stewart, Burgess, Saxby, Anderson, and Goudie – were not just random individuals but core members of a late-nineteenth-century cultural and political movement aimed at repositioning Shetland as a unique indigenous culture that had, for centuries, flourished in the remote, bounded isles of their "old world." "Burgess" was James J. Haldane Burgess, a distinguished scholar of Scandinavian language and literature and a beloved author of prose fiction and poetry centred on his island's distinct culture and history. There were three of his novels in Teit's collection.[11] "Anderson" was Basil Anderson, a poet revered for his poems in Shetlandic, his island's dialect. Anderson's *Broken Lights* was also in Teit's book collection.[12] "Saxby" was Jessie Saxby, a renowned Shetland writer who published dozens of books on the island's history and folklore.[13] She and "Gilbert Goudie," a prominent Shetland antiquarian (and the fifth name on Flaws's list) had co-edited Anderson's *Broken Lights.*[14] "Stewart" (the first name on the list) was George Stewart, the author of *Shetland Fireside Tales,* the first book to feature print versions of the local spoken dialect.[15] Stewart had helped Saxby and Goudie with the production of Anderson's posthumous *Broken Lights.*[16]

From the mid-1870s on, this group of Shetland literati had used their stories, poems, and histories to promote a new image of Shetland rooted in its Scandinavian past.[17] For some of its proponents, the renaissance heralded an independent and more democratic Shetland, free of the class division and oppression that had come with the transition from Danish to Scottish rule in the fifteenth century. Arthur Laurenson, a prominent Lerwick merchant and a keen member of the Shetland cultural movement, articulated this position in a *Macmillan's Magazine* article in 1875: "[The Shetland islands] ... are at this moment, properly speaking, Danish islands, over which Great Britain holds, what is called in Scotch legal phrase, a bond or disposition in security. The Danish crown may at any time resume possession by discharging the bond."[18] Laurenson and others had pursued Scandinavian languages and literature as a way to affirm Shetland as a true Norse "heimland." In his OSA articles, Flaws placed Teit fully on this path:

> To better connect the heimland with the fatherland, and to better explain many things that he [Teit] could not otherwise reason out alone, as we must remember he is his own teacher, he concluded that he must acquire the Scandinavian language. We were only too glad to be of any assistance in the

matter of procuring the books, and hope he may soon prove master of the language.[19]

The signature that Teit used for his OSA submissions ("J.A. Teit" rather than "J.A. Tait)[20] was a public manifestation of the historical depth of his sense of belonging.[21]

The pencil and ink jottings in the margins of Teit's Shetland books added more weight to this. In 1891, he had inscribed "James Alexander Teit, borarn ipa St. Magnus dae, 1864 i Lerwick, Shetland" on the inside cover of his copy of Burgess's novel *Rasmie's Büddie.* His father's inscription in another book a decade later – "to James A. Tait ... from his loving father, John Tait, June 1901"[22] – suggested that Teit's newly minted Scandinavian surname (along with a birthdate expressed in Shetland dialect) was not a break with his family but rather a larger repositioning. A few pages into his copy of *Rasmie's Büddie,* Teit had penciled in "Yae – Dat'll be tru" next to Burgess's line "Ye'll finn da bits o poiems farder ower."[23] As *Rasmie's Büddie* was Shetland's first full-length exposition of poetry in Shetlandic intended to demonstrate to the outside world the dialect's capacity for higher thought and contemplation, Teit's notation was his affirmation. An inscription in Teit's copy of Burgess's novel *Tang: A Shetland Story* was a direct link to the inner circle of Shetland literati because Burgess had not only autographed the book ("J.J. Haldane Burgess, Lerwick Shetland, 2/6/02)" but also inscribed a personal note in Danish: *Jakob Teit, med forfaterens venligst hilsner* ("Jakob Teit, with the author's friendliest greetings").[24]

Beneath a photograph of Basil Anderson in the latter's *Broken Lights,* Teit had inscribed, in jet-black ink, "Basil R. Anderson, (a 'skald' of Thule), born in Unst. Shetland Islands, 6th August 1861. Died 7th January 1888."[25] On a blank end-page of the book, he had hand-copied – in the same black ink – an Anderson poem he had found in a recent issue of the OSA. The two entries, executed in fine calligraphy, seemed a fitting complement to Jessie Saxby's introduction to the book – the sad story of the poet's tragedy-laden life. The son of a fisherman who had died in a *haaf* (deep-sea) fishing accident, leaving his pregnant wife and five children destitute on Shetland's remote north island of Unst, Anderson had died prematurely in Edinburgh just as he was launching a unique line of indigenous Shetland poems.[26]

It was now clear to me that Teit, on arriving in Spences Bridge in the 1880s, had entered a geopolitical space that was strikingly familiar. The densely forested and hot, arid mountains were far from the bare hills, swirling windscapes, and frigid seas he had left behind, and Spences Bridge was certainly not Lerwick. Nevertheless, there was a common resonance, especially in the political sphere where the local Nlaka'pamux peoples, recently dispossessed of their land base, were deploying foreign concepts of land "rights" and "title" to assert their sovereignty. It seemed more than coincidental that, on the other side of the Atlantic, Teit's Shetland friends and colleagues were deploying ancient Norse land rights as a way to detach themselves from Britain and reclaim their rights to their island land base.[27] From his new home at Spences Bridge, Teit found ways to engage with both political cultures and initiatives.

There is much debate in today's academic sphere about the global history of colonization and the conquest of place and space through "exodus and diaspora." The advance of globalization and trade often sparks revitalization among those anxious to salvage meaning in their local, place-based spheres as a way to offset the disorientation produced by the influx of people and goods from far away. Postcolonial scholars have addressed the colonial mentalities that permeate conquered spaces, leaving locals with feelings of inferiority and a self-image as subalterns to colonial masters long after their country achieves formal independence from the imperial centre. Cultural studies scholars ask how grammars of "difference" help locals create and maintain their own collective meanings and identities.[28] So what might a Shetland migrant take with him when he leaves home, and what strategies might he deploy to hold on to his roots?

To Shetland

Teit's Canadian story is wrapped up in these issues that are so alive today. To understand them requires seeing them as he saw them: through the lens of a remote island archipelago on the other side of the Atlantic. And so, in May 2006, I flew from Victoria to Edinburgh, took a train from Edinburgh to Aberdeen, and then sailed by the overnight Northlink ferry from Aberdeen to Lerwick. The last sea leg of my journey was almost as long as the first two air legs combined.

Because of a cancellation the previous day due to weather, the ferry was packed. As we pulled out of Aberdeen, all talk in the passenger lounge was about the unusually placid waters. The gale-force winds had given way to dead calm. We were lucky, I was told, because the sea stayed calm for the full 340-kilometre voyage, allowing us to glide into port well-rested and nausea-free. For a first-time visitor such as myself, the sight of the granite-faced "Lerrick" framed against a clear blue sky instilled relief at a twelve-hour voyage completed and anticipation of a passage begun.

By pure coincidence, I arrived in Lerwick on the eve of a major international conference on Jakob Jakobsen, a distinguished Faroese (Danish) philologist who, in the mid-1890s and again in 1912, had combed Shetland for traces of an ancient Norse (Norn) dialect spoken on the island prior to the Scottish takeover in the mid-fifteenth century.[29] Two of Jakobsen's books, *Det Norrøne Sprog Pa Shetland* (his doctoral dissertation on the Shetland dialect published in Denmark in 1897) and *Shetlandsøernes Stednavne* (his book of Shetland place names, published in Denmark in 1901), were in Teit's book collection. I had thumbed through their endless pages of word lists and place names, noting Teit's marginal jottings, and then promptly placed them back on the shelf.

Like Flaws's newspaper article, the Jakobsen conference opened another window on Teit. From Jakobsen's birth in February 1864 in Tørshavn, Faroe (two months before Teit's birth in 1864 in Lerwick, Shetland), to his untimely death at age fifty-four in 1918 (four years before Teit's untimely death at age fifty-eight in 1922), to his political ideals and his ethnographic goals, I saw more connections than I could count.[30] The main one was a geographic connection: childhoods spent on small, remote islands (one in the North Sea and the other in the Norwegian Sea, both closer to Norway than to Great Britain) that were physically, culturally, and historically related. Another connection was their passion for indigenous languages, especially those of their remote island homes. Jakobsen grew up speaking Faroese, a resident North German language descended from an Old West Norse language spoken in medieval times; Teit grew up speaking Shetlandic, a Lowland Scots English dialect with similar North German/West Norse roots. According to Faroese historian Marianna Debes Dahl, the Jakobsen family business – a bookshop on the waterfront of Tørshavn (Faroe's equivalent of Lerwick) – offered a unique linguistic experience to its late-nineteenth-century Shetland visitors. During their frequent stopovers at the port of Tørshavn, Shetland sailors and fishermen often congregated in the shop, and "so similar were their two languages at the time," Dahl writes, "that Jakobsen senior and the rest of the Faroese staff in the shop were able to communicate with the Shetlanders."[31]

A doctoral degree in linguistics at the University of Copenhagen offered Jakobsen an opportunity to turn those Faroese-Shetland exchanges in his father's shop into serious academic study. On completing several projects on his Faroese dialect, he set his sights on a trip to Shetland to see what survived of the Norn language there.[32] He spent two years (1893–1895) interviewing dialect speakers across the islands. In addition to identifying the unique "peculiarities" of Shetland's Scots-English speech, such as *d's* and *t's* for the *th* sound, the dropping of *g* in the suffix *–ing*, the use of *du* and *ye* as forms of address, he identified ten thousand Norse words and noted that more than half were still in use.[33]

From the Tait family letters, I could see that Teit in British Columbia had monitored the progress of Jakobsen's Shetland project.[34] He had obtained Jakobsen's books as soon as they were available and peppered them with pencil comments, corrections, and additions. He was clearly enthralled to see, for the first time, a full academic study of his much-maligned dialect. And Jakobsen's quest for Shetland dialect enthusiasts had taken him into Teit's circle of close friends and family.[35] Indeed, he could well have had Teit's cousin John Irvine and his friend and former schoolmate J.J. Haldane Burgess in mind when he observed, in an 1893 submission to a Faroese newspaper, that "everywhere I have met with the greatest courtesy and sympathy for my project. People here seem to have expected that some Scandinavian philologist or another would come to rescue the remains of the old 'Norn' or 'Norse.'"[36] Both Irvine and Burgess were key dialect enthusiasts at the time.

In this same report, Jakobsen expressed a political orientation to his work in Shetland that aligned with Teit's orientation to his work on Nlaka'pamux language and culture:

> The more I study this ill-treated speech and attempt to weld the fragments together, the stronger I feel its close affinity with my own mother-tongue, the stronger my love for it and the greater the hatred of the Scots and English who have methodically stunted its growth and future development ... But one may admire the old dialect's tenacity, which has lasted a long way into this century, if only in distorted form, despite persistent pressure for 400 years from the world's most powerful language – English.[37]

The finale of the Jakobsen conference – an evening of poetry and stories performed in dialect by Shetland poets and storytellers – brought the connections between Jakobsen and Teit full circle. Lawrence Tulloch, a storyteller from the northern isle of Yell, took to the stage with the story of "Jan Teit and the Bear," which he described as a story that Jakob Jakobsen had recorded in 1894 from an old storyteller, Thomas Tait, who lived on the outer isle of Fetlar. It was a special story, he said, as it was Shetland's *only* surviving story from Norwegian times. I knew from Teit's letters to his Uncle Robert Tait in New Zealand that Teit had pursued his family members for this very story.[38]

I could see why the story might interest him. In addition to a matching surname and a rich ancestral link, the story's main protagonist was a Fetlar man who had challenged central authority by slaying the Norwegian "skat" (tax) collector over a dispute about his tax payments (paid in butter). The collector had angered Jan Teit by accusing him of overstating his butter's weight. Teit was ordered to Norway to have his case decided by the king. Instead of having the accused executed for his misdeed, the king challenged him to track down an unruly bear that was causing him trouble and bring the bear back alive to him. With the help of an old woman and a large stash of butter, Teit managed to catch the bear and deliver it to the king. The king then ordered Teit back to Shetland with the bear. Teit did as requested and deposited the bear on an island off Shetland's northern shore.[39]

From Haaf Fishers to Merchants

On my first morning in Lerwick, I purchased a small, soft-covered book, *Toons and Tenants: Settlement and Society in Shetland, 1299–1899,* at the local bookstore on Commercial Street. This volume filled many gaps in my knowledge of Shetland history.[40] Its author, Brian Smith, was the head archivist at the Shetland Museum and Archives, who had also helped out Sigurd during his 1992 Shetland visit. I had contacted Smith a year or so earlier with long lists of questions, all of which he had generously answered. As the co-organizer of the Jakobsen conference, he was running everything, from the formal talks and dinners to tours of the countryside. A highlight was the sneak preview of his soon-to-open museum facility on the town's waterfront. Watching Smith in his various roles – including a dialect presentation at the final evening event – was to see a living connection to the Shetland fervour of Teit, Burgess, and others a century earlier.

Smith's *Toons and Tenants* confirmed the word that I was hearing on the street – that life under Scandinavian rule from the ninth to the fifteenth century was more agreeable than life under Scottish rule. The islanders during the earlier period had lived relatively free lives as tenant farmer-fishers in a network of "toons," or "small peasant townships." They were subject to a collection of "lesser and greater" landlords scattered across the landscape, but unlike the eighteenth-century landlords, these early proprietors had not yet formed a consolidated force with large manorial holdings.[41] A robust trade with merchants from northern Germany provided the islanders with outlets to exchange their fish, farm produce, and handmade hosiery for hooks, lines, hemp, tar, linen, tobacco, spirits, and other items from Europe.[42]

This pattern continued until the seventeenth century, when a series of crises – famines, epidemics, landlord bankruptcies, and the collapse of the local governmental system – threw Shetland into disarray. The breaking point was a virulent smallpox epidemic in 1700 that claimed a third of the islands' population.[43] The islanders had just begun to recover from the epidemic when the British government imposed a Salt Tax that effectively terminated the German Hanseatic fish trade.[44] The loss of the commercial trade forced tenant fisher-farmers to resort to fish instead of cash for rent payments and supplies. In some cases, they had to supplement this with butter and farm produce. Several enterprising landlords capitalized on the situation by purchasing and leasing the recently bankrupted estates and implementing a new "fishing tenure" system that gave them full control of large tracts of land along with rent-rates and fish prices. Some gained control of the island's mercantile, fish curing, and banking sectors as well.[45] Such takeovers spawned a system of debt bondage that stripped local tenants of their independence and turned them into wards of their landlords.[46] Anyone who resisted or rebelled faced eviction. This story resonated with stories of land dispossessions, the reserve system, and the Indian Act in Teit's new home in British Columbia.

The fishing-tenure system was the backdrop to James Teit's family history. His paternal grandfather, James Tait (born in 1790), and James's first wife, Catherine (born in 1792), were members of a generations-old *haaf* (deep-sea) fishing community on Fetlar, one of Shetland's northern islands.[47] The haaf fishery was an enterprise that drew on an indentured labour force of some three thousand men and four hundred to five hundred fishboats concentrated along the coast.[48] It dominated the Shetland economy for over a century and imposed huge risks and hardship on the local fisher-farmer families from May to August of each year. In fleets of thirty-foot-long wooden boats (*sixerns* as the locals called them, after their six pairs of oars), men and boys rowed out to sea (assisted by a single sail), to distances of up to forty miles, often in vicious weather, to fish for cod, tusk, and saith (the large white fish that could be easily split, cut, salted, and dried for sale on the international market). It took all hands to lay out the baited lines at seven-mile distances and depths of fifty to one hundred fathoms and then haul them in by hand.[49] The goal was two or three such trips per week, each lasting twenty-four hours or more. The crews returned to designated haaf stations on the shoreline and handed over their full catch to their landlords. Only at the end of the fishing season in August, with the last of the season's catch delivered, were tenants free to fish for their families. Even then they faced restrictions, as their landlords allowed them to fish only for lesser fish – haddock, piltocks, and sillocks – for their family consumption.

A merchant-laird measured his wealth by the size of his tenant base: the larger his base, the larger his cod catch and the larger his return on the international fish market. His demands took a toll on family life by removing all able-bodied men from their homesteads ("crofts") at the very time that those homesteads needed them to help with food cultivation and harvest. It was especially hard on the women. With their older sons, husbands, and fathers at sea for most of May, June, July, and August, they had to run the family farms on their own. In her study of Shetland women's history, University of Glasgow historian Lynn Abrams concludes that Shetland's unusual division of labour in the eighteenth and nineteenth centuries turned it into a "women's world" that "operated with very distinctive female rules, stories, and understandings."[50] With women in the countryside working in the fields, carrying peat, and gutting fish, and their counterparts in Lerwick running boarding houses and working as house servants, laundresses, and dressmakers, much of island life was literally running on women's energy.[51] It was the antithesis of the privatized situation on the mainland, writes Abrams, where women were largely confined to "the home and parlour, the servants' quarters, [or] the factory."[52]

A series of poor harvests, a lull in the international fish market, and a steady loss of tenants to the Napoleonic wars and the Greenland whaling ships in the late eighteenth century weakened the fishing-tenure system. A slump in the cod and herring fisheries in the 1830s and '40s prompted some landowners to consider agriculture as a more lucrative economic option than fishing.[53] The appearance in the 1860s of large, motorized vessels ("smacks") capable of covering longer distances at faster speeds also changed things in the fishing industry, as did the emergence of the inshore herring fishery.[54] The transition to herring had started slowly in the mid-1870s with 50 herring boats pulling in 1,100 barrels of herring. Seven years later, when Teit was seventeen and living in Lerwick, there were 276 boats pulling in 59,586 barrels of herring.[55] The herring boom placed extreme pressure on Lerwick and other fish-curing centres by drawing thousands of fishermen and female labourers from mainland Scotland to work in the fish-curing and shipping sectors.[56] A fishing accident in 1881 that claimed the lives of fifty-eight fishers spelled the beginning of the end of the old

Lerwick's Commercial Street, c. 1895. Teit lived here with his family until his departure for Canada in 1884. | Photograph by Robert Ramsay, #Y00055, Shetland Museum.

haaf fishery. With its connection to that fishery, Teit's family, like many others throughout the island, felt the impact of its demise.

In my exploration of the nooks and crannies of Lerwick, I was surprised to learn that much of the town's built environment, which I had thought of as old, was, by Shetland standards, new. It had come with the 1870s and '80s herring boom that transformed the town from a small fishing port, with one narrow street lined "with rather plain, shed-like buildings of undressed stone," into a good-sized Victorian town.[57] During Teit's adolescence, there were three major construction projects underway: an upscale residential suburb named New Town, replete with rows of stately new residences and villas; a large, gothic baronial-style Town Hall with ornate stained-glass windows; and a fancy new promenade, the Esplanade, along the waterfront to replace the old piers.[58] There was much debate about the Esplanade because many of the older Lerwegians could not imagine their foreshore without the old piers. Along with architectural additions and upgrades, the boom gave rise to a locally produced newspaper, the *Shetland Times,* an improved ferry service to the mainland, a faster and more efficient postal service, and a rash of athletic and social clubs offering everything from tennis, bowling, curling, golf, boating, and swimming to chess groups, music societies, and horticultural societies.[59]

Teit's family was enmeshed in all this change. His grandfather James had moved his family from their centuries-old fishing community on the outer island of Fetlar to Lerwick sometime around 1817.[60] It was a common transition at the time, especially for Fetlar islanders, due to the autocratic actions of a resident laird, Arthur Nicolson (1794–1863). Nicolson had inherited a large piece of Fetlar property in 1805. A ruthless "improver," he gradually bought out the smaller proprietors on the island until, by mid-century, he owned 74 percent of Fetlar's land base.[61] He controlled his large tenancy with an iron fist. In 1820, he built a grand Gothic mansion, Brough Lodge, on his Fetlar estate. For his many dependent (and insecure) employees who participated in its construction, the house was a stark lesson in class inequity.[62] At the end of the workday, they left the ornate, ostentatious Nicolson estate and returned to their overcrowded, two-room croft houses.

When Greenland-bound whaling and sealing ships docked at Lerwick at the turn of the nineteenth century and advertised for crew members, many young islanders sought them out as a way to escape the bondage of lairds and merchants such as Nicolson. According to the Tait/Teit family history, this was the route by which Teit's grandfather, James, got to Lerwick. Nicolson's response to the loss of tenants such as James was to issue an ultimatum in 1826, demanding that his tenants stay home to fish or face eviction.[63]

The drain of young men had started earlier – during James's childhood in the 1790s – with the Revolutionary and Napoleonic wars between Britain and France that drew thousands of Shetland men – many press-ganged – into the British Royal Navy. The drain continued with the Greenland- and Davis Strait–bound whaling and sealing ships, the gin-smuggling ships, and the British merchant marine. Those who returned to Shetland often arrived with cash in their pockets and new job prospects.[64] Some joined the fishing sector as agents for the Greenland whaling ships, while others took jobs in the smuggling trade and the merchant marine. Those with literacy and navigational skills had the best options. James Tait appears to have been one of the latter, because he moved easily from Fetlar into Lerwick's fish-curing and mercantile sector. James and Catherine had likely attended school on Fetlar, where, according to Shetland historian John Graham, the Edinburgh-based Society in Scotland for Propagating Christian Knowledge (SSPCK) had provided two schoolteachers between 1796 and 1826.[65]

Life in Lerwick was tough for the young Fetlar couple. Shortly after settling in the town, they lost a year-old baby girl. Four years later, James lost Catherine. She died in February 1826, leaving him with two young children.[66] The couple's exodus from Fetlar was timely, however, because Nicolson had acted on his 1826 ultimatum to build stone-wall enclosures on his estate. On their completion, he evicted the resident tenants and proceeded to fill the enclosures with sheep. At his death in 1863, Nicolson had sent approximately three hundred tenants into potential vagabondage.[67] The clearances were a catastrophe for an island of nine hundred people, the majority of whom had never lived anywhere else.[68] A second even more vicious wave of clearances occurred in the 1860s. While some of the evicted families found new homes and livelihoods on the sheep farms, many ended up in Lerwick with few employment prospects.

Eight months after Catherine's death, James married Joan Laurenson of Lerwick and had eight more children.[69] The couple's fourth child, John, born in 1833, would later father "my" Teit. James Sr. lived in Lerwick until his death in 1870 at age eighty. James Teit (born in 1864) was only six years old at the time, so he would not have known his grandfather well, but because Joan Tait survived her husband by sixteen years, she was part of Teit's inner family circle in Lerwick all through Teit's youth (she died two years after his departure to BC). Teit's aunt Ursula Tait Irvine (his father's half-sister) was also a part of his inner family circle, as she lived in the town until her death in 1895. These and other family members were Teit's links to his family history. Ursula gave him direct access to the Fetlar side of the family history, as she was born there during the Nicolson regime.[70]

Social Reform and Philanthropy

Although they were never wealthy, Teit's grandparents, James and Joan, lived comfortable lives in the middle-class, mercantile sector of the town. Their position in the community offered their children (Teit's father, John, and his siblings) educational opportunities and upward mobility that James Sr. could not have imagined in his own childhood.[71] Their son Robert (born in 1831) became a prominent town contractor with major projects – the town's first steam sawmill, the Widow's Home, St. Olaf's Church Manse, and the Robertson's Buildings on Union Street. James's daughter, Ursula, from his first marriage to Catherine, joined the town's elite social sector through her marriage to William Irvine, a successful banker. Son John (born in 1833) followed his father into the grocery business and, like Robert, became a "prominent man in town," serving as a longtime "ruling elder" of the United Presbyterian Church and an active member of the town council and the school board.[72]

By Shetland standards, John (Teit's father) married well: to Elizabeth Murray, a teacher from Aberdeen who worked as a governess to the children of his half-sister, Ursula. John had started out on a secure footing as the proprietor of a grocery shop in Lerwick. After nine years, he sold his grocery business in 1873 and moved to Aberdeen to open a new grocery shop in the city. His wife, Elizabeth, was undoubtedly the main reason for the move, as she had grown up in an Aberdeen grocer family. Things did not go well for John and Elizabeth in Aberdeen, however.[73] Four years into the new business venture, John was so heavily in debt that he had to abandon it and return to Lerwick to work as the manager of a shop owned by Hay & Co. It took years to pay off his debts, which created major tensions within the family. In a letter to his brother Joseph in 1880, John wrote that he was "not only poor" but still trying to pay off his "debt."[74]

Lerwick during John Tait's youth in the 1830s and '40s was marked by contrast. On one side was a growing prosperity propelled by the influx of foreign ships, seamen, and permanent residents. Between 1791 and 1821, the population had increased from 903 (356 of whom lived on the periphery) to 2,224.[75] The commercial sector of the town had also expanded. According to an 1849 report, there were "21 drapers and hosiers, 3 tailors and clothiers, a baker, 13 grocers and spirit dealers, 1 ironmonger and 11 general merchants" in the town.[76] Two enterprising Shetlanders, William Hay and Charles Ogilvy, had capitalized on the new cash flow in the community by establishing Shetland's first bank in 1821.[77] With these changes, a new middle class began to close the gap between the small upper-class landlords and the mass of poor tenant farmer-fishers.[78] Shetland was becoming a true capitalist economy – those with cash made money, and not just with goods but with capital itself.

This side of town flourished at the expense of the rest of the town. According to Abrams, Lerwick in the mid-nineteenth century had "some of the worst housing conditions in Scotland."[79] Many residents were widows who had lost their husbands to haaf fishing accidents; others were dispossessed tenant fisher-farmers. A series of harvest failures, a lull in the herring fishery, and several fishing accidents in the 1840s threw many parts of the island into disarray. Unable to cover its debt loads, the Shetland Bank declared bankruptcy in 1842. The numbers of paupers and beggars on Lerwick's streets spoke to the rising poverty in the town.[80]

By the mid-1840s, a group of concerned citizens decided it was time to tackle the poverty. They founded a paupers' dispensary in 1846 to provide free medicine to the poor, and in 1847 they established (through the Lerwick Local Destitution Committee) a soup kitchen to feed the poor.[81] Arthur Anderson, a wealthy expatriate Shetlander, had paved the way by founding the Shetland Fishery Company in 1837 to help local fishers become "free agents." He then endowed a Widows' Asylum in Lerwick to house women whose husbands had been killed in fishing accidents.[82] Like many of his peers, Anderson had spent his teens in the British Navy fighting in the Napoleonic wars. A move into the international shipping sector after the war culminated in a permanent directorship in the powerful P&O shipping company, which made him independently wealthy. He served as the Liberal Member of Parliament for Orkney-Shetland from 1847 until 1852. Ever grateful for the education he received as a boy in Gremista, he took a special interest in improving the education of the youth in Shetland.[83] In 1853, he helped fund a school on the outer island of Skerries. He used personal funds to cover its teachers' salaries. In 1859, he offered to fund the construction of a new school for the children of Lerwick, and the Anderson Educational Institute opened its doors in 1861.[84]

Although Anderson had played a major role in the founding and building of the new school, Teit's father had laid the groundwork for it. Indeed, without John Tait's efforts there might not have been such a school, or at least not at this early date. In 1855, concerned that the poor children in town lacked access to schooling, John Tait and five of his colleagues launched the Lerwick Instruction Society, a free night school, to address this gap.[85] In addition to raising funds to cover the cost of room rental and supplies, they offered their weekday evenings to teach in the school. John Tait did double duty by serving as the school secretary.[86] The volunteer effort was a major success. In short order the teaching corps expanded from six to thirty volunteers, and the student body grew to two hundred children. It was "a remarkable enterprise," writes local historian John Graham, as the volunteers were busy shop-keepers, shop assistants, and clerks, who had to extend their twelve-hour workdays by two hours to contribute to the school. Because the youngest students struggled with the school's hours – 10 p.m. to midnight –Tait and his colleagues pushed for an "Early Closing Movement" in the town's commercial sector to allow the school to run from 8 to 10 p.m. They later opened a special day school for the five- to seven-year-olds and drew on the women in the community to serve as its teachers. The success of this volunteer effort convinced Anderson to throw his energy – and funds – into establishing a full-scale academy in the town.[87] The Anderson Educational Institute would serve John and his wife, Elizabeth, well. Their eight children passed through its doors.

Shetland Renaissance

Arthur Laurenson, a prominent Lerwick merchant, was an influential figure in the town during Teit's adolescence. A close friend of Teit's father and a keen volunteer in the latter's night school, Laurenson had launched his own educational initiative in Lerwick in the 1860s.[88] He founded the Shetland Scientific and Literary Society in 1861 to enhance the cultural life of Lerwick. In addition to establishing a museum and a library in the town, Laurenson's goal was to use the society to bring scholars to the island to give lectures on subjects of interest.[89] A series of lectures on Scandinavian topics drew Laurenson into Norse literature and Scandinavian languages, which in turn focused his attention on his island's history and his family history.[90] He undertook a family history project that extended back seven generations to a Magnus Manson on the isle of Unst.[91]

Convinced of the value of this work for the larger community, Laurenson turned his personal study into a public campaign. One of his premier achievements was the naming of the new streets of New Town after Norwegian royalty – King Harald Street, St. Olaf Street, King Eric Street;[92] another was the installation of Norse-themed stained-glass windows in the new Town Hall.[93] Both projects were underway in Lerwick before Teit left for Canada. In addition to encouraging "educated Shetland families" to acquire copies of "the Sagas," Laurenson encouraged all schools throughout the islands to display "a Map of Shetland" featuring the "Norse names." "I think it would be most valuable," he wrote to his Shetland friend and fellow Scandinavian scholar Gilbert Goudie, "by way of teaching the people the topography and history of their native land to get our islands' geography imprinted on children's minds at an early age."[94] In the 1870s, Laurenson published provocative articles on the impact of British colonization on Shetland:

> All the ancient laws and customs of the island have been set at nought. The odal system has been changed to the feudal: all the native rights and claims nullified or abrogated without the consent of the people of the islands, and without the concurrence of the other Treaty power. These things have been

> done, and no redress has followed; but the right to have them undone or atoned for still remains.[95]

Laurenson was a keen speaker of the Shetland dialect. Indeed, according to a letter to his Shetland niece, who was heard speaking "West Country Scotch" during a trip to the mainland in 1879, he badgered the youth around him to follow suit:

> Now, my dear child, I just put it to you whether you shouldn't soften it down a little before you come here. No doubt a West Country Scotch accent *is* a charming acquisition, and will add a grace to your lips, but you must know that we are not accustomed to it up here, and it might be too much for us at first ... The general public might not appreciate it so well.[96]

No scolding was necessary for John Tait's eldest son, James, however. At sixteen, he was, according to his father, "fairly set upon being a real Shetlander [and] likes nothing to be done that would alter old Shetland customs."[97] At nineteen, Teit had embarked on a family history project that would have made Laurenson proud. "For his age," John Tait wrote to a relative, "I don't think you could have got hold of one so full of Shetland news. He knows lots of folks whom I did not know and ferreted out all our relatives beginning with generations before our great grandfather and tracing the descendants in every branch – all of which he committed to paper."[98] In a letter to his Uncle Robert (his father's brother) in 1903, Teit recalled interviewing his Aunt Catherine (his father's sister) "a good deal (about her mother's people)" before leaving Shetland.[99] Teit's younger brother, Tom, was on a similar path. In a letter exchange shortly after Teit's departure for BC, the two brothers discussed their mutual love of Shetland and their efforts to sustain that love from a distance.[100]

Four years in the large, bustling city of Aberdeen may have fuelled the two boys' passion for Shetland. John and Elizabeth Tait had moved there in 1873 when Teit was nine. They returned to Lerwick when he was thirteen. It was a difficult time for the family because, in addition to John's failed business venture, they lost three infant children. A year-old child, Joan, died in 1872 on the eve of their departure to Aberdeen; a newborn, William, died at birth in Aberdeen in February 1874; and another year-old child, William, died in January 1876. After these losses and the anonymity and fast-paced life of Aberdeen, a return to the intimacy and familiarity of Lerwick seems to have been a welcome relief for all. In a letter to his brother

The town of Lerwick, c. 1880s. The large land mass in the distance is the isle of Bressay. | Photograph by George Wilson, Photograph #Z00003, Shetland Museum.

Robert, John Tait suggested that this was certainly the case for his two eldest children, James and John: "Neither would go back to Aberdeen if they had the offer of the city to themselves." Three years after their return to Lerwick, according to their father, they were still "summing down Scotchmen and praising Shetlanders."[101]

Radicalization

The family's return to Lerwick was well-timed for son James. The Scottish Education Act, passed in 1872, had made school attendance compulsory for all children to the age of fourteen, which meant that he shared classrooms with children from all sectors of the town.[102] He entered the Anderson Educational Institute under the leadership of a new principal, John Allardice, a young Scot with a master's degree from the University of Glasgow. Within a few years of taking up the post, Allardice graduated some of the highest academic achievers in the island's history.[103] Fifteen

Teit (far left) with his friends Alexander Moar, John M. Irvine, Alexander Ratter, William Irvine, and Joseph Hunter, c. 1880. | Courtesy of Sigurd Teit.

of his senior students won first-place standing in the 1881 Glasgow University examinations. One student, James Haldane Burgess, stood first of 607 candidates.[104] Teit, who left the school a year earlier (at age sixteen), had won prizes in "Mathematics" and "German and General Excellence."[105] Many of Allardice's students carried on to careers as writers, journalists, physicians, and academics. Teit left school to apprentice with his father, who was the manager of the town's Hay & Co. grocery store.[106]

For a budding Shetland historian, life outside the classroom in the 1870s and '80s was just as formative as life inside the classroom. In addition to Laurenson's Scandinavian projects, numerous other historical projects were underway. James Goudie, the town provost who served for a time as the secretary of Laurenson's Scientific and Literary Society, worked on a history of Lerwick that traced the genealogies of the town's "leading residents" back three hundred years.[107] He also assembled a large home library of

Shetland books.[108] William Brown, a local shop-owner, converted a corner of his shop into a mini-museum featuring Shetland and Greenland archaeological artifacts.[109] Teit's father, John, participated in his own way. By the time of his death, he had completed "perhaps the most complete history of Lerwick, going back for a period of over a half a century."[110]

The testimonies of the nationwide 1872 Truck Commission sparked a political awakening in Shetland that would continue to build throughout Teit's adolescence. The old "truck" (barter) system that had sustained the fishing-tenure system in the eighteenth century had moved in the nineteenth century into the hands of the local merchants.[111] It was particularly hard on women who produced knitted shawls, jumpers, and veils for merchants because, in return, the latter offered them non-negotiable credit paid in goods or notes rather than cash.[112] Only rarely did merchants offer cash to the women.[113] The Truck Commission was the UK's attempt to liberate local producers from such servitude. The publication in the *Shetland Times* of the transcripts regarding this "crippling system" was a lesson in local history.[114] The Napier Crofters' Commission (Royal Commission of Inquiry into the Condition of Crofters and Cottars in the Highlands and Islands) a decade later provided yet more first-hand testimony of the effects of the island's high rents and insecure land tenures on its inhabitants. The Napier Commission hearings were underway in Shetland during the summer before Teit left for British Columbia. Although there is nothing in the archival record to show its direct impact on Teit, there is evidence of its impact on his adolescent circle.[115]

Historian Bronwen Cohen writes that Teit's school colleague James Haldane Burgess was "radicalized by the evidence given by the Napier Commission when it sat in Shetland in 1883 ... In as much as the injustices in Shetland society could be seen as historical, then they could be seen in terms of Norse-Scottish conflict," she writes, "and Burgess tended to view Shetland life from this perspective."[116] It is more than coincidental that two core members of Teit's inner circle (i.e., Burgess and Alexander Ratter) embraced socialism as they moved from adolescence into their twenties. As historian Brian Smith explains, "Ratter & Co." entered their twenties as a "clever" young group of "workers who had a romantic and rational view of the world and its possibilities ... When realism and romance knock sparks off each other all sorts of interesting things can happen."[117] Among those "interesting things" was the rejection of bourgeois depictions of their island as a "low" culture of crass dialects and quaint, illiterate fisher families. Teit's cohort celebrated Shetland as a "high" culture of authenticity, depth, and richness.

The Truck and Napier Commissions pursued liberal reform as a means to unshackle the feudal past and mitigate some of the evils of industrialization, but the wealth of the new economy had not improved the lives of the general populace. That world was still filled with inequity and contradiction. The modernizing processes slowly removed some of the injustices of the past (most notably, the haaf fishery and the truck system) and introduced new economic opportunities, political openings, and educational options but at the expense of age-old attachments to the land and to the mutuality of self-sustaining communities. New injustices of displacement, unemployment, poverty, and homelessness now took their place. As so many at the time wondered, why must the resolution of old injustices entail new ones? Why must the price of so-called progress require such unsettling?

Teit's letters suggest tension between father and son on some of these issues. A devout member of the Church of Scotland (the Kirk), the senior Tait's expectation was always that his children would follow his example.[118] Such was not the case with son James, however. On arriving in British Columbia, Teit not only ignored his father's appeals to study the Bible and attend church services; he rejected Christianity outright. In his role as the enumerator for the 1901 Canadian national census at Spences Bridge, he listed himself as a "freethinker," a religious designation that would have horrified his father.[119]

Rooted in a philosophical movement that took hold in England in the late seventeenth century, the freethinker movement sought higher "truths" through logic, reason, and empiricism rather than Church dogma and literal biblical interpretation. An anti-Christian *Freethinker* magazine founded in the early 1880s fuelled the movement.[120] In a letter to his uncle Robert, Teit alluded to differences with his father on the subject of religion: "Although I could not agree with him [his father] in all his beliefs regarding religion and politics, still I have no fault to find, for I know he was sincere in his beliefs and acted as he thought was right. Besides there is a continuous evolution in these things, and no two generations view them in exactly the same light."[121] The sudden death of his father in 1904 seems to have instilled feelings of guilt and self-doubt: "We have lost much in father," Teit wrote to his uncle, "for he was a man of very kind heart, and noble character. When I compare myself with him I see how defective I am, and realize how far I shall fall short of being a true man."[122] The death may also have evoked memories of his various dealings with his father, especially during his first years away from home. A major crisis erupted in his family home in Lerwick on March 22, 1884 – just two months after his departure from Shetland – when a letter arrived from a thirty-four-year-old widow named Joan Hughson (also known as Joan Johnson), who claimed that her five-day-old child was the son of their son James. Although she had not registered James as the father, she had given her son middle names, "Robert James Tait Johnson," that spoke to his paternity. In her letter to John and Elizabeth Tait, Joan had asked for their son's address so that she could request child support from him.

It was a "sad, sad piece of information," wrote the senior Tait to his son, and it required some explanation, especially as he had heard that Joan was a "notoriously bad character." He explained that, after receiving the letter, he and Elizabeth had invited Joan to the house, where they had discussed the issue with her. They gave her some baby clothes but told her that they would withhold financial support until they had heard their son's side of the story. In his letter to James, John urged his son to read the Bible, where he would find that "fornication is peculiarly heinous in God's sight." He hoped that God would give him "grace to repent of this great sin."[123] He stressed that if Hughson's baby was his child, "however bad [the mother] may be," he had a responsibility to support it.[124] His father's letterbook was silent on the issue until June 24, when he wrote to Joan Hughson to say that he had finally heard from his son, James, who "denies the paternity of your son."[125] John Tait asked her "not to trouble him with letters." According to the Shetland census records, Joan had another child, a six-year old boy, at the time, whose father had died at sea. Like many women in the town, she earned her living by knitting.

Teit's explanation seems to have satisfied his father, because John Tait made no further mention of Joan Hughson or the child in his letters to his son until September 17, 1888, when he notified James in a short postscript that "Joan Johnson or Hughson died last year [and] I don't know where her child is."[126] According to the census records, the orphaned child, Robert Johnson, lived with his grandmother (Joan's mother) in Lerwick until his mid-teens, when he moved to Leith, outside Edinburgh, to work as an apprentice grinder.[127]

Mass Exodus

Teit, like many Shetlanders, was deeply affected by the mass emigration that ravaged the island during his youth.[128] It had started as a trickle in the 1860s and grown into a torrent by the 1880s. According to one estimate, some 2,000 Shetlanders left the island between 1861 and 1871, and another

4,567 left between 1871 and 1881.[129] Some were forced out by the hardship of island life; others were lured away by newspaper articles and emigration officers offering assisted passage to better lives in new lands.[130] Many were displaced tenant farmers and impoverished fisherfolk. A significant number were members of the merchant and professional classes anxious to escape the uncertainty and instability of the Shetland economy. The positive stories that flowed in from the first wave of emigres – especially those who settled in New Zealand following the 1860s Otago gold rush – enticed many to leave.[131]

Years into his life in British Columbia, Teit described Shetland as a place that he loved but was forced to leave because of a lack of work: "I am still a strong lover of Shetland ... but there is so little chance there for a man to do anything outside of two or three lines which of course are not suitable to us all."[132]

The exodus razed Teit's family. Two of his uncles – his father's half-brother, Thomas, and his full brother, James – were among the first departures. Neither fared well. Thomas died of sunstroke in Calcutta in 1848, and James died of yellow fever in Trinidad in 1853. Subsequent family migrants had more success. Teit's uncle Robert emigrated to New Zealand in 1874 with his wife, Janet, and their seven children. They settled in Wellington where they established a large family estate, "Taitville," and prospered.[133] They were joined by Teit's aunts Catherine and Elizabeth and his uncle Joseph. Teit's aunt Barbara emigrated to Australia and died there. His uncle Isaac died in London, England, in 1899.

Teit was the first of his siblings to leave Shetland. His brother Thomas soon followed with a move to Edinburgh to study law. His brother Isaac moved to Liverpool, England, to work on ships sailing to Cuba and the United States. After a job in Marseilles, he moved to Montreal, where he worked as a consulting engineer in the shipbuilding sector. Teit's brother Harry moved to Africa but later, like his brothers Isaac and James, emigrated to Canada, where he spent two decades working in towns throughout northern Ontario. Harry moved to Spences Bridge in 1921 and died at Lytton in 1937 of alcoholism. Teit's sister Alice moved with her husband to Edinburgh, and his sister Katherine moved with her husband to southern England. The last family holdout was Teit's brother John, who stayed in Lerwick to work with his father. After his father's death in 1904, however, John packed up and moved to Australia.[134] In the space of one generation, an entire extended family that had rarely travelled more than a few miles from their small, Fetlar island home had scattered to the far reaches of the empire.[135] It was a massive exodus that included thousands of families like the Taits. As historian Marjory Harper explains, between 1825 and 1914, Scotland lost approximately two million men, women, and children to non-European destinations.[136]

According to John Tait, a migrant story in the Tait household caught the attention of son James at an early age. It had been his son's childhood dream to join his uncle, John Murray, in Canada. The seeds were likely sown by James's mother, who had used her brother's colourful letters from British Columbia to entertain her children on their sick days. In 1883, when nineteen-year-old James was three years into his apprenticeship (with his father) in Lerwick's Hay & Co. grocery shop, Murray sent word to his sister that he had a clerkship in his Spences Bridge store that he could offer to one of her sons. James was the natural choice. As John Tait explained to Murray, James's "sole desire, since he was a child, has been to go to you. Where a man's heart is, there he works with a will."[137] Murray made it all possible by sending the family $200 to help with James's travel costs. On January 29, 1884 (the day after the annual Up Helly Aa festival – described in more detail in Chapter 7), Teit stood on the pier bidding farewell to his sorrowful parents and downcast siblings, wondering, like so many others on the pier, if he would ever see them again.

Teit's father had spent weeks organizing the logistics of his son's long trip to British Columbia. In addition to lining up two travel companions who were also heading to Spences Bridge (from Aberdeen), he had arranged a stopover at the home of his cousin, Captain Gilbert Tait, who lived in Birkenhead, across the Mersey River from Liverpool, the site of Teit's departure dock.

Diaspora

In Birkenhead, Teit gained a taste of the Shetland diaspora. Uncle Gilbert was a retired sea captain, long separated from his Shetland roots after a life travelling the high seas. He spent much of Teit's visit reminiscing about his life on the Auld Rock. Old Gilbert may even have seen an image of himself in his nineteen-year-old nephew, speaking eloquently in the Shetland dialect and quizzing him about Shetland family history. Gilbert had taken flight from his island home when, at a similar age, he had joined the crew of a Greenland whaling ship.[138] In a letter to another uncle some years later, Teit described what transpired at the Gilbert Tait household during his visits (one in 1884 and another in 1902):

> [Cousin] Sara used to say she was glad when I came there [Liverpool] because I conversed so much with her father about Shetland. He seemed to enjoy thinking and speaking of Shetland and his younger days, and would brighten right up. He often told me he could lie back in his chair and in his mind's eye roam over every bit of Fetlar and follow every hill, dale, house, field, "burn, wick, njo, noost," tc. [N]othing could escape him, for he remembered every stone along the shore the same as if he had left it yesterday. He said one of his great pleasures was to think of Fetlar.[139]

Teit's early letters from British Columbia suggest that, in his new setting, he offset his nostalgia by seeking out and socializing with fellow Shetlanders. A reception held in his honour in 1904 in Nanaimo attests to his success at making connections with expat Shetlanders, because the event was packed with Shetland couples and their children.[140] In a letter to his younger brother Tom in 1888, he explained how he had forged connections with Shetlanders everywhere:

> The Shetlanders in America stick together better I think than those at home. You ought to join the Udal League. I am secretary of it for B.C. There is now an Ork&Shet Newspaper in America and an Ork&Shetland Society, one each in Chicago, Boston, Hamilton and Toronto and 3 others forming. Some of them already number over 100 members. We are in reality here a distinct nation <u>as we ought to be</u>. Very few Orcadians and <u>no</u> Shetlanders join the Caledonian, St. Andrews and other Scotch Societies in the large towns through America.[141]

The Chicago-based *Orkney and Shetland American* newspaper linked Teit to the larger North American diaspora and its news. The paper's editor, Magnus Flaws, who was close in age to Teit, had founded the OSA to ease his own feelings of nostalgia and loss as he settled into his new home of Chicago:

> These storm-bathed islands have a history of which my people might be proud. To be born in them inspires a love that never dies; to be raised in them creates incidents that are never forgotten, and character formed that in most cases is the secret in after life. It is this love and these fond recollections that prompts the publication of this paper.[142]

Teit's letter to his brother Tom, who had recently relocated to Edinburgh to study law, suggests that Tom also missed Shetland and sought out links to help him through. He had written to Teit in the fall of November 1888 to say that he had joined the Edinburgh chapter of the Orkney and Shetland Association and attended lectures by the beloved Shetland writer Jessie Saxby.[143] He also wrote poems about Shetland, one of which he included in his letter to Teit. Teit praised his brother for his poetry and noted that the poem had captured "the right theme (Love of the Old Rock)." He suggested that one of Saxby's poems, "Pull together brother Islesmen," be "committed to memory by each one of us."[144]

The Udal League (later named the Udal Rights Association) gave Teit another link to the international Shetland diaspora. As he mentioned in his letter to Tom, he was secretary of the B.C. Udal League. Founded in 1887 by Alfred W. Johnston, an Orkney-island architect based in London, England, its goal was to reintroduce some of the old medieval Norse governmental institutions to Orkney and Shetland.[145] Johnston, an avid historian of Orkney, had followed the Home Rule movement in Ireland, as well as the Norse Viking revival in Britain, and concluded that both had potential for Orkney and Shetland.[146] He was inspired by the work of Samuel Laing, an Orcadian scholar who, in the early nineteenth century, had brought attention to the old Norse udal law as the "background to a totally just" and "supremely democratic society," and therefore "worth transplanting from Norway to the west."[147] Through his study of the Icelandic sagas, Laing had concluded that the old "udal tenures" and "peasant proprietorship[s]" represented in the sagas appeared to be "genuinely free institutions" that offered a "vigorous and virtuous alternative to an enervated Saxonism."[148]

News of Johnston's Udal League inspired Teit to join the Udal League in British Columbia. He would later correspond with Johnston about his Fetlar family history.[149] Johnston's Norse initiatives lost momentum when a new generation of university-trained medieval historians argued that medieval Norway was not "a workers' paradise at all" but an "aristocratic society" controlled by the "Lords of Norway."[150] Teit was not party to such critiques as they appeared after his death.

Teit was formed by the islands' history, from the Scottish takeover of Shetland in the mid-fifteenth century to the clearances of the fisher-farmers in the nineteenth century. Such processes of exclusion affected both the Old World and the New. In his New World setting, Teit faced an issue that he had not faced at home. Now he was a member of settler Canadian society; long a product of colonization, he was also a participant in the process. Colonization was a cultural as well as a material process – emigrants brought not just skills and materials but also ideas and values into new worlds and communities. Teit's story can be understood only in light of the push and pull of the forces of colonialism and dispossession.

And So, to Fetlar …

During my second week in Shetland, I organized a trip to Fetlar to find Strand, the ancient seat of the Tait family. As I was booked to give a talk on James Teit at the Wind Dog Café in the village of Gutcher on the island of Yell (across from the isle of Fetlar), I had another reason for going. I was joined by my nineteen-year-old son, Patrick, who had arrived in Lerwick, fiddle in hand, a few days earlier to take in the town's music scene.

We rented a car in Lerwick and drove an hour north through rolling, heather-clad moorland to the ferry port of Toft. From there, we caught the twenty-minute ferry to the island of Yell. Because it was the peak of the lambing season, our drive along Yell's single-lane road to Gutcher was a delicate exercise in dodging sheep. The next morning, after breakfast with our B&B hosts Margaret and Lawrence Tulloch (which itself was a treat, given Lawrence's performance of the "Jan Teit and the Bear" story at the Jakobsen conference a week earlier), Patrick and I headed to the parking lot kitty-corner to the B&B to catch the ferry to Fetlar. A half hour later we were on Fetlar's main road, heading toward what we hoped was Strand. According to our map, it was at the far end of the island. Despite extensive signage along the road, few names matched the names on our road map. Some road signs gave no indication at all of what they were marking. When an "Everland" sign popped into view, we knew we were close, as Teit had referred frequently to that name in his letters to his uncle Robert. Still, there was no sign for Strand. In fact, there was nothing at Everland beyond the sign and a long driveway leading to a lone house. And so, of course, we drove up the driveway, parked, and knocked on the door.

A forty-something man in a full blue coverall opened the door and eyed us curiously.

"We're looking for Strand," I said.

"Then you've arrived," he said. "This *is* Strand!"

The man's muscular build, his blue eyes, reddish hair, and ruddy complexion caught me by surprise. Could this be a genome of the place, I wondered. He introduced himself as Peter Coutts and invited us to park our car in his driveway and explore the place. Before closing the door, however, he asked what had brought us to Strand. I explained my story of the Shetlander whose family had once lived at Strand, whereupon Peter asked us in for tea – and an afternoon at his kitchen table poring over copies of the old family letters that I had brought with me.

Peter recognized all of the family names and place names scattered through the letters.

"Where's Byden?" I asked.

"It's right over there," he replied, pointing to a nearby knoll outside his kitchen window.

He was delighted to read the parts of Teit's letters that referred to an old "tradition" that "people of [Tait's] name [had] all descended from a common ancestor [&] at one time held a great deal of land all over Fetlar."[151] Peter's wife, Angela, who was bottle-feeding lambs in the adjacent yard when we arrived, soon joined us at the kitchen table. She and Peter were extremely busy with lambing, rising most mornings at 4 a.m. to assist with the birthing. Patrick and I were excited to learn that not only were they both born and raised on Fetlar, but they were committed to a permanent life there as crofters. They told us they were part of a small, tight-knit community of approximately seventy people on the island, most of whom were crofters.

Peter offered to take us on a tour of Strand, so we bundled up and headed downhill to a large bay surrounded by green, rolling hills and beaches. His destination was a stately-looking, two-storey stone house on the shoreline. The house was in complete disrepair and missing its roof. Known as Smithfield, it was built in 1815 by the son of a merchant fish-curer, Gilbert Smith, who was universally hated by the local fishermen for his cheating and exploitative management of his estate. A Fetlar woman cast a spell on Smith and his stone house after learning that his father had betrayed the whereabouts of her two young sons during the Royal Navy's search for recruits in the Napoleonic war.[152] Smithfield fell into ruins within two generations.[153]

After our walk, Patrick and I headed to Funzie Bay, an old haaf-fishing station close to Strand. There we sat and imagined the scenes that played out in the lives of Teit's grandfather, James, his wife, Catherine, and his uncle, Captain Gilbert Tait. Could this even have been one of the places that Teit's uncle Gilbert reconstructed, rock by rock, with his eyes closed, in his Birkenhead sitting room? At the Wind Dog Café in Gutcher that evening, I chronicled the British Columbia side of the James Teit story to a room filled with local Fetlar, Yell, and Unst folk. It was a story I had told many times in British Columbia, but here, in this far-removed place that Teit called "home," it felt so very different.

Back in Lerwick, Patrick packed up his fiddle and headed off to a music jam at the local lounge while I headed down the tight, flagstoned lanes to the historic Commercial Street. As I passed the old stone lodberries (the sea doors along the shoreline for unloading boats) at the "South End," I pictured Teit in his Twaal Valley cabin under the dim light of a gas lamp reading aloud – in Shetlandic – passages from his friend James Haldane Burgess's novel *Tang* and revelling in characters like Auld Erti, who saw the world as he did:

> Yes, it's the poor as has to siffer, and the ministers is cled in fin linen and fares scrumptiously every day, as the Scripters says. And owld Mann's bit o boy can lie in his bed till ten o'clock in the morning, and the likes of me which his owld drukken father made his money off has to be toiling and slaving like this. But there's a day of recknin coming; yes, there's a day of recknin.[154]

4
Encounter

I tell you, if I should not become really famous one day, I shall not know what to do. It is a horrible thought to envision for myself a life spent unknown and unnoticed by the people.

– Franz Boas, in a letter to his sister Toni, September 5, 1875[1]

Although German-born and deeply rooted in the intellectual traditions of his homeland, Franz Boas more than any other man defined the "national character" of anthropology in the United States ... There is no real question that he was the most important single force in shaping American anthropology in the first half of the twentieth century.

– George W. Stocking Jr., *A Franz Boas Reader* (1974)[2]

Three months into his 1894 field season, Boas yearned to return to his family in New York City. It was his sixth trip to British Columbia in less than a decade and he had spent much of it fighting depression and fending off his demanding supervisor, Horatio Hale. His travel itinerary had left little time for repose. He had started out in the southern Interior in September and worked his way north to the Nass River Valley in October, then south to Vancouver Island in November. By early December, he was back on the train, heading east to Spences Bridge to check on Teit's Nlaka'pamux report.[3] Having allocated a portion of his meagre research budget to this unknown prospect, there was much at stake.

It was all good news at Spences Bridge. Teit was a hundred pages into the report and confident that he could finish it within a couple of months. With this settled, the pair set out on horseback for another tour of the local countryside.[4] "We went around all day long up the hills and down the hills, from house to house, to make measurements," Boas wrote enthusiastically to his parents.[5] On day three, he and Teit took the train to Lytton to do some work in the reserve communities adjacent to the town. A highlight was ferrying across the Fraser River and hiking along the westside wagon road to the Stein reserve, where the local chief "called all the members of the tribe into his house" to make speeches in his visitors' honour.[6]

That afternoon, speeches were not a high priority for Boas. His contract demanded body and head measurements. Although he didn't elaborate in his letters on what it took to convince the chief's guests to submit to his measuring tools, we can be sure that the task generated questions: Your friend wants to do what? Measure my head? Calculate the distance from my chin to my forehead? Examine the shape of my nose? He will pay me for this? Despite the strangeness of the request, the session apparently went well because Boas left Spences Bridge the next day with 462 measurements in hand.[7]

In his family letters, Boas noted the help of an "informant" from "the Shetlands [who had] bummed around here a lot in all kinds of capacities."[8] His snapshot of Teit as a backwoods, jack-of-all-trades "informant" entered the annals of anthropology with a vengeance in 1969 when University of Connecticut anthropologist Ronald Rohner published English translations of Boas's letters and diaries from the West Coast. Henceforth, if anthropology's historians mentioned James A. Teit at all – which they rarely did – they drew on Rohner and depicted him as an obscure, untrained amateur in a one-sided exchange with a professional expert. That this image of Teit circulated through Boas's current and later generations of students and associates suggests that Boas himself allowed it. (Given the reality, Boas surely had an obligation to correct such an unfair characterization.) Instead, University of California (Berkeley) anthropologist Robert Lowie, a former student of Boas, was able to describe Teit in his 1937 *History of Ethnological Theory* as a "squaw man settled in British Columbia,"[9] who had supplied Boas with the data that "led to a series of splendid monographs on Salish tribes."[10] University of Washington anthropologist Verne Ray described Teit in a 1955 source as a "local sheepherder," who "furnished" Boas with the information that enabled him to "put together the admirable ethnographies of the Canadian plateau."[11] In 1959, Marian Smith, a former student of Boas, compared Teit's relationship to Boas to that between a lab "technician" and a scientist. Teit was the technician who gathered on-the-ground ethnographic data that liberated Boas, the "trained anthropologist," to focus on the real work of ethnographic analysis.[12] This characterization taints Teit's reputation (or lack thereof) to this day.

In fact, the young man that Boas encountered at Spences Bridge in the fall of 1894 was a seasoned and sophisticated ethnographer in his own right. He had logged ten years of Nlaka'pamux language study and cultural immersion and initiated several of his own ethnographic field projects. Boas had completed a year of fieldwork in the Canadian Arctic (Baffin Island) and six two- to three-month field trips in British Columbia, Washington, and Oregon, but he was still struggling with the logistics of such work. The meeting of the two ethnographers in 1894 was not, therefore, as Rohner and others have suggested, a meeting of a great anthropologist and a field hand, but rather an encounter between two very different but potentially complementary scholars: one an urban, classically trained scholar and organizer; the other a community-based intellectual and man of action. Each, in his own way, benefitted from the other.

Franz Boas's Ethnographic World, 1894

Although Teit and Boas looked worlds apart at that first meeting in the Twaal Valley in September 1894, they would soon discover they had more than a few experiences in common. In addition to being close in age (Boas was six years older than Teit), both were new immigrants trying to forge permanent homes in their new North American settings. Just as Teit had spent ten years "bumm[ing] around ... in all sorts of capacities," so too had Boas. When he arrived on Teit's doorstep in the fall of 1894, he had changed cities and jobs approximately six times, and he was still without permanent employment.[13]

Like Teit, Boas was raised in an educated, middle-class family with progressive, liberal values. His father, Meier Boas, like Teit's father, was a businessman, and his mother, Sophie, was, like Teit's mother, a teacher. In addition to creating a warm and secure home environment for their children (Boas had one older sister and two younger sisters), Meier and Sophie Boas had encouraged intellectual pursuits, especially in the spheres of politics and history. Just as Teit would later acknowledge the influence of his father's social activism on his own life, Boas would acknowledge the same of his parents: "The background of my early thinking was a German home in which the ideals of the revolution of 1848 were a living force."[14]

Boas's geopolitical roots, however, carried him in a different direction than Teit. The Boas family resided in Minden, Westphalia, a province of

Prussia that later became part of Germany. As a major commercial hub and military centre with a history stretching back twelve hundred years, Minden was the antithesis of Lerwick. The Boas family was Jewish, but like many Jews in the city, they were secular Jews. The Prussian educational system was a formative experience for all children in the country due to its practice of segregating students at an early age according to ability. Boas made it successfully into the prestigious Gymnasium, a nine-year academic high school program that aimed to prepare its students for university and the elite professions, but he struggled in its competitive environment, missing close to two years of schooling due to anxiety, headaches, and general ill health. In his absences, however, he pursued his own interests, such as learning to play the piano, reading the literary classics, and studying folklore, botany, and zoology.[15] The combination of the rigorous Gymnasium curriculum and his self-designed home study turned him into a polymath of encyclopedic breadth, although to the detriment of social skills. Unlike Teit, who spent his teens surrounded by extended family in a town-and-country setting populated by working-class and merchant families, Boas spent his teens largely in a city setting with his immediate family. As he described it at age nineteen: "I spent my early childhood happily with my sisters in my parents' house."[16]

In 1877, after an extra year at the Gymnasium to compensate for his absences, Boas enrolled in mathematics and physics at the University of Heidelberg. A transfer to the University of Bonn in his second term introduced him to the new field of geography, which he carried into his doctoral program. He completed a doctoral degree in physics in 1881 at the University of Kiel with a dissertation that examined the ways in which different organisms perceived their environments through their senses.[17] On assessing his job prospects, he decided that, in light of the explosive growth in global exploration, the newly emerging discipline of geography would open more doors than physics.[18]

His Jewish heritage inhibited his career options in Germany as Chancellor Otto von Bismarck had joined forces with the virulent anti-Semite Adolf Stoecker and his Christian Social Workers' Party and unleashed a wave of racism that targeted Jews. In 1880, an anti-Semitic petition called for restrictions on Jewish immigration, the exclusion of Jews from the judiciary, and the removal of Jewish teachers from schools and universities.[19] Stoecker's racist agenda affected all young Jewish scholars in Germany in the 1880s, but particularly Boas, who identified as a German intellectual rather than as a Jew.[20] It concerned him that some of his own classmates at Kiel had signed the petition. His transition from the elite natural sciences (physics and mathematics) to the lower-status social sciences (geography and psychology) also dampened his job prospects.[21]

On completing his degree, Boas moved back to Minden to fulfill his compulsory military duty in the Prussian Army. He used his free time to continue his study of geography and psychophysics and develop a research proposal that he hoped would lead to ethnographic work, ideally in the Arctic. He returned to Berlin after his military duty, where Adolf Bastian, a distinguished senior scholar at the city's Royal Museum for Ethnology, helped him secure a spot on a German research expedition bound for Baffinland (Baffin Island). In preparation for the trip, Boas studied English, Danish, and Inuit languages and familiarized himself with the latest in photographic and anthropometric technology. He also studied Baffin Island maps in anticipation of joining an "Eskimo" migration along a previously unexplored route.[22]

Boas spent a year on Baffin Island, but it was far from the experience he hoped it would be. In one of his letters, he described it as "looking into hell."[23] In addition to failing to answer many of his original research questions, it exhausted him both physically and emotionally. There were many enriching experiences, such as living with the local Inuit in their igloos, travelling with them by dogsled, eating raw seal meat, and sitting through long storytelling sessions. But there were also many terrifying experiences. On one spring trip through heavy fog and snowstorms, he and his travelling party lost their way and spent several days and nights without food. In addition to hunger and snow blindness, Boas dealt with swelling in his face and a painful toothache. His interactions with the local people were often strained, especially after an Inuit shaman accused him of causing a diphtheria outbreak. With great effort, he managed, on his return to Germany, to turn his notes into a monograph, *The Central Eskimo,* but he was never happy with it. "My ignorance of the problems," he wrote, had created many "gaps."[24] Boas's reservations aside, the project was "extraordinary for its time," writes historian Douglas Cole. Not only did it "break ... with almost all practices of previous polar expeditions in its emphasis upon a detailed study of a limited region over an entire year," but it was also the first major study by a "one-man expedition living largely off the land."[25]

As the sting of his Arctic experience subsided, Boas saw it in a more positive light. His focus on "cartographic surveys, meteorological observation, place-names, and travel and trade routes" introduced him to the potential of applied geography; his interviews with the Inuit about their seasonal cycles and their language, myths, and songs introduced him to the potential of on-the-ground fieldwork; and, most importantly, his observations of human culture in this remote setting gave him a new outlook on race.[26] It had impressed him that the Inuit

> enjoyed life, and a hard life, as we do; that nature is also beautiful to them; that feelings of friendship also root in the Eskimo heart; that, although the character of their life is so rude as compared to civilized life, the Eskimo is a man as we are; that his feelings, his virtues, and his shortcomings are based in human nature, like ours.[27]

The most important outcome of the Baffin Island trip was convincing Boas of the importance of anthropology for salvaging "knowledge from ... doomed peoples" before it was lost.[28] Thus did the reluctant child of the German Gymnasium take his first steps toward his destiny as the "father" of American anthropology.

Instead of returning to Germany, Boas sailed south to New York City to spend six months with his American fiancée, Marie Krackowizer. He and Marie had met the previous summer while she was holidaying with her family in Europe. He hoped to use part of his visit to assess his job prospects in North America. On his return to Berlin, Boas wrote up his Baffin Island notes and supported himself with a small teaching job at the Humboldt Academy and a temporary cataloguing job at Berlin's Royal Museum for Ethnology. His larger concern, however, was how to get himself back to North America.

The arrival at the museum of two ethnographic collectors, J. Adrian Jacobsen and his brother, Fillip Jacobsen, with a touring troupe of nine Nuxalk men from Bella Coola, British Columbia, gave him an idea.[29] He organized interviews with the troupe members to see what they knew about the museum's Northwest Coast artifact collection, and after the interviews he organized a trip to see the place that had produced this cultural assemblage. In the fall of 1886, at his own expense, he spent three months in British Columbia conducting interviews in communities throughout the South Coast – mainly Vancouver Island. He returned to Germany with 140 artifacts, which he promptly sold to cover his costs.[30] He hoped that the trip would give him an entrée into the North American anthropological community. "I will do everything," he wrote to Marie, "to force the people over there to recognize me."[31] He had made a step in this direction by attending the annual conference of the American

Association for the Advancement of Science in Buffalo, where he met two seasoned ethnologists, Horatio Hale and Frederic Putnam, both of whom would later serve him well.

Good fortune followed his North American trip when Nathaniel Hodges, chief editor of the New York–based *Science Magazine,* invited Boas to join his magazine's geography division.[32] The timing was perfect. With a tangible job offer in hand, Boas had what he needed to marry Marie and establish a home in New York City. Marie was the daughter of prominent members of the city's German expat community known as the "Forty-Eighters." Having escaped Germany after the failed 1848 revolution against the government's conservative autocracy, this group of middle-class liberals and working-class radicals had formed a national diaspora that included Marie's recently deceased father, Ernst Krackowizer; Boas's uncle, Abraham Jacobi, a prominent New York City physician; Ottilie Assing, a highly regarded abolitionist; Carl Schurz, a fierce opponent of slavery; and Felix Adler, founder of the Society for Ethical Culture, among others. The Forty-Eighters, writes anthropologist Herbert Lewis, "celebrated reason, freedom, free speech and thought, 'truth,' and human rights, especially the rights of the individual versus the state."[33] Many Jews were attracted to this strand of European liberalism because of its opposition to the conservative, anti-Semitic, Christian-national coalition of agrarian and industrial interests that underpinned the autocratic regime of Chancellor Bismarck.[34] Boas's mother, Sophie, had been an ardent supporter of the revolution, as had Rudolph Virchow, one of Boas's mentors at the Berlin museum. According to historian George W. Stocking, "Virchow was as close as any man could be to Boas' model of the natural scientist." He was "methodologically conservative" but "institutionally activist, and politically liberal."[35]

Having established a home base in New York City and a field base in British Columbia, Boas turned to the academic writing that he would need to secure an academic position in the United States. As Herbert Lewis writes, this was "the heyday of racial formalism and racial determinism, the belief that cultural, moral, and historical differences could be explained by differences of 'blood' – by race."[36] By placing Anglo-Saxon Europe and America at the top of the racial hierarchy and other cultures at the bottom or inching their way slowly upward, this scheme embodied Western economic and political values and institutions, much as neoliberalism has done today.[37] In addition to supporting the state's "anti-Negro, anti-immigrant and immigration" policies, racial formalism's widely shared truth-claim justified the concept of the "white man's burden," with its attendant responsibility to colonize the world and civilize the lower races in the inevitable path of evolution and history. When cultures assert unilateral and absolute power over other cultures, they often do so by positioning themselves as fully "human" in relation to those "non" or "sub" human cultures.[38] In the United States, this took the form of "Jim Crow laws, racial segregation, and anti-black and anti-foreigner agitation."[39]

Boas used his editorial position at *Science* to challenge this model of culture. He started with a critical review of the arrangement of exhibits at the United States National Museum in Washington. He had visited the museum in 1887 to study its Northwest Coast collections and found them "scattered in a dozen different directions" according to type and use.[40] How useful was it, he wondered, to group similar items from various corners of the globe to show that "like causes will produce like effects." Instead, in two *Science* articles ("The Occurrence of Similar Inventions in Areas Widely Apart" and "Museums of Ethnology and Their Classification") he argued for grouping artifacts according to their individual geographies and histories – their "culture areas" – to highlight their spatial "relatedness" and meanings.[41] Such an arrangement, wrote Boas, would show that "like effects do not necessarily have like causes."[42] He also felt that such an arrangement would downplay the personal biases and preferences of museum curators, who often had too much say in categorizing items as "high" and "low" forms of culture.

With funding from the British Association for the Advancement of Science (BAAS), Boas took a two-month leave from *Science* in the summer of 1888 to continue his fieldwork in British Columbia.[43] It was a good year all round, as in addition to solidifying his reputation as a field-based ethnographer, Boas saw the release of his monograph *The Central Eskimo* by Washington's Bureau of Ethnology. His good fortune did not last long, however. On his return from British Columbia, Hodges terminated his *Science* position due to lack of funding, though the BAAS offered him another British Columbia field contract for the summer and early fall of 1889. When he returned to New York City, he moved his young family to Worcester, Massachusetts, to take up a docentship (lectureship) in the newly founded Department of Psychology at Clark University.[44] The Smithsonian's Bureau of Ethnology funded a summer-long leave to undertake fieldwork on Chinookan languages in Oregon and Washington State. To maintain his connection to British Columbia, he used some of the funds to return to Victoria and the Fraser Valley.[45]

The situation at Clark did not go well, however. Boas had proposed a longitudinal study of children in the Worcester schools to trace the effects of geography, environment, and nutrition on human development by studying the relationship of head size to mental capacity. Clark's president, G. Stanley Hall, had approved the project but withdrew his support after it caused a sensation in the local newspaper. Hall then denied Boas a raise in his salary and refused him an unpaid leave to work on the installations for the upcoming Chicago World Columbian Exposition. Some of his fellow faculty members faced friction with the autocratic Hall, and, with eight of them, Boas resigned from the university. In response, the University of Chicago offered jobs to all except Boas, as it already had an anthropologist on staff.[46]

Boas was not adrift for long. Frederic Ward Putnam, head of Harvard University's Archaeology and Ethnology Department and director of its Peabody Museum in Cambridge, Massachusetts, was now in charge of overseeing the anthropological exhibits for Chicago's 1893 World Columbian Exposition. Boas was one of the few scholars with expertise on the Northwest Coast and without a job, so Putnam hired him as a full-time assistant on the installation work. Again, Boas hoped that the job would lead to a permanent curatorship at Chicago's soon-to-open Field Columbian Museum. The job with the World Columbian Exposition was an exciting opportunity, as the Northwest Coast installation included a large collection of artifacts and the live participation of a group of fifteen Kwakwa̱ka̱'wakw adults and two children from Fort Rupert, British Columbia. The head of that delegation, George Hunt, would soon become one of Boas's closest research collaborators.[47]

Boas enjoyed the academic side of the Chicago installation, especially the work on the Kwak'wala language with George Hunt. Because Hunt was fluent in English, Boas could communicate with him without the aid of a translator.[48] Boas disliked the logistical side of the project, however, as it made him feel more like a "circus impresario than a scientist."[49] "Nothing," writes Douglas Cole, "had ever caused him more worry and unpleasantness," and he could not wait to see the end of "the damned fellows."[50] After the fair closed, Boas helped Putnam move its artifacts to the new Field Columbian Museum with the full expectation that he would soon become their permanent curator.[51] Instead, the museum hired William Henry Holmes, a senior employee of the Bureau of American Ethnology, as curator of the collection.[52] Devastated, Boas retreated to Marie's family compound at Lake George in a state of complete "exhaust[ion] and near nervous collapse."[53]

To help himself through this difficult period, Boas returned to the critique of evolutionism that he had initiated in his 1887 *Science* articles.

His plan was to develop this into a full "history of mankind." By "trac[ing] the history and distribution of every single phenomenon related to the social life of man," he would prove that "civilization is not something absolute, but that it is relative, and that our ideas and conceptions are true only so far as our civilization goes."[54] "We learn from the data of ethnology," he wrote, "that not only our ability and knowledge, but also the manner and ways of our feeling and thinking is the result of our upbringing as individuals and our history as a people."[55] Now, of course, he had an ideal testing ground for his ideas: his Northwest Coast field site. By studying the physical characteristics, languages, and ethnology (customs and beliefs) of this region, he was confident that he could reconstruct the dynamics of the region's ancient past. One of his first goals was to compile a systematic catalogue of mythic elements from the Northwest, drawing on his mathematical and statistical skills to show how foreign materials and ideas were modified by pre-existing ideas and customs. His larger goal was to replace the ruling evolutionist paradigm with a new argument for "diffusion and 'acculturation.'"[56]

Teit's Ethnographic World, 1894

Boas's head was swirling with these ideas when he arrived at Spences Bridge in 1894. This was the complex and conflicted man that Teit had met in the Twaal Valley that September day. Teit's head was also swirling with ideas, as he had long been drawn to the "science" of culture but in ways that were more political than psychological, more experiential than theoretical or comparative. Through Antko and her relatives on the local Cooks Ferry reserves, he had witnessed from the inside a vibrant culture suffering under the trauma of population loss while it continued to endure the totalizing colonial oppression of racism, inequality, marginalization, and dispossession. His determination to understand the roots of this oppression had already set him on his own anthropological path. Unlike Boas, who pursued anthropology as the struggle of an educated elite against the forces of racism, fascism, and international conflict, Teit pursued it as the collective struggle of disenfranchised local peoples against imperial elites.

Diasporic connection was a driving force for both Boas and Teit. In Boas's case, the diaspora was the German intellectuals who had fled from Germany to America when their 1848 campaign for liberal transformation failed; for Teit it was the Shetland expatriates who left home out of economic necessity and then dreamt of an indigenous cultural renaissance in their *heimland.* There were core differences of course – Boas's diasporic allegiance was rooted in the "high" culture of urban-based knowledges, and Teit's in the so-called low culture of communal knowledges – but there was a shared antipathy toward racial injustice at all levels.

This was the foundation on which Boas and Teit established a working relationship. The arrangement gave Boas the ethnographic data he needed to advance his academic theories of cultural difference, and it gave Teit the public platform and financial support he needed to assist his Nlaka'pamux friends in their fight against settler colonialism. It enabled Boas to stay where he wanted to be – in his urban, institutional base in New York City – and it allowed Teit to stay where he wanted to be – at "the Bridge" in rural British Columbia.

Over time, their differences would take them in opposite directions. For Boas, anthropology was an academic pursuit aimed at rescuing data on Indian languages, mythology, arts, and culture before they disappeared. "One can already now predict," he wrote in 1889, "that the Kwakiutl ... are heading for their extinction."[57] With assimilation his remedy for the survivors, Boas saw little value in designing an anthropology rooted in the present day. "The sooner these aborigines adapt themselves to the changed conditions," he wrote, "the better it will be for them in the competition with the white man."[58] As a fully functioning participant in Nlaka'pamux life, with a spouse from the community, Teit could not entertain such a perspective: nor was it in his nature. On arriving in Spences Bridge in 1884, though still very much a Shetlander, he was soon drawn to the contemporary issues that plagued the local Indians. When Boas encountered him in September 1894, he was a decade into investigating the source of some of the problems, although not, of course, on the scale of Boas. For one, he didn't have the funding that Boas had. Boas's request for a full report on the Nlaka'pamux was opportune because it allowed Teit to systematize some of this work in writing. Boas's talk of turning the report into a published monograph gave him an outlet to communicate these issues to a broad, international audience.

A New Story of Population Decline

Teit had barely arrived at Spences Bridge in the spring of 1884 when he noted the population loss that had occurred in the surrounding Nlaka'pamux communities. Not only was nothing being done to understand its roots or try to repair the damage, but some newcomers blamed the declining numbers on the Indians themselves. To find answers to this problem, Teit began systematically recording the births and deaths in and around his local Spences Bridge community.[59] By January 1893, he had a decade's worth of data, which he summarized for Boas in his 1895 Nlaka'pamux report. Based on his data and analysis, he concluded that colonization, writ large, was the source of the depopulation. "Where there is much association with the whites," there was "a very high mortality" rate.[60]

Teit recorded the population of the Spences Bridge Band in 1884 as 144 ("not including 13 temporary residents from other tribes or bands") and noted that over the course of a decade there had been an increase of 53 (43 births and 10 transplants from other villages) and a decrease of 89 (30 deaths of infants and children, 42 deaths of adults, and 17 transfers to other communities). He attributed the high death rates of infants and children to introduced diseases (most notably measles), and the similarly high death rates in the adult population (eighteen- to fifty-year-olds) to consumption (tuberculosis). He noted that venereal diseases ("introduced by the whites") and "whiskey and its concomitant evils" had caused the deaths of many young people, as well as the "birth of weak children, and some sterility among some of the women." White settlement was also a factor, as the closer a community was to a settler town, the higher was its death rates. He highlighted the CPR town of North Bend as a prime example. The death rates in that town, he noted, were considerably higher than the death rates in more isolated communities.[61] He concluded with a pointed attack on the federal government: "If the Indian Department would provide for resident physicians for the Indians, the conditions might be materially improved."[62]

In addition to compiling statistics on depopulation, Teit sought out elderly Nlaka'pamux community members for their perspectives on the declining numbers. What he learned from this group was that the decline had started with the 1858 Fraser River gold rush. The gold rush brought miners, they said, and the miners brought smallpox. There had been earlier smallpox epidemics, but they were nothing like the one "that was brought into the country in 1863," which claimed "thousands throughout the interior of British Columbia."[63] Teit's elderly interviewees estimated that, prior to 1858, the Nlaka'pamux peoples living along the Fraser River between Spuzzum and Lytton had numbered approximately two thousand. Some recalled this stretch of the river as so crammed with people that it looked like "ants about an anthill." The corridor along the Thompson

River from Lytton to Ashcroft, they said, was similarly packed with people. Meanwhile, when Teit started recording the numbers in 1884, he counted only seven hundred people living along the river between Yale and Lytton, suggesting a 66 percent drop in population in just one generation.[64]

According to Teit's interviewees, the smallpox epidemic had sent "panic-stricken" people fleeing "to the mountains for safety" with "large numbers ... drop[ping] dead along the trail ... their bodies ... buried or their bones gathered up, a considerable time afterwards."[65] Some of the infected victims had retreated to their sweathouses, "expecting to cure the disease by sweating, and died there." The communities in and around Spences Bridge had been especially hard hit:

> It was early in the spring when the epidemic was raging and most of the Indians were living in their winter houses, under such conditions that all the inhabitants were constantly exposed to the contagion. The occupants of one group of winter houses at Spences Bridge were completely exterminated; and those of another about three miles away, numbering about twenty people, all died inside their house. Their friends buried them by letting the roof of the house down on them.[66]

Teit's findings challenged the popular belief that the Indians were sources of their own decline. To the "many [who] suppose that the decrease among the Indian tribes in general is chiefly due to the dying-off of the old people and to the sterility of the women," he wrote, their view was not supported by the evidence.[67]

Teit appealed to his readers to consider the psychological effects of such sudden and extreme loss. If the Nlaka'pamux did not appear "as proud-spirited as they were ... [or if they did not] take as much interest in games, athletic exercise, and fun, as formerly," he wrote, it was because the impacts of "disease and the knowledge that they are doomed to extinction" had a "depressing effect" on them. "At almost any gathering where chiefs or leading men speak, this sad haunting belief is sure to be referred to."[68] The eldest members of the group had much to say about the dramatic change that came with the miners:

> The Indians say that formerly they were very healthy, and were seldom subject to disease. Very few died in childhood, and many lived to an extreme old age. It is said that their ancestors were taller than the people of the present-day. They were also stouter, stronger, hardier, and more active and

> agile than is the case now. Many men were exceedingly fleet of foot, and others excelled in leaping and in wrestling, owing to careful training and to frequent practice when playing games ... Insanity and imbecility were and are almost wholly unknown.... Natural diseases were generally cured by the use of certain medicines.[69]

In one of his first letter exchanges with Boas, Teit described the trauma of population loss as so raw in some households that it was all people could talk about. He had visited one Nlaka'pamux elder in the Nicola Valley in 1895 to ask about an old Athapaskan language that the man supposedly knew well, but the man was so haunted by the spectre of smallpox that he could talk of little else:

> When a child he (his father) contracted small-pox like many more of his tribe that stayed in the Similkameen at the time. The band of Indians among whom he stayed all died including his parents. A band of Okanagans came along and picked up the child, the only living being left, and raised him amongst themselves. He stayed with them until a lad when he went back and stayed with the remnants of his people on the Similkameen and Nicola. He bore the marks of the smallpox on his face. This happened a very long time ago when the smallpox was raging amongst the Indians of the States.[70]

A New Story of British Columbia

While working on his 1884–1894 depopulation study, Teit initiated an oral history project with a similar objective. I discovered this while doing research at the Anthropology Archives of the American Museum of Natural History (AMNH) in New York City in the fall of 2002. Having exhausted the archive's Teit holdings, I had decided to sift through several boxes of Boas's miscellaneous field notes. I had just started in on a big box when I spotted a sixteen-page document in Teit's handwriting titled "Narratives of Old Pa-ah, 1893." The date leapt off the page because it was the first piece of tangible evidence that showed Teit systematically recording Nlaka'pamux stories *prior* to meeting Boas in 1894.[71] Everything to this point suggested that Boas had launched Teit's work on stories.[72]

The document's contents – seven first-person narratives by three Nlaka'pamux elders, Pa-ah ("PA-ah"), Tsilla-gheskit ("Chill-ah-GES-kit"), and Nanoza ("Nan-OH-za") – opened a new window on Teit.[73] Unlike

Teit sketched this portrait of Tsilla-gheskit (whom he refers to as Tsila-gheskit) sometime in the 1890s. He likely intended it to accompany the stories that the Nlaka'pamux elder told him in 1893. | ACLS collection, American Philosophical Society.

Boas and his colleagues, who approached such narrators as bearers of myth but not history, Teit had approached them as bearers of both myth *and* history. All three elders spoke of the nineteenth century as a period they knew well because they had lived through much of it. Tsilla-gheskit described himself in one of his stories as "getting to be an old man when the white miners came to the country," and "a middle aged man" when he saw "the first gun." Pa-ah described himself in one of his stories as having been a "young man" when the "only whites in the country were Hudson Bay men."[74]

Unlike Boas, who stripped the narrators' names and community affiliations from stories, and changed their first-person tellings into the third person, often in order to turn strings of similar stories into a single composite story, Teit did the opposite. As he explained to Boas at the outset of his work on stories: "I will state ... the names of the principal parties who related [the stories] and I will write them [the stories] as near to the way they tell them as possible."[75] His transcription of a story by Pa-ah about a Secwépemc raid on a Tsilhqot'in campsite illustrates this well. He not only acknowledged Pa-ah as the narrator of the story, but also included Pa-ah's account of how and when he had learned the story – i.e., not many years ago at an Indian gathering at N-talls-iten (Green Lake) from an elderly man named Kakgha. Teit also included Pa-ah's comment that the attack at the centre of the story was rare for the time, as "the whites had been in the country for quite a long time [and] consequently the old fighting amongst the Indians had died down." He introduced the key protagonist of his story, Kakgha, as a short and rather stout man, who had arrived at the gathering with an ugly wound in the breast. The wound was Pa-ah's hook for the story.

All three narrators peppered their stories with names of local people and places, which Teit carefully recorded, even if, at times, they were tangential to the central storylines. For example, Pa-ah interrupted one of his stories to explain that Antko's father, Nsowghin, had participated in a calculated ambush to avenge the death of a relative. In another story, he stopped to explain that the chief protagonist – a Nlaka'pamux man named Tlimmenghin – was the husband of ninety-nine-year-old Wowkto and the father of Mary Ta-homilthkin, who is married to Pierre Audap. He described Tlimmenghin as a jolly fellow who "talked too much about everybody and everything" and often bragged about his prowess with bears. His characterization helped launch his story of Tlimmenghin's terrifying encounter with a grizzly bear. The dynamism of Teit's transcription/translation spoke to his effort to capture in writing – and in English – the vibrancy of Pa-ah's narration:

> It was late in the fall when snow was on the highest mountains. Suddenly a large Cinnamon stepped out of the bush at his side. [Tlimmenghin] raised his gun to fire but it would not go off. She made right for him, the 2 cubs almost as large as herself coming out behind and sitting down in the open. He had no time to do anything. He tried to club her but she struck his arm and knocked the gun out of his hand. He did not have time to draw his knife before she closed on him. She soon stretched him out. The two cubs

> came out right to his side. He lay still expecting to be chewed up between them. Suddenly one of the cubs made off into the bush. The others looked around and hastily followed.

With blood "streaming from his wounds [and] his arms and breast ... badly torn [and] each side of his belly ... laid open so that his bowel was visible," Tlimmenghin dragged himself up the mountain to where his wife was digging roots. She saved his life by helping him limp down the mountain. In his initial work for Boas on stories and storytelling, Teit had stressed his commitment to creating "free translations" that "preserve the true sense and meaning of the stories ... as if written in Indian."[76]

Teit's three elderly narrators offered a new interpretation of nineteenth-century British Columbia history. In contrast to the settler historians, who characterized the early to mid-nineteenth century as an era of progress – discovery, exploration, settlement, and wealth – this group portrayed it as a period of regression – upheaval, violence, hardship, and loss.[77] Things got so bad, they said, that the Nlaka'pamux had welcomed the "advantages of law and order" introduced by whites from 1858 on because they thought it might end a half century of internal violence that had become unbearable. "If you were not always ready either to run or fight," Tsilla-gheskit explained, "you were liable to be killed at any time." He noted that "the Indians when eating used always to have their bow and arrows or gun across their knees and when they lay down it was alongside them." It seemed more than significant that guns, alcohol, and horses featured prominently in this 1893 collection of stories. Tsilla-gheskit highlighted horses as a major trigger of conflict due to the rampant "horse-stealing" amongst the Indians. People with horses, he said, had to be constantly monitoring their animals. Alcohol was another trigger. According to Pa-ah, alcohol killed Tlimmenghin in the end. After a night of drinking, he fell off his horse and died. Guns were all through these stories.

Murder was also a major focus of the stories in the collection. According to the narrators, murders in the early nineteenth century were long and nasty affairs due to the obligatory reprisals that followed, sometimes years after the fact. As Pa-ah explained, the majority of Nlaka'pamux murders during his lifetime arose from internal conflicts within the Nlaka'pamux community. The old inter-tribal conflict, he said, had largely died out with the arrival of whites. It had not completely disappeared, however. As mentioned, one of his stories was about a retaliatory raid by three Secwépemc men that had taken place in Tsilhqot'in territory two years earlier (i.e., in 1891). Pa-ah had heard about the attack from a

Nlaka'pamux man named Kakgha who had participated in the raid. Kakgha had told him that he and two companions had trekked into Tsilhqot'in territory in search of an occupied campsite. When they finally found one, they ambushed it at night, killing most of its inhabitants. Things went according to plan until they made their exit, when Kakgha took a bullet to the chest. On seeing him lying unconscious in a pool of blood, his two companions grabbed his musket and ran. In fact, Kakgha was not dead. Miraculously, he regained consciousness and crawled slowly home, where, over time, he recovered and lived to tell his story to Pa-ah and others.

Pa-ah told Teit another story about the more common form of feuding that he had grown up with: blood feuds triggered by conflicts within his Nlaka'pamux community. His story featured a man named Shoomahiltsa, who wreaked havoc on his own home community in the 1850s (prior to the gold rush). He was "the cruelest and the worst Indian that I ever knew," Pa-ah noted, and "a man without feelings," who murdered many men and abused some of his wives so badly that he drove several of them to suicide. When he fancied a woman, he would think nothing of murdering that woman's husband and then taking her by force. When his community could stand it no longer, a group of men devised a plan to kill Shoomahiltsa. They waited until he and others had gathered at Botanie Mountain. On seeing him wander off by himself, they followed him and stabbed him with a knife. "The country was well rid of him," explained Pa-ah. In fact, everyone at the time "felt glad except some of his immediate relations," who felt compelled, through the old protocols, to avenge his death. One of the relatives was the deceased's nephew (a namesake), who shot a Lytton man two years later in revenge; another was Antko's father, Nsowghin, who killed a second man a year later to revenge the death. These two killings, according to Pa-ah, "settled ... the score."

Several of the Nlaka'pamux chiefs, according to Pa-ah, tried to mitigate the violence by making eloquent and persuasive speeches aimed at convincing their people to put down their weapons in the pursuit of peace. He noted that Ea-men-chooten, the famous chief who had greeted Simon Fraser at Lytton in 1808, was one such chief, whose dexterous speechmaking had foiled many a battle. Ea-men-chooten's grandson, Shigh-pentlam ("Sha-PEENT-lum"), was another famous orator and peacemaker. Early in his role as chief, he had travelled from the village of ʟlkamtci'n (Lytton) into "Lillooet" territory with horses and gifts "to make a treaty of peace" with the "Lake Lillooets" (the peoples who lived around the lakes known today as Seton and Anderson Lakes). His negotiations ended a long string of paybacks for old scores.

Given the knowledge today of the effects of fetal alcohol poisoning and the extent to which alcohol consumption was encouraged by the HBC in the early to mid-nineteenth century, it is quite possible that, by the 1850s, alcohol was a key factor in the behaviour of unmanageable and disruptive adults like Shoomahiltsa.[78] Tsilla-gheskit described the situation as so bad by the mid-nineteenth century that it took the white man's law to calm things down. "I think it was good for the Indians that the Whites came into the country and law, peace and order was brought in," he told Teit. "It gave those who did not want to be bad, a chance to be good and peaceable." It also gave the communities "a chance to ... live easier & better."

Teit's elderly narrators recalled that, during their lifetime (i.e., 1830s to 1890s), many of their people had relied on skilled speakers such as Shigh-pentlam to help them resolve differences. It was Shigh-pentlam who negotiated a peace treaty between his people and the miners in the summer of 1858 when a confrontation erupted between the two groups and threatened to explode into a full-scale war (Chapter 2). The first missionaries in the region took note of Shigh-pentlam's influence and decided it would serve them well to make him an ally. They baptized him and appointed him a "chief in church affairs," Pa-ah explained, but he "did not altogether prove satisfactory" because he was slow in learning the church "prayers" and reluctant to give up gambling. Pa-ah, who had known Shigh-pentlam well, considered him "the greatest chief of the Thompson Indians."

Both Pa-ah and Tsilla-gheskit highlighted the impact of the gold rush as catastrophic. Before the rush, Pa-ah explained, "the only whites in the country were Hudson Bay men," and because they were based upriver at Fort Kamloops and rarely travelled downriver to the junction of the Thompson and Nicola Rivers to trade, they were largely out of sight. In the few instances when traders did appear – to trade for salmon – they were usually "half-breeds" (as he put it). Pa-ah noted that "he had been a grown man for many years when the other kind of white man ... the gold miners ... came." Unlike the traders, the miners "came in large bodies" and interacted with the locals without respect, he said. Missionaries soon followed. The first missionaries, according to Pa-ah, were Roman Catholic "priests" who taught a few prayers and then left. "Mr. Good of [the] English church" arrived ten years later, and he stayed and taught the people more "prayers and all about the creation tc. tc." Both Pa-ah and Tsilla-gheskit noted that they could "remember before the Indians here started the *kwoy-ghoot yaemit*" (the priests' form of prayer).

According to Pa-ah, the stories of strange white newcomers triggered a flurry of religious activity as people tried to figure out who such people were and how their presence might change things. The Nlaka'pamux sought out their southern neighbours, the Similkameen and Okanagans, for information because some of these groups were known to have met and travelled with white traders:

> The Similkameens and Okanagans commenced telling the Indians here about the priests and what the priests over in their country and on the other side [of the US border] used to tell them. Afterwards I remember some of the Indians here in their dancing used to cry out *Katsas skwasts, skuzas ea-as spiteenisums* (The name of the father the son and the holy Ghost). Some of them also commenced to say the same when they eat or when they went to work or to travel or do anything at all.

Over time, long-distance travellers began turning up in Nlaka'pamux territory with stories about the whites they had seen in southern regions. "Paul, the great chief that used to be at Kamloops," explained Pa-ah, spent extensive time travelling on the "American side," where he had picked up "bits of prayers." As more news of whites and their "priests" filtered northward, the Nlaka'pamux added new rituals to their feasting, fasting, and dancing:

> Some of the chief men used to keep time by cutting notches in a stick. Once every week the Indians around here used to assemble men and women and have a big feast together. A good part of the day however they fasted and put in the time by dancing continually. Lifting up their hands to god. Praying, talking and singing or chanting as they danced. Some used to dance for hours or until they dropped. They used all to be painted while dancing. Most of the Indians around here observed those rites.

Pa-ah noted that such rituals died out when "the white miners came to the country."

Religious Responses to Whites

In his 1895 report for Boas (which Boas edited and released in 1900 under the title *The Thompson Indians of British Columbia*), Teit included more detail about these large-group rituals. Unlike the ancient individualistic guardian spirit practices that revolved around solitary encounters between individuals and their spirit helpers (see Chapter 6), these new rituals were large, public affairs led by priest-like leaders known as "prophets." Prophets had had dreams and visions that gave them special powers to communicate directly with an all-powerful deity who presided over the world of humans from an upper "spirit-world" (also described as "land of the shades" or "land of the dead"). Most prophets had been "raptured" by near-death experiences that had transported them to this upper spirit-world, where they had encountered a supreme being who gave them messages – sometimes positive, sometimes negative – to carry back to the world of the living. In the case of positive messages from the upper world, people danced excitedly while offering "prayers of thanks to the chief." In the case of negative messages, people danced in a frenzied state and made "supplications for mercy."[79] Some of the prophets' stories paralleled the stories of the death and resurrection of Jesus Christ.

Teit noted that some prophets returned from the upper world with stories about "the coming of the whites," who would bring new material goods and foods such as "whiskey, stoves, dishes, flour, sugar, etc.," while others returned with terrifying stories about "epidemics" that would wipe out Indians altogether.[80] The latter stories sometimes included news of a fast-approaching apocalyptic end of the world that would reunite all the living people with their dead relatives. When prophets announced that they had new stories to tell, people travelled for miles in large groups to hear them. Teit described one Nlaka'pamux prophet, Pê'lak, who had a large following. Having worked as a guide with the Hudson's Bay Company brigades, he had learned much about whites. In his prophecies, he emphasized "the great changes that would take place, even going into minute details." Some of his predictions – for example, that "the Indians ... would 'die out like fire' on the appearance of the whites" – had a terrifying effect.[81]

With the onset of the gold rush, according to Teit, the large prophet dances began to die out. The prophets, however, continued on. Teit noted that three prophets had visited Nlaka'pamux territory between 1880 and 1891. One was a man from the Fraser Valley who came to Lytton to pray and perform "sleight-of-hand tricks." The local Indian doctors may have killed him, because he died shortly after returning home. Another was a woman from the Nicola Valley who travelled "throughout Spences Bridge and Nicola" recounting stories of her trips to the "land of souls."[82] The third prophet was an Okanagan woman from the United States who visited the Nicola Valley in 1891 and declared that she was the "savior of the Indians." She "preached against the whites, and wanted the Indians to follow her to battle against them." She retreated when she encountered opposition from the local chiefs. "Had she come twenty years earlier," Teit wrote, "it is difficult to say what might have been the result, as even now she has more than one admirer among the upper divisions of the tribe."[83]

In pursuing stories of early- to mid-nineteenth-century prophets and prophet dances, Teit tapped into a cultural phenomenon that would take historians and anthropologists several decades to appreciate.[84] Larry Cebula, professor of history at Eastern Washington University and the author of *Plateau Indians and the Quest for Spiritual Power, 1700–1850,* argues that prophets were powerful sources of knowledge during the fur trade. Through their religious dance ceremonies, they offered Indians a "window into white society."[85] By harnessing the white traders' spiritual power, people believed that they could protect themselves "from disease, improve their material condition, and forge a new and stronger connection to the spirit-world."[86] Indeed, Cebula suggests that the trade in prophecy stories was so important that it surpassed the trade in material goods. In his study of fur traders' letters and journals, Cebula found that many of the early fur traders and missionaries on the North American plateau often mistook this large-group religious fervour for an ancient Indian religion. On hearing Indians speak of an afterworld presided over by an external, all-powerful deity, for example, many traders assumed that they had encountered peoples with an ancient belief system similar to their own. As Cebula argues, however, these stories were variants of their own religious stories that the locals had picked up while serving in trade company brigades or from living near trading posts. Pa-ah's stories corroborate Cebula's claim that the plateau peoples had actively pursued knowledge of whites and their religion during the fur trade. Teit's work on the prophecy movement was one of his most important ethnographic contributions. Instead of trying to separate the deep past from the recent past, as Boas tried to do, he documented the porous mix of the old and the new in the Nlaka'pamux world.

Consider Pa-ah's statement to Teit that "as far back as I remember, the Indians believed in a god unseen or a great over ruling spirit," but "they also believed in a great number of spatakel [animal-people] stories handed down from generation to generation." One belief, he explained, was "that everything on earth was killed or petrified one time long time ago except the Coyote and that the Indians and all the animals had descended from him." This made Coyote "next to or almost equal to God." For Pa-ah, "as far back as I remember" was approximately 1830–1840. In this light, it is understandable that, in a discussion of religion, he might pair his belief in "a god unseen or a great over ruling spirit" with a belief in the trickster-transformer Coyote. After all, the prophecy movement had filled his childhood and adolescence with stories of an unseen god inhabiting an upper world. Traders and missionaries had reinforced this world with their biblical stories of Jesus Christ and God. In one of his first letters to Boas in the spring of 1895, Teit described the mix of beliefs shared by people in his Nlaka'pamux community: for example, a belief that the "Chief of their Ancient World" – an "old man" – was "the same god as that of the 'Whites,'" and that this old man was "the only person gifted with greater magic than the Coyote." In a possible version of the second coming of Jesus Christ, people believed that this old man would one day reappear "on a cloud of Tobacco smoke." They also believed that Coyote was alive in a "house made of ice," and that he too would return one day soon and would "bring back the Indians' dead."[87]

Missionaries as "Bad Medicine"

Shortly after completing his final report for Boas in the early spring of 1895, Teit compiled a report on the status of Christian missionization in and around Spences Bridge and sent it to Boas. Concerned that his candid commentary on such a sensitive topic might cause offence in "some quarters," Teit asked that Boas not include it in the published monograph.[88] The thrust of his report was that, despite years of proselytizing in and around Spences Bridge, the missionaries had made few inroads into the community. He explained that, if asked, most of the Nlaka'pamux would say that they appreciated the missionaries' emphasis on "good" over "evil," but that they disliked their indoctrination program. It was "bad medicine," some said. Teit noted that many Nlaka'pamux people at Spences Bridge resented the missionaries' interference with established practices and customs. If asked about this, they would "say that the Indians were far more religious, and more moral, before the coming of the missionaries." They "ridicule the marriage laws of the whites and missionaries, and pronounce them so far as they affect the Indians as a miserable failure." Many Nlaka'pamux wished for a return to the marriage system of the old days:

> When a man took a wife, she staid [sic] with him, as a rule, for life. There were comparatively few instances of separation or divorcement among them, in strange contrast to the present day. Now ... a man often marries so that he can have a wife who cannot very well leave him ... regardless of his moral conduct. And the same with women. While others, again, pay no attention

> to the marriage laws, but separate from their lawful husbands and wives, and live with others at their pleasure, and the law and the priests can only talk.[89]

Teit noted that many of his Nlaka'pamux neighbours and acquaintances ignored the missionaries' teachings. Some paid the latter lip service by attending church, saying prayers, refraining from hunting on Sundays, and saying grace before lunch, while maintaining and emphasizing their own traditions and beliefs in their homes. There, instead of Bible stories, they taught their children their traditional stories.

Contrary to the missionaries' well-worn claim to have purged Indians of their old ways, Teit stressed that "every individual of the tribe" at Spences Bridge held a "strong belief in the medicine man." The ultimate irony, according to Teit, was that in all their years of missionary work among the Nlaka'pamux at Spences Bridge, all the missionaries could claim as their converts were the most problematic people in the community – people who were "changeable and hypocritical, often very immoral, especially in a quiet way, and [are] generally fond of whiskey, and altogether a rather dangerous character." Such persons took "great pains to show the missionaries and whites that [they are] well up on religion, and a little better than his neighbors."[90] In other words, despite years of hard work and proselytizing, the missionaries' agenda was, at least in Teit's eyes, a failure.

Social Entrepreneur

As much as Teit appreciated the old world of the Nlaka'pamux, he also understood the challenges and demands of the current world. Through his clerkship at his uncle's store and his life with Antko, he knew the extent to which the local Nlaka'pamux economy was now dependent on the cash economy. When Boas asked him to collect traditional artifacts and crafts in the community, his response was that there were too few excess goods in local households to support such a project. "Most Indians here have one or two skins but will not sell them," he wrote. "Each family dressed enough skins for moccasins and gloves, but no more."[91] He also noted that some items, such as archaeological remains, were out of bounds because of the "horror" that people felt toward "hand[ling] human bones."[92] He described weapons as similarly out of bounds "owing to a strong superstition prevailing that by giving their ancient weapons into the possession of the whites, the latter obtain power over them which they may use to the Indians' harm."[93]

As he thought more about Boas's request, however, Teit had a change of heart and sent out the word that if people had old artifacts, buckskin or basketry work to spare, he had a buyer for them. Antko could well have been behind this, as she was a major contributor to his first collection. According to his letters to Boas, the project quickly took an imaginative turn. Assisted by Antko and her close circle of female friends and relatives, Teit assembled a small collection of "over thirty articles of ethnological value." He was surprised to find that the women were "far more obliging than the men in making or selling" these goods.[94] His "accession" notes attest to this as they included items that were typically made by women – for example, dressed skin clothing, baby carriers, and root diggers.[95] Because he noted the makers' names in his first financial statement to the American Museum of Natural History, we can see exactly who made what: Antko contributed a mat, a bone awl, beaver teeth dice, two buckskin sacks for gambling sticks, and a piece of buckskin;[96] Waght-ko contributed a doeskin; Kagh-peetsa, two pairs of leggings, a woman's shirt, and three pairs of moccasins; Whaz-eenik, a mat and a sage-bark cloak; Hy-ses-ka, a buffalo skin mat; Wagha-neenik, a grass mat; Whal-eenik, a birch-bark carrier; Helasa'tko, a baby carrier; and so on.[97]

Teit offered the women good prices for their handmade goods. We know this from his financial statement, in which he listed what he paid: $2.50 to Whal-eenik for her birch-bark carrier; $5.50 to Hy-ses-ka for her buffalo skin mat; $2.50 to Helasa'tko for a board carrier; and so on. He paid Antko $6.15 for her contributions, and Kagh-peetsa, $17.00 for hers. Given that $17 was half of Teit's own monthly wage (equivalent to nearly $500 today), this was significant.[98] In his exchanges with Boas about the costs of the various artifacts, Teit explained that prices would have to be scaled according to the time and work involved in making them. Baskets, he stressed, had "a recognized value and price" and could not "be bought under the regular price except under special circumstances."[99] A commitment to fair trade ran through all Teit's letters to Boas. When Boas expressed his interest in making plaster casts of Nlaka'pamux facial features, Teit responded that he might be able to "persuade someone or another to undergo the operation," as long as "the persuasion" was "backed with a liberal sum."[100]

Teit's motives for this "sellout" to Boas were clear. At the time, the Nlaka'pamux women's access to the cash economy was largely restricted to the domestic and labouring sectors of the economy, most notably the hop-picking camps, canneries, and farms. In promoting artistic work for pay, Teit introduced a new employment niche. As it gained momentum beyond the local community, it grew into a women's working collective.

By February 1897, women had contributed more than his budget could handle. "It is a pity there is no more money to procure other articles of importance," he wrote Boas, "as the Indians are just commencing to take an interest in the matter, and are now anxious to make or sell anything that I wish to get ... Several Indians have brought to me lately some things of particular interest and of splendid workmanship."[101]

To meet the growing surplus, Teit pressed Boas for additional funds to pay for their offerings: "The Indians are anxiously waiting [for payment] while others I have paid with my own money."[102] Three years into this collecting project, he noted resistance within one wing of the community. "Some of the chiefs and others in council," Teit wrote, "talked strongly against the people selling any of their former articles."[103] According to his accession lists, however, the women ignored the chiefs' protests and carried on submitting work to Teit. By now, it was not so much a case of contributing "former articles" as it was making new articles.

Teit also ignored the chiefs' warnings. He devised novel ways to reduce the women's costs, such as purchasing dressed skins from local suppliers to "outsource" the labour-intensive tasks of hunting, skinning, and tanning that impinged on the women's duties in the home, and thus provoked pressure from the men.[104] Teit's work here blurred the constructed ethnographic categories by displacing "authentic" (i.e., precontact) items with new items produced on demand. He also provided women with an alternative to the standard forms of wage work that required them to move away from home (sometimes as far as the Coast to work in canneries and hop-camps) and that paid them little. This new sphere of work involved domestic production (baskets and buckskin clothing made at home) that was done and paid for on a flexible, per-piece basis. Teit also mixed what was once a "traditional" subsistence and craft practice with commercial manufacture.[105] Indeed, a testament to the financial rewards that local people reaped from such work came from a researcher who arrived ten years after Teit's death and reported to Boas that Teit had "spoilt the people" by paying "them far too much."[106] For its time, this women's work "co-operative" was a major innovation, and many of the North American museums – from Ottawa, New York City, Chicago, Washington, and Boston to Victoria – purchased its work, which still exists today in display cases and storage vaults, often with the label "traditional Nlaka'pamux craft." It shows Teit in his first surreptitious incarnation as the Indians' (women's) agent!

Teit revelled in his Nlaka'pamux fieldwork for Boas, and his success offered the latter some relief from what he described to Marie as "5 months of loneliness" equal to the "hell" he had experienced in Baffinland.[107] It may also have offered Boas some space. On returning to New York City, he gathered up his family and moved to Washington, DC, to work on a Kwakwa̲ka̲'wakw life-group diorama for the city's National Museum.[108] On its completion in May, he moved Marie and the children to Germany for a six-month visit with his family.

Good News for Boas

While in Germany, Boas received good news from Frederic Putnam, his former Chicago employer. Putnam was the new head of the Department of Anthropology at the American Museum of Natural History (AMNH) in New York City, a position that he held jointly with Harvard's Peabody Museum in Cambridge. In his new position, he urged Morris Jesup, president of the AMNH, to agree to a cross-appointment for Boas between the museum and Columbia University. On hearing of this, Boas's wealthy New York City uncle, Abraham Jacobi, made a secret contribution of $1,500 to boost the Columbia University side of the proposal. This sealed the deal. On December 6, Putnam sent Boas a formal offer of an assistant curatorship in ethnology and somatology at AMNH. Boas accepted the offer on January 1, 1896.[109] A temporary lectureship at Columbia soon followed.

Finally, at age thirty-eight, after years of struggle, Boas had permanent employment in New York City. His situation improved again three years later when Columbia University converted his temporary teaching position into a permanent professorship. With their prestigious research programs and bright graduate students, these two prominent institutions, Columbia University and the American Museum of Natural History, facilitated Boas's rise to pre-eminence in the anthropological world. Twenty-five years after Boas's death, historian George Stocking would conclude that "there is no real question that he was the most important single force in shaping American anthropology in the first half of the twentieth century."[110]

Two geographical nodes – one in New York and the other in British Columbia – would consolidate Boas's career. With two seasoned ethnographers – George Hunt on the Coast and James Teit in the Interior – working for him at the British Columbia end, Boas was free to stay in New York City and tackle what he saw as the real work of anthropology.[111]

5
Paper Mountain

It is clear that fieldwork could be quite irritating to a Germanic professor bent on making every moment count for scholarship.

– George W. Stocking Jr., "Franz Boas and the Culture Concept" (1968)[1]

Boas turned up again at Spences Bridge on June 4, 1897, with a research plan that far surpassed all those of his former trips. He had spent months mapping it out in letters to Teit, who had reassured him that it was all doable.[2] His itinerary had him spending a couple of weeks working on ethnographic projects in and around the village and then travelling some three hundred kilometres north by pack train to Soda Creek (via Big Bar, Dog Creek, and Alkali Lake), followed by another five hundred kilometres west across the Chilcotin plateau (through Riske Creek, Hanceville, Puntzi Lake) to Bella Coola, measuring and interviewing Secwépemc and Tsilhqot'in peoples along the way. On paper, it looked like an anthropological dream project: weeks of fieldwork, much of it on horseback, through uncharted ethnographic terrain with a seasoned ethnographer/translator and backwoods guide leading the way. Because of the scale of the project, Boas brought along two New York City colleagues, Livingston Farrand and Harlan Smith, to assist him.

The Spences Bridge part of the project ticked along like clockwork. The New Yorkers spent ten full days measuring and photographing Nlaka'pamux men, women, and children; purchasing and cataloguing artifacts; conducting interviews on the design patterns of baskets, jewellery, and masks; plaster-casting Nlaka'pamux head and facial features; and recording songs on a new, portable phonograph that Boas had brought with him from New York. The recording project was one of the first of its kind in North America and a highlight that sparked a full-on theatrical performance, with "ecstatic" singers "act[ing] out all their stories and ceremonies while they sang."[3] Harlan Smith made several excursions to outlying areas with knowledgeable elders to inspect the local archaeological sites.

Teit and Antko facilitated much of this work. In addition to offering their Twaal Valley cabin for interviews and song-recording sessions, Teit translated for the Nlaka'pamux participants and helped Boas with the note taking.[4] Antko joined in on several of the projects and encouraged some of her friends and relatives – Kagh-peetsa, Whal-eenik, Kil-kal-oos, Hy-ses-ka, and Silka-peskit – to follow suit.[5] At the end of it all, Boas reported to Marie that everything had been so well orchestrated, with so many people turning up at designated times, that he and his two colleagues could "not work quickly enough to finish with them."[6] Although he was "dead tired," it had not really required "much effort" because Teit "had prepared everything for us very well."[7] For the next five weeks, Teit would continue in this role, facilitating for Boas the first off-grid ethnographic survey of inland British Columbia.

The road trip started on June 12 at Teit and Antko's ranch, with Boas and Farrand teaming up with Teit, three Nlaka'pamux guides, and nine horses – four for riding, and five for carrying tents, blankets, food, and cooking gear. Smith was left behind to undertake archaeological surveys at Lytton and Kamloops.[8] With Teit managing the logistics, Boas and Farrand had little to do but settle in for the ride. Teit had told them to bring only their own blankets and mosquito repellant. "Regarding the camping outfit, you will not need to buy any of it," he wrote, as "I will furnish it all."[9]

The first day on the road went smoothly. As Boas described it in a letter to Marie, it was "very good" because it kept him "outdoors all the time" with "no intellectual work worth mentioning."[10] His knees ached a little, but overall the horseback riding was easier than expected. He loved the scenery, especially the mountains, as they reminded him of the Alps. Things began to sour on the second day due to incessant rain and a tense ride along a steep trail overhanging the Fraser River. "Travelling is no fun this way," he wrote Marie.[11] By day five, he declared his situation as "terrible" due to more rain and thick swarms of mosquitoes.[12] On entering Tsilhqot'in territory, Boas experienced some encounters reminiscent of past trips: "I find it very hard to get along with these people ... [and] I will be very glad when we finally reach the coast."[13]

The traverse across the Chilcotin plateau proved even more challenging than the first part of the trek as, in addition to rain and wind, they had several serious mishaps. While riding across a long stretch of swampland,

Teit and Antko at their Twaal Valley cabin in June 1897. This was one of a series of portraits, mostly mug shots, that Harlan Smith took at Spences Bridge at the request of Boas, who wanted them to supplement his anthropometric measurements. Boas later published a selection of the photographs in a special Jesup North Pacific Expedition volume on ethnographic portraiture. He published the photos without the names of the individuals featured in the photos. | Photograph #11686, courtesy of the Division of Anthropology, American Museum of Natural History.

Teit and four Scottish clients fording a river somewhere in the Chilcotin–Cariboo in the fall of 1901. | Photographer unknown, courtesy of James M. Teit and Sigurd Teit.

three of their horses slipped into a hidden sinkhole, requiring all hands to drag them out. Their next crisis was a raging river that could not be crossed on horseback. They spotted a canoe on the opposite bank, but by the time they built a raft and poled over to retrieve it, they had lost the better part of a day. To get the horses across the river, they had to form a line and coax them with "sticks and by shouting."[14] Boas complained bitterly in his letters about the time lost to such ordeals and more generally about the long hours spent making and breaking camp.[15] Often his only option for fieldwork was at an adjacent Indian campsite at the end of the day. After three weeks of this wet slog through overgrown, mosquito-infested wagon roads and horse trails, he wrote to Marie that he was "fed up with these trips into the wilderness."[16] There was no turning back, however.

On the second-to-last day, Boas rode ahead to Bella Coola to meet up with George Hunt, his Tlingit/English contact from Fort Rupert on Vancouver Island. He had booked Hunt for some ethnographic work at Bella Coola, but he was so far behind schedule that he worried Hunt could easily have come and gone. He was relieved to arrive in the village and find Hunt waiting for him. While Boas nursed his scrapes and bruises and organized his work schedule with Hunt, Teit rested his horses, tallied up his expenses, and restocked his saddlebags with food supplies. Three days of this and he and his Nlaka'pamux crew-members, Dick and Sam, headed for home. Like Boas, Teit kept a journal, but it was more of a trip log – reports of the weather, the mileage, the routes and camping spots – than a personal diary. According to his log, he made the trip from Bella Coola to Spences Bridge in a record twenty-seven days despite losing a day and a half at Puntzi Lake searching for his horse, Old Charley. He noted steady rain for the first four days and extreme heat (and thick dust) for the remainder of the trip.[17]

Teit arrived home to his other life: a hunting party from England had booked him as its guide and the party members were on their way to the designated meeting place in the central Interior.[18] He loaded up his pack horses, saddled up his riding horse, and headed off. By late November, he had logged another 1,157 kilometres, much of it along the same trails he had taken with Boas and Farrand.[19]

Meanwhile, at Bella Coola, Boas settled into a routine that he had so missed on the road trip: mornings spent with Hunt recording and reviewing Kwak'wala texts; afternoons spent doing the same (through an interpreter) with members of the local Nuxalk community; and evenings spent walking and chatting with Hunt.[20] He left Bella Coola by steamer on August 5 in a much happier state, as he was well rested and his suitcase was filled with 244 pages of dictation and 72 pages of song notes.[21]

The Jesup

The stakes were high for Boas on this trip. He had some anthropometric measurements and linguistic work to wrap up for the British Association for the Advancement of Science (BAAS) but because Horatio Hale, his hawkish BAAS supervisor, had died the previous December, the pressure associated with this work had lifted, allowing him to focus on his own field project – the Jesup North Pacific Expedition. The "Jesup" had come with his new job as assistant curator of ethnology and somatology at the American Museum of Natural History in New York City. Shortly after taking up the job, he had approached the museum's president, Morris K. Jesup, with a proposal to undertake a large ethnological and archaeological study of the North Pacific rim. Jesup liked the proposal so much that he offered to fund the whole thing himself. It was, he said, "the greatest thing ever undertaken by any Museum either here or abroad."[22]

The Jesup was the perfect project for Boas because it gave him a vehicle to test his new theories of "cultural diffusion." To uncover the "mutual influence between the cultures of the Old [Asia] and of the New [America],"[23] he proposed a full ethnographic survey of the North Pacific rim, "from the Amoor River in Asia, and extending northeastward to the Bering Sea, thence south-eastward along the American coast as far as [the] Columbia River."[24] As part of this survey, he would undertake in-depth studies of individual groups within the rim to highlight their "customs in ... relation to the total culture of the tribe practicing them ... [along with] their geographical distribution [in relation to] neighbouring tribes."[25] The larger goal of the project was to determine "with considerable accuracy the historical causes that led to the formation of the customs in question and ... the psychological processes that were at work in their development."[26]

Boas had a good reason for launching his Jesup project at Spences Bridge. With Teit facilitating all facets of the fieldwork, both in and around the village and on the long road trip, he knew that he would be guaranteed good results. He also knew that with Teit handling the communications with Indians, both in the village and on the road trip, there would be few of the usual delays and awkward negotiations that were typical of his past field trips. This was not, however, how Boas described Teit's role in his 1898 AMNH field report. He wrote that Teit was one of two local assistants (the other was Charles Hill-Tout) who had helped with a variety of general tasks associated with the Interior research. Boas gave Teit slightly more credit than Hill-Tout: "The great familiarity with the language of this area which Mr. Teit has acquired during a long period of residence there, and the deep interest he is taking in the Indians, make him a most valuable assistant in the investigation."[27] He wrote that Teit had "collected notes on the Thompson River Indians" prior to the New Yorkers' arrival,[28] and that he had taken part in the road trip. As he put it, "While Mr. Smith was conducting his investigations at Kamloops, Mr. Boas and Mr. Farrand, accompanied by Teit, started on a lengthy trip northward."[29] With this wording, Boas placed himself and Farrand at the helm of the road expedition and Teit as the follow-up sweep.[30]

The arrangement, in fact, was the reverse. The New Yorkers relied fully on Teit, a seasoned ethnographer, translator, and backwoods guide with more experience and expertise than the three of them combined. He had put months into preparing things for Boas. When Boas mentioned that he was bringing along a camera with hopes of photographing the villagers, Teit replied that he was "preparing the Indians here for your taking their pictures," adding, "I think you will have no trouble getting a lot of both men and women."[31] When Boas mentioned his desire to make plaster casts of Nlaka'pamux head and facial features, Teit responded that he was preparing the local people for that too, warning that it would cost more than the photography because it was an awkward procedure that required more of his neighbours' time.[32] When Boas suggested a road trip, Teit mapped out the route and explained that he would be pleased to organize guides, food, tents, sleeping gear, and horses and lead the expedition to its destination.

Boas knew full well, in June 1897, that at Spences Bridge he had an outstanding resident ethnographer with advanced linguistic skills. It was obvious that Teit had a bond with the Nlaka'pamux community that was rare for this time period. Boas had not only observed Teit's field skills in communities in and around Spences Bridge and Lytton in September and December 1894; he had also spent close to two years sifting through Teit's hundreds of pages of handwritten field notes – on Nlaka'pamux subsistence patterns, rock art, social life, religious practices, and storytelling – for two forthcoming monographs, *The Thompson Indians of British Columbia* and *Traditions of the Thompson River Indians.*[33] And he had seen the results of Teit's first field trip to the Nicola Valley to collect data on an extinct Athapaskan language that was once spoken in the valley. In addition to all of this, Boas had processed hundreds of artifacts – and accession notes – that Teit had sent to the museum at his request. To present Teit to his museum colleagues as a "valuable assistant" who had collected a few notes on his behalf was hardly fair – but it was a prelude of things to come.

By comparison, Boas's Jesup teammates were novices. Harlan Smith was a twenty-five-year-old curator of archaeology at the AMNH with little formal training beyond some "erratic study" at the University of Michigan and a few archaeological jobs in Ohio and Kentucky.[34] As a member of the prestigious Jesup expedition, his most important asset – and one that had helped launch his archaeological career – was the support of Frederic Ward Putnam, curator of Harvard University's Peabody Museum of Archaeology and Ethnology. Putnam had met Smith in 1891 and recommended him for jobs on archaeological digs. He later helped Smith secure a job with the Chicago World Columbian Exposition and, following that, a job with the AMNH. Boas considered Smith a reliable young "fellow" with a big heart but lacking in intellectual depth. He doubted that Smith would ever make much of a contribution to anthropology.[35] In addition to wanting to please Putnam, Boas thought he could use Smith to help with the mundane tasks such as labelling and packing up artifacts, making plaster casts, and organizing photographic negatives and wax cylinders for shipment home.[36] Boas also saw Smith's archaeological skills as useful.[37]

Livingston Farrand was also an unusual choice for the Jesup. An adjunct professor of psychology at Columbia, he had a stellar academic record that included an undergraduate degree from Princeton, a medical degree from Columbia College of Physicians and Surgeons, and postgraduate studies in Cambridge and Berlin. In 1897, he was teaching a course in ethnology at Columbia with hopes that it would lead to a permanent academic position in the emerging discipline of anthropology. Because he had had no ethnographic field experience, he saw the Jesup as a way to enhance his eligibility for such jobs. Morris Jesup was not keen on including Farrand, but Farrand was so determined to go that he offered to cover some of his own expenses.[38] Boas liked the idea of including Farrand, partly because he knew Farrand would provide him with good company and conversation on the long road trip.[39]

A Full Backcountry Life

The road trip was a turning point for Boas. In thirty-eight days of travel over hundreds of miles of terrain during the friendliest of seasons, with all the logistics meticulously managed by Teit, he and Farrand had had little success. Bad weather was one thing; empty villages and resistant Indians were another thing altogether. The final straw was encountering a young man who accused Boas of trying to kill him with his measuring tools. It was clear to Boas by the end of the road trip that James Teit was much better suited to such work than he.

Boas ended his 1897 field season with an offer to Teit of five months' funding for fieldwork. With Teit's report on the "Upper Thompson" peoples (those in the communities along the Fraser River from Lytton to south of Lillooet, the Thompson River from Lytton to Ashcroft, the Nicola River from Spences Bridge to the Nicola Valley, and the Coldwater River from Merritt to the Coquihalla Valley) now complete, Boas asked Teit to write a parallel report on the adjacent "Lower Thompson" peoples (the communities on the Fraser River from Spuzzum to Siska – just below Lytton). He also wanted reports on the adjacent "Lillooet" peoples, who lived in communities between the town of Douglas on the Harrison River and Bridge River in the north.[40]

Teit welcomed Boas's proposal because it was work that he could easily combine with his new life with Antko in the Twaal Valley. The couple had put in an orchard and a large vegetable garden and were seeing the first results of Teit's foray into guiding. His 1897 trip into the northwestern

Chilcotin region with paying clients from England had successfully launched his career as a guide. Because this work took place in the fall, it allowed for ethnographic fieldwork in the spring and summer months, and report writing through the winter. Teit suggested $50 to $60 per month to cover his wages and $20 to $30 per month to cover expenses incurred during the summer field trips. He added that he would try to cut costs by camping out with Indians wherever possible.[41]

With the arrangement settled, Teit made two trips by train to visit the Nlaka'pamux communities at Spuzzum, North Bend, and Boston Bar.[42] The second trip turned into a festive affair as he arrived in the middle of a three-day community gathering that was "plenty of fun" and an ideal way to meet "a great many Indians belonging to this part of the country."[43] He was especially pleased to bump into a "very well posted ... old friend," a knowledgeable chief, who gave him a full day of his time.[44] By the end of the two trips, he had "a good many ... stories" and a large number of artifacts.[45] This was good news for Boas who, prior to meeting Teit, had never experienced anything like such success in the region's reserve communities.

The "Lillooet" assignment was more challenging because it was off the CPR line, in an area he had not previously visited.[46] On August 31, after a month of preparation, Teit loaded up his pack horses and rode north along the Fraser River to the town of Lillooet. From Lillooet he rode ninety kilometres southwest to Douglas, an old gold-mining town at the head of Harrison Lake.[47] It was slow going – ten days at eighteen miles per day. Due to rough trails and a lack of grazing land along the way, the journey was very hard on his horses. It was worth the effort, however. As Teit explained to Boas, the peoples along the route – in the communities of Douglas, Skookumchuck, and Pemberton – were the "most tractable & kindest I was ever amongst. I had no difficulty with them in any way."[48] He left with 122 pages of notes "on the customs," a good collection of "stories," and over a hundred cultural artifacts. He was so pleased with the trip that he recommended to Boas that he consider working there himself. He offered a piece of advice that spoke to his employer's quick dashes in and out of reserve communities on the 1897 road trip. To connect with these peoples, Teit wrote, "you want to take your time."[49]

Teit returned to "Lower Lillooet" territory the following June, but he left Spences Bridge on a sad note as Antko, who had been so much a part of his life in the Twaal Valley, had died three months earlier of pneumonia, and he missed her terribly. It had been a difficult year due to Antko's slow and painful decline. In a letter to Boas the previous October, he mentioned cutting Antko's long hair to relieve her of some of the pressure around her head. In his notification to Boas of her death, he described it as a "great blow" as she had been "a good wife to me and we had lived happily together for over twelve years."[50] In his note to Harlan Smith, he described the death in similar terms: "I feel rather lonely and cut up," he wrote, and it will take "a long time ... to get over" it.[51] His decision to undertake most of the trip alone and on foot rather than by pack train may have been partly to help him deal with his loss. Besides the train trip to Agassiz and a boat trip across Harrison Lake to the town of Douglas, he spent most of this field trip walking. It started with a hundred-kilometre hike from Douglas to the villages of Skookumchuck and Pemberton.

Again, he reported good results to Boas. In addition to "some very fine baskets" and other items, he compiled "a very good collection of stories." He noted that he now had a total of sixty stories from this group.[52] On his return home, Teit faced a mountain of demands from Boas. In addition to finishing the "Lillooet" report, Boas asked him to compile a Nlaka'pamux dictionary. Having delegated Harlan Smith to undertake two weeks of archaeological fieldwork in the Nicola Valley, he asked Teit to help with that as well. Boas also planned his own trip into the Nicola Valley to take more measurements in the spring of 1900, and he wanted Teit to join him.[53] At the end of the Nicola Valley trip, Boas asked Teit to undertake a full report on the Secwépemc. With this request, he knew that he was asking a lot of Teit because the field research required pack-train travel along the route that had caused him such grief in 1897.

Despite the challenges of getting into Secwépemc country, Teit accepted the assignment and headed out with his pack horses on July 21.[54] He had personal plans for this trip, however, that he withheld from Boas. He took along his Spences Bridge hunting companion, Percy Inskip, to sneak in some hunting on the side. The pair made a broad sweep through the northern Secwépemc communities of Big Creek, Churn Creek, Dog Creek, Lone Cabin Creek, Bighorn Ranch, and Canoe Creek before returning to Spences Bridge on November 4.[55] In his reports to Boas, Teit wrote of spending most of the time at a campsite at Churn Creek with his old friend "Big Billy" (Sixwi'lexken), who was a treasure trove of stories.[56] According to his trip log, he and Inskip had devoted more time to hunting (and cutting up and drying meat) than they did to ethnographic work. In his communications with Boas, however, Teit highlighted his excellent ethnographic returns – some seventy artifacts and "the great majority or nearly all the stories remembered by the Fraser River Shuswap."[57] Given that storytelling was largely an evening activity, he had likely used his after-dinner campfires to work on Boas's projects as a way to free up the daylight hours for outings with Inskip.

As on the 1897 Jesup road trip, Teit and Inskip experienced many days of heavy rain and muddy trails. In a letter to Boas on August 5, Teit described the river as still so high from a spring flood that it was a challenge to get his horses across it.[58] In mid-October, he noted long delays due to more rain and mud.[59] They rode home through a snowstorm. If Boas had any reservations about missing this trip, Teit's description of his dietary fare put them to rest. "We are living on dried venison and potatoes until we get to Clinton," Teit wrote. "I would not buy any more of the very expensive and exceedingly bad grub of Dog Creek stores."[60]

Teit had been home for only three weeks when he received a note from Boas urging him to write up his Secwépemc notes. He replied that he could not write the report without completing a full field survey of Secwépemc territory:

> I think it will be a wise thing if you can see your way clear to send me as early as possible next summer to the Shuswaps of Canim Lake, Upper North Thompson and Shuswap Lake ... If this were done, I would be able to write out a paper on the whole Shuswap tribe in the same way as the Lillooet and Thompsons have been dealt with.[61]

Teit soon realized that it would be at least two summers before he could consider the Secwépemc fieldwork. Shortly after sending this proposal to Boas, he decided to organize a six-month trip to Shetland. He also agreed to organize and lead a massive guiding trip into the Chilcotin. To get his supplies, crew, and thirty horses into the Itcha Mountain range (364 kilometres from Spences Bridge) by September, he had to put them on the road in mid-July. And to ensure he and his four Scottish clients linked up with his crew and horses in the Itcha Mountains by September, he had to leave Spences Bridge on the first of August. He took a different route than his crew. He met his clients in Vancouver and travelled with them by steamer up the coast to Bella Coola and then by stagecoach across the Chilcotin plateau to Itcha.[62] He estimated that the hunting trip would occupy him into November, at which point he hoped to pack up again and head to Shetland, getting there by Christmas.[63] Because the hunting trip ended late, it pushed his Shetland departure back by a month, which pushed his return from Shetland to July.[64] He notified Boas when he got home that he had such a backlog of work that it would take until at least the following spring to get to the Secwépemc fieldwork.

Six days after unpacking his overseas bags, Teit saddled up his horse and rode over to the Nicola Valley to collect "myths" for Boas. It was a disappointing trip as the storytellers he hoped to work with were away. He managed to find an old friend, Baptiste, who gave him some stories, but he warned Boas that Baptiste's stories were so "peculiar" that he should study them for their value in showing how stories get "localized" and how "Indian conceptions are engrafted onto Whiteness" rather than as examples of authentic myths.[65] As if to warn Boas that he was working to full capacity, he outlined what he had on his plate:

> I got two Nicola Lake Indians to promise to make a full-sized tule canoe this fall. I am going out hunting with two Americans on the first of Sept. and will be back about the 10th of October. Then I go out with an Englishman hunting for one week & after that go back in the mountains for two weeks or more to assist my neighbours to make a dam for irrigation water. After that I intend to tear down part of the store and build a small cottage at the back of same (close to the river). During my spare time I will write off the balance of the Shuswap myths & all the Thompson & Nicola ones. About January I will be able to go to the Lower Fraser and make your collection. As soon as the grass is long enough for feed on the plateau (abt 1st or early in May), I will go to the North Thompson and finish up the Shuswap.[66]

The two Americans were Sam and John Pirie of Chicago's Carson, Pirie and Scott Department Store, who had hired Teit to take them hunting on the Chilcotin plateau. The dam was a local community project involving much time and many hands; and the "small cottage" project was a construction project aimed at creating an "office" for Teit to house his artifact collections and his books and notes. He hoped to build the office out of recycled wood and windows from his uncle John Murray's trade store. Murray had died in 1896 and bequeathed his old trade store and an adjacent piece of his property to Teit. He left all of his financial savings to the Salvation Army.

On Christmas Eve, Teit sent Boas the first of what would soon become a long string of explanations for delays in ethnographic production. He wrote that he was dealing with an attack of rheumatism that had slowed his progress on ethnographic assignments.[67] Despite the pain, he headed out in the early spring to undertake an ethnographic survey of the Coast Salish peoples of the Lower Fraser Valley. The trip was a disappointment as he found the resident Stó:lō peoples not only resistant to working with him but focused on getting big money for the work.[68]

From his perch in New York City, Boas seemed oblivious to the impact of his demands on Teit, because three months later he proposed putting him on a five-year retainer that would push him even harder:

> I should like very much to be able to continue your work in the whole region, which you know so well, and to push it a little more rapidly than we have been doing these last few years. Could you not make some estimate, say, for a period of about five years, including in such an estimate of the expenses for field-work during such period and a salary for yourself.[69]

Teit may have inadvertently triggered this proposal with his offhand remark in a letter to Boas a few days earlier about a ten-day collecting trip in the Nicola Valley with Dr. Charles Newcombe of Victoria that was sponsored by Chicago's Field Columbian Museum.[70] The mere mention of Chicago was anathema to Boas, and only partly because of his lingering resentment over the loss of the 1893 Chicago job. George Dorsey, an employee of the Chicago museum, had been spotted a few years earlier at Namu on the Central Coast, which infuriated Boas because he saw the move as encroaching on his own field base. In a letter to Marie at the time, Boas had complained that "these Chicago people simply adopt my plans and then try to beat me to it."[71] Boas had warned George Hunt at the time to stay away from Dorsey.[72] Word of a Chicago presence in the Nicola Valley suggested more interference from Dorsey. The last thing Boas needed or wanted in the summer of 1903 was to lose Teit to Dorsey and the Chicago Field Museum.[73]

Boas's five-year proposal was a windfall for Teit, as it offered the stability and security that he needed at the time. Teit suggested a salary of $400 per year for himself and $150 for wages for his consultants and assistants (and an additional $300 for food, expenses, and collections).[74] He used the first of the funds to tackle the overdue Secwépemc fieldwork and spent July travelling through the North Thompson, Canim Lake, and Shuswap Lake regions, interviewing people on language and culture, and collecting artifacts. He returned home on August 3, via Kamloops and the Nicola Valley. Again, if Boas had regrets about missing this trip, Teit's descriptions of mosquitoes and mishaps put them to rest:

> I had a very fair trip so far as weather etc is concerned but had mosquitoes very bad especially on the North Thompson. We swam the horses across

> the river at Little Fort about 70 miles above Kamloops & nearly lost one there. We also nearly lost three other horses, two of them by a bridge breaking away beneath us. I managed to bring them all back however in good condition and without a single sore on any of them.[75]

To the Stikine and a New Sphere of Ethnography

As with his previous trip into Secwépemc territory, Teit did double duty on this trip by combining it with a side project for the Canadian Pacific Railway (CPR). The latter assignment had materialized during his stopover in Montreal in January 1902 en route to Shetland. Before boarding the train to New York City, he had looked up an old acquaintance, Joseph Heckman, a CPR engineer whom he had befriended at Spences Bridge in the 1880s. Knowing of Teit's knowledge of BC's topography and wildlife and his high reputation as a guide, Heckman had invited him to Montreal's CPR office to discuss the tourism potential of the region. Teit left the meeting with a contract to write a formal report on British Columbia's wildlife, aimed at giving tourists "an idea of the country, its climate, [and] its game both large and small."[76] Teit's many trips through southern and central British Columbia had introduced him to this world. Heckman's proposal gave him an opportunity to systematize his knowledge in writing.

A guiding contract in the fall of 1903 with W.C. Neilson (his client from the previous Chilcotin trip) helped Teit fill a large gap in his knowledge of British Columbia. "I am going out on a hunting trip to the Stikine on the 7th Sept," he wrote to Boas, "and have got to canoe it about 200 miles upstream. I expect to be back in early November."[77] As Teit had never been that far north, the trip presented a new set of challenges. The most difficult part was the 260-kilometre canoe trip required to get himself, his crew, and his gear up the Stikine River from its mouth in Wrangell, Alaska, to the town of Telegraph Creek. Teit had ordered a cedar-lined Peterborough canoe from Ontario, to be delivered to Vancouver. He picked it up himself and transported it via steamer to Wrangell.

As the Stikine is one of the continent's fastest free-flowing navigable rivers, the canoe trip was a feat in itself. It took Teit eleven days to paddle upriver, even with the help of two highly skilled boatmen: Alex (Buck) Choquette at Wrangell, one of the Stikine's most experienced river pilots; and Joe Martel, Teit's good friend from Spences Bridge, who also had extensive river experience. At Telegraph Creek, Teit sought out local outfitters to secure riding horses, pack horses, supplies, and local guides and wranglers. With this settled, he headed into the mountains with his crew and clients. In addition to helping with the river trip, Martel served as the camp cook. At the end of it all, Teit described the Stikine trip as a major success despite encountering "very rough disagreeable weather and a good deal of hardship."[78] In addition to introducing him to the Stikine Valley, it gave him the data he needed to complete his CPR report on the wildlife of British Columbia.

Teit spent much of the following winter drafting his CPR report. In the style of his ethnographic reports, he documented in detail the behavioural patterns, physical features, and habitats of the province's large game – grizzly bears, black bears, moose, elk, deer, caribou, mountain sheep, mountain goat, cougars, antelope – along with its small game – birds and fish. Knowing that the CPR wanted to attract sport hunters to British Columbia, he characterized the region's "country, its climate, [and] its game, both large and small and the range of different varieties,"[79] as highly suitable for hunting. However, he also pitched the region as an excellent destination for what is now called "non-consumptive tourism." He mentioned naturalists, botanists, geologists, mineralists, tourists, artists, ethnologists, philologists, and anthropologists as groups that would find much of interest in British Columbia. Given the richness and diversity of his expertise in all spheres of the province's biology – from wildflowers to grizzly habitat, from their Latin nomenclature to their English and Indigenous names, from the grasslands of his southern home to the vast mountains of the north, and everywhere the rivers – this orientation was a "natural" for Teit.

As in his reports on the human culture of the region, Teit highlighted the negative impacts of colonization on the province's wildlife. He stressed that the settler population caused serious grizzly bear decline through the use of poisons around homesites and ranches. He also identified the fur trade as a problem for grizzlies. "Since their skins became of commercial value," he wrote, "the Indians have persistently hunted and trapped them (this may be said of all kinds of bear) so that they have become considerably reduced in numbers." He closed his report with a scathing critique of the CPR's policy of shooting grizzlies found wandering within a 1.5- to 2-mile radius of its track (along the Thompson River) without considering the fragile status of grizzlies in that area. His message was that the grizzly bear population was in trouble and many constituents in the province – including the CPR – should be held responsible. This he wrote in a document funded by, and intended to promote, the CPR!

Teit knew the status of grizzly bears first-hand as he had travelled through much of the province's grizzly bear habitat. The situation he described along the CPR tracks was occurring in his own neighbourhood. How he felt about, and justified, his own role in the grizzly bear hunt (as a hunting guide) is missing in the archival record. His perspective as a naturalist in a land he loved, and also as a hunter in a time and place where hunting was a way of life, on the other hand, is well-documented in his correspondence with A. Bryan Williams, BC's first provincial game warden.

Shortly after Williams's appointment to this post in 1905, Teit pushed the latter to implement stronger conservation measures in over-hunted areas across the province. Among his suggestions were special hunting permits required of all guides, along with sworn affidavits at the beginning and end of their trips declaring exactly what they had killed and where. He also advocated for restrictions on the sale of game in regions that had been over-hunted. In areas like the Nicola and Similkameen Valleys and the US/Canadian border, where large game had been "practically exterminated," he recommended a ban on hunting for a number of years to allow for some recovery. He highlighted the Similkameen Valley as a problem area due to the sale of heads of "undersized (young)" sheep.[80]

Back to Boas

While writing up his Secwépemc report, Teit received yet another outsized request from Boas. With the "Thompson" and "Lillooet" reports in hand and the "Shuswap" report in progress, Boas now wanted a report on the "Okanagan." Teit responded with his usual enthusiasm: "You can depend on me trying to get as full information as possible on the ethnology and traditions of these people. Personally, I feel much interested in the work, and will try to take an elderly man with me from this region, who is well acquainted with the Southern dialects, and interested in old things."[81] He left home with his pack horses on June 28.

Leaving home this time was a new experience, however, as three months earlier Teit had married twenty-three-year-old Leonie Josephine (Josie) Morens and moved in with her family at the 84-Mile Ranch, just north of Spences Bridge. Hence, instead of an empty log cabin, he now left a full and busy household that included not only Josie, but also Josie's mother, Franchette Morens, Josie's younger sister, Pauline, and her brother, Leon. The Morenses were a family he had known well, as they lived directly below his Twaal Valley ranch. Pierre, the head of the household, was one of the oldest settlers in the region, having arrived in the early 1860s from the Savoie region of France. Shortly thereafter he acquired a large tract of arable land on which he built a roadhouse and established a farm.[82] Pierre died in 1897, leaving Franchette and her three teenaged children to run the farm on their own. (After over a century of activity, most recently as a roadside fruit and vegetable stand, the old Morens house burned down in April 2018).

Teit began his Okanagan trip with a stop in Nicola Valley to interview people. He then headed south and set up a camp at Ashnola in the Similkameen Valley, where he undertook a month of interviews before circling home via Vernon, Kamloops, and the Nicola River.[83] Having been forewarned of rampant horse theft along the Okanagan River near the border, he was relieved to return without losing any of his eight horses. He was also relieved to return with extensive field notes. He followed this trip with a six-week hunting trip in the Chilcotin.

By the spring of 1905, Teit was running in all directions to keep up with Boas's escalating demands and deadlines. An eye problem, likely caused by long winter nights of writing under dim gas lamps, forced him to request a break. He notified Boas in August that he had completed his "Shuswap" report (350 pages of text and 100 illustrations) but it had come at a cost: "My eyes got sore last spring when I was nearly finished the Shuswap M.S. and since have been getting worse if anything, so the Doctor has told me to quit reading & writing as much as possible for several months."[84] He wrote that he was heading north into the Cassiar mountains for his annual hunting trip and hoped that it would relieve his eyes. Years later, after repeated eye problems, he would describe hunting as a tonic to both his eyes and his soul: "I find [it] acts as a great relaxation & my eye is always better after a trip looking at long range and resting from writing, reading, tc. Relieves them."[85] He returned from the hunting trip to a major life transition. On Christmas Eve, Josie gave birth to their first child, Erik.

Homer Sargent

Teit's long months in the remote mountains guiding wealthy European and American hunters had benefits beyond a seasonal wage. In the fall of 1906, one of his American clients, Homer Earl Sargent Jr., decided to donate funds – via Boas – to support Teit's ethnographic research. A thirty-one-year-old electrical engineering consultant from Chicago, Sargent

This photograph is from an album that Homer Sargent sent to Teit after their 1904 hunting trip into the Chilcotin–Cariboo. The rider in the fringed buckskin jacket on the left is Teit; the rider in the western jacket and Irish peaked cap is Jimmy Kitty (Nlaka'pamux) of the Cooks Ferry Band. The cover photograph (of Teit and Jamie Wanemkin) was taken on the same trip. | Photograph by Homer Sargent, courtesy of James M. Teit and Sigurd Teit.

Homer Sargent, Teit's client, on the Chilcotin–Cariboo hunting trip in 1904. Teit likely snapped this photo at Sargent's request as the camera belonged to Sargent. | Courtesy of James M. Teit and Sigurd Teit.

had degrees from Yale and MIT and a large inheritance from his recently deceased father, Homer Earl Sargent Sr., who made his fortune in the railroad business.[86] Having hired Teit as his guide for two hunting trips – one into the Chilcotin in the fall of 1904, and the other to the Stikine in the fall of 1906 – Sargent Jr. saw Teit as a good investment. On the recent Stikine trip, Sargent had watched Teit train a young Tahltan man, Little Ned, in the logistics of guiding. He had also spent many nights around campfires listening to Teit and Little Ned exchange stories. (Ned would later adopt Teit's surname and become one of the Stikine's top guides.)

Sargent presented his proposal to Boas in New York City in January 1907.[87] He started with an offer of $500 to cover Teit's field expenses for research with the Salishan- and Sahaptin-speaking peoples of Washington State, Idaho, Oregon, and Montana. He made only one request: that Boas not reveal the name of the funder to Teit.[88] In April, with the arrangement settled, Boas informed Teit that he had secured funds to cover field research south of the border.[89] As much as Teit welcomed the new support and the prospect of fieldwork in the United States, he could not commit to a summer start date, as he had booked a fall guiding trip into the Stikine with four American hunters.[90] It was a wise decision, as the preparations for the Stikine trip consumed much of his summer, and the trip itself consumed much of his fall.[91] He arrived home on November 1, just in time for the birth of his second child, Inga.

A year into Sargent's financial offer, Boas and Sargent decided to divert some of the funds to a side project on basketry. Boas saw the move as a way to support his new research on primitive art, while Sargent saw it as a way to build a collection of Indian baskets.[92] Sargent had recently moved to Pasadena, California, where he took note of a basket-collecting movement that was sweeping across the southwestern United States. In addition to acquiring baskets for his personal collection, he decided to create a basket collection in his name at Chicago's Field Museum. Boas wanted to use the basketry project to collect data to support his emerging theoretical premise that artistry in primitive settings would tend toward conservatism – imitation and replication – until such time as a gifted individual emerged and pushed the local makers in new and more creative directions.[93] Because he lacked the linguistic expertise to work one-on-one with the basket makers, he would need Teit again to gather the data he needed to develop his "individualistic" hypothesis.

Teit responded with his usual enthusiasm: "Re the basketry designs, I will find out all I can about them." He noted his plans to contact two basket makers at Spences Bridge and others at Nicola, Lytton, the Fraser

Canyon, and North Bend.[94] In May, Boas sent Teit a list of questions to take to the basket makers. The main one was to find out how the women laid out their designs and adjusted their patterns to the available space. The mathematician in Boas wanted to know if the women counted out their stitches or if they "put in the coloured patterns merely by eye."[95] With each set of questions, Boas became more mired in the modernist empiricism in which he was trained as a physical scientist. He wondered "how the first colored stitches are put in and how the zig-zag lines, diamonds and triangles are planned out so as to meet as evenly as possible."[96] To elicit insider perspectives on notions of what is good versus bad in basketry design and execution, he asked Teit to seek out "really good basket-makers" and ask them to assess – and critique – the works of their fellow basket makers.[97]

With the addition of a basketry project to his two ongoing projects – a study of Nlaka'pamux language and family genealogy with John Whistemnitsa, which was funded by the Smithsonian,[98] and fieldwork in the northern United States, funded by Sargent – Teit's assignments for Boas again piled up. He tackled the US assignment in May, travelling by train and stagecoach through Washington, Idaho, and Oregon to visit the Colville, Kalispel, Spokane, Coeur d'Alene, Nez Perce, Yakima, Warm Springs, and Umatilla reservations (see Map 3, p. xxi).[99] He reported to Boas from the Coville reservation that the people there were "glad that I have visited them, and also to know that their history is to be recorded as the White man's is."[100] He returned home via Revelstoke on June 24 to continue his linguistic work with Whistemnitsa while he prepared for another guiding trip to the Stikine.[101] The Stikine trip introduced him to George Adsit, a respected hunting guide with whom he had a close affinity. Adsit had arrived in the region some years earlier to run the trading posts at Nahanni and Teslin Lake, and had married a Tahltan woman, Aggie. Through Aggie, he learned the Tahltan language and immersed himself in her culture.[102] Teit wrote a glowing review of Adsit to Boas and suggested that with his depth of knowledge about the Tahltan, he would make an ideal ethnographer.[103]

These two back-to-back trips – one through the northern United States and the other through northern British Columbia – underscored the fragile state of the environment south of the border. At the end of the US trip, Teit informed A. Bryan Williams, the provincial game warden, that, according to the Indians he interviewed, "deer (2 or 3 kinds), elk, antelope and even moose were plentiful at one time," but "there is nothing there now owing to the Gov. of those states doing nothing for game protection until it was too late."[104] Having helped Williams compile a full inventory of the province's wildlife, Teit knew that, without protection, the same situation could easily occur in British Columbia.[105] He was particularly concerned about the fate of the prairie chicken and willow grouse.

Teit started the 1909 field season in mid-May with a trip to the mouth of the Kootenay River in southeastern British Columbia to interview the resident Ktunaxa peoples. From there, he carried on to Washington and Idaho to undertake more work on the Colville, Spokane, Kalispel, and Coeur d'Alene reservations before heading to a new destination: the Flathead reservation in Montana. The Montana visit introduced him to Michel Revais, a blind octogenarian with a vast knowledge of plateau history and fluency in six languages, including English and French. Raised at Fort Vancouver in the 1830s by a Kalispel mother and a French Canadian/Kalispel/Pend d'Oreille father, Revais had spent his youth travelling with trade brigades and much of his late life working as translator.[106] After another round of fieldwork with the Ktunaxa, Teit arrived home on July 19, just in time for the birth of his third child, Magnus. The baby was only nine days old when Teit headed off again, this time to the Stikine for another guiding trip.

Through the late fall and winter, Teit divided his time between writing up his field notes for Boas, working on his in-laws' farm, and helping the local chiefs mount a political campaign to address their outstanding land problems (see Chapter 7). In early May, he undertook his final US field trip for Boas: a survey of the Quinault, Chehalis, Nisqually, and Lummi reservations in western Washington State (see Map 3, p. xxi). After two months of interviews, he returned home to spend July writing up his notes and continuing his political work for the chiefs. In early August, he was off again to the Stikine on another guiding trip. His client on this trip was Homer Sargent, whom he now knew as his secret benefactor.[107] With letters flying between Sargent and the curators at the Field Museum, Boas felt that it was only a matter of time before Teit would discover who was behind the funding. "I have always felt awkward during the last three years," he wrote Teit, "because I have not been able to tell you that the funds for the work you have been doing for Columbia University were given by Mr. Homer Sargent." Sargent "did not want you to know it, and so of course I could not speak about it."[108] Sargent had purchased a Kodak camera to use on the hunting trip, and his plan was to leave it with Teit at the end of the trip. He felt it would be difficult to train Teit in the mechanics of the camera without explaining that he planned to leave it with him for use as an ethnographic tool.

Out of Balance

The Nlaka'pamux chiefs added a vast new slate of responsibilities to Teit's workload in the summer of 1910 when they approached him to help with their campaign to resolve their land-title issue (see Chapter 7). This put him on the road for weeks at a time as he travelled from reserve to reserve to educate people about the objectives of the newly formed Indian Rights Association, whose aim was to settle the land-title issue in the British courts. At the peak of this intensity, perhaps not coincidentally, Teit received, out of the blue, in February 1911, a written offer of full-time work from Boas. His first response was hesitation.[109] He replied that he might be persuaded to consider an eight-month arrangement of six to eight hours per day, but a full-time commitment was out of the question as it would interfere with his ongoing "Indian political work, and [his] ... hunting."[110] He also noted that his eyes could not tolerate full-time written work, but Boas was unmoved, throwing in perks, such as vacation time and extra funding for fieldwork and interpreters' wages.[111] Teit had certainly proven his worth with four monographs (*Traditions of the Thompson River Indians, The Thompson Indians of British Columbia, The Lillooet,* and *The Shuswap*) published and a fifth one (*Mythology of the Thompson Indians*) on its way. As the general editor of these works, Boas benefitted directly from them.

Teit tentatively accepted Boas's offer on March 16, 1911, but only on condition that Boas pay him as much as he averaged during his "best years at other work."[112] Based on his packing and guiding wages ($5 to $6 per day), he stated that he would need $80 per month while working at home and $100 per month while in the field. He asked for six weeks of vacation time.[113] At this stage, the negotiation was still an abstraction as Teit had a year's worth of political commitments to the local chiefs and a pre-booked guiding trip to the Stikine to complete before he could consider taking it on. Having worked his way up to recognition as the province's "premier" guide, he was now in high demand.[114]

Edward Sapir

Boas had a specific reason for extracting a full-time commitment from Teit, but he kept it to himself: his former graduate student Edward Sapir had just been appointed to the headship of the new Anthropology Division of the Geological Survey of Canada (GSC) in Ottawa, and he was scouting around for employees.[115] Knowing that Teit would be high on Sapir's list

Teit on a tight section of trail on the 1904 Chilcotin–Cariboo trip. | Photograph by Homer Sargent, courtesy of James M. Teit and Sigurd Teit.

of eligible recruits, Boas, ever the monopolist, worried about maintaining his own arrangement with Teit. He was right to worry. After discussing the situation with Sapir, Boas realized that his offer of long-term, permanent employment could not begin to compete with Sapir's federal government budget, which guaranteed his employees good wages and long-term financial security. In April, Boas wrote to Teit and explained that it "would not be right on my part to ask you to give up your other engagements for a few years unless I could see that you were going to have a permanent appointment later on."[116] He made one final request of Teit, however, that he knew would keep him on his tab for a while longer: "I suggested to [Sapir] that as long as the appropriation which I have at my disposal lasts, you continue to work for me."[117]

In mid-November, with Boas fully apprised of the situation, Sapir sent Teit a formal offer to join his Anthropology Division staff (indicating an annual salary of $1,500 plus another $1,000 for field expenses and interviewees' wages). Teit accepted on condition that it offer long-term security.[118] He also asked that it allow him to work from Spences Bridge (as an "outside service" employee) rather than from Ottawa.[119] Sapir agreed to all of his conditions. Their first order of business was to figure out exactly what Teit's "appropriations" to Boas were and how long it would take for him to complete them. Early in their negotiations, Sapir had asked Teit about this and was surprised to learn that Teit "did not know."[120] Boas, on the other hand, knew exactly what Teit owed him. When Teit contacted him for clarification, he responded that, according to his records, he owed him a paper on the "distribution" of the Salish tribes, a supplementary paper on the Thompson Indians, a paper on basketry, and field trips "for the next year or so" in Salish communities on the American side of the border, some of which extended into Canada.[121] He also noted the $2,800 from Sargent that was earmarked for fieldwork.

A trip to Ottawa with the Indian Rights Association in January 1912 gave Teit an opportunity to discuss this situation with Sapir. Although nothing survives of their exchange, Teit's next move suggests that he and Sapir strategized on how to loosen Teit's ties to Boas. On his way home from Ottawa on January 21, Teit penned a long letter to Boas, explaining that he understood "perfectly" the need to complete the supplementary paper on the Thompson, but that he had reservations about the others. He wrote that although the original plan for the basketry project was to complete a full study of the basketry of western and eastern Washington, "it would take a good deal more field work before a paper on same would be possible." Because the bulk of his basketry research focused on Nlaka'pamux basketry, he felt it might be more effective to treat it as a chapter in his Thompson supplementary notes. He noted that there was simply not enough field material for either an Okanagan mythology collection or monographs on American Salish peoples.[122]

Meanwhile, Teit was so keen to embark on his first assignment for Sapir – a field project with the Tahltan in the Stikine Valley – that he overrode Boas's condition and spent the early summer of 1912 planning a two-month trip to the Stikine.[123] On August 2, he left Spences Bridge for Telegraph Creek.[124] He received notification from Sapir a few days later that a cash advance of $750 was on its way.[125] Teit arrived at Telegraph Creek on September 1 as an ethnographer rather than a hunting guide. At a meeting the next day, the Tahltan outlined what they wanted him to cover, and they appointed one of their knowledgeable members, Dandy Jim, to work with him. Two days later, Teit embarked on the project with Jim and his two colleagues, Big Jackson and Slim Jim. After six weeks of daily interviews with Jim and others, he packed up two hundred pages of ethnographic notes, one hundred pages of stories, dozens of rolls of photographic film, a collection of plant specimens, and sixty-one wax-cylinder recordings of songs and headed home.[126] Sapir was pleased with his results but wondered why his artifact collection was so small. Teit replied that because the Tahltan had had negative experiences with a collector – Lieutenant George Emmons – who had pillaged their community for artifacts, often behind their backs and without recompense, they were against selling "old things" to outsiders. Out of respect, he had accepted only what individuals had offered him during his last week of his stay.[127] With much work still to be done, he proposed a follow-up field trip into the Yukon border region to work with Kaska and Tsek'ene peoples. Sapir agreed as long as Teit agreed to submit his Tahltan report before embarking on the new study.[128]

The Paper Mountain Grows

On his return from the Stikine, Teit worked fiendishly to meet his two employers' demands. It was a tricky juggling act. To report progress to one, he had to report delays to the other. It also involved tricky financial negotiations. When he was on Boas's payroll, he had to drop off Sapir's.[129] Teit's method of dealing with Boas during periods of low productivity was to ignore him, which placed Sapir in an awkward position, as Boas would contact Sapir for an explanation. On hearing that Teit had dashed off to the Stikine, for example, Boas asked Sapir about it. Sapir feigned ignorance: "I was rather surprised to learn that you did not know of Teit's departure for Northern British Columbia on work for the Geological Survey ... I took it for granted that his decision to begin work for the Survey had been made with your knowledge."[130]

On Boxing Day 1912, after a long stretch of silence, Teit finally faced the dreaded task of sending Boas a progress report. He began by explaining that, in addition to letters going missing in the mail while he was in the Stikine, he was tied up with family responsibilities at home as Josie had been ill. Her decline had started with a stillbirth the previous March (they named the infant Rolf and buried him next to his grandfather on the Morens property). She was much improved, he wrote, so he was now back on track and making good progress on his long overdue "Thompson paper." He continued to push back on Boas's request for a monograph on the American Salish groups on grounds that he had insufficient data for such a monograph, especially as there was no time for additional fieldwork.[131] "It seems too bad," he wrote, "to publish a report ... [that] will be half or three quarters full."[132]

Teit devoted much of January and February to the basketry project, complaining in letters to Sapir that it was consuming "most days, almost all day, and up to 11 & 12 at night," and that it was frustrating work. In addition to cataloguing some five hundred baskets, he had to canvass basket makers across Nlaka'pamux territory for their perspectives on their design patterns.[133] With each letter, Boas increased the intensity of his requests. "I should like very much to get a detailed list of all the patterns that every basket-maker makes, at least in a few of the villages," he wrote to Teit in January 1913.[134]

From Boas's New York City base, this may have seemed like a reasonable request. At Teit's end, however, it was a logistical – and theoretical – nightmare verging on "foolishness." His response to Boas on January 21, 1913, suggests that it was akin to asking jazz musicians and African drummers today to explain their improvisatory styles according to Western metrics and notation. This was not the first time that Teit had tried to convey to Boas that his "up to date New York City methods do not always work out in the wilds of BC":[135]

> I note all you say re. additional information on the designs. I find only a few women who enter into this subject seriously. Some of them look upon the questions as a kind of foolishness, and for that reason are hard to get full information from. Another difficulty is the great number of variations of designs, these being described rather than called by special names, and if the variation is not well known, or rather called by say a descriptive design name which is in use, different women will describe it in different ways, and it often is not clear what is meant. As a rule they will not attempt to mark the design on paper saying they cannot do it well enough.[136]

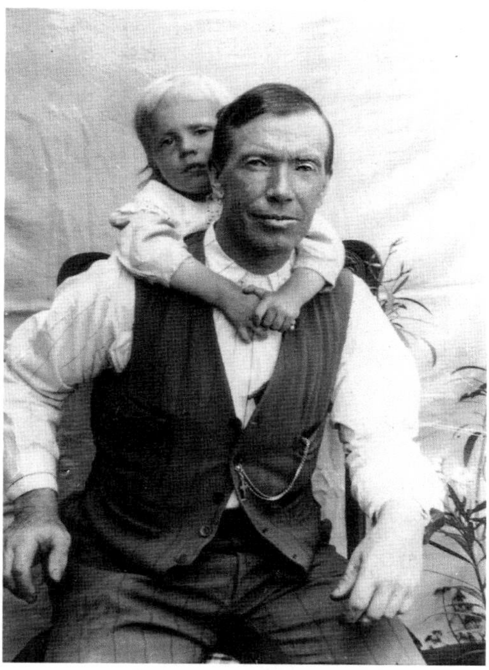

Teit with son Magnus, c. 1912. | Teit family collection, courtesy of Sigurd Teit.

Nevertheless, Teit soldiered on, even offering to go to the Potatoe Garden (Shackan) reserve (a half-day ride from Spences Bridge), and stay there "for say a week, and make a house-to-house visitation of the basketmakers."[137] He ended this letter with a request of Boas that spoke to his growing frustration with the entire project: "I have to charge a little higher wages for this year as the cost of living has gone up so much," he wrote. "I have also been working very cheaply all the years past. Not that I consider myself very highly or any better than formerly or even worth the wage, but I have to live & even the Ottawa wages is really none too much as living is going up all the time & I have a wife & family to keep."[138]

While working on the basketry project, Teit chipped away at his other assignments for Boas. A month after his request for a salary increase, Teit sent Boas eighty pages of field notes on the American Salish groups – the Coeur d'Alene, Pend d'Oreille, Sanpoil, Flathead, and Okanagan.[139] He then wrote up his notes on Nlaka'pamux stories.[140] In April 1913 it was more travel – to the Nicola Valley to interview more basket makers, and then over to the Kootenay region for two weeks of research on the Ktunaxa language.[141]

Teit's domestic situation added to his workload. He and Josie now had three children under the age of eight. As a member of a busy farming family that required all hands for the annual pruning, planting, harvesting, irrigating, watering, and winterizing, it was often difficult to justify jaunts to Spences Bridge to interview elders and write reports while Josie and her sister and brother toiled away in the fields and orchards at home.[142]

In March, Sapir added yet more stress to Teit's life by reminding him of his plans for a second trip north as well as his plans for a song-recording project at Spences Bridge. The problem was, as Teit explained in his response to Sapir, that he was so "busy with Boas's work" that he had little time to do much else.[143] He even doubted he would have time to make the northern trip. The song-recording project was out of the question.

In fact, Teit was wrong about the song project. As soon as he set up the phonograph in his "office," his Nlaka'pamux friends came in droves to try it out. Some may have done so out of curiosity about this new innovation in recording technology that could capture and play back their voices. Others may have come because they had contributed to Boas's phonograph project in 1897 and wished to continue on with Teit's. Still others may have come because of the stories Chief John Tetlanetza had told them about his contribution to a song-recording project in Ottawa in 1912. Indeed, Tetlanetza had been so impressed with the technology that he purchased a phonograph for himself! By June, Teit had filled over a hundred empty cylinders with songs, which he promptly sent to Ottawa along with a large file of handwritten explanatory notes.[144] This was the collection that had so enthralled me in 1977, and that Teit's daughter, Inga, had remembered sitting on the large desk in her father's "office."[145]

Teit's Kodak camera also attracted the attention of the Nlaka'pamux community. Teit used it for ethnographic purposes, but his Nlaka'pamux friends, in particular the women, used it for family photographs. The trove of photos of mothers dressed in their finest outfits, with their babies and toddlers sitting in their laps and their older children standing by their sides, attests to this.

Teit faced pressure on all sides, particularly from Sapir, who wanted him to cut his ties with Boas. "It must be unsatisfactory to yourself to be under obligation to two parties at the same time," he wrote. "For my part, I should prefer ... that you free yourself of all previous obligations at your earliest opportunity, so as to be able to devote all of your working time to ourselves."[146] On hearing that Teit's finances had fallen to an all-time low, Boas had stepped in with a surprise advance of $500. For some reason, which isn't altogether clear in his correspondence, Teit interpreted Boas's advance as marking the end of their working relationship. In his thank-you letter, he wrote that "after all these years I will miss my working with you."[147]

There was trouble on other fronts as well. The Canadian Northern Railway had surveyed a rail line along the north bank of the Thompson River, and its right-of-way passed right through a property that Teit had inherited from John Murray, forcing him to tear down the building he had constructed in 1902 from wood and windows salvaged from Murray's old trade store. (John and Jessie Smith had purchased the old Morton House and its adjacent orchards from Teit in 1897. Because that structure also stood on the CNR right-of-way, it too had to come down).[148] To make the best of a bad situation, Teit decided to construct a family house – an arts-and-crafts bungalow – on a new lot above the old property.[149] He also built a small cottage on an adjacent lot next to the bungalow to serve as his office. Again, Inga remembered her father's efforts to salvage windows, the old double doors, and other fixtures for the office.

Collapse

The construction project was all-consuming. To save costs, Teit worked alongside his carpentry crew. In addition to the house and "office," he needed a new barn and a fence. During his "free" time, he wrote up his Tahltan field notes and helped his Nlaka'pamux colleagues with their political campaign. In the middle of it all, he suffered an attack of "rheumatism" that paralyzed his shoulders, his neck, his right arm, and his right foot. He also had a recurrence of the old eye problem. At one point, his eyes were so bad that he could not read or write.[150] By early August 1913, his legs were so swollen that he could not walk. On his good days, he worked on his basketry notes for Boas.[151]

Once again, Teit had to explain his delays to Boas – and this was just the beginning. Typhoid fever from polluted drinking water had struck the town and, while sanding and oiling the floors of his new house, he and his son were hit, sending both to the Ashcroft hospital. Months later, he notified Sapir that he was recovering at home, but was as thin as a rail, and still on a liquid diet. His doctor had insisted that he cancel his trip to the Stikine. The timing could not have been worse, as his new house and barn had drained his finances.[152] Instead, Teit proposed an excursion closer to home to work with the Tsilhqot'in and Wet'suwet'en peoples.[153] The route he proposed was the one that years earlier had sent Boas running.

But such travel was out of the question, as typhoid and rheumatism had ravaged Teit's body. He squeezed in a few hours of writing from his bed.[154] Sapir gave him an advance on his annual salary and field expenses.[155] Boas dropped in (his first visit to BC in fourteen years) to urge Teit to complete his outstanding reports on the US Salish groups and finish his supplementary paper on the Nlaka'pamux. In August 1914, Teit started in on the paper even though he was deathly ill and flat broke.[156]

To keep his family afloat, he had one option – to sell off his personal collection of some five hundred Nlaka'pamux artifacts. This only added to his stress, as each item had to be carefully labelled, documented, and packed. He offered the collection to Sapir,[157] but Sapir had to turn it down because the federal government had frozen his budget due to the war effort. He recommended that Teit send him the collection and wait out the war, after which funds would be released to pay for it.[158] Because he needed the funds, Teit offered the collection to George Heye, a collector in New York City who had set up his own museum. Heye wanted only the oldest items, which would have meant breaking up the collection. Teit did not want to do this, so in the end he sold the full collection to Charles Willoughby, assistant director of Harvard University's Peabody Museum in Cambridge, for $1,500.[159]

By September 1914, Sapir was growing restless. He had waited three years for Teit to wrap up his work for Boas, and his patience was wearing thin. "When do you think that you could definitely finish up all your work for Dr. Boas?" he asked. "I have been hoping for a long time that you would be able to start in devoting all of your working time to the Survey, as was the original understanding."[160] Teit gave Sapir an honest reply: "I am almost afraid to make any definite statement. I have done so before & found myself wanting owing partly to sickness and loss of time I had not foreseen."[161] He also explained that Boas's expectations were proving "rather difficult to work up,"[162] but that if Sapir would grant him just one more extension, he would do his best to return to the Ottawa work in good time. He noted that his collection of Tahltan stories and song notes from the previous year was almost ready to go to press.[163]

Teit had just posted this response when he was summoned to Vancouver to serve as a witness in a court case. He used the trip to meet with the members of the Royal Commission on Indian Affairs.[164] By December, he was ahead on Boas's projects,[165] but so far behind on Sapir's that he had to request a deduction in pay.[166] Sapir did not take kindly to the request. "I do sincerely hope that you will be able to take up work for us more continuously than heretofore," he wrote in March. "I feel that from now on, any obligations you have [to Boas] ... should ... be assigned a secondary place."[167] Meanwhile, Josie was nine months pregnant with their fourth child, Sigurd, who was born on March 6, 1915. Two days later, Sapir posted his letter.

The Final Stikine Trip

In early June 1915, Teit notified Sapir that he was well enough to undertake the second field trip into northern British Columbia. In fact, he was still weak from typhoid and dealing with yet another attack of rheumatism in his foot. He was also recovering from an abscessed prostate.[168] Nevertheless, he downplayed his ailments and left for Telegraph Creek at the end of the month, with plans to stay until November. It turned out to be a good decision as it plunged him into a field experience that, even by his own standards, was unique.

He spent the first week at Telegraph Creek working with his Tahltan co-worker, Dandy Jim, while he awaited a pack horse to carry their gear inland. With the gear loaded, he and Jim spent five days hiking the 120-kilometre trail to the head of Dease Lake.[169] From there, they took a lake boat to Porter's Landing at the far end of the lake. Teit's initial plan was to descend the Dease River 290 kilometres to its junction with the Liard. However, on hearing from others that the people who lived around Lower Post, near the Dease–Liard confluence, had scattered to the wind, he decided to stay at Porter's Landing to work with two of its local residents, Albert Dease, a knowledgeable forty-five-year-old Kaska chief, and his wife, Nettie. Teit and Dandy Jim were well-rewarded by their three weeks with the couple, who regaled them with songs and stories. Fully saturated, they then hiked seven hours to Mosquito Creek to work with their old guiding friend George Adsit and his wife, Aggie. After another productive visit, they returned to Porter's Landing for more interviews with Albert and Nettie Dease and others, before catching the boat back across the lake. From there, they trekked back to Telegraph Creek, where Teit rented a small cabin for the next five weeks. One can only imagine the scene as groups of local Tahltan people turned up to discuss – with Teit and

Teit (front, centre) heading down the Stikine River to Wrangell, Alaska, after a two-month hunting trip with Homer Sargent in the Cassiar mountains in the fall of 1906. | Photograph by Homer Sargent, courtesy of James M. Teit and Sigurd Teit.

Dandy Jim – Tahltan leadership practices and protocols, clan structure, crests, and potlatches. Teit had his phonograph with him, so there was lots of singing. His camera helped him capture the gatherings in many photographs.[170]

Winter arrived early that year, shutting down commercial boat travel on the river. Again, Teit rose to the occasion and hand-built a twenty-four by five-foot flat-bottomed scow equipped with six oars. It held ten people and their gear, along with Teit's camping outfit, notebooks, artifact collections (approximately 150 items), cylinder recordings, and phonograph. He also carried a large bale of "valuable furs" from the local outfitters and between $20,000 and $25,000 worth of "gold dust" pulled from Pike's Thibet Creek mine.[171] After settling his passengers, Teit took the steering oar and, through heavy snow, navigated the scow downriver to Wrangell in a record four days. It was an onerous journey as two feet of snow fell on their campsite during one night. A second scow was not so lucky – its passengers abandoned ship partway down the river. Teit arrived in Vancouver on November 1, dreaming of another Yukon trip the following year. Alas, the voyage along the river in his handmade scow would be his last trip on the Stikine.[172]

Teit had no sooner arrived at Spences Bridge than he faced the problem that had plagued him prior to the trip: a letter from Sapir urging him to "devote" himself "fairly uninterruptedly henceforth to the working up of [his Tahltan and Kaska] notes for publication in the form of memoirs."[173] Then came the worst of all crises: his mother-in-law, Franchette Morens, the matriarch of the family, and his children's only living grandparent, died suddenly on December 7, 1915.[174] Teit spent the next month at the family ranch consoling Josie and her two siblings. On the heels of their mother's death, Josie and her sister, Pauline, and the children contracted the flu. While struggling through all of this chaos, Teit managed to write up 130 Tahltan and Kaska stories, which "occup[ied] about 200 pages." He mailed these, along with a preface and annotations, to Sapir at the end of January.[175] A month later, he wrote to Sapir about his struggle to meet the demands of two employers: "I have so much to do between your work and Dr. Boas ... If I was through with the latter I would be able to do your work more leisurely and therefore in better time. I am working as hard as I can to get through with it but it takes longer than I expected and I do not want to do any skipping."[176]

By spring the local chiefs had organized another trip to Ottawa. They wanted Teit to join them, so he was off again. He arrived in the nation's capital to bad news. Sapir informed him that the Canadian government had frozen all funds for ethnographic fieldwork due to the war effort, so plans for the next season's trip to the Stikine were off.[177] Teit used the delay to work on his Tahltan report for Sapir and the American Salishan reports for Boas. In early November, he mailed off the latter (excluding the maps) to Boas.[178] Having complained to Sapir about the time lost to "Boas's work," he was relieved.[179] In fact, most of Teit's time was now being spent on the chiefs' political campaign (see Chapter 8).[180]

At the end of November, Teit notified Sapir that he had completed Boas's work: "I finished the paper for Dr. Boas on the Coeur d'Alene about the middle of the month, and am now engaged on work for you."[181] He

From Tsilt-ghaskit per Wk. 30th J

$ cts. $

Im-pess (brother of Skim-mēn) was a noted fighter
N-kaz-öwa (brother of Hatl-melst) hung at Lytton
S-kwu-oo (name of Indian who stabbed Tagksa)

ACCOUNT OF POSTAGE COLLECTED ON NEWSPAPERS

at ______________ in 187 .

NAME OF SUBSCRIBERS. NAME OF PAPER. No. of times published per Week. QUARTER ENDING 31st March. 30th June. 30th September. 31st December.

$ cts. $ cts. $ cts. $ cts.

From Tsilt-ghaskit

Im-pess (brother of Skim-mēn) was a noted fighter
N-kaz-öwa (brother of Hatl-melst) hung at Lytton
S-kwu-oo (name of Indian who stabbed Tagksa)
S-hegh or S-sē-ghegh, Kwol-sīlighin, Kwol-teskit, prominent men or chiefs around Cooksferry and neighbourhood formerly. Kwol-teskit was a great orator

S-sē-ghegh, So-whogh-igh-ghin, Kina-moz-selst, Tidlē-ī, Shooma-hiltsa were all related to the Shuswhaps and had Shuswhap blood. Shooma-ghatko The only living descendant of S-sē-ghegh. Antko the only one of So-whogh-igh-ghin Whal-ānik & sons the only ones of Kina-moz-selst. Kul-sha-mēn the only one of Tidlē-ī.

Salish-esket was a great speaker at the old Indian way of worship

Kloogh-teskit } all half brothers — Whoy-pelst only living son
Kwil lan-ītsa } — Kwiltan-ītsa do
Whīst im-nītsa } — Whīstim-nītsa do

Tsala's father and Hai-seska's mother brother and sister and younger brother and sister to Tsili-gheskit

Hai-seska and Kwiltan-ītsa ft same father but different mothers.

Old Whīstim-nītsa when he died had 3 wives, one of them a Lillooet he and his wives and children and several others were all living in one house near the site of Nelsons old house (ghlīt-ko one of his wives with her two children was away in the mountains at the time). One night they all got poisoned by eating out of a copper kettle an 10 out of 12 died. Hatl-melst and Tsala were the two that recovered.

7 — Whoy pelst's brother was the first Indian here to get the small-pox. The great majority of the Indians at the Mouth of Nicola where he lived died of it. Some of those who were able took to the mountains. His mother dropped and died at the crossing of Teval Creek. His brother half way up and his sister at Long Jack [illegible]

◄ A typical page of Teit's field notes. Here he is listing the names of people in the local Nlaka'pamux community, including Antko, with various family and community affiliations. The most important detail is Teit's acknowledgment of Tsilla-gheskit (whom he refers to as Tsili-gheskit here) as the source of this information. See Teit's sketch of Tsilla-gheskit (p. 102) and Teit's recounting of the elder's stories in Chapter 4. | "Salish Ethnographic Materials, 1908–20," Slb. 7, American Council of Learned Societies Committee of Native American Languages collection, American Philosophical Society Library.

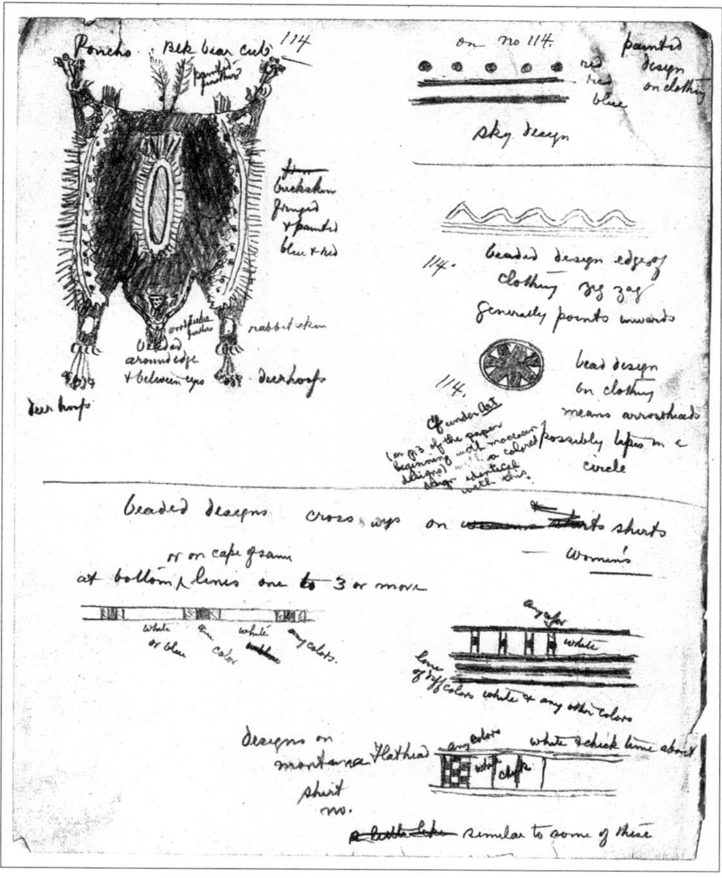

Another page from Teit's field notes. Note his skill in sketching items in his collections. | "Field Notes on Thompson and Neighbouring Salish Languages, 1904," Slb.7, American Council of Learned Societies Committee of Native American Languages collection, American Philosophical Society Library.

had no sooner written this than he wrote again to report that he had "just received a letter from Dr. Boas who says he is waiting for the maps so I will drop your work for a few days and finish them."[182]

Basketry

Two months later, in February 1917, Teit faced yet another tense exchange with Sapir. Boas had written to ask him to return to the basketry project; in order to do this, Teit had to request a three-month salary suspension from Sapir. Sapir replied that he thought it "unpolitic" of Boas to make such a demand at this time.[183] Teit responded that he felt obligated to say yes because Boas had had a recent brush with cancer and "there seems a strong possibility that [he] may not last very long."[184] Teit noted that he would "hurry it" up by allotting two, rather than three, months to Boas.[185] Reluctantly, Sapir agreed.[186]

In fact, the last thing that Teit wanted was to return to the basketry project, as it was his least favourite of Boas's projects. One by one, he sent the women's responses to Boas. Because they were not the sorts of responses that Boas wanted, he decided to add his Columbia research assistant, Herman Haeberlin, to the project. Haeberlin had completed his doctorate under Boas and spent two field seasons working with Coast Salish basket makers in and around Puget Sound, so Boas felt that a shift to the central Interior basket makers would suit him well.[187] He explained this sudden change in plans to Homer Sargent (who was funding it):

> I think you will understand me if I say that, although I value Teit very, very highly and have the greatest respect for his persistence and clear judgment, some of the theoretical questions are naturally removed from his interest; and since it is impossible to stay with him long enough to explain [to] him all their bearings, the material that he sends us must necessarily be re-arranged here and be discussed here. I think therefore that the best way of doing the present piece of work would be for him simply to send us his notes without trying to discuss them himself.[188]

He had explained this earlier to Teit as the simple addition of an anthropological assistant to the project. Teit welcomed the addition, seeing it as a way to extract himself from the project. As he explained to Sapir, "I then thought the matter would be off my hands except perhaps for the answering of some queries or giving a little additional information now and then as Haeberlin proceeded with the writing up of the subject."[189] Haeberlin visited Spences Bridge at the end of June 1917 and spent four days discussing basketry with Teit, who took him to meet some of the local basket makers. Haeberlin had floated the idea of treating the art of Nlaka'pamux basketry as Western art historians treated the so-called high art forms in "civilized" settings, and when he was with Teit, he expressed interest in pursuing the Nlaka'pamux basket makers with the same sorts of questions about problems of form and composition that art historians might ask artists in Western contexts.[190]

Because the basketry work extended well past the two months that Teit and Sapir had agreed on, there were further delays on both fronts. "I would have been through before," he wrote Boas in October, "but my time has been very much broken one way and another."[191] On sensing that Boas was dissatisfied with his contribution to the project, Teit went on the defensive: "I think the number of designs I have got together is more than any single investigator could obtain in the field except he took a very long time." He added that he felt that his collection of "design names" was "nearly complete for the tribe."[192] It had little impact. In his letters to Haeberlin, Boas continued to complain about Teit: "I got two bunches of Teit's material," but it represented "very little of what we want ... There is very little to tell us here."[193] This would be one of the last communications with Haeberlin. A month later, on February 12, 1918, the young ethnographer died suddenly from a diabetic attack. Teit was deeply saddened by the death as he had enjoyed his four days with Haeberlin the previous summer.[194]

Teit saw Haeberlin's death as marking the end of the basketry project. On March 14, he mailed the last of his basketry notes to Boas and wrote to Sapir to say that he felt so "relieved ... to have [the basketry project] off [his] hands."[195] Once again, it was not to be. On the same day Teit posted his letter to Sapir expressing relief that the basketry project was over, Boas posted a letter to Spences Bridge asking Teit to record his "observations on the way in which the older women teach young girls to weave baskets. There must be a lot of criticism and definite instruction in regard to the way of holding the material, evenness of coils and so on."[196] Two weeks later, Boas notified Teit that he had found a replacement for Haeberlin: she was a young female student, Helen Roberts.[197] A classical pianist by training, Roberts had come to Columbia in 1916 to pursue a master's degree in anthropology under Boas. She had previously worked with Haeberlin on a Coast Salish song project and had undertaken some research on southwestern basketry. She would later turn Teit's Salishan basketry notes into her master's thesis.[198]

In June, it was back to Sapir, who delivered bad news. R.G. McConnell, Deputy Minister of Mines, had decided to reduce Teit's GSC contract by 60 percent ($600 per annum instead of $1,500). Teit was now well known in federal and provincial government circles as a harsh critic of the policies of the Department of Indian Affairs, and both Sapir's Anthropology Division (which included Teit) and the Indian Department were under McConnell's jurisdiction. "It is obvious that his name hardly impresses the administration," Sapir wrote to Boas.[199] This news was yet another blow to Teit, who was now fully dependent on his government salary to support his wife and four children. "Perhaps I am too obscure? ... or it may be I am not the right kind?" he wrote to Sapir. "[If I were] something they consider valuable," he added, "I would be a success ... [but] their point of view is different from ours."[200] Instead, Teit returned to the seasonal work of his early days – prospecting, working on local ranches, picking fruit, digging potatoes, and haying.[201] The Interior chiefs relieved some of the pressure by offering him a salary for his work on their behalf. "The Indians have given me a job for a time," he wrote to Sapir. This "may come in handy seeing the Gov. does not deem my services of much value, evidently?"[202]

The next crisis was the Spanish flu epidemic that was raging across the world. Teit noted that it claimed "as many as 28 and 40 per cent of those Indians contracting it."[203] In the spring of 1919, Josie and her sister, Pauline, and two of their children contracted it, and Pauline died. As one of his "most valued friend[s]," her death hit him hard.[204] Meanwhile, Josie, who was pregnant with their fifth child, caught pneumonia in the wake of her sister's death and spent a month in the hospital.[205] During her absence, two of the children contracted mumps.[206] Miraculously, everyone in the family, including the new baby, Thor, survived. But its toll on Teit was visceral, especially as he was now suffering from a "partial[ly] detach[ed] ... retina," which he was told was "uncurable."[207]

Boas again piled on the stress with more demands on the basketry project. In addition to long lists of questions,[208] he sent Teit boxes of coloured pencils and pads of paper with a request to take these to the basket makers and ask them to draw out and colour in their imbricated basket designs.[209] Boas's student, Helen Roberts, only added to Teit's stress by treating him in a belittling manner. In the spring of 1919, Teit was so frustrated by her notes that he ceased responding to them altogether and contacted Boas directly. On detecting this change in one of Teit's postcard communications to Boas while the latter was on holiday, Roberts wrote an angry response to Boas: "Mr. Teit has written [in] a post-card that he was writing to you what he could find about rhythm, so I suppose I am still out of favor. I had written that you were away. He sent in some more utterly irrelevant data on some realistic designs, which are really not important enough to include at this late date."[210] Roberts's comments referred to Teit's efforts to extract answers to Boas's questions from noted Nlaka'pamux basket makers Tsóstko, TSEKENêlEMEX, and Pelpíltko, and others.[211]

In July, Sapir shocked Teit with news that the Geological Survey had decided to terminate his contract altogether because of the expense of the war.[212] To soften the blow, Sapir told Teit that he was trying to negotiate a new arrangement that would pay him on a piecemeal basis for Tahltan manuscript material as he submitted it.[213] The proposal offered Teit little consolation, however, as he was so busy working on the chiefs' political campaign that he had no time for piecemeal ethnographic work.[214]

The timing of Sapir's news could not have been worse. Josie was ill again, this time with appendicitis.[215] On hearing of Teit's dire situation, Boas wrote to say that he was seeking external funding on his behalf. He noted that he would first need an update on his outstanding assignments. A lingering sore point. Teit replied that he had reports on Nlaka'pamux ethnobotany, place names, and genealogies, and that he was working on a preliminary report on the Snare Indians and some linguistic notes and ethnologies of the Tahltan and Kaska.[216] He added that because the chiefs were now paying him (at the rate of $6.50 per day for his time), it would be a while before he could complete these projects.[217] Boas then contacted Sargent, who offered to fund the ethnobotany project, the place-names project, and the personal names project.[218] Two weeks later, Sapir had some good news for Teit: his superiors had approved Sapir's proposal to pay Teit in instalments of $300, $250, and $200, respectively, on delivery of three sections of the proposed Tahltan report. Sapir added that he could offer an additional $125 on delivery of a Kaska report.[219]

Through all of these negotiations, Teit wrote repeatedly to Sapir about his anger with the federal government's termination of his contract. Perhaps the reason the museum let him go, he wrote to Sapir, was "that people in general are more interested in finding out about the dead and their history than investigating the living ... It seems there is a tendency among the powers that be in Ottawa to cut out anthropological work altogether or at least to pare it down so that it just merely exists ... What can we expect from the class of people who are in power? They cannot be expected to advance anything except they see dollars in it."[220]

A Dire Diagnosis

Although buoyed by the renewed support of Boas and Sapir, Teit was now so consumed by the chiefs' political campaign that he could not consider moving ahead on their respective assignments. The political work had involved extensive travel: in September 1919, a trip to Prince Rupert on the North Coast and to Aiyansh, a village located a hundred kilometres north of the town of Terrace, to attend meetings;[221] in March 1920, a trip to Ottawa for three months of meetings – with a quick return trip to Vancouver in May for another meeting, then back to Ottawa (see Chapter 8).[222] As the chiefs' representative on the government's Ditchburn Inquiry, Teit was now on the road full-time, undertaking a last-minute cross-check of the McKenna-McBride Commission's report.

In a letter to Boas, he explained that he had been "overworked" all year long by the "Allied Tribes of B.C. in connection with their land and other rights," which had left "little time to work on the papers [he] had on hand for yourself and Dr. Sapir." He also noted that he had been "handicapped by sickness."[223] In a letter to Sapir three weeks later, he explained similarly that the political work had stretched him to the limit and that he was now dealing with an illness that had hit him during a meeting in Victoria a few weeks earlier. He attributed the illness to "a severe chill" that he had picked up while sitting outside in the cold. As hard as he tried, he could not shake it.[224] His weight dropped by thirty pounds. In mid-February, he was so weak and emaciated that he was hospitalized for twelve days.

With little improvement by March, Teit's doctor in Merritt suggested taking him to Vancouver for tests.[225] The diagnosis was dire: "cancer in a lower bowel where it is very difficult to operate."[226] The "pressure on the bowel seems most serious at the present as it will ultimately stop anything from passing through," Teit wrote to Boas.[227] "They have thus given me up, and I am under sentence of death," he wrote Sapir.[228] Word was that he had two or three months to live. Not one to wallow in self-pity, the diagnosis sent Teit into a frenzy of work to finish off his reports for both Sapir and Boas. On March 22, he mailed sixty pages of linguistic notes on the Tahltan, Kaska, and Tlingit to Sapir.[229] Two days later he mailed his Tahltan notebooks to Sapir, noting that his goal was to continue writing up material as long as he was able, but that if he should die before finishing it, he hoped Sapir would complete the task for him.

On hearing of Teit's diagnosis, Homer Sargent sent a telegram to Spences Bridge offering to finance a trip to the Mayo Clinic in Rochester, Minnesota, for a second opinion.[230] In his weakened state, a grateful Teit took the train to Rochester, where a medical team confirmed the original diagnosis and recommended a return to Vancouver for radiation therapy. Between April and August, with more funds from Sargent, Teit made three trips to St. Paul's Hospital in Vancouver for x-ray treatments.[231] Initially the radiation ravaged his body. By summer, he was down to 117 pounds and largely bedridden.[232] He used his good days to write up his notes and organize his collections. In mid-July he shipped more cylinder recordings and song notes to Sapir.

By early fall, after twenty days of radiation, Teit suddenly rebounded.[233] An x-ray showed him to be cancer-free. He was so improved that some of his doctors even questioned the original diagnosis.[234] Buoyed by this news, Teit informed Boas in November that he had resumed work on the ethnobotany manuscript. He told W.E. Ditchburn, Chief Inspector of Indian Agencies, that he wanted to return to his work on the Ditchburn-Clark Inquiry (see Chapter 8). The latter work, as he told Boas, paid so well he could not afford to give it up.[235] His energy spurt was short-lived. Seven months later, he was back at St. Paul's with a recurrence of the original problem.[236] Boas visited Teit at Spences Bridge at the end of August and wrote to his older sister, Toni, that it was a "very sad" visit as "an old companion of my travels is dying of cancer."[237]

Teit died two months later, on October 30, 1922, in Merritt. He was fifty-eight.

6
Dwelling

As all American anthropologists are aware, Teit's "Thompson River Indians" ranks as one of the very best monographs on any single American tribe.

– John Swanton, *American Anthropologist* (1907)[1]

In 2010, the town of Princeton, BC, threw a party to celebrate its 150th birthday.[2] It was a festive affair on the Labour Day weekend that included street theatre, storytelling circles, and gold-panning demonstrations. A highlight was the unveiling of a heritage plaque honouring Susan Moir Allison (1845–1937) as a "person of national historic significance." Susan had settled in the Similkameen Valley in 1868 after her marriage to John Fall Allison, a gold rusher who established the first cattle ranch in the valley.[3] She joined John's household shortly after the birth of his third child with a local Similkameen woman, Nora Yakumtikum. This side of the family history was not noted in the dedication, even though some of Nora and John's descendants were in the audience.[4]

Instead, the focus was on Susan Allison's pioneering "firsts": the first white woman to settle in the Similkameen Valley, the first white woman to give birth to a white child in the valley, and the first settler to publish profiles of the local Similkameen Indians. For a novice writer, she did well, publishing two articles on Similkameen history and culture in British academic journals in the 1890s,[5] and a long narrative poem about a Similkameen chief with an American press in 1900.[6] She wrote a memoir late in life that the *Vancouver Sunday Province* serialized in 1931. Two Vancouver artists – Barbara Pentland (a composer) and Dorothy Livesay (a poet) – were so inspired by the memoir that they collaborated on a chamber opera, *The Lake,* based on the story. It premiered on the CBC in the mid-1950s. In 1976, University of British Columbia historian Margaret Ormsby published an annotated version of Allison's memoir, *A Pioneer Gentlewoman in British Columbia,* in UBC Press's colonial and provincial history series.

In her introduction, Ormsby described Allison as the "only authority on the life and customs of the Indians of the Similkameen region."[7] Jim Prentice, federal Minister of the Environment, echoed Ormsby in his speech at the plaque unveiling in Princeton, citing Allison as a "fine example of our government's commitment to honouring women in Canada who have contributed to our understanding of this great country's rich history and culture." Her work, he said, "remains a respected source for both Aboriginal and non-Aboriginal scholars and communities."[8]

Allison certainly deserves praise for her pioneering firsts, but not without critical reflection. One of her key messages was that settler Canadians need not worry about extracting land from the Indians in the Similkameen Valley, because Indian life in that valley was all but gone. In a nation built on assimilation, this was good news to Allison: "I know from personal experience that the Similkameen Indians of to-day are totally different both physically and mentally from what they were thirty or even twenty years ago."[9] If they survive "the civilizing process," there will soon "be little or no distinction between a Similkameen Indian and his white brethren."[10] She noted with relief that the old, earthen winter homes – those "dirty, unwholesome dens, harbouring every kind of filth and disease" – had been replaced by "good warm" log houses, some within range of newly constructed churches.[11] She explained that the old Similkameen belief in "an Almighty Spirit, the Creator of all things, and Master of All" had facilitated a smooth transition to Christianity. She described Indian women as so embarrassed by their old-style life that many had given up hunting "lest the white settlers should laugh at them."[12] She was pleased to report that the men, who were formerly aggressive thieves and prone to cruelty, were now "peace-loving" and "trustworthy." Allison attributed this dramatic shift to the "generous land allotments" of the government reserve system. "They have too much property to wish for war," she wrote.[13]

Allison wasn't alone in profiling BC's resident Indians in British journals in the 1890s. Charles Hill-Tout, an Englishman who arrived in Vancouver in 1891 to work at an Anglican boys' school, wrote in the 1899 *Report of the British Association for the Advancement of Science* that "the primitive customs of the Thompson, like those of their neighbours have for the most part given way to new ones borrowed from the whites."[14] He described Nlaka'pamux culture in the 1890s as so far gone that it could only be retrieved through its "folk-tales."[15] In his report to the *Journal of the Royal Anthropological Institute,* he described land clearances as beneficial to the lives of the lazy Okanagan Indians:

> They now live on reserves, some of the finest tracts of country having been set aside for their use. I cannot say that they have taken much advantage of their opportunities. With rare exceptions here and there, and generally where the infusion of white blood makes itself apparent, they are content to muddle along in their old hand-to-mouth style of living. They display little or no concerted action in their labours ... If they showed any energy or enterprise they might all be wealthy, or at any rate well-to-do, in a few years.[16]

By 1915, the message was clear that it was time to replace the lazy, indolent Indian with the assimilated Indian, ideally one with good Christian values and a strong work ethic. Those who resisted needed to be "subjugated" or stamped out.[17] CPR publicist and author F.A. Talbot summed up the sentiment in his 1912 book, *The New Garden of Canada: By Packhorse and Canoe through Undeveloped New British Columbia:* "The red man of today is a keen hunter, but withal a lazy lout."[18] English travel writer John B. Thornhill proposed a radical solution to the Indian problem in his 1913 book, *British Columbia in the Making.* Because the Indians hold "all the best lands in the province – quite 20X what they possibly require ... I think I am right in saying that everybody would be pleased if they segregated sexes and let them die out altogether."[19] The region's resident historians, Alexander Begg, John Kerr, and Oliver Cogswell, concurred. Since Indians had "played no role in British Columbia's development," they had no place in its history. They were peoples of a "timeless past" whose history existed "in myths."[20]

Teit, of course, had little tolerance for such white supremacist rhetoric. In a letter in the fall of 1893, he noted the lack of "books or essays on Indian tribes of this country by reliable authorities," and the existence of newspaper articles filled with "errors" and displaying "little knowledge of the subject."[21] In his correspondence with Franz Boas and, later, Edward Sapir, he highlighted Charles Hill-Tout as one of the worst offenders.[22] In three monographs published between 1900 and 1909 by New York City's American Museum of Natural History, Teit characterized the "Thompson," "Shuswap," and "Lillooet" peoples of south central British Columbia as the opposite of Hill-Tout's characterizations: they were intelligent, hardworking, and strong, bearers of a traditional socio-economic system that was leagues beyond that of so-called civilized Western society.

In 1906, Teit and Boas issued a public critique of Hill-Tout. The catalyst was an article that Hill-Tout had published on the peoples of the Upper and Lower Lillooet region ("the Statlumh," as Hill-Tout called them) in a British journal the previous year.[23] After reading the article, Teit compiled a long list of criticisms and mailed them to Boas, noting in his cover letter that "H.T. has done wrong in trying to make a study of Lillooet culture tc. at Douglas. The extreme end of a tribe where it borders another tribe always shows a mixture of ideas, customs, tc.tc."[24] Because Teit's monograph on the "Lillooet" was at the printer, Boas arranged to have the critique inserted – in his (Boas's) name – as an appendix.[25]

Starting with Hill-Tout's choice of the town of Douglas as his primary field base and "Captain Paul" as his primary informant, Boas highlighted, point by point, the problems associated with using a border town as the reference point for the full group. Douglas, he explained, was as much a Fraser Delta (i.e., Coast Salish) community as it was a "Lower Lillooet" (i.e., Interior Salish) community. He also challenged Hill-Tout's assertion that the "Lower Lillooet" guardian spirit complex was a form of "totemism." This was not only wrong but demonstrated a complete lack of understanding of the basic principles of totemism. He highlighted other flaws, such as Hill-Tout's listing of "Liluetō'l" and "Xailô'laux" as place names when, according to Teit, they were "the name of a band" in the former case, and "the name of a people" in the latter case.[26] Boas concluded by stating that Teit's findings were far more credible than Hill-Tout's, as he had made four trips through "the country between [the villages of] Douglas and Pemberton – twice on horseback, once on foot and once by canoe," visiting "every one of the villages" along the way with "Chief James of Pemberton," who had a solid knowledge of their names.[27]

Teit likely had both Hill-Tout and Allison in mind with a comment in his 1909 monograph, *The Shuswap,* about the dangers of ethnographic whitewashing:

> At the present day, the characteristics of the tribes are described more from the white-man's point of view. Thus, on the whole, the Shuswap are considered religious, because they pay attention to the observances of the Christian religion; progressive because they copy the example of the whites very closely in all essentials; industrious, because they work extensively on their own reserves, and labor for the whites.[28]

Such criticisms by a well-published Canadian ethnographer and a leading American anthropologist should have done serious damage to Hill-Tout's academic standing, but such was the hegemony of white supremacy within the scientific establishment in Canada at the time that seven years after Boas's scathing review of Hill-Tout's 1905 Lillooet report, the Royal Society of Canada, an institution representing the country's intellectual elite, elected Hill-Tout to its presidency.[29]

It was a different story south of the border, where Boas's circle of students and associates pursued a new critical, anti-racist, and professional anthropology. On hearing of a federal government initiative to establish an anthropological research institute in Ottawa, Boas worried that Hill-Tout, as one of the few published ethnographers in Canada, might well be a serious contender for the institute's directorship. To block this possibility, he described Hill-Tout in a letter to Reginald Brock, the Director of the Geological Survey of Canada (GSC) tasked with hiring the head of the new anthropological unit, as an anthropologist with "a most remarkable ability of exasperating every one with whom he comes into contact ... [and one] who is thoroughly unscientific in his conclusions."[30]

Members of the new American anthropological community read and admired Teit's work. From his base at the Smithsonian Institution, John Swanton, a former student of Boas, summed up his colleagues' views in the 1907 issue of the *American Anthropologist.* "As all American anthropologists are aware," he wrote, James Teit's *Thompson Indians* "is one of the very best monographs on any one single tribe."[31] Edward Sapir echoed Swanton a few years later in a letter to the head of the GSC. Teit's "well known monographs on the Thompson River Indians, Shuswap and Lillooet," he wrote, were "models of their kind."[32]

As much as Swanton, Sapir, and others admired Teit's published work, however, they overlooked the unique style of fieldwork that underpinned it. Frank Cushing was the new model of fieldwork. An American anthropologist who had lived continuously with the Zuni peoples of New Mexico from 1879 to 1884, Cushing had used this experience to advocate for a more engaged and reflexive relationship between the anthropologist and his subjects of study.[33] As a self-conscious undertaking by a sojourning outsider (ideally a sojourner with academic training), his approach aligned well with the urban, academic affiliations and allegiances of the new anthropological community. In contrast, Teit was an amateur, but a unique one. His field methodology had required no formal academic training (indeed, it might have suffered from it), and there was nothing "sojourning" about it. The "field" was his home; so-called ethnographic informants were his relatives, neighbours, and friends; and "participant observation" was his daily practice.

As such, he was on a path that, decades later, the German philosopher Martin Heidegger (1889–1976) would eulogize as the art of "dwelling:"

> But in what does the essence of dwelling consist? ... To dwell, to be set at peace, means to remain at peace with the free, the preserve, the free sphere that safeguards each thing in its essence. *The fundamental character of dwelling is ... sparing.* It pervades dwelling in its whole range. That range reveals itself to us as soon as we recall that human being consists in dwelling and, indeed, dwelling in the sense of the stay of mortals on the earth.[34]

What Heidegger describes here is what Teit had always known and practised, from his youth in Shetland to his life in Spences Bridge to his first work with Boas. His was a life close to the land and its people, and a commitment to sparing – that is, to safeguarding and preserving – "dwelling in its whole range." This was the lived foundation for his anthropology of belonging. It led him not to high philosophy but to strong practice, to what is now defined (clinically) as "participant-observation" and, later, to political praxis, all of it decades ahead of its time.

A Tableful of Contents

A week after meeting Teit in 1894, Boas mailed him a letter outlining what he wanted him to include in his Nlaka'pamux report. He listed everything under the sun – the locations of the "divisions of the tribe," descriptions of local "dialects and villages," stories of "migrations," descriptions of various house types, household utensils, and industries (such as basketry, creation of stone implements, wood carving, dressing of skins, preparation of food supply, hunting and fishing practices); concepts of war, trade, government; marriage customs; rituals surrounding birth, puberty, death, and shamanism; a description of the local sign language; restrictions around food and work; "customs regarding sickness, Indian doctors and witches;" and all "beliefs regarding the soul." To top this off, he asked Teit to make a collection of "myths" and "traditions."[35]

Despite the scale of the assignment, Teit took it on, and within five months mailed Boas a 216-page report.[36] While Boas praised the report for its breadth, Teit worried about its gaps.[37] "I do not pretend to call it a complete paper," he wrote.[38] "As it stands, there is hardly any subject included within the scope of the paper but which I could deal with in far greater detail if I wished to."[39] To allay Teit's concerns about the gaps, Boas sent him funds to extend his work on the Nlaka'pamux into the Lower Division (a collection of communities along the Fraser River between the villages of Spuzzum and Siska). Again Teit completed the work promptly and sent Boas a second report. Boas turned the two reports into a single monograph, *The Thompson Indians of British Columbia,* and published it as the fourth in his twenty-seven-volume Jesup North Pacific Expedition monograph series. Teit would spend the rest of his life working on his "Supplementary Notes on the Thompson" with hopes of seeing it appended to the 1900 monograph. Alas, it never happened. As with the larger collection of his field notes that Boas destroyed after Teit's death (see Chapter 9), most of these notes have disappeared.

The *Thompson Indians* was an exciting addition to the literature on Native North America. With its 250 pages of text, 200 drawings and illustrations, and 56-item Table of Contents, it was one of the most comprehensive portraits of North American Indian life on record. You have "a right to feel gratified with the reception of your Memoir," Boas wrote shortly after its publication. "The reviews are not only very good, but I find that the contents of your descriptions are used extensively in all new books treating of the general subjects of anthropology."[40] Six years later, as Swanton noted in the *American Anthropologist,* the monograph continued to lead the way. It was far from an amateur effort.

After three decades of studying Teit's *Thompson Indians,* I can attest to its precision and subtlety, and its value as an endless source of insight and illumination. A few months ago, while thumbing through the introductory chapter looking for details about a particular place name, I had one of those revelatory moments. Instead of characterizing the Nlaka'pamux land base as part of a bygone era, as Hill-Tout, Allison, and others were doing, Teit characterized it as their still-functioning full home (their "habitat," as he called it in appropriately Heideggerian language). As if to challenge the power and legitimacy of the new settler maps, he superimposed his own hand-drawn map of the full Nlaka'pamux traditional territory onto the official "British Columbia" map and listed beside it the key Nlaka'pamux place names within that territory. In addition to English translations of those names, he noted their precise locations. To access such information required multiple trips to the places bearing those names; to verify the meanings embedded in the place names required tracking down people knowledgeable about them. The end result was a vibrant visual and discursive portrait of the southern Interior as a large, living, and wholly Indigenous landscape. It was also a form of "community mapping" that is popular today, but a century ago was an insurgent challenge to the imposition of new maps asserting the colonial presence.

Teit's description of the place name Tûxezê'p illustrates this well. He listed it in the monograph as a village site on the east side of the Fraser River, one mile above Lytton, and noted its Nlaka'pamux name as a "shortened form of xûzē'êp, [meaning] 'sharp ground or place for pitching lodges,' so called from small sharp stones around there."[41] To locate Tûxezê'p on a map required a trip to the place of sharp stones and also a careful mathematical calculation to determine its exact distance in miles from the starting point (Lytton). It also required tracking down and interviewing the people who knew and used that place to determine its full cultural meaning within the community. And this was just one of dozens of such place names.[42]

Chapter 3 ("House and Household") gave context to the place names. As if to distinguish the fluidity of Nlaka'pamux housing from the fixity of its settler-colonial counterpart, Teit described Nlaka'pamux housing as an ever-changing system of moveable lodges scattered across the full territory and utilized according to the seasons. He noted that for approximately eight months of the year, people lived in temporary "lodges" near their multiple foraging, fishing, and hunting sites.[43] Of these Nlaka'pamux lodges, he highlighted the summer lodge as their primary dwelling. It was a round (or sometimes square) teepee-like structure, fifteen to twenty feet in diameter. A dozen or so long poles created the framework over which a deerskin was draped. The structure could be easily taken apart and reused. He noted that in 1900, many older people still lived in such lodges, some for the full duration of the year.[44] Hunting lodges were also common. These were simple structures made of "light poles covered with fir or spruce branches." Unlike the summer lodges, hunting lodges were used for only a day or two at a time and abandoned, as hunting parties moved continuously across their territory, some for up to eight months of the year.[45]

Given the weight that the Canadian courts now place on "occupancy" as the basis for title claims, Teit's description of Nlaka'pamux occupancy as dependent on movement and moveable lodges spread across the full territorial base – touching that base sensitively, that is, through careful cultivation, selective harvesting, and managed forest fires – challenges the settler-colonial model of occupancy as a permanent and continuous physical presence in a discreet spot. For years, scholars, lawyers, and others have seized on the Nlaka'pamux winter home as the primary marker of Nlaka'pamux occupancy – likely because, of all the types of traditional housing, it is the closest to western housing. In fact, as Teit notes, the primary "house" in the Nlaka'pamux world was the mobile summer lodge that extended across the full territory, and this form of "housing" defied all notions of fixity. Unlike the court decisions that have long redefined Indigenous occupancy in terms of small fixed locales, the recognition of which would not interfere with colonial "resource extraction," Teit's depiction of occupancy as a broad and fluid concept is a challenge to the modernity that these courts represent. Again, it is strikingly close to Heidegger's concept of "sparing," which "safeguards each thing in its essence ... [and that] pervades dwelling in its whole range."[46] Teit's Chapter 6 ("Travel and Transportation") gives additional context to the fluid forms of "housing" utilized by the Nlaka'pamux over the seasons.

Teit allotted several pages of his monograph to the winter home, or the "kekule-house," a "semi-subterranean hut" that bordered the main rivers and lakes throughout Nlaka'pamux territory.[47] His point was not that it was the most important house, but rather that it was the most structurally complex dwelling.[48] Because there were numerous kekule houses still in use when he arrived at Spences Bridge in 1884, he knew these "houses" well, both from the inside and out. He noted that by 1890, all but one had disappeared. A year later, it too was gone, its occupants opting for a log house.[49] In contrast to Susan Allison's description of kekule houses as "dirty, unwholesome dens," Teit described them as important communal dwellings that shielded their occupants from the frigid winter conditions. "They were extremely warm" inside, he wrote, with their "inmates ... scantily attired."[50] He noted that they could be easily constructed in a day or two by groups of twenty to thirty people (mostly women). With the first signs of spring, people headed off to their summer lodges in the back hills.

In addition to sketching a kekule house near Nicola Lake, Teit sought out people who had built such houses to explain how they were constructed. His detailed descriptions reveal his own knowledge of joinery:

> The braces and rafters were securely connected with willow withes. The rafters did not meet in the centre. The side-rafters rested on the ground and on the outside of the main rafters, at the place where these were supported by the uprights. The rafters were either notched for the reception of the braces, or they were simply tied on, while the butt-ends were embedded in the ground. Horizontal poles (d) from one to two feet apart were tied to the rafters and side-rafters. They formed the support for the roof-covering.[51]

His drawings and notes have inspired several kekule replicas. One of the first appeared at the Royal BC Museum's First Peoples' Gallery in Victoria, and another at the Secwépemc Museum in Kamloops. A new pit-house has been added to the Tuckkwiowhum Village at Boston Bar. In 2009, Nlaka'pamux architect Lynda Ursaki used Teit's drawings as inspiration for the Chief Tetlenitsa Memorial Outdoor Theatre at Spences Bridge.

Teit's chapter on "Manufactures" addresses the specialized technology – items such as arrow flakers, antler wedges, stone hammers, adzes, axes and knives, skin scrapers, and tweezers – that the Nlaka'pamux used to make baskets, headdresses, necklaces, mats, and buckskin bags, dresses, moccasins, and hats.[52] His chapter on "Subsistence" explains the roles that these items played in daily life. The segment on bag-net fishing, for example, illustrates not only Teit's eye for detail but his skill at translating complex activities into written text:

> The net is made of bark twine woven in large meshes. The size of the mouth is about equal to the space enclosed by a man's extended arms with the middle fingers touching each other. This bag is fastened on a hoop, generally of fir or cedar, which has a long, straight handle of the same material. Around the hoop are small horn rings, to which the bag is attached ... A string, to which a small piece of stick is fastened at one end, for a handle, is attached to the bag, and this is held in the hand of the fisherman while manipulating the net. When he is sure of a capture, he lets go the piece of stick, when the weight of the fish causes horn rings to come together, and thus close the mouth of the net. The fisherman then draws the net ashore, pulls the stick, thereby opening the bag, and throws the fish out. It is then put into a rather larger circular hole made by scraping away bowlders, which are piled around the sides, leaving a clear space of pebbles, sand or gravel in the centre.[53]

Unlike Susan Allison and Charles Hill-Tout, who characterized such practices as "primitive" remnants of a dying past, Teit presented them as sophisticated practices of a living present. He made strategic use of verb tense to make his point:

> When two or three men *hunt* together, they generally *start* simultaneously at a distance of a few hundred yards from each other, to walk over the prescribed ground, and *meet* occasionally at given points for consultation. If the party is large, the general method employed is that of driving. A leader *is chosen* to direct the hunt, generally one of the more experienced men, and one *who knows* well the ground to be hunted. In winter, one of the larger gulches may be chosen, as the deer frequent such places during the cold weather. Some of the best marksmen *are stationed* at those places for which the deer are expected to make. The rest of the party, who are the drivers,

> *then make* a circuit to the top of the gulch and come down in a line in the shape of a crescent, walking about a hundred yards apart.[54]

> Roots *are threaded* on strings of bark or grass and hung up to dry. Service-berries, soapberries, wild cherries, huckleberries, raspberries, bramble-berries, and rose-hips *are dried* by being spread thinly upon mats exposed to the hot rays of the sun ... Dry roots *are cooked* in the following manner: A circular hole *is dug* in the ground to a depth of two feet and a half, and large enough in diameter to contain the roots to be cooked. Into this hole *are put* four or five flat stones, – one in the centre, and the others around the sides. Above these *is piled* a heap of dry firewood, on which *is placed* a quantity of small stones.[55]

Chapter 7, on "Warfare," cast new light on the history of conflict in southern British Columbia in the late eighteenth and early nineteenth centuries. As if to challenge the popular stereotype of vicious Indian warriors, tomahawks in hand, launching regular attacks on their "tribal" neighbours from time immemorial to the present, Teit stressed that, except in a few isolated cases, there had been *no* inter-tribal warfare in Nlaka'pamux territory for close to a century. From "the arrival of the fur-traders [in 1811]" until 1858, he wrote, "regular tribal wars, in which one whole tribe was arrayed against another, were very rare."[56] With sources such as Pa-ah and Tsilla-gheskit (see Chapter 4 of this book), he knew that he was on solid ground in making such claims because both elders spoke from first-hand experience (Pa-ah was seventy-five years old in 1895, and Tsilla-gheskit, in his nineties).[57]

Teit stressed that, according to the stories passed down from the previous generation, the inter-tribal "warfare" in Nlaka'pamux territory prior to 1811 was not only short-lived but also specific to three groups within the Upper Division. "It seems likely," he wrote, "that most of the [large inter-tribal] wars [that] were carried on during the last and the early part of the present century [i.e., the eighteenth and early nineteenth century]" involved mainly the Upper Divisions (i.e., the Lytton, Spences Bridge, and Nicola Divisions). The other Nlaka'pamux groups – the "Upper Fraser" peoples (from Lytton to just below the town of Lillooet) and the "Lower Thompsons" (from Spuzzum to just below Siska on the Fraser River) – claimed that they had "never sent out any war parties" against their neighbours.[58] Their immediate neighbours to the west, the "Lillooet," claimed similarly that they "seldom went on war-expeditions."[59] A key variable that distinguished the aggressors from the non-aggressors was the introduction and adoption of the horse.[60] Teit wrote that the main aggressors, i.e., the Upper Nlaka'pamux peoples, were skilled horsemen in the late eighteenth century, whereas their less-aggressive relatives, the Upper Fraser River and Lower Fraser River Nlaka'pamux peoples, and their neighbours, the "Lower Lillooet" peoples, were not horse people.[61] This created problems, he wrote, as those with horses tended to look down on those without horses; in picking battles, they preferred horse people to non–horse people.[62] This was why so much of the inter-tribal fighting involved the Upper Nlaka'pamux and the neighbouring Secwépemc. Both groups were skilled horse people, so when they battled with one another, they did so on equal ground, so to speak. This helped explain not only the source of some of the inter-tribal fighting, but also its geographical distribution. As if to remind his readers that much of the evidence for inter-tribal "warfare" had come through storytelling, which thrived more on entertaining its audiences than preserving historical facts, Teit noted the prevalence of blood and gore: "Many are the stories told of exploits of these war parties some of which make conspicuous their endurance, courage and prowess; but these tales oftener recount the most revolting cruelty and the basest treachery."[63]

Teit reiterated here what old Pa-ah and Tsilla-gheskit had told him in 1893 about group conflict: that the large inter-tribal wars of the late eighteenth century had largely died out with the arrival of the traders in 1811, but this was not the end of the conflict.[64] The inter-tribal battles were quickly replaced by internal (intra-tribal) fighting – mainly "blood feuds between families" – which tended to be just as vicious as the inter-tribal fighting of the previous era (see Chapter 4). The "most trivial quarrels and insults often ended in bloodshed," Teit wrote. In fact, it was so bad that "no person's life was perfectly safe."[65] "No man went unarmed, and he was always ready to shoot, or guard against being shot." In addition to bows and arrows, many people carried guns – some with their barrels cut off to conceal them under their clothing. In his discussion of this more recent phase of internal conflict, Teit highlighted a point that Pa-ah and Tsilla-gheskit had made in their 1893 storytelling sessions: the internal conflict was so pervasive and unbearable by the mid-nineteenth century that the Nlaka'pamux chiefs had welcomed the "advantages of law and order" introduced by whites as a way to end the conflict.[66] It seemed more than coincidental that the stories of both the inter-tribal conflict of the late eighteenth century and intra-tribal conflict of the early nineteenth century included recently introduced guns, horses, and alcohol.

Teit's Chapter 10, on Nlaka'pamux social organization, challenged the settler-colonial claim that the plateau peoples lacked formal forms of governance.[67] According to his interviews with elders, the Nlaka'pamux peoples practised a sophisticated form of communal governance grounded in consensus. In contrast to the top-down, bureaucratic Western model introduced by the Indian Act, the Nlaka'pamux model enabled mobility without hierarchy. Teit found no evidence of entrenched "hereditary chiefs or ... recognized nobility," and no evidence of authoritarian decision-making bodies. Instead, leadership was dispersed through the community. Families, for example, appointed family heads to facilitate decisions at the family level. Only when faced with problems that extended beyond the family did such heads seek outside help. In such cases, they turned to a special chief (an orator) whose job was to help them settle multi-family or large-group conflicts. Except in cases of small, family-maintained fishing stations, eagle nests, and tobacco patches, land was communally held and managed by extended family units with lateral systems of decision making and power dispersed through a diversity of leaders.

Teit noted that the "chief" who came closest to the new Department of Indian Affairs–appointed chief was the "chief orator." The difference was that this chief was just one among many chiefs designated to help manage and regulate important activities such as hunting, fishing, food gathering, feuding, and healing. He wrote that hunters, for example, appointed a respected member of their group to serve as the chief of their hunting expeditions, and that female plant specialists and cultivators appointed a respected member of the group to serve as the chief of their berry-picking or root-digging expeditions. The group designated a special "war chief" to help them resolve conflicts that required retaliatory raids. Indian doctors handled all forms of illness. The chief orator had one of the most delicate leadership roles because, unlike the other chiefs, he was a skilled speechmaker. As such, he had the power to sway the group in whatever direction he wished, or, as Teit put it, to "influence" the group in ways he thought desirable. There were protocols to prevent undue influence, however. Not only were the chief orators expected to work toward "peace and harmony"; they were also not to "act ... in matters of public interest without obtaining the consent of all their people." More importantly, they were expected to demonstrate their allegiance to the larger group by hosting ceremonies at which they distributed gifts to their members. "The more liberally [one] gave of [one's] riches," Teit wrote, "the more highly [the chief orator] was thought of." Thus, it was in a chief orator's interest to host lavish feasts with no expectation of return. Teit's depiction of Nlaka'pamux leadership was the antithesis of that presented by Charles Hill-Tout, who wrote in 1899 that Nlaka'pamux "village communities" were "ruled over by ... hereditary chief[s]," of which the chief at "Tlkumtcin (Lytton)" was "lord paramount."[68]

Teit's chapters on the Nlaka'pamux life cycle and spiritual worldview underscored the importance of the large land base in maintaining the social, political, and economic well-being of the group. In contrast to Christianity's despiritualization of nature and its emphasis on an all-powerful transcendent deity residing high above the earth, he described the Nlaka'pamux belief system as grounded in a pervasive spiritual power emanating from the earth itself. It was a form of "nature-worship," Teit explained, that treated the physical world as alive with subjectivity (to use today's term) and spiritual power. It was a "post-human" perspective (again drawing from current terminology) in which animals, trees, birds, flowers, insects, rivers, and rocks behaved as fully fledged "people" with their own languages, thought patterns, and souls. As Teit noted, "animals and everything that grows, such as trees and herbs, and even rocks, fire, and water ... have souls."[69] The difference between the human and the non-human in this sphere was that the latter had direct access to the earth's powers while the former did not. In order to gain access to the earth's powers – a necessity for survival – human people were expected to seek out and align themselves with non-human persons, and they were expected to do this *early* in life through a long and rigorous training process. It was a requirement of the transition into adulthood. Because Teit had rejected Christianity – a heretical act in most settler-society spheres at the time – he was able to appreciate the Nlaka'pamux concept of the soul or *anima* of the earth and its beings in ways that many of his anthropological peers did not. This explains why his account of Nlaka'pamux puberty training was, and still is, one of the fullest on record for Indigenous North America. His findings completely contradicted Hill-Tout, who the previous year described Nlaka'pamux puberty-training "customs" as all but gone. The most he could report on girls' rituals was that "when a girl arrived at puberty she must withdraw herself from a time and live apart by herself."[70]

Teit stressed the importance of childhood training in the maintenance of a well-balanced and fully functioning culture. He wrote that young children, from toddlers to puberty, enjoyed full days of unlimited and unsupervised group play. At the first signs of puberty, however, they were plucked from this scene by their parents and other adult members and subjected to a rigorous educational program aimed at preparing them for adulthood. The parents' goal was to help their young daughters and sons connect with a "manitou" or "guardian spirit" (for lack of better terms in English). A boy began his training "generally between the ages of twelve and sixteen," when he "dreamed for the first time of an arrow, a canoe, or a woman." Under the supervision of parents and relatives, the boy then embarked on a period of ceremonial isolation and practice that required time in "the mountains ... fasting, sweating, and praying." In the warm weather, many boys stayed in the mountains for a month at a time, fasting and vomiting to purify their bodies. The goal was to have a dream or vision in which an "animal or bird" offered itself to the boy as a "protector or guardian spirit." As Teit explained, "Besides helping him and protecting him from danger, [such protectors] became his mediums, imparting to him power and magic, also knowledge concerning the world of the living and that of the dead."[71] Songs were a necessary part of the process as they were the vehicles by which the trainee called up his protectors.[72]

For girls, the training practices and rituals were slightly different. At the first signs of puberty in a young daughter, the parents took her "into the wilder parts of the mountains to allow her a better opportunity to perform the required ceremonies." There they built a small, conical hut as a base for performing prescribed activities, such as painting rocks and stones, digging trenches, and making miniature baskets and other items. At dusk, she left her hut and hiked up to "a peak or the top of a hill," where she made a fire around which she danced and sang until sunrise. Then it was back to her hut for another round of specialized activities. Teit wrote that twice a day the young female trainee was expected to wrap herself in a heavy blanket and run back and forth to a specified target. After four months of this training, she and her parents returned to their community.[73]

One of Teit's elderly Twaal Valley neighbours, Waght-ko, told Teit stories about the rocks she had painted at "Skai'tōk," a training place for girls that was a mile northeast of Spences Bridge.[74] Teit sought out the rock and photographed it. He also made hand-drawn sketches of the images, which he took to Waght-ko for explanations. He included this medley of information and images in his *Thompson Indians*. It was a rare body of specialized knowledge. As Teit noted, people rarely spoke of the dreams or vision experiences associated with their paintings. Because of this, there is little in the published anthropological record on rock painting. In contrast, Waght-ko opened up to Teit about her paintings, animating a collection of discreet crisscrosses, zigzags, and squiggles through her stories of puberty training. She explained that two lines crossing at right angles stood for trail crossings, and four short lines running downward from a horizontal line stood for four special sticks that girls placed at trails as offerings. She described other markings as identifying the locations of food supplies, the girl's isolation lodge, parts of an unfinished basket, and so on.[75] Teit's interviews with elders about the rock art panels along the Stein River contradicted Hill-Tout's claim that the Nlaka'pamux peoples "had no knowledge of the significance of the rock paintings" along this river.[76]

At the end of their training period, boys and girls returned to their communities, where they were treated as young adults. For girls, this meant helping their mothers and others with the construction and maintenance of the summer and winter lodges, gathering food, tending the hearth, cooking and storing winter provisions, making clothing, and caring for the younger children. For boys, it meant joining their fathers and uncles on hunting and fishing expeditions. According to Teit, these were not fixed gender roles, however, as men often participated in the women's work spheres and vice versa. Both sexes were expected to marry soon after their puberty training. Although by the late nineteenth century the common form of marriage was a union between one man and one woman, earlier marriages often involved one man with "two to four wives, sometimes all sisters."[77]

Teit included a detailed account of death and burial rituals in his chapter on the Nlaka'pamux life cycle. He knew this subject well. As he explained to Boas, "Although having repeatedly seen Indians dying, or shortly before death, I have never yet happened to see one who seemed to be in distress, or had much fear of death; and in life they talk to one another of death with the utmost composure, and do not seem to dread it in the least, neither do they try to avoid talking of it."[78] With Antko's death on March 2, 1899, he experienced the Nlaka'pamux death rituals and protocols as an insider. In a letter to his parents, he explained that "fifty or sixty people" had camped at his house for the three-day wake and funeral.[79] There was no mention of the long slate of rituals expected of Nlaka'pamux widowers: the laying of the body on a platform outside the house, the hiring of women to prepare a special feast of the deceased's food supplies, and the ritual vomiting and wailing of the women. In a letter eight months after Antko's death, he wrote of hosting a large feast, the centre of which was a "paying" ceremony that had required him to stockpile "money, blankets, horses, etc," to give away at this ceremony.[80] In the pages of his soon-to-appear *Thompson Indians,* his parents would learn more about the paying-off ceremony – for example, the thanking of the messengers, the grave-diggers, the cooks, and all others who had helped with the funeral.

Boas wrote the concluding chapter to Teit's *Thompson Indians.* Instead of commenting on its substance, however, he expounded on his new theory of cultural diffusion. His main point was that Teit's findings pointed to a culture of borrowers rather than innovators. The "Thompsons," as he called them, were bearers of a "very simple" social organization, he wrote, with a "remarkably limited" slate of religious ideas and rites that were "influenced ... to a great extent by their eastern neighbors, [and] to a less[er] extent by the tribes of the coast."[81] He had detected only two instances of innovation. The first was the "beautiful" cedar-bark basketry tradition of the Upper Thompson peoples; and the second was the weaving tradition, using mountain goat wool, of the Lower Thompsons. Boas explained the former as a case of borrowing from the more creative Athapaskan basket makers when the latter group migrated through the south central Interior region on their way to California. He was less certain about the origin of the wool-weaving tradition of the Lower Thompsons, other than that it was the "same in principle as that applied by the Upper Thompsons in making rabbit-skin blankets and mattings."[82]

The irony of Boas's analysis was his failure to see his own role in it. He had asked Teit in 1894 to make a collection of traditional items, and he had highlighted baskets and textiles as priorities. The women, on discovering that their baskets and buckskin creations could generate a good income, had responded by making bulk batches of baskets and buckskin clothing and delivering them to Teit. As the more complex and ornate baskets and textiles yielded higher prices than the plainer ones, many chose to make fancier ones. By 1900, many were aware of the basket-collection craze on the Coast and what their female counterparts in that region were earning from their baskets. As UBC historian Paige Raibmon has shown in her study of the 1890s Puget Sound hop fields, basket sales were high in and around the hop-picking camps.[83] Some of the Nlaka'pamux women in the Fraser Canyon worked in the Fraser Valley hop camps.

When Boas examined the Nlaka'pamux women's baskets (many of which came from the Fraser Canyon communities) at the receiving end in New York City, he could not help but notice their increasingly complex designs.[84] Ignoring what would have been obvious to Teit, he turned these differences into a research problem. Indeed, Boas's three-page conclusion spoke volumes about the differences between his scientistic orientation and Teit's communitarian orientation. It also cast new light on Boas's critique of racial formalism and evolutionism, as it showed him applying the very modernist, social evolutionary framework for which he criticized "amateurs" such as Hill-Tout. He made no mention of Teit's efforts to contest the ethnocentric values that dominated the ethnographic portraits of Indians at the time.

More Monographs

With reports on the upper and lower "Thompsons" in hand, Boas asked Teit to compile parallel reports on the neighbouring "Lillooet" and "Shuswap" peoples.[85] He needed such reports on contiguous plateau groups to complete his three-stage research objective.[86] The Nlaka'pamux reports gave him stage one: a detailed study of "the customs and traits of a single tribe." Parallel reports on the adjacent "Lillooet" and "Shuswap" peoples would give him the data he needed to advance to stage two – an exploration of the customs and traits of neighbouring groups, noting the distribution of shared cultural "elements" with the first group. With all three groups covered, Boas could advance to stage three – the search for general laws of cultural development in the plateau region of northwest North America. In his proposal to Morris Jesup in 1896, Boas had presented this as the central goal of his Jesup North Pacific Expedition. As hard as he tried, however, he was unable to fulfill this objective in his own work on the coast. Despite years of research on the Kwakwa̱ka̱'wakw, he never wrote a full ethnography for the group.

Teit moved quickly on his "Lillooet" and "Shuswap" assignments. Having seen how Boas edited his Nlaka'pamux report, he now had a clearer idea of what his employer wanted in these reports – and what he didn't want. For example, Teit had peppered his report with Nlaka'pamux names and terms, only to discover that Boas removed all of them at the publication stage. And Teit had titled his report "N-kla-Kap-mugh," only to discover that Boas changed it to "Thompson," the name that Simon Fraser had given to the river in honour of his colleague David Thompson, an explorer for the Northwest Company. As Nlaka'pamux territory included several rivers and lakes beyond the Thompson River, the term was inaccurate. With its colonial roots, "Thompson" was inappropriate for other reasons as well.

This was not the first time that Teit had seen such changes at the publication stage. In December 1894, Boas had asked Teit to take a trip to the Nicola Valley to investigate the status of an extinct Athapaskan ("Tinneh") language that was once spoken there. In April, Teit saddled up his horse and rode over to Nicola, where he tracked down three elders said to have some knowledge of a few old Tinneh words. Over the course of several letters, Teit described in detail the complex back-and-forth exchanges he had had with these elders in his efforts to initiate a discussion of Tinneh vocabulary. He started with his interactions with an old man named Aāp'kîn:

> [Aāp'kîn] was very uncommunicative and I had to do a considerable amount of talking to get the desired information from him. He would not say anything at all until he had gathered all his friends together so that they should hear what he said. He then indulged in a great deal of speech making (necessarily causing me to do the same) before he gave me any words or other information.[87]

He found another man, TEkwo'xux̲kîn, even more resistant. "Although quite friendly, I could make nothing out of him":

> I tried different kinds of tactics getting him to make a bow and arrow for me and paying him double what it was worth but to no purpose. His wife also advised him to tell what he knew but ... he would not give me any words of the language which he says he knew better than Tcuieska, Timskolaxan or any other living Indian.[88]

As it turned out, all that TEkwo'xux̲kîn would discuss with Teit was the impact of a smallpox epidemic on his family history.[89] In summarizing Teit's notes for his article for the *Report of the British Association for the Advancement of Science,* Boas ignored all of this contextual detail and instead highlighted the abstract Tinneh word lists that Teit had elicited, along with a generalized account of Tinneh history. Boas mentioned only one of Teit's four Nicola Valley consultants by name, and only because of his unusual tattoos. He reduced the others to a cohort of "four old men."[90] It was a pattern that Teit had seen in his first work with Boas. In 1897 at Spences Bridge, for example, Boas had photographed and recorded (on wax cylinders) a group of Nlaka'pamux men and women, and Teit had carefully documented their names. On publishing the photographs and songs, however, Boas had removed all of the names.[91] What was important about these ethnographic exercises was the generalizable data they yielded, not the people behind them.

Teit completed the "Lillooet" and "Shuswap" reports quickly, allowing Boas to include them in his Jesup monograph series (*The Lillooet* in 1906 and *The Shuswap* in 1909). In both monographs, Teit adhered to Boas's instructions to "use as few Indian words as possible in writing out the chapters."[92] The two monographs followed the template of *The Thompson Indians* with a couple of exceptions. Instead of including his own preface, conclusion, and special-topics chapter as he did with *The Thompson Indians,* Boas issued *The Lillooet* as a stand-alone text under Teit's name but with an appendix in his own name; and he published *The Shuswap* as a standalone text by Teit with a preface in Teit's name.[93] Apart from establishing the format for these works and then editing the final reports, Boas had very little to do with the ethnographic process or drafting. This was Teit's work, full stop.

Teit's 1909 "Preface" gave readers their first glimpse of the elusive author behind this unique series of monographs on the plateau peoples. In addition to introducing himself and his primary consultants, Teit used the preface to introduce readers to the geographical scope of his fieldwork:

> At the request of Dr. Franz Boas, I made a journey with pack-train in 1900, and visited the western and northern bands of Fraser River, spending almost all the summer and fall among them. I was previously acquainted with this region, having made several hunting and exploring trips through it in 1887, 1888, and 1892, my journeys extending far into the Carrier country. I also accompanied Dr. Boas on his visit to all the western Shuswap bands, and across Chilcotin country to Bella Coola in 1897. During the season of 1900, I collected the bulk of my information from several old men in the vicinity of Canoe Creek and Dog Creek. In the summer of 1903, I made an extended trip by pack-train across Canim Lake, and thence to North Thompson River.[94]

He noted that his primary consultant on the 1900 trip was Sixwi'lexken and his primary consultant on the 1903 trip was George Sisiu'lax. He described Sixwi'lexken as "a very intelligent" and well-travelled man who "was particularly well posted on the history, traditions and customs of the people," and who had taken "great interest in relating everything he knew." In his concluding chapter, "Myths," Teit acknowledged Sixwi'lexken as the narrator of fifty-two stories represented in the volume.[95] Acknowledging one's research collaborators is now standard anthropological practice. In 1909, however, it was a rare gesture.

Teit used both monographs to reiterate the central message of *The Thompson Indians:* that British Columbia's plateau peoples were fully functioning members of an ongoing *living* culture that was under assault by settler colonialism. As in *The Thompson Indians,* he highlighted the devastating impact of the smallpox epidemic on both groups. "During the great smallpox epidemic," he wrote, "[the Lillooet] suffered more than any other tribe." Their population, which in 1858 was nearly 4,000, dropped to 1,600 by 1900.[96] He described a similar situation for the Secwépemc.

Based on interviews with "an intelligent old Indian" who had travelled extensively throughout Secwépemc territory in 1850, enumerating "almost all the bands of the tribe,"[97] Teit concluded that a series of introduced diseases had decimated "whole villages" along the Chilcotin and Fraser Rivers. Through "the introduction of the white man's laws, which recognized no tribal boundaries, and precluded the possibility of war and retaliation," the vacant lands had been quickly snapped up – without resistance – by neighbouring Tsilhqot'in peoples and white settlers.[98] The "settlement of the country by the whites, and the consequent change in the manner of the living of the Indians, with the attendant introduction of new laws, of whiskey, of venereal and other diseases," further "hastened their decrease," he wrote. More losses followed, such as outbreaks of "measles, scarlatina, whooping-cough, and influenza," along with tuberculosis and high child mortality. Teit estimated that the population in Secwépemc territory in 1909 was "less than one-third" of what it had been fifty years earlier.[99]

As in his *Thompson Indians,* Teit criticized the Department of Indian Affairs for its role in the population loss. He wrote that many reserves in Lillooet territory were very small and "hardly sufficient in many places to grow enough potatoes and other vegetables for their own use."[100] Such deterritorialization had forced people out of their home communities to the mouth of the Fraser River to work in salmon fishery or to the Cariboo to work as packers for whites. Others worked on "white man's ranches" as labourers and domestics.[101] With mass deaths and migration outward, the settler communities claimed the right to determine territorial boundaries. "Some whites," Teit wrote, "believe the Shuswap never had any permanent settlements west of the Fraser River, while others think that they at one time occupied nearly all the Chilcotin country extending in a continuous line to the Bella Coola, but that they have gradually been driven out of that country." This was "altogether wrong," Teit wrote. He then noted the impact of the "white man's laws, which recognized no tribal boundaries," and of mass deaths due to smallpox, which stripped the land of its inhabitants.[102]

Teit used both monographs to challenge the stereotype of the savage Indian warrior perpetually prone to war. Through his interviews with elders, he learned that the "Shuswap" and "Lillooet" peoples had not been the vicious fighters that the settler population had made them out to be. Of the many divisions within these two groups, only three (the Fraser River, Kamloops, and Bonaparte "Shuswap" Divisions) had perpetrated wars. He noted that the "Lillooet" peoples, for example, had tried to resolve inter-tribal conflict through intermarriage and gift-giving rather than physical violence.[103] The HBC was clearly a factor in the fighting, as those communities with the closest contact with the HBC (i.e., the Fraser River, Kamloops, and Bonaparte Divisions) tended to be more aggressive than the communities more distant from the post. The latter, Teit wrote, "seldom engaged in war, and acted only on the defensive."[104] As mentioned earlier, it was significant that the war stories that survived into the late nineteenth century included frequent mention of alcohol, horses, axes, war clubs, and guns obtained from the fur trading post.[105] This suggested that the presence of a trading post in the middle of Secwépemc territory was a key factor in these conflicts. Unlike the Nlaka'pamux inter-tribal battles, which had died out early in the nineteenth century, Teit noted that the "Shuswap" battles persisted into the mid-century.[106]

Teit's quest for historical and ethnographic specificity was new for its time, and it was diametrically opposed to Boas's quest for common-denominator culture in a nebulous precontact time period. To show the impact of an HBC post in the centre of Secwépemc territory, Teit wrote that "half" of the "Shuswap" had adopted log cabins "before the Thompson thought of erecting one,"[107] and that they had adopted western-style clothing – bold-coloured woolen leggings, shirts, coats, mittens, and socks – well before the Nlaka'pamux.[108] He also noted that, unlike the Nlaka'pamux, who maintained their old annual subsistence cycle well into the nineteenth century, the "Shuswap" had spent three-quarters of the year trapping furs in "distant grounds" for trade at the post.[109] They had traded "furs of all kinds, dressed skins, moccasins, dried roots and berries, dried meat, fat, dried salmon, dogs and horses," for "woolen blankets, cloth, glass beads, steel traps, flintlock muskets, powder, ball, shot, axes, tomahawks, steels and flints, knives, tobacco, iron, copper kettles, brass, finger-rings, bracelets, etc."[110] He noted that the Secwépemc were quicker to convert to Christianity than their neighbours. In addition to erecting "some of the largest and finest churches of all the tribes of the interior," many believed "in heaven, hell, purgatory, and a judgment day, as taught by the priests."[111] Sixwi'lexken ("Big Billy"), Teit's elderly consultant at Churn Creek, corroborated this by stressing in his conversations with Teit that "the Coyote and Old Man stories" of his youth had largely been replaced by "Bible and White man stories." The Coyote stories had survived, he said, because of their entertainment value – people enjoyed "the tricks narrated in them."[112]

A contract in 1912 to write a chapter on the plateau peoples for the multivolume series *Canada and Its Provinces: A History of the Canadian People and Their Institutions* offered Teit his first opportunity to publish a piece independently of Boas, and in a Canadian rather than an American source. Up to this point, all but one of his publications had been edited by Boas and published under the auspices of the American Museum of Natural History or the American Folk-Lore Society. Robert Glasgow, head of an American publishing company, had launched *Canada and Its Provinces* as a way to create the Canadian equivalent of the hugely popular US-based *Encyclopedia Americana*. By the time of its release in 1914, *Canada and Its Provinces* had expanded to a twenty-three-volume set, with 153 chapters by 90 authors. Glasgow's goal with this series was to offer Canadians a general history of their country through a series of special-interest chapters on politics, economics, immigration, natural resources – and "Indians." The editors paired Teit's chapter, "Indian Tribes of the Interior," with Edward Sapir's "Indian Tribes of the Coast" and placed both in the final volume, *The Pacific Province*.[113]

Instead of rooting his chapter in the precontact era, as Boas had encouraged him to do, Teit focused on the postcontact period and its imprint on the earlier period, allowing him to challenge popular stereotypes, such as the notion of lazy Indians endowed with too much land. He wrote of the plateau peoples at the centre of his chapter as of "high general intelligence" with "excellent" speaking skills. He noted subtle differences from group to group: the "Shuswap" were "reticent and self-contained"; "the Ntlakyapmuk," "more sociable, obliging, outspoken, and easy-going."[114] He noted the absence of social hierarchy, such as "privileged classes," "hereditary nobility," "clan systems," and "secret societies," and a complete absence of "private property." "The earth and all that grew upon it," he wrote, "and all the game and fish of the country, were the common property of the tribe." On gender roles, he wrote that men managed the political affairs of the household and community, and women managed the domestic affairs of the home. According to the rules of inheritance, however, when a woman died, her daughters inherited her household belongings. There were few "restrictions on marriage." The plateau peoples, he wrote, practised a high form of egalitarianism sustained by the communal bonds between humans and nature. The essence of plateau religious life, he wrote, was a "sort of animism, or nature-worship based largely on the belief that a certain mysterious power pervaded all nature, its manifestations varying in different objects as to kind and degree."[115] It was the goal of every individual, he wrote, "to obtain as much as possible of this power from those animals and objects in nature that appeared to possess it in the greatest degree or that manifested the type of power considered the most valuable." The sun, the dawning of the day, certain mountain peaks, thunder, rocks, and trees were major objects "of veneration," he wrote, as was the "spirit of the sweat-bath."[116]

All signs of cultural decline or weakness among the plateau peoples should, Teit argued, be set against the backdrop of settler colonialism:

> The sudden changes in their methods of living, forced upon them by new conditions, resulted in the breaking down of almost all their laws and customs and in the loss of authority by their elders and chiefs. The removal of the old restraints undermined their power of resistance and left them practically without protection against the evils of the white man's civilization. They had no guidance or protection from the white men who had forced the new conditions upon them, and the change of life was too abrupt and far-reaching for them to adapt themselves to it with readiness.[117]

He highlighted smallpox and "other epidemics, venereal diseases and intoxicants introduced by the whites" as major causes of depopulation. "All the interior tribes have decreased in number since the advent of whites, and at the present time are only about one-third as numerous as in former times." He provided concrete numbers to support his point:

> Sixty or seventy years ago the Indian population of the interior was probably at least 38,000, of which about 20,000 were Salish, 12,000 Athapaskan, and 6000 were other stocks. The present population is estimated at 11,500, divided about as follows: Salish, 6000 or less; Athapaskans, between 3000 and 3500; Kutenai, between 500 and 600; Kitksan, between 1100 and 1200; Tlingit and others, about 200.[118]

Tetlanetza Speaks Back

In the spring of 1916, Teit joined his Nlaka'pamux friend Chief John Tetlanetza on a new ethnographic project. The setting was the Victoria Memorial Museum in Ottawa. The two men were there with a delegation of chiefs to lobby Prime Minister Robert Borden and Deputy Superintendent General of Indian Affairs Duncan Campbell Scott on their land-title issue. It was their second trip to the nation's capital, and things were not going well (see Chapters 7 and 8). At the invitation of Edward Sapir, Tetlanetza and Teit spent their free days at the city's Victoria Museum, discussing subjects that were not allowed in their sessions with officials from the Department of Indian Affairs (DIA) and other federal government departments. With Teit translating by his side, Tetlanetza described in detail his community's traditional governmental structure around land tenure.[119] What is more significant is that he did this without making a single reference to the entrenched DIA categories that had enveloped his community – i.e., terms such as "Indian Act," numbered "reserves," "band chiefs," "Indian agents," "game and fish wardens and regulations," and "elected chiefs and council."

Tetlanetza began by explaining that his account pertained only to the Spences Bridge Division of Nlaka'pamux territory and not to the Lytton Division or the Fraser Canyon Division. Teit interjected to explain that when he arrived at Spences Bridge in 1884, the population of the Spences Bridge Division was 300. Three years later, it had fallen to 240; in 1916, it had dropped to 100. Based on interviews with the oldest members of the community, Teit estimated the base population prior to the downturn had been approximately 1,000. In other words, this was a 90 percent attrition rate over three generations.

Tetlanetza explained that much of the decision making in his division was handled by a "head chief" and a council of "family heads." The head chief was charged with facilitating decision making for the full division, but such a chief could not make unilateral decisions on his own. His role was to work with the council of family heads to bring that council to consensus. Each family within a division appointed a head to represent it in family affairs. Tetlanetza explained that in 1916, Whistemnitsa was the head chief of the Spences Bridge Division.[120] He noted that the general rule was that when such a chief died, he would be replaced by his son. This was a flexible arrangement, however, because if a group felt that the chief's son was unsuitable for the job, it was free to appoint a close relative – the chief's nephew or younger brother – in his place. If no close relatives were available or suitable, the group was free to choose someone "without regard to inheritance." Whistemnitsa had been such a choice, Tetlanetza explained, as he was only "indirectly descended" from his predecessor, Chief Shoona-mitza, the head chief of the division at the time of the arrival of the whites.[121]

To illustrate how this system operated on the ground, Tetlanetza described the constitution of each of the thirteen families in his Spences Bridge Division. He explained that Whistemnitsa was the head of Family #4, and that he served a double leadership role as he was also the head chief of the division. His family consisted of his mother, his wife (who was originally from the Lytton Band), and an adopted daughter, all of whom lived under a single roof "across the river." Family #8 was a larger family headed by Ghleeghimkin (who was "half Shuswap"). This family included his wife (a member of both the Spences Bridge and Lytton Divisions), a married daughter and her husband (from the Fraser Canyon Division) and child, plus another daughter (a "half negro") from Ghleeghimkin's previous marriage and her three children. (This daughter's mother was originally from the Lytton Division.)[122] Family #5 was headed by Whal-eenik whose husband had died the previous winter.

Tetlanetza described a rich range of community protocols and decision-making practices associated with the annual food-production cycle. "The fruit, berrying, and root-digging [grounds]," he explained, "belonged to [the] whole band as a unit" and thus "were under the charge of the head chief, or chief of the band." Everyone "understood that it was against the law to interfere with the service berry patches" until a designated man or woman declared that the berries were ready for picking. At that point, all the girls and women arrived at the designated picking grounds at the same time and held a ceremony to offer thanks "to the crop of berries" and to ask for abundance the next year. They did this for huckleberries, tobacco, and certain roots that "were all products of the earth and related to a kind of earth deity." The community approached its fishing sites, hunting grounds, soapstone outcroppings, and paint deposits in a similar way.

There were a few exceptions of note. Because the maintenance of deer fences, salt licks, eagle nests, family fishing stations, and certain tobacco patches involved the work of individual families, such families often gained the exclusive right to such areas. Deer fences were a good example because they required considerable labour to build and many were "back in the hills" or in the mountains. All domestic animals, such as horses and dogs, were uniquely regarded as "private, moveable property."

There was flexibility within this system. Special "rights" to fishing sites, eagle nests, and deer fences, for example, were often subject to change. For example, if a family abandoned its fishing station due to changes in the river, another family could move in and claim it as theirs. In cases where families died out, the last direct heirs could select a relative to inherit the family fishing station, deer fence, salt lick, or eagle nest. Some of these rules applied to the common land as well. Adding to Tetlanetza's explanations, Teit noted that if "a woman travelled in the mountain and found some valuable patch of roots, for that season only, she had the first right owing to her discovery." She would allow others to use her patch but only if they recognized her more prominent role in the patch. A head of a family, according to Tetlanetza, did not have the power to "alienate the property of the family under him."

To illustrate how this system functioned at the family level, Tetlanetza listed the cultural protocols associated with harvesting various essential foods. What emerged from his account was a cultural blueprint that ensured equitable access for each family to everything it needed. Family #2, for example, had a fishing station and an eagle nest near its home base and a deer fence twelve miles away, on the opposite side of the river. Family #3 had the same rights and privileges as Family #2 because the two families were closely related.

Tetlanetza's account of his community's land-tenure system sat dormant in the bowels of the Victoria Memorial Museum (later renamed the National Museum of Man, the Canadian Museum of Civilization, and, most recently, the Canadian Museum of History) for a full century while the federal and provincial governments chipped away at "land claims." Until the recent Supreme Court of Canada Tsilhqot'in decision in 2014, the judiciary bypassed the importance of the multiple temporary winter village sites scattered across the territory to highlight what it viewed as the more permanent pit-houses located along lakesides and riverbanks, even though the former were just as integral to an assertion of Aboriginal title as the latter. As in the case of the Old World land clearances, dispossession in south central British Columbia was a prerequisite to establishing a capitalist economy and a modern state. To assert state sovereignty, there was a need to mis-recognize the fluid cultural understandings of home and household shared by human and non-human alike, and made manifest in the physical and spiritual realms. The Nlaka'pamux and their colleagues across the province had to be corralled and confined to small land allotments and kept there. Teit's monographs, and his efforts to document concepts of land tenure explained by named, knowledgeable chiefs such as John Tetlanetza, challenged this process by highlighting the importance of what Martin Heidegger later termed "dwelling in its whole range."[123] Herein lies the value of Teit's ethnographies. Unlike Boas, who saw his Jesup research project as generating data on the "mind of the primitive" for academic analysis, Teit saw it as documenting for posterity the anthropology of "dwelling" – as lived and understood by its members.

7
Capital of Resistance

There was a big meeting here [Spences Bridge] which broke up yesterday. Members of the Carrier, Chilcotin, Shuswap, Kootenay, Okanagan, Ntlakyapamuk, Lillooet & Stalo tribes were there to the number of about 450. Also several chiefs from the south coast, and one man each from the Spokane and Coeur d'Alene.

– Letter from James Teit to Edward Sapir, August 2, 1912[1]

In the fall of 2009, Chief David Walkem of the Cooks Ferry Band announced his plans to build an outdoor theatre at the junction of the Nicola and Thompson Rivers. He had hired his niece, Lynda Ursaki, a professional architect, to design it and was pleased that she intended to incorporate elements of the Nlaka'pamux kekule house (the winter home) into her design. Walkem wanted the theatre named in honour of John Tetlanetza, the Nlaka'pamux chief who represented the Cooks Ferry Band in the land-title battles of the early twentieth century. He chose a May 2010 opening date in order to commemorate the centenary of a Memorial that Tetlanetza and a delegation of Interior chiefs had presented to Prime Minister Wilfrid Laurier in Kamloops. Because Teit had played a role in the Memorial, Chief Walkem invited me to speak at the opening ceremony.

I sensed the excitement around the project in my phone calls and emails with two old friends, Lynne Jorgesen and Bernadette Manuel. Members of the Upper Nicola Band, both had ancestral ties to the Interior chiefs involved in the early political campaign. Bernadette served on the organizing committee of the opening ceremony. We met up in Merritt on the morning of the event and spent the hour-long drive to Spences Bridge reminiscing about our long connections: my meeting Lynne in Merritt in the early 1980s, when I was interviewing her great-grandmother, Nellie Guitterrez, about songs, and Lynne was editing the Merritt-based *Nicola Indian* newspaper. I reminded her of her efforts back then to educate her people about the political resistance that was now being commemorated at the theatre's opening ceremony. Lynne and Bernadette had joined forces in the 1990s, when Lynne took a research position with the Upper Nicola Band's cultural heritage division. Two decades of battling BC Hydro, Kinder Morgan, and various other intruders on their territory had turned them into cultural warriors.

It was gridlock in the parking lot as hundreds of people filed into the theatre. I wondered about the local townspeople around the corner and what they knew of their community's role in the political protest that was being commemorated that afternoon. So much of the town's history had faded. The fruit stand at Hilltop Garden Farm, the old Morens homestead where Teit lived for years, was the last remaining of the dozen or so fruit and vegetable stands that once lined the highway above the town. Several shuttered gas stations and motels were all that survived of the Trans-Canada's golden years. Their demise had come with the four-lane Coquihalla Highway that opened in 1986, offering a more direct route from the Coast to the Interior. The historic Spences Bridge Inn on the south side of the Thompson – the inn where Boas had stayed on his first night in the village in September 1894 – still offered rooms, but its owner struggled to keep it afloat. Jessie Smith's old fruit-packing house was one of the town's few successes. A resident farmer had converted it into a popular café and music venue. The local public school had been similarly retooled. After the decision to bus the community's handful of children to Ashcroft, the town's seniors turned the building into an activity centre for their quilting bees, basket-making workshops, and bridge tournaments. The CPR and CNR cars were still running along the old tracks, but they carried mainly freight – mostly coal – instead of passengers. The old single-lane bridge that connected the two sides of the town was slated for demolition, which infuriated most of the townspeople, who used it every day. The famous steelhead run that once attracted fly-fishers from around the world was, like the Spences Bridge Inn, almost gone. River-rafting was now the main draw, offering tourists thrilling rides down the Thompson River to Lytton from spring until fall.

The scene inside the theatre mirrored the mayhem in the parking lot. Master of ceremonies Raymond Phillips of Lytton calmed things down by announcing the start of the ribbon-cutting ceremony to rededicate the four-page 1910 Memorial. In the speeches that followed, Chief Walkem and others highlighted the document's continuing significance. In my talk, I pointed out the importance of the town of Spences Bridge as the centre of the political resistance and the roles that James Teit and John Tetlanetza played. Given the demands on Teit in the summer of 1910 (described in Chapter 5), it is difficult to imagine how he found time to work on the chiefs' political campaign. Until recently, few knew much about this side of his life. As one scholar concluded in 1980, "What Teit really knew about the Indians, their inner life and aspirations and how their politics connected to their tribal past will never be published ... It was never written down. It was not asked for."[2] The details of Teit's political activism have indeed faded, but the thread of the story can still be found in the petitions, memorial statements, translated speeches, and letters in which he had a hand.[3]

Socialism Now!

The seeds of Teit's political activism were sown during his youth in Shetland. A return to his island home in 1902, after an eighteen-year absence, rejuvenated those seeds. He arrived in Lerwick on January 26 and the next day learned that a group of his former schoolmates had joined the Social Democratic Federation (SDF), Britain's first Marxist political party, and recruited over one hundred members to their socialist cause. They were within a few months of launching the Lerwick Literary and Debating Society to attract more members.[4] With one of their members now on the school board and another (Teit's old school friend Alexander Ratter, who appears in the photograph on p. 77) close to winning a seat on the town council, they were inching their way into the town's governance bodies. The local booksellers carried the SDF newspaper, *Justice,* and Robert Blatchford's socialist magazine, the *Clarion.* Blatchford was a British writer and a prominent socialist campaigner, who, in addition to editing the *Clarion,* published a series of popular books on socialism. According to Shetland historian Brian Smith, Blatchford's *Merrie England* had "circulated all over Shetland" in the 1890s.[5] The hub of socialist activity was Lerwick:

> Socialism began to crawl out of nooks and crannies here and there in the town. David Sutherland's shop, opposite what is now Hepworth's, became a hotbed of sedition. Sutherland was a native of Unst, who set up a shop in Lerwick as a watchmaker (he gave his name, incidentally, to the House of David, 92 St Olaf St.); his shop became a centre for a select group of young Lerwegians whom Sutherland badgered for hours with his revolutionary ideas. In exactly the same way William Strong Eunson's shops, in Market Street and at the South end, became nests of rebellion. A blind Lerwick

> poet called James Haldane Burgess began to drop in at the south end shop [where] ... "they ... talked of how to right the world."[6]

Burgess had been stricken blind as a graduate student in Edinburgh in the mid-1890s but it had barely slowed him down. He returned to Lerwick where he worked as a tutor and a writer. He also became one of the town's most active socialists, opening his family home (Nort Kirk Kloss) on Queen's Lane to a political discussion group known as the Nort Kirk Kloss forum.[7] As one attendee wrote of the forum, "in a book-lined room, without a fire and with windows and doors wide open ... [Burgess] would sit, in his great-coat, his violin on the table, face aglow with the message of social deliverance, the pleasant voice using his beloved dialect, to Shetlander and stranger alike."[8]

Teit visited Burgess throughout his 1902 stay to rekindle his friendship and catch up on local politics. If Teit sought out Burgess on his first day back at home on January 27, he would have found his old friend preoccupied with preparations for Up Helly Aa – an annual torchlight procession of guizers (men in masks and costumes) that culminated with the burning of a galley ship. Due to start the next day, Up Helly Aa was one of the highlights of Burgess's year, especially as it was now a vehicle to promote socialism.

Teit knew the earlier versions of Up Helly Aa well, as its squads of masked working-class revellers had rolled burning tar barrels past his family home on Commercial Street annually at Christmastime. During the five years his family lived in Aberdeen, Lerwick's town council banned the tar-barrelling part of the ritual and moved the date to late January. When the family returned to Lerwick in 1878, Up Helly Aa was in the hands of a new generation of "clever young men" who saw it as a vehicle to right the wrongs of the world. In 1882, when Teit was seventeen and living in Lerwick, they elected his friend Alexander Ratter as Up Helly Aa's first "Worthy Chief Guizer" (or the "king of misrule"). In 1889, they adopted a proposal by Burgess to introduce a Norse longship (soon termed a "galley") to the procession.[9] A year later they added a new Up Helly Aa song by Burgess, featuring lyrics that extolled Norse freedom fighters as models for contemporary Shetlanders. In 1899, the Up Helly Aa committee added a satirical placard (a "Bill") "ridicul[ing] local councilors, public figures and institutions."[10] As historian Callum Brown writes, "It was a festival that retained its rights to process the streets at night by torchlight, led by its inverted 'king of misrule' (who in the Edwardian period was appropriately enough often a Marxist), and to satirise the elites and the events of the day."[11]

Teit's trip to the northern island of Yell to interview Laurence Williamson about his family history took him into yet another sphere of Shetland's politics. This "great genealogist of the North Isles" (as Teit called Williamson)[12] could not recount his island's history without cloaking it in his contempt for the clearances that had dispossessed his family of their old Fetlar homestead:

> My whole life in one of its leading aspects has been the beholding of the drama and history of our 9 or 10 Fetlar families and individuals beside who flit to Yell (to say nothing of those who flit elsewhere) ... And it has been a very sorrowful history and spectacle – In short it has been chiefly a prolonged funeral with each family – those left of them in Yell are now in wreck and hastening to extinction.[13]

Teit was clearly inspired by his political "education" in Shetland, especially the initiatives of his socialist colleagues, because within a week of returning to BC, he notified Burgess to say that he was reading socialist literature and excited by its messages: "Now I understand better what socialism is and what good news it has for people."[14] He thanked his friend for giving him a copy of Robert Blatchford's *Britain for the British,* reporting that he had finished it and passed it on to his friends. Blatchford's *Merrie England,* he wrote, made such "sense to all who wish[ed] to hear about [socialism]."[15] He also expressed delight at seeing letters by James Robertson and Frank Pottinger in his copies of the *Shetland News.* He noted that he was tracking down socialist writings by American and German authors in order to learn more, and he reported that the socialist cause in North America was progressing well:

> It is wonderful the progress socialism has made in America within the last 12 months or so. At the last presidential election in the U.S. the socialists polled almost half a million votes, an increase of 400 per cent within two years ... There are now about 400 soc. magazines and newspapers printed in the States, and socialist literature is being distributed in tons.[16]

He also enclosed several issues of a popular local newspaper, *Lowery's Claim,* noting that he thought his friend would "enjoy reading it" as its "editor talks very straight on so called religion and other subjects."[17] Teit described British Columbia as ripe for socialism: "The government is very rotten and will have to take a walk soon [as there is] a good deal of dissatisfaction with the existing order of things ... religious ideas are also changing ... People think more for themselves and are not so much led by the nose. They recognize that form and dogma is not religion."[18] In a later letter, he reported enthusiastically that "the first socialist has been voted into the [British Columbia] legislature and [a]nother very nearly got in at a by-election."[19] This "all shows," he wrote, "that people are now wakening up."[20]

The newly elected MLA was James Hurst Hawthornthwaite, an Irish immigrant and former employee of the British-owned Vancouver Coal Mining and Land Company, Ltd., in Nanaimo.[21] A staunch anti-capitalist, Hawthornthwaite had won his seat in the BC Legislature on February 18, 1901, as an independent Labour candidate on a platform of "socialism, pure and simple."[22] Much of his support had come from Vancouver Island's coal miners, who were reeling from record-high death rates and intolerable working conditions in the local mines. They had organized worker strikes such as the province had never seen. It was hard to ignore class inequities when miners headed into the dark, damp underground while their employers indulged in highly visible above-ground "galas, automobiles, [and] stately homes."[23] The ultimate insult was the election of James Dunsmuir, the autocratic owner and manager of Vancouver Island's R. Dunsmuir and Sons mines, to the premiership of the province in 1900.[24] When the death rate in Dunsmuir's collieries soared to a record high in 1901, many mine workers joined a rash of disgruntled workers from across the province in support of the newly founded Socialist Party of British Columbia (SPBC).[25]

Immediately upon his return to British Columbia from Shetland in July 1902, Teit sought out British Columbia socialist organizations, and he encouraged his friends and neighbours to follow suit.[26] The August 9 issue of the *Canadian Socialist* newspaper listed him as an enthusiastic "Comrade Teit" from "Spences Bridge," who was fully "in favor of socialism and wishe[d] to understand its aims better."[27] He reported that the movement was "gaining ground and if a socialist [were to] run in the Yale-Kootenay district next election, I think he is sure to go in." He appeared in the pages of the November 1 issue of the *Western Socialist* newspaper as an active party canvasser.[28] By the spring of 1903, the SPBC singled him out as a noted "hustler" and praised him for his success in recruiting new members.[29] Sam Anderson, a Shetland expat based in Vancouver, described Teit as one of a group of expat Shetlanders who spent time at the Socialist Party of Canada headquarters in Vancouver.[30]

Getting to the One Percent

Having spent close to two years in the powderwork division of the Northfield Mines near Nanaimo, Teit knew the miners' grievances first-hand. Like many working-class British Columbians, he had turned to mining after his other lines of employment – a clerkship in his uncle's trade store and two seasons of hunting and trapping in northern British Columbia – had run dry.[31] The exodus of construction crews and engineers from Spences Bridge after the completion of the CPR in 1886 had sapped the town of its temporary economic energy.[32]

The CPR was the new engine of the BC economy. As the historian Martin Robin reports, with the fur trade "fast becoming a faded relic of a romantic past," and fish quickly replacing furs as the province's primary resource,[33] "the big men came in droves, consum[ing] the little men according to the rules of the cannibal game which flourishes in all growing capitalist economies."[34] Building on its teams of surveyors in the 1870s and its armies of engineers and construction crews in the 1880s, the CPR in the 1890s was the largest of the big-man enterprises. It owned a conglomerate of huge land assets (millions of acres of provincial land and timber grants), large hotels, telegraphs, steamships, and express lines.[35] The transfer of the CPR's western terminus from Port Moody to Granville (renamed Vancouver) transformed the latter overnight from a village into a booming metropolis offering state-of-the-art shipping facilities and banking and trade outlets. With travel times reduced from months to days, the provincial forestry sector expanded from 27 sawmills in 1881 to 224 mills in 1911, and the mining sector expanded from gold and coal to include silver, copper, lead, quartz, and zinc in a network of new mining towns – Nelson, Rossland, Trail, New Denver, Slocan, Sanden, Kaslo, Grand Forks, Phoenix, Greenwood. The Okanagan's orchards grew from 7,500 acres in 1900 to 100,000 acres in 1907.[36] Cattle ranching consumed thousands of acres of rolling rangeland in the south and central Interior.[37] Because only 5 percent of British Columbia's 250-million-acre land base was suited to agriculture, resource extraction – mining, logging, and fishing – dominated the province's economy.[38] By the 1890s, the majority of British Columbians earned their living as longshoremen, fishers, miners, loggers, and cannery workers. The growing frustration of workers across the province produced a two-fold increase in local unions,[39] as well as a series of strikes in the railway, fishing, and mining sectors between 1900 and 1903.[40]

During Teit's employment at the Northfield mine, his co-workers at the nearby Wellington Colliery carried on an eighteen-month strike.[41]

In the midst of this unrest, the SPBC merged with the Socialist Party of Canada (SPC) in December 1904.[42] It was a bold move, given the radical agenda of the SPC at the time:

> First, that capitalism could not be reformed and attempts at amelioration had no place in the class struggle; second, that trade unions could not benefit all workers in the short run or any workers in the long run; and third, that class conscious political action was the only means by which the proletariat could destroy the wage system and establish the co-operative commonwealth.[43]

Many SPC members supported the idea of forming a "proletariat ... force of arms" aimed at "driv[ing] the capitalists out of power."[44] In 1909, D.G. McKenzie, a coal miner who spent his evenings editing the *Western Clarion* newspaper, used his editorials to radicalize workers: "Pick up the revolutionary club and go after the earth, and the first thing you know you will have palliatives galore from the cowardly capitalist tribe fleeing for their lives from the wrath to come."[45] In a letter to a Shetland friend in 1908, Teit expressed his allegiance to McKenzie's platform with a prescient reference to the "one per cent":

> I would not advise any one to emigrate to this country except they had considerable money. The state of this country at the present time for the working or wage earning class is simply rotten, the country is swarming with idle men, and war has set in to the teeth between labor and capital. Wages are going down and the price of commodities such as food tc are going up steadily. To make matters worse the Salvation Army and emigration & other agents of the Capitalist Class are bringing out poor people from England and other European countries on false information and dumping them wholesale in this country with what result you may imagine. This great America is certainly a wonderful country, and has undergone a wonderful development, but what is the result? All the wealth of the United States & Canada ... is in the hand of a very few men representing the giant trusts and corporations. 7/8 of the wealth is owned by 1 per cent of the people whilst 99 per cent own 1/8. And these conditions are rapidly becoming worse. Things cannot continue this way, and there will be a great revolution in this country within the decade. It must come as sure as day follows night.[46]

If the situation for working-class British Columbians was dire, the situation for Indians was disastrous. When Teit arrived in BC in 1884, Indians formed approximately half of the province's population; by 1911, however, they were approximately 6 percent of the total population.[47] With no treaty negotiations beyond fourteen land-purchase agreements on Vancouver Island and one treaty in northeastern British Columbia, they argued, with justification, that the settler Canadian project in British Columbia stood on stolen land. As noted in Chapter 2, the colonial administrations had placed them on small, scattered reserves and, from 1866 on, amended the land laws to prohibit them from pre-empting land without government permission. Meanwhile, the government allowed incoming settlers to pre-empt large tracts of land without such permissions. British Columbia's entry into Confederation in 1871 added further complication by placing Indians under the jurisdiction of the federal government and their lands under the province. The latter decision precipitated major friction between the two governments as they argued over how large the reserves should be. The federal government offered a small reprieve in its 1876 Indian Act by inserting a provision stating that a reserve could not be reduced in size without the band's consent.[48]

Tensions between the federal government and provincial governments over the land issue escalated in 1906 when the federal government amended the 1876 Indian Act to encourage bands to surrender some of their unused lands. This exacerbated the long-standing issue of who had proprietary rights over such land surrenders.[49] Premier Richard McBride articulated his position in legal terms when he passed an order-in-council in February 1907 that stated the Indians had only a "right of use and occupation" of their lands, and Ottawa had "no proprietary rights in the reserves."[50] In the case of surrenders, the entire benefit must go to the province. The surrender of a piece of Tsimshian reserve land near Prince Rupert in 1907 brought this issue to a head. The dispute, as legal historian Hamar Foster notes, "was significant because Article 13 of the Terms of Union that ushered British Columbia into Confederation in 1871 provided that a disagreement between the Dominion and provincial governments about Indian lands in B.C. could be appealed to the imperial secretary of state for the colonies."[51] The situation peaked a year later when the provincial government announced that it was terminating all land allotments for reserves.[52] When McBride declared, in the wake of this decision, that, should Indians relinquish their claims to reserve lands, the province would sell off such lands to white settlers at bargain rates, the chiefs across the province erupted in anger. As Foster explains, it was now clearer than ever that the "authorities in British Columbia" looked on Indian rights to the land "as legally non-existent ... beyond the temporary right to occupy them."[53]

The Nisga'a chiefs of the Nass watershed responded by founding a political organization – the "Nishga Land Committee" – in 1907 to consolidate their position on these decisions.[54] A group of coastal chiefs followed suit two years later by founding a parallel organization, the Indian Rights Association.[55] The Nlaka'pamux, Secwépemc, and Syilx chiefs founded the Interior Tribes of British Columbia (ITBC) around the same time to consolidate their challenge to multiple settler intrusions on their territories. The opening of the CPR in 1886 had triggered a spike in foreign land purchases across southern British Columbia. One land purchase on Secwépemc territory, near the eastern border of Nlaka'pamux territory, was beyond anything yet seen. A London-based speculator bought two thousand hectares of prime land east of Ashcroft in 1907 for a planned community (the "Walhachin project") of 150 electrified residences, a hotel, tennis courts, a polo field, and a golf course.[56] This gentrified community was to sustain itself by growing and exporting fruit. In a letter to Boas a year after the Walhachin purchase, Teit described a forthcoming meeting that was aimed at contesting such incursions:

> I may say that in southern BC there is considerable dissatisfaction & unrest amongst the Indians at present, the settling up of the country & changing of conditions is restricting the Indians more & more to their small reserves, etc. They are also of the opinion that they are very much neglected & kept in an inferior condition. When I return home about 30 Thompson, Shuswap & Okanagan chiefs are to meet at Spences Bridge to hold a big "talk" preliminary to sending a big "paper" to Ottawa recounting their grievances.[57]

Steeped in Resistance

The Interior chiefs had a long history of political protest. In his 1912 *Mythology of the Thompson Indians,* Teit described a "big talk" that took place at Lytton in the summer of 1858 when "hundreds of warriors from all parts of the Upper Thompson country ... assembled" for the purpose of "blocking the progress of the whites beyond that point, and, if possible, driving them down the river."[58] As described in Chapter 2, this conflict threatened to erupt into a full-scale war between the Nlaka'pamux and the miners, especially when the neighbouring Secwépemc and Syilx chiefs sent word to Lytton that should the Nlaka'pamux decide to fight the miners, they were fully prepared to assist them. At the last minute, the head chief at Lytton, Shigh-pentlam (or Cexpē'ntlEm as Teit sometimes spelled it), convinced his colleagues of the merits of a peaceful resolution. This served Governor James Douglas well, as he was on his way to Lytton to negotiate a truce when he learned that Shigh-pentlam, "on behalf of his people," had persuaded the Nlaka'pamux to "allow ... the whites to enter the country."[59] "Nobody now knows the exact agreement or promises made by either party," Teit explained.[60] Through interviews with elders, Teit pieced together a rough account of Shigh-pentlam's side of the exchange. Some of this exchange appeared in a volume of stories published in 1917:

> Chief Cexpē'ntlEm, in talking to the whites (in 1858) told them they had entered his house and were now his guests. He asked them to treat his children as brothers, and they would share the same fire. He did not know that they would afterwards treat his people as strangers and inferiors, and steal their land and their food from them. Had he known it, there would have been war, and the land would have been red with blood. They [Douglas's entourage] asked him where his house was. He [Cexpē'ntlEm] said "You are in it. The centre of my house is here at Lytton. The fireplace is right here, and you are sitting by it. The doors of my house are at Spuzzum, at Laha'hoa [Fountain], at StlE.z [Ashcroft], at .stcē' kus [Quilchena], and at Tcutcuw ī'xa [near Hedley]. Between these places is our tribal territory, from which we gather our food." This is why Lytton was considered the chief and central place of the tribe, and our head chief was there.[61]

For some reason, the published version excluded the following segment:

> I know of no white man's boundaries or posts. If the whites have put up posts and divided my country, I do not recognize them. They have not consulted me. They have broken my house without my consent. All Indian tribes have the same as posts and recognized boundaries, and the chiefs know them since long before the first whites came to the country.[62]

Shigh-pentlam's peace treaty was short-lived. Conflict erupted again when the British government dispatched the Royal Engineers to survey the southern and central regions of the Interior for townsites, roads, bridges, and Indian reserves. A major altercation took place in 1864 at the junction of Homathko River and Mosley Creek. During construction of the Bute

Inlet Wagon Road from the Coast to the Cariboo, a party of Tsilhqot'in murdered seventeen members of a road construction crew and three members of a packing crew. It had started with an argument between the ferryman on the Homathko River and a group of Tsilhqot'in over the latter's request for food. When the ferryman refused their request, the Tsilhqot'in murdered him and stole the food. They then went on a killing spree that resulted in nineteen deaths. One member of the construction crew had stirred up trouble by threatening to infect the Tsilhqot'in with smallpox as punishment for the theft.[63] It ended badly for the Tsilhqot'in. Eight of their chiefs were called to a meeting with government representatives. On arriving at the meeting, six were charged with murder and five were hanged. Two of the survivors were later tried in New Westminster, and one was hanged. This brought the total number of hangings to six.[64]

The 1860s was a difficult decade for the Interior peoples because of the government reserve surveys that had taken place on their territorial lands. By 1861, a dozen reserves had been surveyed between Yale and Lytton; by 1864, another dozen reserves had been surveyed along the Thompson River to Kamloops and along the Fraser River to Soda Creek.[65] As noted, the colonial government in 1866 had amended the land laws to prohibit Indians from pre-empting land without government permission. Meanwhile, members of the settler population could pre-empt up to 160 acres of Crown land on the Coast and up to 320 acres in the Interior. With settlers acquiring large tracts of the best agricultural lands – often with adjacent water rights – the reality of strict confinement to Indian "reserves" assumed new meaning.

To contest such land theft, Indians needed politically supportive and skilled English translators. Initially, they turned to the handful of missionaries who had learned the basic rudiments of the local languages as a way to teach religion to their new converts. Beyond this select group, however, there were few skilled and sympathetic translators to be had. In 1868, a Nlaka'pamux chief, Naweeshistan, appealed to J.B. Good, the Anglican missionary at Lytton, to help him prepare a written petition to Anthony Musgrave, governor of the Colony of British Columbia, protesting the reserve allocations in the Nicola Valley and the settlement of "lands and resources that belonged to Natives."[66] The request yielded positive results. In addition to helping Naweeshistan draft his petition, Good submitted his own letter of protest to the land surveyor, Peter O'Reilly. O'Reilly responded by accusing Good of stirring up trouble in the Indian communities. "The Natives were happy with their reserves," O'Reilly reported to the missionary's church superiors, "until Good stepped in."[67] A second group of Nlaka'pamux chiefs approached Good the following year to help them draft another letter of protest to Musgrave and Joseph Trutch, Chief Commissioner of Lands and Works, about the Lytton reserves. As with his earlier letter, Good backed the chiefs, arguing that the surveys represented "only a small fraction of [Nlaka'pamux] territory, leaving the door wide open to settlement."[68]

British Columbia's entry into the Canadian Confederation in 1871 triggered a new round of dispossession by "superimpos[ing] a new constitutional rigidity and years of Dominion-provincial acrimony on the Native land question."[69] "There was trouble from the beginning," writes Cole Harris, as federal and provincial governments argued back and forth over how much land to allocate to reserves. At the chiefs' end, "lands were being pre-empted from under their eyes, a process launched with little more than a few scratched lines on a slip of paper, but that, in the eyes of the settler who happened along and of the law that backed him, created enduring property rights."[70] Protests erupted across the province as local chiefs internalized the realities of the new land transactions. One of the most serious protests occurred in 1874 near Kamloops when a group of seven Secwépemc chiefs gathered to plot war against the whites. Like the Nlaka'pamux leaders at Lytton a few years earlier, they appealed to their local missionary, Father C.J. Grandidier, to help them. He drafted a letter on their behalf that challenged the very idea of reserves.[71] He also submitted his own letters of protest to the local newspapers, arguing that "title had not been extinguished."[72]

Such petitions and threats of violence finally forced the federal and provincial governments to respond. In 1876, the two governments established a provincial-federal Indian Reserve Commission aimed at finalizing reserve surveys throughout the province. Angered by the premise of the commission, representatives of reserve communities in the south central regions assembled at the Head of the Lake, in Okanagan Territory, to organize an attack on the settler communities. When word of the attack reached Victoria, the commissioners raced to Kamloops, where they negotiated separate land agreements with individual chiefs as a way of breaking up the chiefs' alliance.[73]

As he moved from reserve to reserve, taking testimony from individual chiefs about their opposition to reserves and their claims to their full territories, Reserve Commissioner Gilbert Sproat began to question government policy. At a meeting with the Nlaka'pamux leaders at Lytton in July 1879, he oversaw the signing of a document meant to attract the attention of "a sympathetic Queen" to their cause. The leaders elected a head chief and thirteen councillors and outlined a series of rules and regulations – around health, education, and community leadership – that, in their view, fulfilled the conditions that whites were asking of them. As Brett Christophers, Douglas Harris, and Cole Harris have argued, this was a landmark document because of its endorsement of "white law" as a way to achieve equality with whites.[74] In the end, however, their initiative backfired by fuelling fears in the settler community of an Indian confederacy. Sproat resigned from the commission in frustration in 1880, allowing Peter O'Reilly (Joseph Trutch's brother-in-law and Ottawa's agent in British Columbia at the time) to take his place. O'Reilly had assigned many of the small reserves that Sproat had challenged.

In 1898, with the majority of reserves now in place, O'Reilly retired, leaving the final details to his colleague, A.W. Vowell, Superintendent of Indian Affairs for the province of British Columbia. Vowell continued assigning reserves and adjusting their boundaries until 1908, when Richard McBride's Conservative government stepped in and refused "all further cooperation" with Indians over reserve lands.[75]

Waves of Protest

Several members of the ITBC were well-seasoned political protesters by 1908. Secwépemc chief Basil David of the Bonaparte reserve (upriver from Spences Bridge) had travelled to London, England, two years earlier with Squamish chief Joe Capilano and Cowichan chief Charley Tsilpaymilt to appeal directly to King Edward VII on their right to title. The trio carried a petition that stated: "In British Columbia the Indian title has never been extinguished ... nor has significant land been allotted to our people for their maintenance."[76] It also demanded a repeal of the potlatch ban and the elimination of newly imposed hunting regulations. David and his two colleagues obtained an audience with King Edward VII, but they were informed beforehand that they could not present their petition to the King because such petitions had to pass through the Canadian government.[77] There is some debate about whether or not they observed this condition.[78] The chiefs stopped in Ottawa on their way back to British Columbia and hand-delivered their petition to the office of Prime Minister Sir Wilfrid Laurier. Buoyed by its potential to resolve the land-title issue, Joe Capilano travelled around the province with the petition to educate his colleagues in reserve communities about its significance.[79]

When news filtered back to British Columbia in December 1907 that *all* grievances concerning title and sovereignty had to pass through Canadian government channels, representatives from the northern and southern reserve communities assembled in North Vancouver to prepare a collective response. The outcome was a decision to send a delegation to Ottawa to argue their case face to face with Laurier.[80] The delegation included Chief Basil David who had been part of the 1906 London delegation. The group arrived in Ottawa in June 1908 and presented Laurier with two petitions. It was a busy month of protest for David, as he joined a second delegation (this one including Chief Louis Clexlixqen of the Kamloops Band and John Chilahitsa of the Upper Nicola Band) a month later for another Ottawa trip, this one to petition for a new reserve in Secwépemc territory.[81] Meanwhile, at home, Joe Capilano's travels with the 1906 petition had attracted so much attention that the provincial police threatened to arrest him for stirring up "serious trouble in the Nass and Skeena districts as well as other unsettled portions of the province."[82]

Capilano's campaign was likely the catalyst for a large Nlaka'pamux strategy session at Spences Bridge on July 25, 1908. On that day, four Nlaka'pamux chiefs, Peter Poghos, John Tetlanetza, William Luklukpaghen, and John Whistemnitsa, along with sixteen colleagues met to draft a petition ("A Prayer of Indian Chiefs") to send to A.W. Vowell, Superintendent of Indian Affairs for the Province of BC, protesting his department's administration of their affairs.[83] The petitioners demanded the immediate removal of their local Indian agent, Archibald Irwin, on grounds of incompetence. They alleged that in Irwin's eleven years as their agent, he had created more problems than he had solved.[84] They also asked for "a properly trained medical man," a day school for Nlaka'pamux children, healthcare for the elderly and infirm, compensation for railway rights-of-way through their lands, and, most importantly, compensation for the "appropriat[ion]" of the land base "by whites without treaty or payment." They concluded on a rhetorical note: "Have we been treated thus because we welcomed the whites as a brother, believed what he said, and asked nothing from him?"[85]

The "Prayer" marked Teit's formal entry into the political sphere – and the beginning of a worklife of unfathomable complexity and commitment. He not only handwrote the document; he signed off as one of its two witnesses. There was "no resisting the Indian appeal," he later explained, as "I was so well known to the Interior tribes and had so much of their confidence, and was so well acquainted with their customs, ideas, languages, and their condition and necessities."[86] Within a year, he accepted their invitation to serve as the secretary-treasurer of their newly founded Interior Tribes of BC. As few of the chiefs could speak or write English well enough at the time to participate in these debates on their lands and lives, Teit played a critical role in their new movement by lending them his ear and his voice. Their signatures on the 1908 "Prayer" spoke to the extent of their English illiteracy: all four petitioners had signed with x's. Such illiteracy placed them in a vulnerable situation, as Teit had explained to Boas a few years earlier. Given that "not one Indian in 200 can sign his name ... it would be easy for me to put crosses and Indian names and no one would know whether they are genuine or not."[87] He noted the fear that many held toward pens and paper: "To them 'touching the pen' is a very serious, and solemn matter," requiring "much deliberation, and explanation – as for instance when they make an agreement with the Government, or with some big tyee about some important matter."[88] Two years into his new role, the southern Interior tribes "elected" him as "their secretary, treasurer & organizer in the movement."[89]

Advocating for Indigenous rights is now common practice. Many of the country's leading lawyers and anthropologists have built entire careers on it. A century ago, however, those who took on such work were blacklisted as "white agitators" and promptly shunned. Some were subjected to police surveillance.[90] In 1916, Teit described some of the risks he faced when he first declared his support for the Nlaka'pamux leaders:

> [My friends] advised me to have nothing to do with helping [the chiefs], that it was a matter for government officials and others to attend to, that I would get no thanks, that I would be branded as an agitator, that the Indian Agents would consider it an interference, and on the whole so many people would misunderstand me and get down on me, my success and standing in the country would be injured.[91]

Government politicians and Indian Department personnel had well-established strategies for dealing with "agitators." As historian Keith Smith explained in his 2009 study of the Kamloops Indian agency, they tended to blame "any disaffection or disquiet" on the Indian front as "fomented and sustained by ... outsiders" rather than the Indians themselves.[92] To admit that Indians were leading the resistance campaign "would not only threaten to expose the actual results of liberalism in Canada, but would also force the admission that the Indigenous people were capable of reasoned opposition to unjust legislation and policy that should only be expected from those granted citizen status."[93]

Such intimidation tactics did not deter Teit. A decade into this work, he insisted that he had no regrets about "what little" he had "done to help these people."[94] On the contrary, Teit saw it as an extension of his ethnographic work. As he explained to the Deputy Superintendent General of Indian Affairs in 1916:

> For many years back when engaged among the tribes in ethnological work ... the Indians almost everywhere would bring up questions of their grievances concerning their title, reserves, hunting and fishing rights, policies of Agents and missionaries on dances, potlatches, education, etc. and ... [as] they invariably wanted to discuss them with me or get me to help them ... I had to listen and give them some advice.[95]

Teit's role with the ITBC in 1909 linked him to a small circle of "white agitators" that included Arthur O'Meara, Charles M. Tate, and a few others.[96] Tate was a Methodist missionary who had spent years working in reserve communities along the Coast and on the Lower Mainland. In 1909 he was based in Duncan on Vancouver Island, where he assisted the local Cowichan chiefs with their land grievances. O'Meara was a newly ordained Anglican clergyman from Ontario who had moved to British Columbia via the Yukon after a twenty-year career as a lawyer. The two clergymen met in 1909 and began strategizing on how to achieve a legal solution to the impasse over the "British Columbia Indian Land Question." They saw major potential in the 1763 Royal Proclamation.[97]

The Royal Proclamation was the legacy of King George III (1738–1820). It promised no more seizures of Indian lands without treaties between the Crown and the affected parties. This had generated a rash of treaties in eastern Canada and the Prairies, but it had stopped at the Rocky Mountains. Apart from pockets of southern Vancouver Island and a small region in northeastern BC, none of British Columbia had been "treatied." Inspired by the potential of the Proclamation to resolve the land problem in British Columbia, Tate and O'Meara drafted a petition on behalf of the Cowichan peoples that asserted that because "the Cowichan valley ... had never been ceded," it "therefore belonged to" the resident Indians.[98] Their Cowichan Petition instilled excitement in reserve communities across the province.[99] O'Meara worked with John M. Clark, a prominent Toronto lawyer known for his legal work on behalf of Indians in Ontario, to help refine the terms of the petition.[100] The two lawyers met in Toronto in March and together drafted what legal historian Hamar Foster describes as "the first legally sophisticated articulation of the doctrine of Aboriginal title on behalf of Aboriginal people in British Columbia."[101] In brief, they argued that "British imperial law, and in particular, the Royal Proclamation of 1763, recognized Aboriginal title [and] [i]n failing to respect this, British Columbia had violated that law." Hence, "the title question should be referred ... directly to the Judicial Committee of the Privy Council" (JCPC) in Britain.[102] O'Meara carried the petition to London, where he hand-delivered it to the Secretary of State for the Colonies.[103]

While the Coast and Interior chiefs strategized about how to reclaim a stolen land base that they firmly believed was legally and rightfully theirs, the federal Department of Indian Affairs (DIA) strategized in the opposite direction: how to reduce the size of existing reserve lands. To this end, in 1909 it hired Methodist missionary John McDougall "to examine carefully reserves in and south [of] the railway belt, as to their area, fitness for agriculture or other purposes, the number of Indians on each, [and] what, in his opinion should be sold."[104] (The railway belt was a strip of land, twenty miles on either side of the CPR rail line, conveyed by British Columbia to the federal government as part of the 1871 Confederation agreement.) Having witnessed the negotiation of Treaty No. 6 (in Saskatchewan) in 1876 and Treaty No. 7 (in Alberta) in 1877, and worked on land surrenders in the Northwest Territories for the DIA in 1905, McDougall had the background for the BC job.[105] In addition to asking him to assess the status of land, the DIA had also asked McDougall to assess "the moral and general condition of the Indians."[106]

McDougall carried out his duties deftly, travelling from reserve to reserve to meet with Indian leaders throughout the south central Interior. The chiefs in Teit's neighbourhood saw his visit as a sympathetic response by DIA to their written appeals for a hearing to air their grievances, so they welcomed him with open arms.[107] In fact, Chief Whistemnitsa was so pleased about McDougall's visit that he asked the Indian Department for additional time in order to "gather a good many chiefs in here from outlying bands including all those along the Thompson River between Savona and Lytton." In his letter (drafted on his behalf by Teit), Whistemnitsa stated that he had heard from "whites" that "Mr. McDougal [sic] is a very good man [who] has been sent here on an important mission" and that, in furtherance of these goals, he would "put every facility in his way to take him around on their reserves, and also enlighten him on every matter that he desires information about." He warned that some of the chiefs had "complaints to lay before him." In addition to requesting additional time to assemble a large crowd, Whistemnitsa asked that the date of the meeting be arranged to accommodate his "No. 1 interpreter," Teit.[108] With the date decided, McDougall appeared and listened to the grievances of Whistemnitsa. He also heard out Whistemnitsa's many compatriots across the southern Interior. His final report, however, was a disappointment. McDougall recommended only two additions to reserves in Nlaka'pamux territory: one in the village of Spences Bridge to compensate for a reserve that had been washed out by a landslide in 1905, and another at Lytton. His recommendations for the neighbouring Secwépemc and Okanagan included reductions of several thousand acres to reserves at Kamloops and in the Okanagan.[109] These were frustrating times for the chiefs.

O'Meara's delivery of the Cowichan Petition to the British Secretary of State for the Colonies offered a glimmer of hope, however, as the Colonial Office studied the document and returned it to Canada with a request for an explanation.[110] In addition to forcing Laurier's Liberal government to respond, this request pushed the government to retain legal counsel, T.R.E. MacInnes, "to investigate and report upon the nature and present status of the Indian Title to certain lands known as 'Indian Lands' in Canada, with special reference to British Columbia."[111]

MacInnes assessed the situation and in August submitted a hundred-page opinion that asserted the provincial government had indeed violated the Indians' rights as there was "unextinguished Indian title in British Columbia."[112] He advised Laurier that, as the Indians' trustee, his government had an obligation and a responsibility to mount a legal case on their behalf. Laurier expressed his willingness to pursue this route, even stating that his government would seek to "facilitate a judicial decision, at the highest level, on Native claims."[113] Because BC's premier, Richard McBride, opposed the idea, Laurier had no choice but to force the Province into court. To initiate this process, he amended the Indian Act "to authorize the institution of proceedings in the Exchequer Court on behalf of the Indians, which would effectively have forced B.C. into court."[114]

Another positive outcome of the Cowichan Petition was the launch of two new political organizations – the Indian Rights Association (IRA) and the Friends of the Indians of British Columbia (FIBC). Both organizations broke new ground by drawing in supporters from the settler community as well as the reserve communities. Their main goal was to help cover the legal costs of having the Indian title case argued before the JCPC.[115] The IRA retained the Toronto-based J.M. Clark as its legal counsel.[116] Teit spent from January to March 1910 travelling to reserves across the province to educate people about the terms of the Cowichan Petition and its judicial goals.[117] In a letter to Boas, he outlined what was at stake:

> The last two weeks I have done very little ... as I have been busy traveling around, and speaking to the Indians so as to get them united in an effort to fight the BC Government in the Courts over the question of their lands ... The BC Government has appropriated all the lands of the country, and claims also to be sole protector of the Ind. Reserves. They refuse to acknowledge the Ind. title, and have taken possession of all without treaty with or consent of the Indians. Having taken the lands they claim complete ownership of everything in connection therewith such as water, timber, fish, game, etc. They also subject the Indians completely to all the laws of BC without having made any agreement with them to that effect. The Indians demand that treaties be made with them regarding everything the same as has been made with the Indians of all the other provinces of Canada & in the US, that their reservations be enlarged so they have a chance to make a living as easily and as sufficient as among the Whites, and that all the lands not required by them and which they do not wish to retain for purposes of cultivation and grazing, and which are presently appropriated by the BC. Government be paid for in cash. The Indians are all uniting and putting up money and have engaged lawyers in Toronto to fight for them, and have the case tried before the Privy Council of England. I came back from Nicola yesterday and am going to Kamloops to address a very large meeting there on Sunday next.[118]

The 1910 Memorial

Teit's educational campaign culminated with an ITBC political meeting on July 15 and 16, 1910, with a large delegation of "Okanagan, Shuswap and Thompson" chiefs, to compose a written "Declaration" in support of the IRA's appeal for treaties and compensation from the BC government for all lands "appropriated, or held by them, including all lands preempted or bought by settlers, miners, lumbermen, etc."[119] The end result was a collective statement that also demanded additions to their own reserves and "permanent and secure title (to be acknowledged by the Government as such) of our ownership of our present reservations, and of such lands as may be added thereto." Echoing the IRA, the Declaration also demanded an airing of the chiefs' claims "before the privy council of England for settlement, and in the event of our obtaining justice as we expect, we ask that such compensation as may be awarded us for our lands, etc. shall be paid to us, half of it in cash, and the other half to be retained by the dominion government, and used, as occasion may require, for our benefit."[120]

The delegation had just signed off on the Declaration and disbanded when news arrived that Prime Minister Wilfrid Laurier was on a cross-country summer rail tour that included a stop at Kamloops on August 25. Having heard that Laurier might be open to settling their land-title case, the chiefs decided it was important to send a delegation to Kamloops to meet with him. With little time to organize another large-group meeting to prepare a collective written statement for Laurier, the chiefs delegated Teit to draft a memorial statement on their behalf. By now, they trusted him to "channel" their views accurately and respectfully. In a rare moment of self-reflection six years later, Teit described the delicacy of his advisory role:

> Were I to recommend [something] strongly myself perhaps they really all would favor it but I don't care to advise as I want a free expression of opinion from them on the matter first of all. I seldom advise the Indians at any time (except when asked for advice). I prefer to give them the information and explain everything as well as I can and then leave them to make their own decisions.[121]

Teit moved swiftly on the chiefs' Kamloops assignment, producing in three days a tight, four-page "Memorial to Sir Wilfrid Laurier, Premier of the Dominion of Canada from the Chiefs of the Shuswap, Okanagan and Couteau Tribes of British Columbia."[122] Because a pre-arranged guiding trip to the Stikine prevented him from attending the Kamloops meeting, he invited the Oblate priest Father Jean-Marie-Raphael LeJeune to stand in his place as translator.[123] Teit knew that LeJeune would do the job well as he was not only fluent in the Secwépemc, Nlaka'pamux, and Syilx languages, but had also introduced a French Duployan shorthand writing system that enabled the speakers of Chinook Jargon (the old trade language) to read and write Chinook. Some of his Chinook Jargon students became so proficient in the shorthand that LeJeune had invited two of them, Chief John Chilahitsa of Douglas Lake and Chief Louis Clexlixqen of Kamloops, to participate in an international shorthand competition in France in 1904. The trip turned into an extended four-month excursion that included, in addition to the shorthand contest in France, trips to London, Rome, and LeJeune's home community in Brittany, France.[124]

After three days of work on the Memorial, Teit mailed it to LeJeune on August 6, with a note explaining how it should be presented:

> I have finished writing out the memorial for presentation to Laurier by the Indians at Kamloops. It is longer than I intended to make it, but it was impossible to give anything like a good statement of the Indian case (as they view it themselves) without dealing at some length. I think I have brought out all the important points every one of which has been emphasized to me by one or more Indians at various times.[125]

He asked LeJeune to "read over" the Memorial to the delegation prior to their meeting with Laurier and to invite "either Louis or Johnny" to supplement it with their own speeches to Laurier.

The Memorial opened by thanking Laurier for his open attitude toward "the Indian rights movement." It welcomed him as the "head of this great Canadian nation" and a descendant of the good-willed, French-speaking whites (in the Memorial's words, "real whites").[126] It then characterized the history of colonization as a century-long struggle between good and evil as resident Indians transitioned from dealing with "real whites" to dealing with bad whites ("other whites"). The "first whites" had arrived with the Hudson's Bay Company traders and were "good" people who "found us happy, healthy, strong and numerous ... [with] each tribe ... living in its own 'house.'" They "did not force their conceptions of things on us to our harm." The next wave of whites, who arrived with the 1858 gold rush, stole land from the Indians and asserted ownership over those lands by laying down laws. "We had never known white chiefs to break their word so we trusted." As more and more groups of other whites arrived in the region, they treated Indians as "subjects without any agreement to that effect ... They laugh[ed] at our chiefs and brush[ed] them aside." With the BC government claiming "absolute ownership" of reserve lands, the chiefs said, "We find ourselves without any real home in this our own country."

Throughout the document, Teit highlighted the non-capitalist, communitarian relationship that the chiefs and their peoples had maintained with their land base prior to the takeover by the other whites:

> The country of each tribe was just the same as a very large farm or ranch (belonging to all the people of the tribe) ... [and on which] all the people had equal rights of access to everything they required. You will see the ranch of each tribe was the same as its life, and without it the people could not have lived ... No one interfered with our rights, nor disputed our possession of our ... own "houses" and "ranches," viz., our homes and lives ... [This all changed when the other whites] commenced to enter our "houses" or live on our "ranches." With us, when a person enters our house he becomes our guest.

There were few terms in the English language that were more enmeshed in the new capitalist economy of BC's Interior than the term "ranch." Thomas William Seward and Thomas Earl owned a huge ranch, Earlscourt, near Lytton; Clement Francis Cornwall and Antoine Minaberriet owned another massive ranch near Ashcroft; and William Ward owned the Douglas Lake Cattle Company, a 110,000-acre ranch, at Douglas Lake. At one point in the 1880s, two brothers, Thaddeus and Jerome Harper owned 38,000 acres of ranch land stretching from the Chilcotin south to Hat Creek and Cache Creek.[127] Such operations, as historical geographer John Thistle notes, were classic corporate holdings with a broad global reach. "The massive Douglas Lake Cattle Company was incorporated by British investors in 1886; the equally enormous Gang Ranch was incorporated by a London, England-based investment agency in 1892; and the British Columbia Cattle Company was incorporated in 1900."[128] The staff required to run these ranches was massive. In addition to a manager and several working foremen, many ranches included an army of cowboys and a support staff, such as cooks and blacksmiths. Some also housed sawmill operators for onsite sawmills, and large numbers of seasonal laborers.[129] Many Nlaka'pamux, St'at'imc, Secwépemc, and Tsilhqot'in men and women worked as labourers on these large ranches. Some of the ITBC chiefs, such as Chief John Chilahitsa of Douglas Lake, had established their own ranches on reserve land. Indeed, for both the new settlers and the Indigenous peoples, "ranching" symbolized both individual gain and communal loss.

The Memorial depicted the corralling of Indian inhabitants onto reserves as a form of collective incarceration through the law:

> They treat us as subjects without any agreement to that effect, and force their laws on us without our consent, and irrespective of whether they are good for us or not. They say they have authority over us. They have broken

> down our old laws and customs (no matter how good) by which we regulated ourselves. They laugh at our chiefs and brush them aside. Minor affairs amongst ourselves, which do not affect them in the least, and which we can easily settle better than they can, they drag into their courts ... They have knocked down (the same as) the posts of all the Indian tribes. They say there are no lines, except what they make ... They have stolen our lands and everything on them and continue to use same for their own purposes. They treat us as less than children and allow us no say in anything. They say the Indians know nothing and own nothing, yet their power and wealth has come from our belongings ... Although we have waited long, we have been disappointed ... We had no powerful friends. The Indian agents and Indian office at Victoria appeared to neglect us.

It listed a long series of impediments to daily life, such as the poor quality of reserve land, the erosion of pasture lands due to fencing, new restrictions on hunting and fishing, and "the depletion of salmon by over-fishing of the whites." The Memorial concluded with an angry charge against the provincial government:

> We condemn the whole policy of the B.C. government towards the Indian tribes of this country as utterly unjust, shameful, and blundering in every way [and demand] ... that our land question be settled and ask that treaties be made between the government and each of our tribes, in the same manner as accomplished with the Indian tribes of the other provinces of Canada, and in the neighbouring parts of the United States.

Teit mailed copies of the Memorial to his Indian Rights Association colleagues on the Coast, as several of them, both "Indians and whites," were "anxious" to see it.[130] It was an important addition to an emerging collective discourse about colonial disempowerment. Although the Memorial remained out of public view for decades, it retained its relevance and, a century later, resurfaced as a collective testament to the just "demand that the Indian land question be settled."[131] In his seminal book *Making Native Space,* Cole Harris described the Memorial as "one of the most remarkable documents to come out of British Columbia before the First World War."[132]

A guiding contract in the fall of 1910 (the trip that prevented him from attending the Kamloops meeting with Laurier) allowed Teit to extend the geographical reach of his IRA and ITBC campaign northward. At a meeting with the Tahltan at Telegraph Creek at the end of the guiding trip, he outlined the activities that were taking place in the south. In response, the Tahltan asked Teit to help them prepare a declaration of support: "We have read the Declaration made by the chiefs of the southern interior tribes at Spences Bridge on the 16th July last and we hereby join them in the fight for our mutual rights."[133] In a letter to LeJeune, Teit noted the strong show of support that the Tahltan had given him at this meeting:

> When up North hunting I talked with the Indians, and had two meetings with the Tahltan tribe just before leaving with the result that they, and the neighbouring Cascas have joined us in a body. They got me to draw up a Declaration for them and 81 of them signed it including their old chief. They are willing to subscribe money whenever called upon.[134]

Red Land, White Politics

By now, politicians and government officials realized that, between Victoria, Ottawa, and Spences Bridge, they had a battle of the "capitals" on their hands. The IRA, the ITBC, and the Nishga Land Committee now worked in tandem – often using Teit as their liaison. In mid-February 1911, Reverend Charles Tate of Duncan organized a meeting at Spences Bridge to solicit support for a planned meeting with Premier Richard McBride in Victoria.[135] Teit assured him he could round up "a deputation of 16 or more chiefs" to attend the Victoria meeting. In a letter to Boas, he wrote that the movement now had so much momentum that it was starting to feel like a unified "one league" affair.[136]

The Victoria meeting drew close to a hundred representatives from sixty reserve communities for three full days of discussion. The goal was to prepare a series of statements to present to McBride. The delegation broke new ground by appointing twenty-five-year-old Peter Kelly, a member of the Haida delegation, as its spokesperson. A graduate of a Methodist residential school in the Fraser Valley, Kelly was unusual in that he was fluent in English and fully at ease with public speaking. He successfully convinced the group that it was time to replace "missionary pleas for grace and favour" with Indians "speak[ing] their minds."[137] The delegation appointed Teit to translate Kelly's speech and McBride's responses into Chinook Jargon so that the non-English-speaking attendees could understand the proceedings.

In his speech, Kelly stressed that he spoke for "the original inhabitants of this land," who held "title to the unsurrendered lands of the Province, which ha[d] never been extinguished, either by conquest or treaty."[138] It was now time, he argued, to refer the land title case to the courts. With Teit as his translator, Chief John Chilahitsa also made a speech in which he stated: "The Indians say that it is their country and if you claim it they want to go to some big court house and have the matter settled."[139] McBride lashed back with a response that shocked the delegation. He stated that the Indians had "no title to the unsurrendered lands" and that he had no intention of taking "the [land] question to the Courts" as there was "no proper case for submission."[140] He stressed that not only were the majority of Indians around the province "well satisfied with their position" but many of their reserves were larger than they needed to be. He blamed the current agitation on the work of "unscrupulous whites."[141]

The Interior chiefs called a special meeting at Spences Bridge in mid-May to organize a collective response. Sixty-eight chiefs "representing the Shuswap, Couteau or Thompson, Okanagan, Lillooet, Stalo or Lower Fraser, Chilcotin, and Tahltan tribes" turned up for that meeting and, with Teit's help, drafted a Memorial to Frank Oliver, the federal Minister of the Interior and Superintendent General of Indian Affairs:

> What we know and are concerned with is the fact that the British Columbia Government has already taken part of our lands without treaty with us, or payment of any compensation, and has disposed of them to settlers and others. The remaining lands of the country, the Government lays claim to as their property and ignores our title. We ask is this the brotherly help that was promised us in the early days, or is it their compensation to us for the spoilation of our country, stealing of our lands, water, timber, pastures, our game, fish, roots, fruits, etc. and the introduction of diseases, poverty, hard labor, jails, unsuitable laws, whisky, and ever so many other things injurious to us?
>
> If a person takes possession of something belonging to you, surely you know it, and he knows it, and land is a thing that cannot be taken away, and hidden. We see it constantly.[142]

Many felt it was now urgent to send a delegation to Ottawa, especially as they had heard, through the newly formed Friends of the Indians of BC, that they had a sympathetic supporter in the prime minister's office.[143] Laurier had a concrete case in view: the impending grant by the provincial government of Bulkley Valley farmland to Boer War veterans. Acting as a trustee for the Indian title-holders, Laurier hoped to launch a federal government lawsuit against a "randomly selected homesteader" as a way to bypass the federal government's need to gain provincial consent before making such a move.[144] Alas, "democracy" intervened. Laurier called a federal election and lost on September 21 to Sir Robert Borden's Conservatives.[145] With the shift to Borden, a staunch British loyalist and supporter of the campaign for "A White Canada," plans for a "contemplated court action" were soon abandoned.[146]

Despite the loss of Laurier, the Interior chiefs carried on with their planned trip to Ottawa, arriving in the capital city in early January 1912 under the auspices of the Indian Rights Association. Accompanied by Teit and their legal counsel, J.M. Clark, they were granted a brief meeting with Borden on January 8. It did not go well. Clark opened the proceedings with a summary overview of the 1909 Cowichan Petition, noting that the petition had been delivered to England and then promptly referred back to Canada for review. After discussions between Ottawa and Victoria, it had been returned to London with a report "of the facts" as the two governments saw them. Clark explained that the gist of those facts, from the point of view of the "Imperial Government," was that the two governments should try to resolve the land question in Canada. Given that the Justice Department (endorsed by Governor General Dufferin) and "the Indian Department in the old days" had recognized Indian title, "that same law," Clark argued, "applies today, or at any rate it is a question for judicial determination."[147] In the endless self-serving irony that is the "Indian land question," a state without title turned to its people without title to render voiceless those with title but with neither democratic voice nor legal standing.

When Clark finished his statement, Teit stood up and announced that four chiefs – John Chilahitsa (Syilx), John Tetlanetza (Nlaka'pamux), Chief Basil David (Secwépemc), and James Raitasket (St'at'imc) – had prepared speeches for the prime minister. One by one, they explained – in their languages, with Teit translating – what their fathers had negotiated with the traders and reserve commissioners. They stressed that they understood the commissioners to be representatives of the Queen, who promised to protect Indians from white encroachment. Tetlanetza explained that problems arose when the commissioners "set aside reserves for different bands of Indians and families" without consideration of the larger "tribe[s]" of which those families and communities were a part.[148] Another problem was the setting aside of reserves "without proper talks with the chiefs." James Raitasket reiterated this point in his speech: "My father never gave land to the whites," he explained. He "never lost it or gambled it away or gave it away, or ever sold it ... I cannot see how the land belongs to anybody except us."[149] His comment drew a heated response from Borden: "Do you claim all the land without exception – the cities and railways and everything else in British Columbia?" Raitasket charged that: "The whole country has been taken from us without treaty or agreement, and without compensation of any kind, and the cities have come later, and the railways later, and these things have been built on our lands."[150]

At this point, Borden turned to Teit. "You might tell them," he explained, "that I am a new chief and that I have not seen any word from the Queen or from the King about these matters ... that men have come to see us as numerous as the leaves that fall from the trees in autumn, and that documents are coming in as fast as snowflakes are falling outside today."[151] He then bid the delegation "a safe journey to their homes and family" and promised to read their documents and send a response to Clark. Clark seized the last word. He explained to the chiefs that the prime minister had "made the greatest sacrifice a white man can make; that is, to do without ... lunch, to hear them."[152] Thus ended the meeting, and the disappointed chiefs returned to British Columbia.

Two months later, with no word from Borden, the ITBC organized a meeting at the Kamloops Indian reserve with sixty representatives of groups from across the province to plan their next move. According to the Kamloops Indian agent, John Freemont Smith, it was a "monster meeting of Indians."[153] The meeting culminated with a strongly worded letter to Borden, demanding a response to their Ottawa visit:

> We sent chiefs to Ottawa last winter so they should petition you in person, and place our statements regarding our claims in your own hands, so you might read them and understand our position thoroughly. You promised us an answer through our counsel as to what you were prepared to do in the matter, but we have heard nothing yet. In all respect, we press for a speedy answer ... If you have no power, nor influence, with the British Columbia Government to accomplish a settlement, we want to know ... We want to stand on our feet. We were never made for slaves. We cannot lie down and be ridden over. We demand our rights, and we expect your help.[154]

It was a frustrating time for Teit and his colleagues, Arthur O'Meara and Charles Tate, as the Vancouver and Victoria newspapers had seized on McBride's claim that the Indian problem was the work of outsiders. An article in the *Victoria Colonist* charged that "Indian title" had "never

This undated photograph could well have been taken at the "monster" political meeting at the Kamloops Indian reserve in March 1912. Seated from left to right are Chief Basil David of the Bonaparte reserve (Secwépemc), Reverend Charles M. Tate, and James A. Teit. Chief John Chilahitsa is the man with wire-rimmed glasses and a dark fur coat, with a large stetson in his hand. | Photograph courtesy of Sigurd Teit.

entered the minds of the Indians until it was suggested to them by officious white people."[155] An article in the *Vancouver Province* depicted Indians as childlike "roaming savages" who never really "possessed settled places of abode for any great length of time and never regarded the soil as of any value."[156]

Dirty Politics

In May, Borden finally broke his silence and appointed Dr. James A.J. McKenna, a long-standing Indian Department bureaucrat, to negotiate an agreement on his behalf with Premier Richard McBride that would resolve the Indian land problem once and for all. McKenna was the ideal candidate for the DIA job. A native of Prince Edward Island, he had served (in 1887) as the private secretary to the then Superintendent General of the Department of Indian Affairs, Sir John A. Macdonald. After a short break to study law, McKenna returned to the DIA, where in 1897 he helped negotiate a settlement with the BC government on the administration of the Railway Belt and the Peace River Block. He then assisted with the negotiation of Treaty No. 8 in northern British Columbia and the District of Athabasca in 1899. In 1901, he moved to Winnipeg to work as the Indian commissioner and chief inspector of agencies for Manitoba and the North-West Territories. According to E. Brian Titley, McKenna was "a staunch champion of his department's repressive policies, supporting residential schooling and the harsh measures taken against traditional dances and Indian appearances at exhibitions."[157]

McKenna moved his family to Victoria in order to have easy access to the premier's office and reserve communities across the province.[158] On August 1, he attended a meeting of 450 chiefs (yet again at Spences Bridge), where he faced a series of heated questions about how the federal and provincial governments planned to resolve the land-title question.[159] It was at this meeting that he met James Teit, the notorious Spences Bridge "trouble-maker."[160] According to Teit, McKenna had arrived at the meeting convinced that outsiders were the source of the Indian problem. He recalled that McKenna's first question of him was to this effect: "Is not this trouble of recent origin, and has it not been stirred up by Whites?"[161]

McKenna's response to the assembled chiefs came on September 24 by way of a joint announcement by Prime Minister Borden and Premier McBride that the two governments had reached an agreement on how to "settle all differences between the Governments of the Dominion and the Province respecting Indian lands and Indian Affairs." They called for a royal commission consisting of a panel of federal and provincial representatives to examine existing reserves with the view of adjusting – with Indian consent – their size.[162] In fact, the commission was not charged with "settling" any of the issues on the Indian side. It was yet another duplicitous delay tactic and a power play on the parts of both governments to accommodate Premier McBride's refusal to deal with the land-title issue. As the key negotiator who helped formulate the deal, McKenna betrayed the Indian cause with a response that was fully in keeping with McBride's position that Indian title "'to practically the whole of the Province' could not be recognized." McBride, as historian Patricia Roy writes, feared that "to look seriously upon the claim of the Indians would mean a revolution in our economic conditions that would be very disastrous indeed."[163] The commission excluded Indian representation completely and insisted instead on a committee composed only of representatives of the two governments. It also insisted on an agenda that adhered to a strict list of pre-set questions. There was to be no mention of title.

News of the McKenna-McBride Royal Commission raced across the provincial landscape like a wildfire. As the chiefs prepared their strategies to challenge it, DIA officials devised strategies to push it forward. Their first line of attack was to shut down the "white advocates." The provincial government hired the Seattle-based Pinkerton Detective Agency to monitor Arthur O'Meara,[164] and the federal government used its DIA channels to monitor Teit. Agent Scott Simpson of Telegraph Creek accused Teit of causing "mischief in [his] quarter" by using his position as Secretary of the Indian Rights Association to encourage the Tahltans not to cooperate with any commissioners "unless advised to do so by the Indian Rights Association." He noted that $250 had been paid out of the general funds as "Lawyers Fees."[165] Simpson also expressed concern that Teit was "coming in this summer" under "the pretext of gathering scientific data, and will no doubt place every obstacle in the way of the Commissioners for a speedy settlement of the land question."[166] He warned McKenna against using Teit as a translator: "It goes without saying that a man of his stamp is not to be depended upon to interpret, seeing that he is directly interested in this society who are working against the interests of the Government ... I considered it my duty to place this evidence in your hands without delay."[167]

T.J. Cummiskey, Inspector of Indian Agencies at Vernon, was so infuriated by the actions of so-called white agitators that he wrote to J.D. McLean, Assistant Deputy Secretary of Indian Agencies in Ottawa, with the prescient suggestion that fundraising on behalf of the Indian protest be made a criminal offence:

> The Indian mind and character, is such that they have a desire for meetings and pow-wows, therefore they are easily gathered together ... If it were a criminal offence for any white man, half breed or Indian to collect funds of any description from Indians individually or collectively without the consent of the Indian Department, it would have a salutary effect on the whole Indian question. I know white men who live practically by this method. I presume if these leaders in the so-called Indian Right's Association, were dealt with under section 109 of the Criminal Code, they would proclaim themselves martyrs ... Something should be done to prevent such gatherings of the Indians ... Many of the chiefs are losing respect for the law which they formerly held. I meet strong indications of this in my travels and I think it is my duty to inform the Department.[168]

Cummiskey knew very well that the public sector would welcome such a move. According to legal historian Hamar Foster, Section 109 of the

Criminal Code worked in his favour as "it made it a crime to incite or 'stir up' any three or more Indians or 'half-breeds' to riotous or disorderly behaviour." Indeed, "it was even enough," Foster explains, "simply to incite them to make any request or demand of government in a disorderly way." Section 109 dated from before Confederation and it was not repealed until 1954.[169] Indeed, prominent writers like John B. Thornhill and others were promoting similar ideas in their books on British Columbia. With Arthur O'Meara and Charles Tate in view, Thornhill noted in his 1913 *British Columbia in the Making* that "there is a real scoundrelly class of missionaries engaged in inventing Indians grievances, and bringing them before the dominion's Parliament."[170]

Teit charged through these accusations undeterred.

8
The Indians' Agent

The attitude of the Indian Department is now that the Indians have no rights ... If no better arguments against the claims of the Indians [on their land-title case] can be produced than those lately put forward by the Dep. Sup. General of Indian Affairs ... then it seems the Indians should have a pretty good chance of success.

– James Teit to Walter Baer, Secretary to BC premier John Oliver, April 28, 1920

The Indian land question in British Columbia took a sinister turn in 1913 with the appointment of Duncan Campbell Scott to the position of Deputy Superintendent General of Indian Affairs. A steely administrator with a "shrewd and supple political sense" and a "meticulous and exacting" work record that spanned three decades, Scott was a perfect fit for the job.[1] He had started in the Department of Indian Affairs (DIA) at age seventeen with a political patronage appointment awarded to his clergyman father by Sir John A. Macdonald for work on the latter's election campaign. He then climbed steadily up the DIA bureaucracy – from a copy clerk to chief clerk in charge of all DIA expenditures, to commissioner for the James Bay Treaty 9 negotiations, to Superintendent of Education, and finally to the top job (a deputy minister, in today's terms).[2]

As a staunch British imperialist, Scott saw assimilation as the answer to the Indian "problem." The "happiest future" for the Indian, he wrote in 1914, is "absorption into the general population." Only through "the great forces of intermarriage and education" "will [we] finally overcome the lingering traces of native custom and tradition."[3] In his previous position as Superintendent of Education, he had pushed for mandatory schooling – ideally residential schooling – for all Indian children. "Without education and with neglect," he wrote, "the Indians would produce an undesirable and often a dangerous element in society."[4] To inculcate a strong sense of Canadian heritage rooted in old world (i.e., colonial) values, he advocated for a national curriculum grounded in the "great deeds" and "heroic sufferings" of the nation's founders.[5] He had little time for his wards' perspectives on heritage or their continuing place in Canada's unfolding history. Like their old hunting, trapping, and fishing way of life, these were remnants of the old life that interfered with their much-needed transition to a new and better life in farming and wage work.

This was but one side of Scott's life. At the end of his workday, the iron-fisted bureaucrat and architect of one of the most aggressive assimilationist campaigns in Canadian history retreated into his other life: that of the erudite writer, musician, and art connoisseur. In addition to serving on the boards of Ottawa's theatre and symphony societies and contributing to the city's literary guilds and arts collectives, he and his wife, Belle, a concert violinist, hosted musical and literary soirees in the music room of their grand Lisgar Street residence. The music room was Scott's pride and joy. In addition to his piano and musical scores, it housed his Indian artifacts, his books, and his oil paintings, watercolours, and prints by prominent Canadian artists such as Emily Carr, Lawren Harris, Walter J. Phillips, Clarence Gagnon, and others.[6] According to one visitor, the feeling in the room was of a "display" that "Scott had prepared for others to see."[7]

Scott's music room doubled as his writing studio. By 1916, he had four books of poetry, a biography, and a novel to his name.[8] His poetry's focus on Canadian themes in the early post-confederation period earned him a place in the literary group known today as "confederation poets." Nineteen thirteen was a banner year for Scott as, in addition to his DIA appointment, two prominent British literary figures, Rupert Brooke and John Masefield, singled him out as Canada's "only poet."[9] Scott relished such praise from abroad because in his own country, as hard as he tried for recognition as a "grand old man of letters," he never fully achieved it.[10] Canada's academic elite were more generous, electing Scott in 1899 to the Royal Society of Canada and awarding him in 1920 a University of Toronto honorary degree. He wore the degree with pride, insisting thereafter on being addressed as "Dr. Scott."

As a top civil service bureaucrat and a core member of Ottawa's arts community, Scott seemed the embodiment of high social standing. In fact, he was the opposite. A "gentleman" bureaucrat known for his "old-fashioned spectacles" and baggy dress suits, he had difficulty navigating his way through most social situations. On meeting him for the first time, Madge MacBeth, an Ottawa writer, noted his "aloof" and "forbidding" manner. By "his own admission," writes his biographer, Brian Titley, Scott "was reticent and difficult to communicate with on any degree of intimacy."[11] His "remoteness," according to writer Sandra Gwyn, was partly the result of a "disconnected and chilly childhood."[12] He was "a child of the manse," she writes, who was raised by a strict Methodist minister father and a humourless Scottish mother. Because the family moved frequently, Scott formed few close childhood friendships. He dreamt of following in the footsteps of his uncle, a successful Montreal physician, but had to abandon the idea because his parents could not afford to send him to medical school.[13]

Given Scott's social reticence, it is surprising that he performed as well as he did in his DIA job. As Deputy Superintendent General of Indian Affairs, he was the administrative anchor of the department as well as its chief policy-maker. With an "inside service" team of 76 employees based in Ottawa,[14] and an "outside service" team of 651 employees scattered across the country, his day-to-day responsibilities required continuous hours of intense social interaction. He was accountable to the federal Minister of the Interior, who held the title of Superintendent of Indian Affairs, though this was in name only. Most superintendents general relied on their deputies to run Indian Affairs.[15] With eight ministerial changes between 1913 and 1932, there was little consistency in the minister's office. As historians Douglas Cole and Ira Chaikin explain, in an area "where few cared very deeply, an entrenched bureaucrat had the liberty to do as he pleased. Indian Affairs concerned few people, most of whom were not even voters."[16]

To help him through his workweek, Scott imported some of his artistic life into his bureaucratic life. He installed a piano with a built-in silencer in a corner of his Booth Building office so he could practise during his breaks,[17] and he mined his DIA case files for inspiration for his poetry. "The surprise, or paradox, or twist of the knife," notes Montreal poet Mark Abley, in a recent book on Scott, "is that while doing his utmost to enforce government control over indigenous people, Scott made them the subject of his most vibrant writing."[18] Literary critic Lisa Salem-Wiseman argues that although his Indian poems expressed a certain sympathy for the difficulties Indians faced, they also supported his assimilationist policies. His poetic subjects, she writes, were the fearful bearers of racial memories and pagan religions. Many were also psychologically and socially damaged peoples who were ultimately doomed to disappear. Scott never portrayed them as his social equals.[19] Literary critic Stan Dragland, who surveyed the full sweep of Scott's Indian poems, notes their lack of social connection: "I have found that the only true recorded meeting of the whole man with individual Natives takes place *in* those poems ... So much of his life was lived without reference to Native people."[20]

Petitions and Agitators

In his new role as head of Indian Affairs, Scott tightened the reins. He sent circulars to Indian agents across the country, demanding more stringent policing on reserves, heftier fines and longer prison sentences for possession of liquor and for holding potlatches, more rigorous investigations into criminal activity, and increased surveillance of Indian schools and agricultural projects.[21]

With the Royal Commission on Indian Affairs (the "McKenna-McBride Commission") underway in British Columbia, Scott faced a steady stream of petitions and protest letters.[22] Knowing that neither the federal government nor the provincial government had any intention of settling the Indian land question in favour of the Indians regardless of earlier promises and precedents, he held firm to the long-established government refusal to discuss it, dismissing all political agitation on the Indian side as the work of "white agitators" who had stirred up otherwise contented Indians.[23] It was a well-worn state tactic that reinforced the popular racist stereotype of Indians as incapable of speaking for themselves.

Meanwhile, Scott's department monitored "agitators" in British Columbia closely. By 1913, it had a large dossier on James Teit. In addition to newspaper reports of gatherings of "Indians ... from all over B.C.," at which a certain "James Teit" was seen "acquaint[ing] them with the government's policy in regard to their land titles," were letters from Scott's British Columbia agents describing Teit's covert movements and activities.[24] T.J. Cummiskey, Inspector of Indian Agencies at Vernon, contacted J.D. McLean, Scott's DIA secretary in Ottawa on November 30, 1912, to complain about meetings at Spences Bridge and Kamloops at which Teit was seen inciting Indians to civil disobedience by removing surveyors' stakes in and around reserves.[25] Cummiskey urged his superiors to find ways to block Teit from entering reserves in his agency.[26] Cummiskey also complained about cards that Teit had distributed to chiefs about an upcoming political meeting in Vancouver. Teit and his activist colleagues, he charged, were clearly living off the proceeds they were collecting from the Indians in the name of such political work. He urged DIA to devise a way to criminalize such activity.[27] Thomas Deasy of the Queen Charlotte agency sent a report to Scott about a meeting that Teit had called with the Haida at which he was seen promoting the agenda of the Indian Rights Association.[28] Scott Simpson of the Stikine agency at Telegraph Creek wrote repeatedly about suspicious meetings and fundraising activities that Teit had organized with the Tahltan.[29] Simpson was concerned that Teit was also using these meetings to urge the Tahltan to "strike" for higher wages from their hunting clients. He had heard from a local outfitter, J.F. Callbreath, that Teit had caused friction in the guiding community by paying his Tahltan crew higher wages than those of other guides.[30]

Such reports often included references to Arthur O'Meara, the legal counsel to the Nisga'a, who was working with Toronto lawyer J.M. Clark to find ways to make a direct appeal to the British Judicial Committee of the Privy Council (JCPC).[31] The two lawyers drafted a petition (modelled loosely on the 1909 Cowichan Petition) that dismissed all provincial land transactions in Nisga'a territory as a violation of the principles set out in the Royal Proclamation of 1763.[32] In May 1913, O'Meara carried the Nisga'a Petition to London, hoping to have it referred to the JCPC. On his return to Canada, O'Meara learned that the JCPC would not consider the Nishga Petition while a royal commission was in progress in Canada.[33] According to Hamar Foster, Ottawa had informed the imperial Privy Council that Indian title was within the mandate of the royal commission when in fact it wasn't, as the BC chiefs learned when they raised it before the royal commission in 1912.

The Nishga Petition was one of the first issues that Scott faced as the new DIA head. Angered by its premises, he recommended that it be submitted to the Exchequer Court of Canada, with the right of appeal to the JCPC, subject to the following conditions: that the petitioners accept a government-appointed lawyer to represent them; that, should their case succeed, they agree to surrender title in return for the customary benefits accorded by the Crown; that they agree to accept, in advance of the release of the McKenna-McBride Commission's final report, any changes to their reserves that the royal commission might propose; that BC's granting of the royal commission reserves (an acknowledgment that, as Hamar Foster points out, "was now nearly 45 years overdue") was to be regarded as having completely satisfied any and all claims the Indians had against the province; and that, if they lost their court case, federal policy was all that mattered and it would "be governed by consideration of [the Indians of BC's] interests and future development."[34] Scott presented the memorandum to his superior, William J. Roche, Minister of the Interior and Superintendent General of Indian Affairs, on March 11, 1914. Roche took it to cabinet, where it was discussed, signed, and released as Order-in-Council PC 751.[35]

News of PC 751's subject clauses, especially the clause that required acceptance of the McKenna-McBride report prior to its release, infuriated chiefs across British Columbia. The Nisga'a called an emergency meeting at Kincolith in December, where they decided to send O'Meara and two chiefs to Ottawa to contest PC 751. They sent two of their members to an Interior Tribes of British Columbia (ITBC) meeting at Spences Bridge to solicit the support of their southern colleagues.[36] The Spences Bridge meeting ended with a written endorsement of the Nishga Petition as a test case for the ITBC rights to their ancestral lands.[37]

Word of these meetings quickly filtered back to Ottawa. A.M. Megraw, Inspector of Indian Agencies for Southeastern British Columbia, notified Scott from Vernon that the "O'Meara-Teit propaganda" was "instill[ing] into many Indians an unreasoning notion that they must negat[e] any and all proposals put up to them by the whites for taking over any of their lands."[38] He noted that Teit had gathered all the Chiefs and Council-men "for no purpose ... but to listen to a few misguided fanatics from the Nass, who were coming there to harangue them and embitter them against the Whites and against the Department." The frequency of these meetings, he explained, had "reached the limit" and "should not be ignored any longer."[39] He expressed concern that the funds that were being raised at these meetings had prevented his Indian charges from settling up outstanding debts to storekeepers. Such agitation, he wrote, was a fast-spreading virus for which Spences Bridge served as the host:

> Any grievance which the Indians of Nass may have should not interest those in this part of the Province, and if Mr. Teit wants to hear them he should go to Naas [sic] at his own expense instead of calling all the Indians to him at Spence's Bridge where he lives ... There is no learning what is said or done at these meetings, but the remarks and attitude of Mr. Teit to Indian Agent, Graham [of Lytton], is ample evidence that the result accomplished is that of sowing discontent among the Indians, and still further impoverishing them.[40]

Agent H. Graham of Lytton issued a similar report:

> I cannot see what right a man like Teit has to send out notices to Indians calling them to Spence's Bridge, and all it does is to excite and make them discontented, and besides, these Indians cannot afford to travel the long distances and live at the Hotel for three days; then some of the old ones will

> be getting Government assistance for food ... I always find that there is a great deal of discontent after these meetings, and they take a long time to settle down again, all sorts of hopes, etc. are put into their heads, which one cannot drive out.[41]

Some of the local missionaries joined in this chorus. Father Lambot, an Oblate priest based at Cranbrook, contacted Scott's secretary, John McLean, about a political meeting called by Teit that had stirred up local Indians who otherwise, he said, would have "a great confidence in the Government at Ottawa."[42]

The Potlatch Ban

In the middle of these heated letter exchanges, Teit's name surfaced in a new context: the potlatch debates. A ceremonial feast marking births, weddings, funerals, and other rites of passage, the potlatch was central to the peoples of the Pacific Northwest, especially those along the Coast. Sir John A. Macdonald's government had passed legislation in 1885 outlawing the potlatch, but Scott's predecessor, Frank Pedley, had largely ignored it.[43] Scott, on the other hand, decided to activate the law on grounds that the potlatch was "an abominable and wasteful aboriginal custom" that blocked his department's reformist, assimilationist policy. Encouraged by several of his West Coast agents and associates, he informed his agents in May 1913 that "should evidence appear conclusive," he would commit "ringleaders for trial."[44]

Through his colleague, Edward Sapir, Teit found a way to challenge Scott's autocratic stand on the potlatch. As the head of the federal government's Anthropology Division, Sapir had heard details of Scott's draconian measures on reserves across the country. A five-month research trip to Port Alberni in Nuu-chah-nulth territory on Vancouver Island in 1913–14 gave him a first-hand look at these measures when he witnessed the slow, painful death of a five-year-old child of one of his close Nuu-chah-nulth contacts. The family had appealed to the local doctor for help, but the doctor was so slow in responding that the child died before he arrived. Sapir knew the death could have been prevented with an earlier medical response. Concerned about the disparity between healthcare delivery to Indians and that provided to the settler population, he appealed to Scott in mid-March to rectify the situation.[45] The archival record is silent on Scott's response.

Edward Sapir in New Haven, Connecticut, c. 1936. | Photograph #2006-00012, courtesy of the Canadian Museum of History.

When Sapir's Nuu-chah-nulth consultants pressed him on another issue – the potlatch ban – Sapir devised a more aggressive plan to extract a response from Scott. He invited a group of scholars knowledgeable about the potlatch – Franz Boas, Harlan Smith, and John Swanton, as well as Teit, Charles Newcombe, and Charles Hill-Tout – to take part in a petition to Scott. In his cover letter, Sapir explained: "When I was out in Alberni the Indians were very much disturbed at the renewed vigor with which the old more or less dead letter potlatch law was being applied ... I have no doubt that a systematic presentation of our point of view ... would do much to assist the Indian[s]."[46] Sapir sent the petition to Scott on March 1, 1915.[47] As a seasoned petitioner, Teit knew what Sapir might face from his government superiors for such an action. To help him through it, he sent Sapir reassuring notes: "I do not think being Gov. employees will matter ... We are not mixing in politics or taking sides openly with any political party. The potlatch as whether it should be or should not be is altogether a non-political question."[48]

The resounding endorsement of the potlatch by prominent members of the international anthropological community sent a powerful message to Ottawa. It had a "sobering" effect on Scott.[49] On receiving the petition, Scott notified William Roche, Minister of the Interior and Superintendent General of Indian Affairs, that the campaign to abolish the potlatch needed to be handled carefully as the Indians were "very loath to give up" a practice so deeply ingrained in their social system, and that suppression would require "some diplomacy."[50] The courts apparently agreed, as judges at the time were handing down suspensions and dismissals rather than convictions and penalties.[51]

Teit's letter was a mainstay of the petition. In contrast to his colleagues' single-page statements, Teit submitted a twelve-page, point-by-point analysis that dismantled Scott's argument for the ban.[52] Teit spared no words, describing the ban as "unwarranted and foolish" and rooted in "prejudice, ignorance, misunderstanding, [and] ... selfishness." The idea of the potlatch as impoverishing individuals and families and encouraging dependence on government subsidies was totally "false," he wrote, because "[n]o one gives either all or most of his wealth away at a potlatch." Should a person choose to do this, he would be considered a "fool" or "crazy." He would also be declared a public "disgrace" for feigning wealth when he had none. "Pretence of this kind and hypocrisy" is a quality that "the Indians scorn." They "are remarkably free of these vices." He wrote that he had "never kn[own] of a case where an Indian crippled himself so he could not carry on his usual avocations." Teit added that he had attended many potlatches, and not once had he seen people distribute items of utilitarian value such as farming tools, harnesses, teams, hay, and seed. Moreover, it was "rubbish," he wrote, to link potlatches to "laziness and improvidence," as organizing a potlatch required hard work and "thrift." To the charge that the potlatch encouraged "immorality and drunkenness ... [and hence] a menace to the safety (and lives and property) of the whites," Teit noted that, in his experience, "disturbances" associated with potlatching in the south central Interior were "exceedingly rare" and certainly "rarer than ... at gatherings of whites." To cast such affairs as a threat to whites was "an echo harked down from early days when the Whites were in fear of the Indians." The potlatch was an integral "part of the Indian organism." If "violently disrupted or suddenly removed," it would have a "detrimental" effect on the whole organism. Teit took direct aim at Scott with one of his points:

> I believe it is inflicting a serious injury and injustice on the Indians, for the Government or anyone else (however well intentioned) to try and abolish ruthlessly or uproot the potlatch or anything else which is a part of the old social organization of the Indians. It is a serious matter to destroy suddenly and by force the social, economic, and other institutions of a people. You are aiming a blow at their life, and if the blow is effective, it means their demoralization. Any white race powerful enough would fight to the bitter end against this.[53]

Nevertheless, behind the scenes, Scott carried on, mounting a new and more aggressive initiative that included a proposal to amend the Indian Act to give his Indian agents the power to act as prosecutors and judges.[54] He also found a way to circumvent Sapir by approaching Marius Barbeau – Sapir's employee and the one anthropologist who had not signed the petition – with a request for an independent opinion on the potlatch. According to historians Douglas Cole and Ira Chaikin, Barbeau's report added little to the controversy as it incorporated no interviews with Indians, made no concrete recommendations, and included no feedback from either the Indians or their counsel.[55]

A Plan for Teit

With reports of Teit's covert activities flowing in from agents across the province, James McKenna decided that it was time to deal directly with the infamous Spences Bridge "agitator." A letter from Chief John Tetlanetza to the royal commission gave him an idea. Drafted by Teit, it had requested a meeting with the commissioners to discuss the terms of Order-in-Council PC 751.[56] Tetlanetza had attached a "draft resolution" from the Indian Rights Association's lawyer, J. Edward Bird, that outlined the terms by which Scott's contentious order-in-council might "be acquiesced with" so as to move "the question of title ... to the courts without delay." The resolution reiterated the chiefs' refusal to accept the clause requiring them to agree to the royal commission's report prior to its release.

McKenna's secretary had read the letter and turned down Tetlanetza's request for a meeting with the royal commission on grounds that the commissioners were not authorized to comment on the order-in-council.[57]

McKenna read the letter, however, and forwarded it to Scott with a new plan, co-option:

> There is some prejudice against Mr. Teit. He may have views in respect to Indians in which all interested in the Indians would not agree [but] I have thought since I first knew him that it would be wise to make of him a friend than an enemy ... Shortly after arriving from Scotland to serve under his late uncle, who was an Indian trader, he took to mingling with the Indians of the country with whom his uncle's chief trading was carried on. He not only thoroughly mastered the language, but entered into the minds of the people, from among whom he took a wife, who died some years ago. His sympathies with and interest in her tribe grew and extended to other tribes. His view-point on the Title question pretty well, I think, accords with the Indian view-point. But his larger range of vision and experience bring into play alongside the Indian view-point the consideration of practicality. I don't believe that he would urge the Indians to refuse attainable good for problematic benefit.[58]

Five days later, Scott informed McKenna that although he disagreed with the attached resolution's "prohibitive" request for large land allotments and special reserves for hunting and trapping, he would try to "establish friendly relations with Mr. Teit." He assured him that "good results" would follow.[59]

Scott then sat down and penned a letter to Teit. "We have only one thought here," he wrote, and "that is to treat the Indians fairly, and I think when all the reasons of the terms set forth in the Order in Council are fully understood, there will be less objection to them." Moreover, "I thought it well to say at once that we had no intention of pressing the proposed agreement on the Indians until the findings of the Royal Commission are known."[60] With this comment, the author of the contentious order-in-council refuted, in writing, the very subject clause that Teit and the chiefs had spent two years contesting.

Teit took two weeks to respond to Scott. After thanking him for "clearing up th[e] point" about having to accept the findings of the royal commission prior to the release of its report, he wrote that "the great question now" was "whether the findings of the Royal Com. (as to land, etc) will be satisfactory to the Inds. or not."[61] As if to hold Scott to his word, Teit stressed that what he now wanted was "to see the Dom. Gov. go on record for its noble and liberal dealing with these poor people in the whole matter of the settlement of their rights." He asked Scott to review the attached resolution carefully, as he (Teit) had called a meeting of all the Interior chiefs on March 15 to discuss the details with them in open council and was certain they would approve it.[62] It was Teit's not-too-subtle warning that, should Scott act against the resolution, he could expect trouble from the chiefs, who were now a strong and unified voice.

Believing that he had snared Teit, Scott now set his sights on snaring Arthur O'Meara. He had met O'Meara briefly in Ottawa in February 1915, when the Anglican clergyman had turned up with two Nisga'a chiefs to protest the terms of his order-in-council, and he was unimpressed.[63] Unlike Teit, O'Meara was a prickly character who was "persistent to the point of stubbornness."[64] Because O'Meara was a valued member of the Nisga'a delegation, however, Scott knew it would be unwise to challenge him in this public setting. In their speeches, the Nisga'a had praised O'Meara for his work on their behalf. They had even suggested that Scott should cover O'Meara's legal costs. In his own speech, O'Meara made reference to his colleague "James Teit" as "one of the best friends of the Indians of British Columbia." He stressed that "probably no other man to be found in the province has a better knowledge of their mind, or is better able to advise them well. In common with myself, he has set before him as the object to be aimed at, an equitable solution of the land question."[65] O'Meara's reference to Teit clearly irked Scott, because immediately after the meeting he sent a letter to McKenna, proposing that they "endeavor to separate O'Meara from Teit in order that the former may have no influence on this large body of Indians." He wrote: "Everybody of influence here is gradually losing confidence in O'Meara ... I believe he is spreading the idea that I am in the pale of the British Columbia Government, which is just one of his stupid ideas."[66]

Separating Teit from O'Meara was not an easy undertaking in 1916, however. The two men were close political allies and shrewd strategists, and both were savvy to Scott's political gamesmanship. Although the restrained and soft-spoken Teit looked, on the surface, like an easy target of manipulation, underneath he was as feisty as O'Meara. Just as Scott had designs on Teit and O'Meara, Teit and O'Meara had designs on Scott. After years of trying – in vain – to gain access to Prime Minister Robert Borden and William Roche, his Minister of the Interior and Superintendent General of Indian Affairs, they finally had the attention of the top bureaucrat in the DIA.[67]

Teit's approach was to feign friendship as a way to extract favours. Given his disdain for government officials, it was not an easy role to play. "You know (as I have told you before)," Teit wrote to a close colleague in February

1915, "I do not have much faith in governments for I know exactly what they are. They are not for the people nor for the good of the people, their advancement, the advancement of science and truth, etc. They are more executives of the capitalist class of their respective countries and represent capitalist interests entirely."[68]

Two months later, on April 29, 1916, Teit and Scott met face to face for the first time. Teit was in Ottawa with O'Meara and members of the ITBC and Nishga Land Committee (NLC). Their goal was to press the federal government to delay the implementation of the royal commission report until the Nishga Petition was settled by the JCPC.[69] It was a busy week in Ottawa. In addition to meetings with Scott, the group organized meetings with Sir Wilfrid Laurier (leader of the Opposition), William Roche (Superintendent General of DIA), and Prime Minister Borden. It was an expensive trip. Teit later informed Scott that he had contributed $500 of his own money (equivalent to $11,000 in 2018) to help cover the delegation's trip costs and hotel expenses.[70] In a letter to Boas, he explained the significance of the trip and its impact on his ethnographic assignments:

> I went to Ottawa with a delegation of Indian chiefs from the Lillooet, Shuswap, Thompson, Okanagon & Kutenai and remained there much longer than I expected. This helping the Indians with their land question ... puts me behind in my ethnological work. Besides it is a loss to me as the Indians cannot afford to pay me excepting bare expenses when I take a trip with them and not even that for all the writing I do for them. However, it is hard to get out of it as there is no one else to help the Indians that they have confidence in, so I suppose I will have to remain losing my time until such time as the question between the Governments and the Indians is settled.[71]

Around and Around

Teit had just returned to Spences Bridge when he was summoned to Vancouver to help resolve a crisis that had erupted within the ranks of the Indian Rights Association (IRA). Its legal counsel, J.M. Clark, had suddenly split from O'Meara and unilaterally informed the Superintendent General of Indian Affairs, William Roche, that the members of the IRA were prepared to accept the terms of the contentious order-in-council.[72] Members of the ITBC, IRA, and NLC deliberated for four days on how to respond to what they saw as a breach of trust – they had *not* agreed to

Edward Sapir took this photograph of Teit and eight Interior chiefs outside the Victoria Memorial Museum in Ottawa in 1916. Back row, from left to right: Eli Larue, John Tetlanetza, James Teit, Thomas Adolph, and William Pascal. Front row, from left to right: James Raitasket, John Chilahitsa, Paul David, and Basil David. | Photograph by Edward Sapir, #36002, courtesy of the Canadian Museum of History.

this. In the end, they fired Clark and founded a new organization, the Allied Indian Tribes of British Columbia (ATBC). They elected Peter Kelly as chair and Teit as secretary of its executive committee. They appointed John Tetlanetza and three chiefs – Charles Barton (Nisga'a), Dennis Peter (Stó:lō), and William Nahinee (Squamish) – to its executive,[73] and retained O'Meara as chief counsel. The newly formed ATBC rallied behind the Nishga Petition as "a test case for the land claims of all the tribes," and denounced the work of the royal commission, demanding reserves of 160 acres per capita, as well as recognition of Aboriginal title and full compensation for alienated lands.[74]

To prevent news of an IRA breakdown from filtering back to Scott, Teit quickly drafted a letter to the Deputy Superintendent General in which he described the Vancouver "conference" as a major success: "Although there was a good deal of dissent on a number of small points, the delegates were, on the whole, unified on the issue of submitting their case to the courts."[75] He wrote that the Interior Indians might be willing "to accept an out of court settlement if a satisfactory one can be found ... The statement makes it clear the Indians intend to press on but actually I believe they will have to wait until the Gov. places the findings of the Royal Commission before them."[76] Teit explained that letters had been sent "to all the tribes in the province," and, on receipt of their responses, he would inform Scott of the results. His goal was to convey to the DIA head that Clark's indiscretion had strengthened, rather than weakened, the Indigenous leadership. He added that the ATBC was drafting new proposals that would "be suitable to the Gov. and to most of the Indians – a compromise as it were between the Gov. proposals and the Ind. proposals." He withheld details of the compromise.[77]

It was a good thing that Teit withheld details from Scott because Scott, at the time, was withholding a major detail from Teit. The royal commission had completed its report and delivered it to Scott, but Scott was keeping the report an in-house secret while he tried to secure the support of the provincial and federal governments.[78] The problem was that as hard as he tried, Scott could not convince the two governments to agree to his accord. The impasse was partly due to a change in the premier's office. Richard McBride had retired in December 1915, and his replacement, William John Bowser, had little interest in the report. Like all government leaders across the country, he was fully preoccupied with the war in Europe.

These were difficult times for the chiefs because they were now desperate for news of the commission's final report (Scott would hold them in suspense until March 1919).[79] In August 1916, the Interior chiefs asked Teit to contact Scott on their behalf for an update on the status of the report. In his letter, Teit warned of trouble at his end should the report contain bad news: he stressed that the communities around him were actively raising funds to cover the cost of protest trips to Ottawa if necessary.[80] He noted that some of the chiefs had asked that "a special official [be appointed to] ... bring [the report] around" to them. "They do not wish the [Indian] agents to place it before them."[81]

Teit used the lull in ITBC and ATBC protest activity to tackle a string of complaints at the local level. Most were complaints that were normally handled by Indian agents. In August, he wrote to Scott on behalf of Chief Jean Baptiste, who asked for compensation for a railroad right-of-way through his Cayuse Creek reserve.[82] Later, Teit wrote on behalf of a Cooks Ferry Band member who asked for compensation for his cattle killed on the CNR tracks.[83] He also wrote on behalf of Duncan McPhail, a physician based at Lillooet, who described "ghastly" medical conditions on the reserves to which he was assigned. McPhail wanted Scott to "come out here and take a look round ... to see matters for himself."[84] "It is a case ... of whites first and Indians afterwards."[85] Teit also used this interlude to present some of his own complaints to Scott: for example, the need for a more reliable system of recording chiefs' signatures to protect them from others signing x's for them without their knowledge. "It would be a good thing if the chiefs who cannot write used thumb prints in signing of papers, petitions, tc."[86] Meanwhile, Teit continued to push Scott for news of the final report. Scott's response was always the same: that there was "nothing very new in the British Columbia Indian question."[87]

A provincial election offered the first hint of promise. Bowser had called the election in July 1916 and lost in September to Harlan Brewster's Liberals. According to reports about Brewster, it seemed that, unlike Bowser, he might be open to discussing the land question. Teit and O'Meara travelled to Victoria in May 1917 to test the waters. In a meeting with Brewster, they learned that "his government might consider the question of Indian title in British Columbia before dealing with the report of the Royal Commission on Indian Affairs."[88] Finally, it looked like they might have an ally in the premier's office.

Military Conscription

The euphoria over the Brewster meeting was soon eclipsed by another problem. In mid-July 1917, Prime Minister Borden announced the Military Service Act, requiring all bachelors and childless widowers, aged twenty to thirty-four, to report for duty by November 17. The act was his government's attempt to augment a depleted volunteer military corps in Europe. It placed Scott in an awkward situation because he had failed to provide input on the status of Indians in the act. Faced with arguments that Indians should be exempt from conscription because of their special status under the Indian Act, the Deputy Minister of Justice, Edmund Lee Newcombe, contacted Scott for advice.[89] Scott replied that the Military Service Act was a legal document that applied to all British subjects, and since there were no "existing treaties" that gave Indians "immunity from military service,"[90] they were subject to it. So convinced was Scott of his position that he sent the Military Service Council a list of all the agents in his department, along with estimates of the numbers of eligible recruits in those agencies. He insisted that all eligible Indian males must register for service by November 17.

News of enforced conscription drew heated responses from reserve communities across British Columbia. The opposition, writes historian Katharine McGowan, "was nearly universal."[91] The head of the Nass agency, Charles Perry, notified Scott to say that the Nisga'a were so enraged by the prospect of conscription that they had made threats on his life. Some were arguing that Indians should fight against, not with, the British.[92] The idea of conscripting Indians infuriated Teit, as he completely opposed the war. "The War is a disgrace for people calling themselves Christian and Civilized," he wrote to Sapir in mid-September 1917. "All these nations ... claim to be fighting for democracy. This is quite ridiculous. Who ever heard of any modern capitalist class fighting for democracy?"[93] A few weeks later he wrote again on the same topic: "I am quite disgusted. I believe socialism alone is the cure. That is to say S. of the true brand."[94]

Well before the conscription bill, Teit had informed Scott of the subversive recruitment practices taking place at Spences Bridge. "Young lads had been lured off and induced to enlist by extravagant stories told to them of the good times they would have seeing the White man's countries, and having White women, and free liquor, tc," he wrote.[95] Some of the recruitment agents were "bluff[ing]" boys by telling them that "if they did not assist in the war" by joining up, "they would lose all their lands, tc." Other agents were using liquor as a recruitment tool. They would intoxicate boys, he wrote, many of whom were underage, and then force signatures from them. Many were heading off without the permission of their parents or their band chiefs and Indian agents. The exodus of young men was taking a toll on elderly parents and single mothers, who needed these boys to run their family farms. Many were asking if the recruits' salaries could be "diverted to parents tc requiring more or less help." He noted that one of the underaged recruits, "Private William Frank," had been taken to "England lately and is now probably in France." He stressed repeatedly in his letters to Scott that, given the unresolved status of the "B.C. Indian question," the very idea of "Indians rendering service by going to the War" was wrong.[96]

Teit and Peter Kelly telegraphed this message to Prime Minister Borden on November 17, 1917, the deadline for signing up. Acting respectively as secretary and chairman of the ATBC, they noted their organization's full opposition to the conscription of Indians in British Columbia.[97] Such "enforced military service," they stated, was akin to "enslavement" by targeting peoples who were denied citizenship and basic human rights while it ignored their unsettled "land question." They concluded with a strong warning: "We are sure any attempted enforcement of the Act against

Indians would be forcibly resisted and probably cause bloodshed."[98] They sent a copy of their telegram to the editors of the *Victoria Daily Colonist*, who published it three days later under the headline, "Committee of Allied Tribes says men regard enforced service as enslavement."[99] Three weeks later, the Duncan correspondent for the *Victoria Daily Times* challenged the Teit–Kelly position on conscription in an article titled "Indians Not Against Conscription Plan." He wrote of attending an Indian meeting in Duncan at which he had observed full support of conscription.[100] Teit fired back with a letter to the editor of the *Daily Times*, stating that he had attended that very Duncan meeting where he observed full opposition to conscription.[101] He wrote that he had consulted with "the Indians of many parts of British Columbia on the matter of conscription," and that he could state "unhesitatingly ... that the Indians of B.C. are against conscription. I have not yet met one Indian in favor of it."[102]

In her study of the Nisga'a response to conscription, McGowan noted Teit's prominent role. "The similarity in language between the petitions, the travels of the secretary of the Allied Tribes around the province, and meetings held at the secretary's home in Spences Bridge," she writes, "all suggest a level of collective interest and concerted action articulated through earlier-established links among Native groups of British Columbia."[103] She highlighted the efforts of Teit and Kelly "to juxtapose the patriotic rhetoric and ideals of wartime with the war's practical/unpleasant realities: how could a government committed to fighting oppression and militarism consciously force a small, disadvantaged, and disenfranchised population into uniform?"[104]

The harder Teit pushed Scott to amend the Military Service Act to exclude Indians, however, the harder Scott pushed his position that the act applied "to all British subjects and as the Indians are British subjects the Act applies to them."[105] Like the Duncan correspondent, he stressed that the majority of Indians supported conscription. There were "some Indians [who were] very worked up over conscription," he noted, but they were in the minority. Most "in other parts of the country [were] obeying the law."[106] Teit fired back with an angry response:

> I may say that the whole idea of force in the matter of conscription is altogether foreign and repulsive to the Indian mind. In the old military systems of these tribes there was no compulsion of any kind whereby a person could be forced to go to war against his inclination or will. The chiefs and ruling bodies had no powers of this kind. Enlistment for war and other services was altogether voluntary. Men were persuaded to go to war or they saw it

> in some way to their interests to do so. Physical force in this was unknown. The Indians nowhere in BC are against the voluntary method although many prefer that none of their people should go to the war.[107]

He stressed that "the non-settlement of the B.C. Indian question also militated against Indians rendering service by going to war."[108]

Scott was unmoved, especially after hearing that the Teit-Kelly telegram had landed in the prime minister's office and stirred up fears of violence should the government proceed with conscription. A Victoria-based lawyer had calmed things down by notifying the federal Deputy Minister of Justice, E.L. Newcombe, that fourteen chiefs on Vancouver Island had opposed the ATBC petition. Scott used this new piece of information to bolster his position that resistance to conscription was minimal in British Columbia, and that the telegram was the work of a small, ineffectual political organization that was more white than Indian.[109] He described Peter Kelly to Newcombe as a highly assimilated Indian – i.e., a Methodist minister; he tossed off Teit as the husband of an Indian woman.[110]

Scott conveyed this information to Newcombe, even though he was aware that it was largely false. Not only did he know first-hand that Teit and O'Meara were powerful political figures in British Columbia. He also knew that there was strong resistance to the bill in that province. His BC agents had sent letters warning him of trouble should he continue to press conscription on the Indians. W.E. Ditchburn, his Inspector of Indian Agencies for Southwestern BC, had stressed that, until the land claim was resolved, the ATBC case against the conscription of Indians was fully valid. He recommended to Scott that in cases where Indians applied for exemption from the draft, they be granted it. Scott's Inspector of Indian Agencies for Southeastern British Columbia, A.M. Megraw, had also reported serious unrest over the conscription issue at Vernon. Scott, however, stood his ground, arguing that if the BC Indians were granted exemption "on the alleged claims against the Crown," it would "savour ... an acknowledgement that they occupied a different position from the other Indians of the Dominion."[111]

Teit was the subject of many of these communications. Megraw, for example, wrote that Teit was fuelling the unrest by disseminating anti-conscription propaganda to Indians under the auspices of the Indian Rights Association. He reported that the situation had gotten so out of hand that, at one point, he had had to send a spy to a meeting at Teit's home at Spences Bridge to record details. When the spy reported seeing Teit advising people to abstain from registering for the draft, Megraw recommended that Teit be arrested under the British Defense of the Realm Act for encouraging Indians to disobey the Canadian law and thus affecting public safety during wartime.[112]

Despite a barrage of "letters, telegrams, and applications for exemption," Scott held his ground. In the end, however, he lost: the federal government introduced Order-in-Council PC 111, which declared that, because Indians had no right to vote, they should be exempt from conscription.[113] It was one of the major losses of Scott's career. In his correspondence with Teit, Scott swallowed his pride and described the decision as one that he had supported. "You can expect a decision before long," he wrote Teit prior to the announcement, "that will tend to remove the difficulty [of conscription]. I cannot say any more at present and this is only for your own information."[114] He noted that he had worked for weeks on it with the Military Service Council.

Teit thanked Scott for this news, but he clearly did not trust it, because he followed up with a long letter explaining the importance of the exemption, noting that the chiefs had "commissioned" O'Meara to go to Ottawa "to express their views to the Gov. and to the heads of the Militia Department (of the Military Service Council) on this matter."[115] On January 23, 1918, Scott notified Teit that the order-in-council had passed on January 17, exempting Indians from combatant military service through application to their Indian agents.[116]

With this announcement, Teit enjoyed one of the first victories of his political career. Because the Armistice was still ten months away, his intervention undoubtedly spared hundreds of lives and families. Still, there would be little time to savour the victory.

Back to McKenna-McBride

Six weeks later, Teit faced another setback. Premier Brewster died suddenly on March 1, 1918, leaving John Oliver, the former Minister of Agriculture and Railways, to take his place. Neither Oliver, a Delta farmer, nor T. Duff Pattullo, his powerful Minister of Lands and the former mayor of Prince Rupert, had any interest in resolving the Indian claims.[117] Scott organized a meeting with Premier Oliver and Arthur Meighen, the Superintendent General of Indian Affairs, in Ottawa in May 1918 to convince the two parties of the value of signing a secret accord. Oliver, however, refused to participate in Scott's behind-the-scenes negotiation and instead unilaterally released the McKenna-McBride report to the public on March 4, 1919.[118]

The report's stringent recommendations – land increases of 87,291.17 acres and cut-offs of 47,058 acres, with the cut-offs consisting of rich agricultural land valued at three times that of the additions[119] – shocked the Indian leadership across the province.

Teit dropped his ongoing work for Boas for what had literally become his "other work" to challenge the report. In private letters to friends and colleagues, he expressed his personal anger: "The Gov. as a whole and the capitalist class which they represent have no appreciation for anything except dollars [sic] are in immediate sight."[120]

Premier Oliver offered a small reprieve by inviting the ATBC to review the report's findings. In response, members of the ATBC gathered at Spences Bridge in June and delegated Teit and Peter Kelly to undertake this task on their behalf. The two men spent much of the summer travelling from reserve to reserve, explaining details about the report's land cut-offs and additions, and soliciting feedback on how these might affect communities and families. They presented their preliminary findings at a full meeting of the executive committee of the ATBC in Vancouver on November 12, 1919, and sent their final report, *Statement of the Allied Indian Tribes of British Columbia for the Government of British Columbia*, to Premier Oliver a month later. The *Statement* was a flat rejection of the commission's report on grounds that it had completely ignored the Indians' comprehensive claim to title. Drawing on interviews with chiefs from around the province, Kelly and Teit documented the inadequacy of the lands added to reserves, the failure to adjust water rights in the Dry Belt region, and the lack of compensation for cut-offs.

The ATBC then stated that its condition for an "equitable settlement" was the acceptance by the two governments of the 1763 Royal Proclamation "as the main basis of all dealings and all adjustments of Indian land rights and other rights."[121] After outlining details, such as assigning each "tribe ... full, permanent and beneficial title" to their lands including bordering tidal and inland foreshores, they outlined a series of individual recommendations, such as 160 acres of agricultural land per person in the Dry Belt along with water for irrigating that land. They concluded with a demand for compensation for the costs of all past and future expenditures of the ATBC in connection with "the Indian land controversy."[122]

The ATBC *Statement* gained wide support, superseding, according to political scientist Paul Tennant, the Nishga Petition "as the authoritative statement of British Columbia Indian claims."[123] It would take more than a century to see even a few of these demands gain judicial recognition.

Bill 13

Both governments ignored the ATBC *Statement* and continued on their original course, with Scott leading the way. Determined to finalize the McKenna-McBride Commission's final report, Scott drafted a land-settlement act which, if passed, would authorize the federal government to adopt the recommendations of the report. His proposal was prompted in part by the Indian Affairs Settlement Act, an initiative by the BC government that empowered the province to "give effect to" the royal commission's report and to settle differences with both the Indians and the federal government.[124] Scott faced a major obstacle, however, in pushing his proposed legislation forward. He wanted to circumvent the McKenna-McBride Commission's recommendation that land could not be cut off a reserve without a band's consent – which was already a requirement of the Indian Act. To this end, he proposed adding a clause to the implementation legislation that would grant the government power to override the consent clause, notwithstanding the Indian Act.[125] Acting on Scott's advice, Arthur Meighen, Superintendent General of Indian Affairs, took Scott's draft proposal to Parliament where, on March 12, 1920, it was introduced as Bill 13, the British Columbia Indian Lands Settlement Act. If enacted, it had the power to strip Indians of their last piece of protection under the Indian Act: band consent as a prerequisite to alienating lands from Indians.[126]

On receiving news of Bill 13, Teit, Basil David, Peter Kelly, and George Matheson (Tsimshian) headed straight to Ottawa. They were joined by O'Meara and their Nisga'a colleague, Peter Calder. The trip was a sad one for Teit, as his good friend John Tetlanetza, who had been such a valued member of the previous delegations, had died two years earlier of cancer. The group stopped briefly in Winnipeg to meet with Dr. Charles Gordon, a prominent Canadian social activist who supported their cause, and attend a meeting of the Social Service Council of Manitoba. They also stopped in Toronto to attend a meeting of that city's chapter of the Social Service Council of Canada and meet with Frederick Loft, a member of the Six Nations reserve and head of the League of Indians of Canada. Loft had spearheaded a Canada-wide protest campaign aimed at "free[ing]" Indians "from the domination of officialdom" in order to "assert their rights as free men under the British flag."[127]

The Ottawa lobby effort was long and stressful. Aside from two weeks at the end of May, when Teit made an emergency trip back to British Columbia to meet with Premier Oliver, he and his delegation spent from

March until mid-July in the nation's capital.[128] In addition to full days of writing letters and articles for newspapers and preparing speeches and testimony for delivery at meetings, they monitored the House of Commons debates from the public gallery. In a long letter to Boas prior to the Ottawa trip, Teit stressed the necessity of putting this "special work," of which he had only "occasionally made mention," ahead of his ethnographic work.[129] After years of undertaking anthropological work for Boas, there was more than a little irony in his cursory reference to his decade-long struggle to help the chiefs fight their battle for cultural survival:

> For a number of years I did work for the Inds. without charge. They simply paying my expenses when I went to meetings tc. As the work has kept increasing of late they have paid me wages for what time I put in for them. Owing to the now high cost of living this spring they raised my wages to 6.50 per day. I do not care to desert the tribes at this time ... but desire if possible to assist them until such time as they get some kind of settlement of their case.[130]

Teit's prominent role in the political arena was undoubtedly a factor in his later marginalization by the discipline of anthropology, where such activism had little currency. And many of his actions were undoubtedly factors in the gradual termination of his contract with the federal government's Anthropology Division: for example, his criticisms of the government while taking a salary from that government; his helping Indians with their land-title case while the federal government asserted that they had no such case; his years of educating Indians about the Western legal process as a way to help them fight that legal process; his translation work in order to help them put their views on the public, political stage at a time when the state argued that Indians were incapable of such views.

The efforts of O'Meara, Basil David, Peter Calder, George Matheson, Peter Kelly, and Teit to draw sympathetic MPs to their cause worked. On March 26, William Lyon Mackenzie King and two fellow MPs, Ernest Lapointe and Jacques Bureau, rose in the House of Commons and challenged the bill.[131] King took the lead by asking the Minister of the Interior, Arthur Meighen, to explain the Indian perspective on the bill. Echoing Scott, Meighen replied that there were some Indians, "or at least some people who represent them," who opposed the bill, but this group was small and ineffective and did not represent the majority. Jacques Bureau then referred to a letter in his possession from a "special agent" of the "Allied Tribes" that stated that large numbers of Indians backed this organization and all were "dissatisfied and [hence] they would like to have a hearing." Meighen retorted that "if there are any Indians who want to be heard in relation to this Bill, I have not heard of it." King then stated that he had a petition in hand from an Indian delegation that "ask[ed] to be heard in reference" to the act. Meighen expressed surprise that the Indians had not given him a copy of the petition. "I don't know why they did not," retorted King, "unless it was, as the Minister has intimated to-night, that he was not inclined to listen to the Indian point of view."[132]

Several MPs jumped to Meighen's defence by charging that the petition in question was the work of a notorious white agitator named O'Meara. "That is not the gentleman I refer to," King responded. King's colleague, Bureau, came to King's defence by listing the signatories to the petition as Peter Calder of the Nishga tribe, George Matheson of the Tsimpshian tribe, Peter Kelly of the Haida tribe, and Basil David of the Shuswap tribe. Cyrus Peck, MP for Skeena, charged that although O'Meara's name wasn't on the petition, he was fully behind it. Indeed, he added, the group of signatories could well be called "children of Arthur O'Meara." King then interjected to say that O'Meara was *not* the "special agent" who had given him the petition; rather, it was another individual by the name of "J.A. Teit." Lapointe turned to Meighen and asked, "Are the four signatories not true representatives of the Indian tribes?" "No, of course they are not," replied Meighen. "I understand there is no Indian agent or missionary or anyone who has anything to do with it who does not denounce the whole movement and denounce the men, or the man, at the head of it." Lapointe expressed surprise at hearing this, saying he knew one of the petitioners, Peter Kelly, personally, and he considered him not only a "gentleman" but a man who was fully "qualified to speak to" the questions at hand. The discussion concluded with a proposal by Lapointe and Bureau that the bill go to special committee to allow the Indians a chance to address the matter themselves. Meighen seized the final word: "What these people claim – or rather what this man claims and what he got others to help him claim – is that in 1874 the original Indian title was not extinguished."[133]

Meighen, of course, had taken his lead from Scott, who had assured him prior to the House of Commons debate that reserve cut-offs without Indian consent would not be a problem as the Indians had no real need for the lands in question anyway. In the end, Scott and Meighen got their way. Despite Mackenzie King's interventions on the chiefs' behalf, Bill 13 sailed through its third reading and received royal assent on July 1. The bill authorized the federal government to implement the McKenna-McBride Commission recommendations without consideration of Indian title, land rights, or past promises and laws.

Bill 14

In addition to Bill 13, the Ottawa delegation faced a second contentious bill, Bill 14, that moved through Parliament at the same time as Bill 13. It was yet another of Scott's draconian measures to "rid [the country] of the Indian problem." As he explained to a special parliamentary committee, "Our objective is to continue until there is not a single Indian in Canada that has not been absorbed into the body politic, and there is no Indian question, and no Indian Department and that is the whole object of this Bill."[134] If passed, Bill 14 would authorize his department to enfranchise an Indian against his will on the basis of a "report by a person appointed by the superintendent general on [a particular individual's] suitability."[135] Among other things (for example, requiring compulsory school attendance for children between the ages of seven and fifteen), Scott hoped to use this bill to eliminate a number of his key adversaries in the reserve communities. In addition to Peter Kelly, he was now sparring with Frederick Loft over the latter's League of Indians' challenge of the harsh policies of the DIA. If passed, Bill 14 would enable Scott to divest Loft of his Indian status on grounds that he was a fully acculturated Indian who was exploiting innocent Indians for personal gain.[136]

After seventeen "special parliamentary committee" meetings that drew heated opposition from Indian delegates, the bill ended up in the House of Commons, with Teit and his colleagues working around the clock to contest it.[137] In addition to submitting articles to newspapers, they lobbied various Members of Parliament. Opposition Leader Mackenzie King was one of the first to respond. He rose in the House of Commons on June 23 and declared Bill 14 an example of the government's "hasty, unreasonable and autocratic method of making laws for [Indians] without consulting [them] and without ascertaining whether these laws will really benefit [them]."[138] He noted Scott's tampering with procedure by limiting feedback on the proposed bill to delegates who happened to be visiting Ottawa during its special committee discussions. When the Minister of the Interior, Arthur Meighen, challenged King on the allegation, the latter demanded a concrete response to the issue of Indian consultation on Bill 14. Meighen

The delegation of chiefs from across Canada who appeared before the parliamentary committee at Ottawa to protest the Bill of Enfranchisement (Bill 14) in May 1920. The photograph was published in the *Montreal Standard* newspaper on May 1, 1920. The backdrop is a canvas image of Ottawa's Parliament Buildings. Teit is in the second full row, second from left; William Lyon Mackenzie King (leader of the Opposition) is in the same row, extreme right; Peter Kelly is in the same row, third from right; Duncan Campbell Scott is seated in the front row, second from right; Arthur O'Meara is on a chair directly between the two men sitting cross-legged on the ground. Chief Basil David (Bonaparte reserve, Secwépemc) is on a chair, third from right (beside D.C. Scott). Information for this photograph was provided by Donald Smith and Hamar Foster. | Photograph courtesy of Sigurd Teit.

fired back, saying that consultation was unnecessary as Indians were "wards" and not "citizens" of the state.[139]

Their heated exchange exposed the raw underside of Scott's secret meddling. MP John Harold stated that he had in hand a report that supported Bill 14, which was "made some time ago by Mr. C.M. Barbeau."[140] Marius Barbeau, of the Anthropology Division, had undertaken an anthropological study of the "Lorette reserve" on the outskirts of Quebec City and concluded that it was a community of Europeanized "half-breeds" who were "suffering considerably because they are not enfranchised."[141] Quoting at length from Barbeau's report, Harold stressed that the members of this reserve "chafe[d] under the restrictions and humiliation" resulting from their reserve status. In Harold's view, the Barbeau report provided an ideal test case for Scott's bill.

Shocked that a colleague in the Anthropology Division would dare to write such a report, Teit contacted Sapir, noting his fear that the case study might easily extend to reserve communities across the country. A similarly surprised Sapir then sent an urgent letter to Barbeau in Hazelton, BC, asking who had authorized the report. If the "narrow-minded" Scott was behind it, he wrote, he had "no right to use our department" in such a "dishonest way."[142]

Barbeau's response arrived a week later. In it, he confessed sheepishly that yes, he had indeed written the report for Scott and that, yes, it had come with a pot of independent funding. He noted that the report should not have come as a total surprise to Sapir as he had informed him about it beforehand. Rather than dwell on his part in the offence, Barbeau shifted the blame to Scott: "I see that you do not have Scott in 'odeur de sainteté'! I have long felt the same way about his tendencies and breadth of mind."[143] While Teit had acted as a double agent in his dealings with Scott through his loyalty to his Indian colleagues, Barbeau had acted as a double agent loyal only to Scott.

Surprisingly, Sapir took a soft stand on Barbeau's betrayal, probably as a way to extricate himself from the wrath of Teit and his colleagues should they discover that he had had prior knowledge of the report. The last thing that Sapir – or Teit – needed in the middle of the Bill 14 controversy was word that the director of Ottawa's Anthropology Division had condoned the infamous report. Instead of making a public spectacle of Barbeau's gaffe, Sapir warned Barbeau privately that he must never again accept "incidental work" or funding from the DIA without his approval, or "we will find ourselves drifting into the position of genteel spies for the Department of Indian Affairs."[144]

To compensate for Barbeau's blunder, Sapir wrote a long response to Bill 14 and sent it on July 13 to O'Meara.[145] In it, he attacked compulsory enfranchisement as an autocratic, "machine-like" method of "handling Indian affairs," and he characterized the whole Bill 14 process as not only unfair and inappropriate but wrong. To address Teit's concern about the nationwide application of Barbeau's findings, Sapir declared that there was "no one general 'Indian' set of conditions." To promote such a thing, he wrote, would "break up the integrity of the tribe" and cause serious "degeneration." He clearly had Scott's secret manoeuvre in view with his final statement. The Department of Indian Affairs, he wrote, should never be allowed to act on its own. It should always do so in conjunction with "the Indians themselves" and/or a "disinterested third party ... [such as] a scientific student or a group of scientific students of Indian customs."[146]

Despite the opposition, the government passed Bill 14 on June 25 and it received royal assent on July 1. Mackenzie King, however, continued to oppose the new legislation, and after he won the federal election in December 1921, Parliament repealed this amendment to the Indian Act. Thereafter, enfranchisement could only take place at the request of the individual concerned. Like conscription, Bill 14 was another major loss for Scott.[147]

Back to the McKenna-McBride Report

Behind the scenes, Scott faced the problem of how to bring the federal and provincial governments to a joint final agreement. In the spring of 1920, while Bills 13 and 14 made their way through Parliament, he had sent a copy of Bill 13 to British Columbia's Minister of Lands, Duff Pattullo, for feedback. Pattullo, who had ignored Scott the previous fall, proposed as an interim measure the formation of a small committee consisting of a federal government representative and a provincial government representative to undertake one final review of the McKenna-McBride report.[148] After holidaying in the Rockies, Scott headed on to Victoria to finalize the proposal with Pattullo. The result was a decision to appoint W.E. Ditchburn, Chief Inspector of Indian Agencies, to represent the federal government and Major J.W. Clark to represent the provincial government in a Ditchburn Inquiry aimed at finalizing the report. In response to complaints from the Indian organizations about the lack of Indian representation on any of the previous committees, Scott and Pattullo approached Teit to fill this gap. In a letter, Scott stressed to Teit that this would be "the only opportunity that the Indians will have to represent their reserve claims to the Governments, and that if they fail to take this opportunity I do not see how matters can be reopened as the agreement to be reached will be considered final."[149] Teit consulted with the chiefs, and with their approval he agreed in mid-October to represent them on the committee.[150] In a note to Sapir, he seemed cautiously optimistic:

> I have now to occupy all my time during the rest of this month and the greater part of next with work for Mr. Scott and the Indians in connection with placing the Indian case before the Board which has been appointed by

> the two governments to investigate the actual needs of the Indians as regards lands, fishing, hunting, etc. This Board of two officials will later make recommendations to the governments and then an attempt will be made to settle with the Indians and if possible settle this troublesome controversy."[151]

A month later, during a meeting of the Ditchburn committee in Victoria, Teit fell ill with what was soon diagnosed as cancer, forcing him to suspend his work for the inquiry while he sought medical attention. After several rounds of radiation therapy in Vancouver and eight months of convalescence at home in Spences Bridge, he rebounded and asked, in the fall of 1921, to be reinstated to the inquiry. Ditchburn agreed, informing him that he and Clark had covered the Babine, Bella Coola, Cowichan, Kwakewewlth, New Westminster, Queen Charlotte, Stikine, Stuart Lake, and West Coast agencies, but the "Kamloops, Kootenay, Lytton, Okanagan, Nass, Skeena River, Williams Lake Agencies" were yet to be covered.[152] Teit headed off to the latter agencies and notified Ditchburn the following January that he had completed written reports for the Okanagan, Kamloops, Lytton, and Williams Lake agencies and had plans to meet with the Tsilhqot'in chiefs at Spences Bridge at the end of the month.[153]

Teit's work for the Ditchburn Inquiry drew him back into DIA surveillance. Agent Fred Ball of the Okanagan agency reported to his DIA superior, J.D. McLean, that Teit was using his Ditchburn Inquiry salary to fund his work on the Indian political campaign. He stated that he had heard this from members of his agency, who had attended a meeting in Vancouver at which they saw Teit raising funds to send "a delegation to England."[154] Indian agent Harry Graham contacted Scott a week later with word of three meetings that Teit had organized – two in Vancouver and another at Hat Creek – that appeared to be aimed at raising funds "to send representatives to Ottawa, and, if necessary, to England."[155] On hearing this, Scott contacted Ditchburn to verify details. Ditchburn responded that he too had heard rumours about "Indians" making "contributions" to Teit at meetings, so he had contacted Teit for an explanation, and Teit had assured him that the fundraising on reserves had nothing to do with the Ditchburn Inquiry or political trips or lobbying. It was aimed at paying back long overdue loans to O'Meara from members of the Friends of the Indians in eastern Canada.[156]

This was not the first friction that Teit had faced in his role as a member of the Ditchburn Inquiry. Several accusations against him had arrived on Scott's desk at the outset of the inquiry. Likely stoked by Indian agent Fred Ball, members of the Penticton and Osoyoos Bands had sent a letter to Scott in December 1920, accusing Teit of "collecting money from them under [false] ... pretext." They stated that he claimed "to represent Indians on said Reservations and also to represent the government at Ottawa." They wanted "to know what authority this man has and if we are to continue to pay him for imaginary help that we never receive."[157] Scott forwarded the letter to Teit with a request for an explanation. The timing could not have been worse, as Teit was dealing with the initial onslaught of the illness that would soon kill him. From "a reclining position," he drafted a letter to Scott denouncing the accusations as "the grossest of misrepresentations" from a group of people who had no understanding of his work.[158] He noted that the signatories had backed the ATBC until several years ago, when one of their chiefs, Ineas George, convinced them to break away. A man whom Teit described as a notorious troublemaker, who had teamed up with "an old Indian dreamer from the American side" who claimed "Jesus Christ" as "his chief," George wielded significant power over a small faction:

> What has made them particularly sore lately is learning that I (who have acted as representative of the Allied Tribes) had been chosen by the Gov. to present the Indian case, point out the needs of the Inds., interview the Indians as to certain of their needs & other matters all with the object of accomplishing a settlement. The leading men and chiefs through the Okanagan are very pleased the Gov. has chosen me for this purpose and it may be they have been rubbing it in a little bit and made the opposition feel particularly sore. I think this soreness is the chief reason for the writing of the letter.[159]

As O'Meara faced similar accusations at exactly this time, the charges against both men were likely part of a coordinated government campaign to turn the Indians against their advocates.[160]

With a recurrence of his illness in the summer of 1922, there was no returning to the Ditchburn Inquiry. Teit grew weaker by the day and died in Merritt at the end of October 1922.

The Campaign without Teit

Teit's death left both the inquiry and the chiefs' political campaign with a gaping hole. Ditchburn responded by hiring Peter Kelly, Ambrose Reid (Tsimshian), and Andrew Paull (Squamish) to finalize Teit's work, but things did not go well. Three months into the trio's work, Ditchburn notified Scott to say that dealing with the trio was a "nightmare."[161] After an "all-wise Providence ha[d] seen fit to remove J.A. Teit," he wrote, the committee of three had produced haphazard reports that recommended everything that the Indians had asked for. Ditchburn wrote that he had no choice but to finalize the report on his own, and he acted quickly to "eliminate all requests for alienated land and those he considered exorbitant or superfluous."[162] In the end, he proposed a number of small reserves, most of which were related to fishing stations.[163]

On July 26, 1923, the provincial government finally ratified the McKenna-McBride report as modified by the Ditchburn report; Ottawa followed suit in July 1924.[164] Meanwhile, the ATBC continued to oppose it on grounds that the case needed to be resolved in the courts. A petition to Parliament in 1926 led to a federal government investigation by a special joint committee of the Senate and House of Commons in 1927 that, as Foster writes, "purported to deal with the merits of the claim [but] ended in dismissing it."[165] Scott was behind the dismissal as he successfully convinced the 1927 parliamentary committee to agree that the reserves of the Indians of British Columbia were "sufficient for their needs," and that the Indians had no claim to title.[166] After a unanimous vote, the committee's decision passed quickly through both the House of Commons and Senate.

With Teit conveniently out of the picture, the government was also able to include an amendment to the Indian Act that struck at the heart of what had for two decades allowed Indians to resist colonialism: the amendment made it an offence for Indians to hire lawyers or raise money "for the purpose of prosecuting any claim against government unless the minister's permission had first been obtained."[167] This legislation marked the end of the long campaign to take the title issue to the British Judicial Committee of the Privy Council. Its ramifications would shackle resistance for decades to come. By the end of 1928, O'Meara would be dead and both the ATBC and ITBC gone.

The ITBC had started losing ground during Teit's illness, when he was too ill to attend meetings, leaving the older chiefs confused and frustrated as they tried, without his assistance, to navigate through the complicated legal discussions and debates in English. According to Peter Kelly, Teit was the glue that held the old ITBC leadership together: "I have never seen anything like it even to this day," he explained. "The Indians trusted [Teit] implicitly ... They would have done anything for him. When he died, the Interior organization fell apart."[168] With the emergence of new-generation leaders such as Peter Kelly and Andy Paull, who were fluent in English and knowledgeable in the Western legal tradition (Paull had apprenticed in a Vancouver law firm),[169] the old leaders felt marginalized. Johnny Chilahitsa of Douglas Lake quit the ATBC in frustration in 1925, and he took a cohort of ATBC members with him. It was the sort of conflict that Teit had overcome many times through the simple act of explaining carefully to the chiefs – in their languages – what was at stake.

Chilahitsa had charged ahead on his own and, like his Okanagan colleague Ineas George a few years earlier, had stirred things up in Ottawa by airing his grievances directly with Scott.[170] The old chief had found a new translator in his niece, Julianne Williams, who had attended residential school where she learned to speak, read, and write English. "Since the death of J. Teit, we Indian chiefs said, or agreed," he wrote, "that we will not take a white man to (interpret) for us Indians to the Government."[171]

Ironically, Teit's death also created problems at Scott's end, as he no longer had a reliable cultural translator to help him deal with the complex communications with the chiefs. Chilahitsa's claims against Kelly and the ATBC strengthened Scott's position that the ATBC was in the hands of a small group of white agitators and "half-breeds" who did not represent the majority population. Teit had spent years successfully challenging this accusation, most recently in a statement before the Senate Standing Committee on Banking and Commerce, in which he explained that "plenty of evidence can be produced to show the Indians have had serious grievances since the early seventies and generally speaking the Governments have ignored them."[172]

Everything came to a head when Chilahitsa arrived in Ottawa in 1925 with his niece, Julianne, to present his grievances to Scott, only to discover that things were not as they were in the old days. Scott treated Chilahitsa with such disdain that, on his return to British Columbia, Chilahitsa retained a Kamloops lawyer, Alex McIntyre, to lodge an official complaint on his behalf to Scott's superior, Superintendent General of Indian Affairs Charles Stewart. In his letter, McIntyre wrote that "Mr. Scott was as offensive as it was possible to be to the unfortunate Indians alone in Ottawa." He "grossly insult[ed] the chief and Mrs. Williams" by telling them they had "no business in Ottawa." The most egregious part of this trip, he wrote, was that Scott had "ordered them out of his office."[173] Stewart forwarded the lawyer's letter to Scott with a request for an explanation. Through his secretary, Scott replied that there was no need to respond to Chilahitsa's letter as "the statements regarding the reception given Chief

Chillihtisa and those who accompanied him to Ottawa last year [were] entirely erroneous."[174]

Scott's dismissal of Chilahitsa paved the way for the final and humiliating dismissal of Chilahitsa, Kelly, and O'Meara – and, posthumously, of James Teit – by the special joint committee in Ottawa in 1927. For years, Scott had argued that the "entire difficulty" surrounding the Indian's claim to title was due to the "'mischievous' agitation by 'designing white men.'"[175] By 1928, with Teit and O'Meara conveniently out of the picture, Scott was free to run wild with this accusation, facilitating the closure for decades to come of the contentious Indian land question in British Columbia.

9
NOttawa

Many stories were told of seals coming ashore, divesting themselves of their skins, and then dancing, gamboling, and enjoying themselves in human form ... I remember that when I was a boy, two or three persons were pointed out as being affected by ... skin-blemishes [unique to the offspring of seal-folk with human beings], which, it was said, proved their descent.

– J.A. Teit, "Water-Beings in Shetlandic Folk-Lore, as Remembered by Shetlanders in British Columbia" (1918)[1]

The long days in Ottawa were hard on Teit and his Indian Rights Association (IRA) and Interior Tribes of British Columbia (ITBC) colleagues. In addition to the political conflict on Parliament Hill, they faced personal discrimination in the streets. Teit was so worried about the racism before the group's first trip to Ottawa in 1912 that he appealed to Edward Sapir for help. "As every hotel will not admit Indian chiefs," he wrote, "I will be much obliged ... if you could locate a suitable stopping place for us that we could go to on our arrival, and let me know soon."[2] Sapir resolved the hotel problem,[3] and he offered his workplace, the Victoria Memorial Museum, to the chiefs as a daytime refuge – and a change of pace. "If they are not too busy palavering with Parliament," he wrote, "perhaps I [and my museum staff] can seize the opportunity to do a little linguistic [and ethnographic] work with them."[4]

Nicknamed "the castle" because of its Scottish baronial edifice – Tudor-Gothic design with rock-faced limestone walls, pointed arch windows, and decorative buttresses – the museum was the new home of the Geological Survey of Canada. The chiefs sought it out within a few days of arriving in the city in early January, and they returned regularly throughout their two-week stay.[5] It was a ten-minute walk from Parliament Hill's Centre Block, where most of their political meetings took place. Their first sight of the museum building was surely a surprise, as it was a mirror image of the Centre Block.

Sapir's employee Marius Barbeau leapt at the opportunity to work with the chiefs. A Rhodes scholar with a newly minted doctoral degree in anthropology from the University of Oxford, he had recently undertaken song-recording projects in Huron-Wyandot communities in Quebec, Michigan, and Oklahoma, so he proposed a song project to the chiefs, and several of them volunteered to take part. This project turned into what Barbeau later described as a highlight of his anthropological career. It was certainly one of his easiest projects, as it required none of the usual travel and logistical issues associated with such work. The chiefs simply appeared at his office with Teit (their translator) and sat down to work. By the end of the visit, John Tetlanetza (Nlaka'pamux), Ignace Jacob (St'at'imc), and Chief Francois (Secwépemc) had filled forty-one wax cylinders with songs and speeches, and Barbeau had filled more than a dozen notebooks with Teit's English translations of the discussion.[6]

Songs and Sovereignty

The discovery of Barbeau's 1912 and 1916 field notebooks in Ottawa a few years ago opened a new window on Teit by revealing, through a third-party observer, details of Teit's ethnographic practice. According to Barbeau's notes, Teit not only translated for the chiefs; he also guided them – in their individual languages – through the intricacies of the discussion, sometimes by sharing his own stories and anecdotes. (Ignace Jacob was the only member of the group who could speak English.) The notebooks also showed Teit guiding Barbeau through the discussion while simultaneously dictating running translations and spelling out Nlaka'pamux names and terms.[7] Teit rarely included such commentary or self-reflection in his own ethnographic notebooks.

According to Barbeau's notes, Tetlanetza, Jacob, and Teit spent much of the song sessions discussing the spiritual significance of their songs and the role of that spirituality in connecting humans to their territorial land base. Barbeau's request for songs may well have been the catalyst, because most of the songs the chiefs chose to sing for him had a spiritual connection to the land. As they were in Ottawa to assert sovereignty over their land base, they may have seen political value in having their spiritual connection to their land base documented by a member of the museum staff. They had learned through their exchanges at the other end of Metcalfe

Street that highlighting such connections in meetings with prime ministers, premiers, and Indian Department officials was not only futile but damaging.

Sᴇɴā'ms (pronounced roughly "shna-ams") or "manitous" (as Teit called them in English) – dominated the discussion.[8] "Of all the things of nature," Tetlanetza explained, "nearly all may be a manitou and speak to a man." Because manitous offered humans special "strength from nature, from the earth," it was essential to connect with them, ideally early in life. In addition to protecting their proteges from danger, manitous ensured that humans had long and healthy lives. "The old people" considered them to be the lifeblood of the culture and believed that "if you have no manitou, you will have nobody to help you in times of need, in times of danger." It was "the school system of the old days," Tetlanetza explained. In addition to long periods of isolation, training involved fasting from four days (the norm) to as long as ten days. Teit interjected at one point to explain that "the longer" one fasted, "the greater" was one's power, particularly as a healer.

Like Tetlanetza, Jacob emphasized the "power" and "strength" of sᴇɴā'ms.[9] "When boys and girls reached the age of ten," he explained, "they went, all alone, out in the woods" to train for this power. "They generally stay by a creek or river to wash themselves everyday. Sometimes they dance there, all alone, pretty nearly all night." He recalled that, as a boy, he had known an old man, an Indian doctor, whose sᴇɴā'm was so strong that it gave him power to control the weather. After a long hot and dry spell, he ordered the residents of two villages into their houses, at which point he "made the Thunder come." "I saw it myself," said Jacob. "A big ball of clouds came, about noon, and ... rain poured down." An hour later and "it was as clear as before."[10] Like Tetlanetza, Jacob referred to the training period as "a kind of schooling" "aimed at helping [i.e., young people] see something" – a deer or a bear or other animals – that would carry them through life. "It is the same as for those who go to school in your country," he told Barbeau. Some "come out to be doctors," while "others to be priests, etc." Tetlanetza noted the parallel with "Christ," who was "40 days in the desert [when] he was on his training."[11]

Tetlanetza explained that although a manitou often looked like a man, and often referred to himself as a man in his communications – as in "I am the man who has lived in these mountains from the beginning of time. It is I who speak to you" – he was not "the same as us, as his powers [were] different and greater." Tetlanetza noted that all communication between humans and manitous was through dreams and visions:

> When after a fast, you dream or have a vision, "what you dream you never forget." In that vision, the being of the vision comes to you as a man would and speaks to you. All at once, in a vision, when you see something coming to you, and which disappears as soon as it reaches you, it is not considered a powerful vision. But when, after a longer fast, you have another vision, the manitou comes and when it reaches you, it talks to you and tells you lots. And when it leaves you, at a few yards distance, it disappears, and the vision is over. Then if you continue training in the solitude, and thinking of your vision and manitou ... it becomes a kind of acquaintanceship. In some cases, the manitou becomes friend[s] with the man; then they become thoroughly acquainted; then the manitou may appear to him frequently and talk to him. The manitou, as a rule, gives advise [sic] ... When the Indian has finished training, he may sometimes not see the manitou in a vision, or at least seldom. But he may see the manitou often in real dreams (not visions).[12]

Such was the chiefs' introduction to the songs they offered Barbeau. To connect with a manitou, they explained, it was necessary to have a dream or a vision that included a special manitou song. Tetlanetza sang two songs into Barbeau's phonograph to illustrate his point. The first was an "Uncle Coyote" song that had come to a Secwépemc boy in a dream. It was a relatively new song, Tetlanetza explained, as it was introduced only "100 years ago." According to the boy's account of the experience, he had been sleeping near a lake when a coyote appeared in a dream and spoke to him: "Wake up nephew, the day has dawned. Listen to the warbling of the birds." The boy opened his eyes but all he could see of the coyote was "dust from his heel at a distance." The song was being sung by a bird – "a diver" that was flying over the lake. The boy learned it and embraced it as his "Uncle Coyote" manitou song.[13] Tetlanetza's second song was a "loon song" (also a century old) that another "lad" had acquired in a vision while training near a river somewhere in "Upper Thompson" territory. This boy noticed a loon dipping and diving downstream while singing a song about visiting his sister at the river's mouth for an extended period and wondering what he should take to her as a gift. He learned the song and adopted it as his loon manitou song. Tetlanetza stressed that this all took place while the boy was awake. It was a vision. "He did not dream it."[14]

Jacob followed with another "manitou song" and a long account of the rituals and protocols associated with it. Jacob's discussion of "manitous appear[ing] to their proteges ... sometimes in the form of a fish, sometimes in the form of a man, etc.," prompted Tetlanetza to sing his own manitou song.[15] He explained that when he was fifteen and undergoing his training, he had had a dream about two sisters who were walking toward him, singing a song and scattering flowers. As the two women got closer, he noticed that one had slightly raised red paint spots on her cheeks, and the other had the same paint spots on her breasts. In his conversation with the sisters, they told him that the spots were scars from "gun-shot wounds," and the song they were singing had saved them. "Perhaps you will obtain that power that we have if you continue to sing this song," they told Tetlanetza. "Then when you are wounded in any part of the body, you paint the wound as we do and you will become well." Teit noted that "manitous almost always (very often) give instructions of that kind regarding painting." He explained that after the sisters told him this, they walked to the "edge of the timber" through "a violent [flash of] snow" that "obliterated all the[ir] tracks." As they disappeared into the forest, they called out, "Our enemies cannot follow us," and changed into two female black bears. It was "like a moving picture"; it all happened as "in a dream; when sleeping," Tetlanetza stated.

Tetlanetza said that he had a second encounter with the bear sisters fifteen years later. He had fallen gravely ill, and the older of the two sisters appeared to him in a dream and said, "You are almost dead ... You are far gone." "Yes," he replied, "I am nearly gone." You need to "eat the soapberry," she said. He woke up, remembered his dream, and told his wife that he needed to eat soapberries. Because their winter supply of soapberries had run out, she ran seven miles to a neighbour's house to get some. Tetlanetza ate the berries as instructed and made a full recovery. "You see," he told his wife, "my manitou still loves me, and helped me."

Eight years later, Tetlanetza had a third encounter with his manitou while working on a road construction project near Yale. He was fast asleep in his tent, when suddenly an old man dressed in "something like a priest's robe" appeared in a dream and asked Tetlanetza if he recognized him. Tetlanetza froze in fear as he could not recall ever having seen the man. The man responded with a dire warning: "If you don't sing the song that I am singing, at noon tomorrow you will die. You must sing my song very well for me." Tetlanetza awoke from his dream singing the man's song and noticed that the old man was standing beside his bed and singing along with him. Tetlanetza's wife, who had been sleeping beside him, suddenly sat up and asked what was going on. Since she could not see the old man standing beside the bed, Tetlanetza told her about his dream. She then joined in the singing. After a while, the old man walked toward a creek about a hundred yards away. On reaching it, he turned around and opened the front of his white robe. "You see my dress," he said. Tetlanetza saw that what looked from a distance to be a priest's white robe was actually the man's long grey hair "running down his whole body, a part of which he had twisted around his waist, which looked like a woven belt ... long hair that he had parted in front when he opened his robe." The man explained:

> Since the world first grew, I have been until now. See how old I am. Yet I remain strong ... The manitous of the mountain peaks, the manitous of the waters, the manitous of the trees, the manitous of the winds, the manitous of all nature are in me, they are my manitous; thus from them, from all nature, I am strong.

Tetlanetza watched as the man walked, still singing, into the middle of the creek and submerged himself in the water: "As the water reached the top of his head, his great mass of grey hair floated as foam on the water. Then his song came from underneath the water, came from the trees, and came from the waters." Singing from underneath the water, the old man issued instructions to Tetlanetza:

> Go over to the ravine where Emilie is ... You go towards the ravine [it was 3 miles away] and in the middle of it you will see two trees growing. There are bushes around the foot of the trees. And then there you will find Emilie, from the place where you are going to die ... You will see their tracks, leaving from that point [referring to the two bears]. You will follow them up, and you will find Emilie.

On hearing the name "Emilie," Tetlanetza knew there was a connection to his manitous, the bear sisters, because they had used that name. It gave him a strange, out-of-body sensation. Teit interjected to explain to Barbeau that what Tetlanetza meant was that his soul left his body while he "sat singing there, during that time." As the old man predicted, "the youngest of the two sisters" appeared in the form of a black bear. There was a bear den there, and the bears from that den joined her in the singing. Gradually they all vanished and the song faded away. Tetlanetza, however, continued on singing the song.

His singing woke the white men in the adjacent tent. "Are you crazy?" one called out. "No," Tetlanetza responded, "I had a dream and I am singing. If I had not sung this song well now, at 12 o'clock, I would have died." His response triggered a round of laughter in the tent, which Tetlanetza and his wife ignored, instead singing through to sunrise. After breakfast, Tetlanetza headed off to work with the others. Around lunchtime, as he trekked along a steep bank, he heard a fellow worker holler, "Look out!" A large log catapulted toward him. It caught him and dragged him for some distance. By all rights, it should have killed him. Instead, it only knocked the breath out of him and bruised his shoulder. Tetlanetza attributed his miraculous survival to his manitous, the black bear sisters.

Not Mirage

Tetlanetza's vison story prompted Teit to tell a vision story of his own.[16] He explained that he was living with Antko in a house on "a long bench" just east of the village, close to the CPR tracks. After supper, she announced that she was going to the "Indian village" to visit her sick friend, Somantza.[17] She asked Teit to meet her on the trail on her return, "[a]bout half past 8." It was midsummer, so the days were long. Close to the designated time, Teit "strolled out" to meet her. Because there were two trails leading to the village – one along an upper bench and the other along the flat near the river – he was unsure which one she would take. Therefore, he chose a place on the upper bench that offered a view of both trails.

He had just settled down on the bench when he noticed "three men standing together right in the middle of the square" below him. It caught him by surprise as the trio seemed to have materialized from nowhere, and none of the three looked familiar:

> It struck me that these people there had appeared there very suddenly because I did not notice them in the square before. I looked at them very closely. Their distance would be about, or a little over, 100 yards. I was looking down on them. They were standing facing each other, quite close together, and they appeared to be conversing and I could see their features quite plainly. They were typical Indians of that region, but still they were strangers to me. I could not recognize any. [There was a hotel on one side, small storehouse on the other, and a shed for wagons – it was before the railroad was built.] One of them was an old man with rather aquiline features and long hair, dressed in "old" Indian style of costume. His back was partly

> turned towards me, the other men were fairly young men and were dressed partly as cowboys. One had a large cowboy hat, a young man. I wondered who they could be. I looked at them for a considerable time; they did not seem to notice me. So I stopped there, stood still, and I whistled at them. They paid no attention, remained in exactly the same position, appeared to be conversing. So I thought I would sit down there and watch them. There was no other living soul around. I sat down and I filled my pipe and lit it. They were still there. After I started smoking I called in Indian to them. They paid no attention.

It seemed strange to Teit that the three men were "exceedingly absorbed" in conversation and yet he could not hear their voices.

He then spotted Antko walking along the lower trail, which meant that she would have "to pass by where those people are" and, in doing so, would have to acknowledge them in some way. It was even more strange when Antko walked past the three men without noticing them at all. Teit whistled loudly to catch her attention, but all she did was look up at him and continue on. How could she "not possibly see me without seeing them?" he wondered. He watched her disappear temporarily behind some buildings, then reappear "where the two trails met" near their house. On glancing back at the square below him, he saw that the three men were gone. He called out to them and ran down the slope to try to find them, but there was nothing. He also checked the ground for tracks: "I glanced around and the tracks were very confused in different directions. I could not make anything out of the tracks. So I hurried over to this wagon shed. Went through there but I could see no sign of anybody. Visited all around there. Could not see a soul. Then I followed up the hill toward our house."

Back home, he quizzed Antko about the people in the square. "What people?" she asked. "I saw no one." As she passed by "that spot," however, she noted "a peculiar feeling." "Those must have been ghosts," she said. "Probably Somantza is going to die."

"That was the way she looked at it," Teit said. And her premonition turned out to be correct because Somantza died "less than 4 days afterwards."

"I have often explained that to Indians," Teit said to Barbeau, "and it was their idea that the vision was connected to the person who died." They "believe that the appearance has been there." Whites, on the other hand, "believe it does not exist." Teit noted that he was with the Indians on this point: "I believe that I actually saw them. It was not mirage."[18]

Teit with three Interior chiefs in Ottawa, 1916. Left to right: Chief John Tetlanetza, James Teit, Chief Paul David, and Chief Thomas Adolph. | Photograph by Frederick Lyonde, Teit family collection, courtesy of Sigurd Teit.

Back to Centre Block

Two days later, Tetlanetza, Ignace Jacob, and Teit joined John Chilahitsa, Basil David, James Raitasket, and Thomas Adolph for a meeting on Parliament Hill with Prime Minister Robert Borden. Their goal was to convince Borden to agree to the submission of their land-title case to the British high courts (as described in Chapter 7). The chiefs wore buckskin jackets and traditional regalia borrowed from the museum's collections for the occasion.

Their lawyer, J.M. Clark of Toronto, initiated the proceedings by giving a full summary of their case. Tetlanetza and Chilahitsa followed with separate speeches (with Teit translating), in which they noted the importance of their ancient land base to their cultural survival. In contrast to the recent session in the museum, they made no mention of the importance of dreams and visions associated with the land base, having learned that sharing details of their relationships with loons, lizards, coyotes, rivers, and mountains with outsiders would hinder their case. The closest they came to revealing this relationship was Chief Basil David's comment: "Our land has been taken and we look upon that as our life – we get all our life from the land."

From Centre Block Back to the Museum

As if to build on Basil David's comment about the relationship between "land" and "life," Tetlanetza immediately returned to the museum to sing four doctoring songs that drew directly from the land. The first was the doctoring song of an old Spences Bridge shaman, ck'min, who had acquired it from a wolf and a hawk; the second was the doctoring song of a Lytton shaman named Ntiltci'nêm, who acquired it from an eel and a bird; the third was a doctoring song of a Nicola Valley shaman, Terapalst, who had acquired it from a ptarmigan; and the last was the doctoring song of a Coldwater Valley shaman, Cpekq'ekqtsa, who received it from a lizard.[19] Tetlanetza also sang a sweathouse song that he described as a vital part of the training exercises.[20] "The priest[s] today, [they] destroy all that," explained Ignace Jacob. "They say it is the devil's work."[21]

Teit interjected again with one of his own stories.[22] It was about the sweathouse, he said, which he had used "many hundred times." He and Antko had set up camp in the Twaal Valley with Chief John Whistemnitsa and his wife. They were fast asleep in their tent when "all of a sudden" they heard someone singing. "I looked out through the tent," Teit explained, and noticed that Whistemnitsa and his wife were "lighting the fire." Moments later, Whistemnitsa called out, "Get up! I had a bad dream; and we must avert the danger." Whistemnitsa instructed his wife to "go and prepare the sweat-bath." Antko headed off to help her fire it up and heat the stones. Whistemnitsa sang continuously all through this. When the women announced that the rocks were ready, he invited Teit to join him in the sweathouse. The women sat at the campfire and continued the singing. In the sweathouse, Whistemnitsa told Teit why he was doing all of this: "This is the 4th time I have had the same dream. The first two times after I have dreamt that dream, a sister died one time, and a friend the next. I was taught to use this song to ward off [potential] ... danger ... That's why I am acting thus." All he told Teit about the dream was that it had come from his manitou. Teit noted that he and Whistemnitsa "sweated there until daybreak," after which Whistemnitsa also instructed the women to similarly "purify themselves."[23]

A few days after this session, Teit and the delegation of chiefs made a final visit to the museum before heading home. On this visit, Tetlanetza broke from songs and offered Barbeau two speeches. The first was a funeral speech, said to have been given by a father at the death of his son; the second was a speech said to have been delivered by a chief to a group of adolescent boys prior to their puberty training.[24] Before leaving, the delegation sang a farewell song to the museum staff. According to a letter that Ignace Jacob sent to the museum after the trip, the group had enjoyed the visits there. Jacob wrote that although he had arrived home with "no answers from the Government," he was pleased to tell his people about the "good & kind people at Ottawa," and the parties that they had held in their honour.[25]

Ottawa, 1916

In the spring of 1916, Tetlanetza and Teit returned to Ottawa for another round of political lobbying. Once again, they sought out the museum on their free mornings and afternoons,[26] but this time it was not the quiet refuge it had been on their previous visit. A fire the previous February had destroyed the Centre Block on Parliament Hill, and the federal government had designated the museum as its replacement during the reconstruction period. Its amphitheatre was now the Commons Chamber, and its first-floor mineral gallery the Senate chamber. Federal MPs, senators, and civil servants shared the hallways and offices with the museum staff.

Such intrusions did not deter Tetlanetza. He arrived in Ottawa eager to contribute a new round of songs and stories to Barbeau's recording project. Having purchased his own Edison phonograph on the previous trip, he was now at ease with the device. Teit was also at ease with it, as he had also purchased one in the spring of 1912 for use at home and on an upcoming Tahltan field trip.

Having had a new encounter with his black bear manitou, Tetlanetza was keen to share details with Barbeau and Teit. He explained that one night, while he was living in a work camp near a copper mine at 8-Mile Creek near Spences Bridge, he had had "a dream" in which a woman "wearing a single skirt came and called him." She was "of dark complexion," he noted, "and in appearance similar to people who are half Indian and half Negro in blood." He noticed that her face was "slightly blue in color as if painted blue." The woman instructed him to follow her into a hole in the rocks near a creek. The hole was "the opening of the tunnel or mine in which he had been working." He did as she instructed and, on entering, spotted a "dark colored baby lying wrapped in an old blanket." The baby was so frightened by his appearance that it turned into a "fly" and flew up into the roof of the tunnel. "Don't be afraid," the woman called out to the baby. "This is your uncle. He will not hurt you." At that point, the woman's skirt fell off "and she became quite naked," and the baby reappeared as "a real baby in her arms." She rocked it and sang a song, which Tetlanetza learned and sang with her. When she finished singing, Tetlanetza asked her not to "harm him." Having seen the baby transform into a fly and then transform back into a baby, he knew that she was "a powerful 'mystery.'" Her response was to start singing. Tetlanetza joined in. When she finished her song, she offered to "take him home." Naked and carrying her baby, she led him to his bed in the camp and disappeared. Tetlanetza awoke from what he thought was a five-minute nap, only to discover that the full night had passed and it was now daybreak. In his mind, the woman and her baby were new manifestations of the black bear sisters. For this reason, he embraced her song as his own. Tetlanetza explained that the sisters always "appeared to him in different forms in his dreams," and although the woman in this dream did not explain it this way, "she always treat[ed] him in the same way by taking him off to show him something." She often appeared as "a very dark woman" carrying a baby. After explaining all of this, Tetlanetza sang the woman's song to Barbeau.[27]

He also sang the dream song of a long-dead prophet named Kwālos, who created a stir when he announced that he had had a dream that transported him to France. He told the people that "his spirit left his body and passed rapidly to the shores of a great lake in the far east where the clouds always hung low along the edge of the water." His spirit rolled along until it came "to a land on the other side of the great lake," where he encountered many "strange people who spoke a strange language very different from the Indian languages." These people were light-skinned, with different colours of hair and eyes, "and many fine clothes and ornaments." Kwālos imitated the sound of their speech and described their large stone houses with "mouths and eyes" and fires burning inside. The houses were surrounded by beautiful flowers. These people had animals who "were like dogs and mixed with the people." They also "had much music and singing" and were "very rich" and "seemed to be happy." Kwālos told the people that "these strange new people ... would come to the Indians sometime soon and then great changes would take place among the Indians." Tetlanetza explained that when Kwālos first told his people about this dream, few took it seriously. He noted that today, however, many people reflect back on Kwālos's dream and "believe his spirit really went over to France," where it acquired knowledge of "the advent of whites."[28]

Tetlanetza also sang a "shaman's song used in doctoring sick people," which he had learned from "an old shaman called 'Flying Squirrel'" of

Nicola. Flying Squirrel had used this song to revive a grandchild who was "very sick" and "emaciated" and on the verge of death.[29]

Stories of women transforming into bears, babies transforming into flies, and old men dreaming their way to France were not new to Teit. He had been raised on similar stories in Shetland. During his years in British Columbia, he had interviewed old Shetland seamen about their memories of his island's old sea lore. In 1918, he had enough material for an article on the topic, which he published in the *Journal of American Folklore*.[30] Like Tetlanetza's stories, the Shetland stories depicted a world populated by powerful "people" who could transform themselves at will into other forms, such as seals and porpoises, and travel long distances at record speeds. "I have heard of *Finns*," or seal people, as "having journeyed to or from Norway in only a few hours," Teit explained.[31] Like the Nlaka'pamux prophet Kwālos, such people had the gift of foreknowledge. Because of this, fishing crews considered it good luck to have a Finn on board. Some Finns lived as ordinary people "all their lives ... without betraying their identity."[32] Because of their small stature, dark complexions, and distinct skin blemishes, however, it was difficult to keep their true identities secret. "I remember," wrote Teit, "that when I was a boy, two or three persons were pointed out as being affected by these skin blemishes, which, it was said, proved their descent."[33]

In 1916, Teit and Tetlanetza initiated a museum project that was directly pertinent to the land-title issue. Having tried unsuccessfully to convince both federal and provincial authorities that the Nlaka'pamux peoples were the legitimate and rightful owners of their large land base, Tetlanetza narrated in full – in his language and at his own pace – an account of his community's traditional land-tenure system, complete with descriptions of the family groupings within that community. He may have been motivated by his frustration with Prime Minister Borden, who had no interest in hearing such stories (see Chapter 7), or by his equally frustrating exchanges with the members of the McKenna-McBride Royal Commission when they interviewed him at Spences Bridge in November 1913 about the social constitution of the reserves in the Spences Bridge Band. That exchange did not allow for a discussion of traditional community protocols. Nor did it allow for a translator of his choice. The commissioners had arrived at Spences Bridge with their own translator, Lily Blatchford. To compensate for this, Tetlanetza and his colleagues hired Teit to double-check her translations.

The 1916 trip to Ottawa would be Tetlanetza's last trip to the nation's capital. He died on April 20, 1918, of stomach cancer. Teit notified Sapir and his museum staff of the death, noting the heavy impact of the loss:[34] "Taking him all round, he was probably the most intelligent chief in the Interior of BC and he can't be replaced by another like him. At least none of the others are quite his equal."[35] Many of Tetlanetza's colleagues contributed to Teit's song project at Spences Bridge, perhaps as a way of supporting the project that their old chief had initiated in Ottawa.

Missing in History

Until a few years ago, the Canadian Museum of History had nothing on file for the 1912 and 1916 Ottawa song sessions beyond a few random notes by Teit and a collection of forty cylinder recordings in Barbeau's name. Given Teit's role in the recording sessions and his compulsive commitment to full documentation at all times (often in duplicate), such a gap did not make sense. Teit had submitted detailed notes on all the songs that he had recorded at his Spences Bridge workshop (and in Telegraph Creek) from 1912 until 1920, and these were all carefully filed under his name at the museum. His notes included his own comments about the song that Tetlanetza had sung for Barbeau in Ottawa in 1916.[36]

The first clue to the missing notes turned up in a collection of stories that Barbeau had published (with Grace Melvin) in 1943 under the title *The Indian Speaks.* In the middle of the collection was a fifteen-page account of Tetlanetza's manitou story. The depth of detail for the story suggested that Barbeau could not have reconstructed it from memory three decades after its telling.[37] A comment by Barbeau in the book's preface suggested that he had relied on notes: he thanked the museum "for the use of unpublished texts in its keeping."[38] Barbeau's liner notes for a 1957 Folkways record, *My Life in Recording Canadian-Indian Folk-Lore,* included another reference to notes. He explained that in Ottawa in 1912, he had recorded a "set of songs and dances ... on the phonograph," and that he had also compiled "a full text with translation and explanation" to accompany those songs.[39] With this, I had it straight from the source that Barbeau had indeed kept notes on the songs.

Another clue turned up in the January 10, 1959, edition of the *Star Weekly Magazine.*[40] Barbeau had published a condensed version of Tetlanetza's bear sisters' song in the magazine, and, unlike the previous version, he included details of how he had acquired the story: "When I was a young ethnologist at the National museum in 1912, a delegation of British Columbia Indians arrived in Ottawa to interview the government on their rankling land question. To while away the time when waiting, some of them came to the museum and I worked with them recording songs and legends." Barbeau mentioned Teit for the first time in this article: as a "guide" from "the Shetland islands," who had served as the delegation's "interpreter." He explained that one day, when he, Teit, and Tetlanetza were alone, Teit informed Barbeau that Tetlanetza wanted to give him his personal vision song as a special gift. It was an unusual offering, Barbeau explained, as such songs were "usually withheld and kept a secret for a lifetime."

In a 1965 CBC radio interview about his career as a folklorist (an interview that the museum reissued in 1982 as a vinyl recording),[41] Barbeau retold the story of Tetlanetza's special gift, but in a very different way than he had told it previously. Instead of a three-way exchange involving Teit, he reduced it to a two-way exchange between Tetlanetza and himself. He made no mention of Teit: "[Tetlanetza and I] worked together and I had great difficulty recording those harsh sounds, sounds of the palate, of the throat, throat rattling we call that, and so forth. It was difficult, but I managed to do it and I kept on recording. I transcribed several of them and I think I wrote good transcriptions." Instead of three singers and forty songs, he described the session as involving "ten to fifteen" singers who sang "sixty or seventy songs." More significantly, Barbeau added a new detail to the story about the special song given to him as a gift. He explained that Tetlanetza had told him that he, Barbeau, would be free to release the song to the public after his (Tetlanetza's) death, and that he would find a way to notify Barbeau of this. Barbeau was pleased to report that Tetlanetza had followed through with this plan:

> Fifteen or twenty years later I was on the Skeena River working with the Tsimshian, an entirely different group of people way up towards Alaska. One night, I was coming back home when there was a man that walked on the track back and forth, and he said, "Are you Mr. Barbeau?" I said, "Yes, I am, why?" He said, "You know you have a friend way down in the Ntlakapamuks territory. He has died and he wants me to tell you."

It took but a minute to see the inconsistencies and inaccuracies in Barbeau's story. First, Tetlanetza did not die fifteen to twenty years after Barbeau recorded his story in Ottawa in 1916; he died two years later, on April 20, 1918, and Barbeau would have received news through Teit, who notified the museum staff of Tetlanetza's decline and of his death. Secondly, Barbeau was nowhere near the Skeena River in northern British Columbia

Marius Barbeau, c. 1957, transcribing songs from a phonograph. If left alone, the cylinders retained their original recording quality. If played repeatedly for transcription purposes, as Barbeau is doing in this photograph, the cylinder gained static, often to the point of obscuring the singers' voices. | Photograph by Chris Lund, #J4840, courtesy of the Canadian Museum of History.

at the time of Tetlanetza's death. According to his biographer, Laurence Nowry, he was in Ottawa preparing for a summer of field research in Quebec.[42] Barbeau would not get to the Skeena River until July 1920, two years after Tetlanetza's death. Third, and most striking, was that Barbeau could not have communicated directly, or at any time, with Tetlanetza without Teit's assistance because Tetlanetza spoke no English.

So how could this have happened? Could Barbeau have become forgetful in his latter years? Or did he feel he could take such liberties because there was no one left alive to challenge him? Teit had died in 1922; Tetlanetza had died in 1918; and Sapir had died in 1939. Harlan Smith, who also knew details of the 1912 and 1916 song sessions, had died in 1940.

Armed with this new information, I contacted the museum's archivists, and this time I was in luck. They had undertaken a full inventory of their

Marius Barbeau holdings and found the missing notes. They were a revelation. A comparison of Barbeau's original handwritten notes, as dictated by Teit, with the published versions, edited and reworked by Barbeau, revealed that Barbeau had not only changed the wording of Teit's dictations but had cut out large sections of Tetlanetza's story. One of his most extensive cuts was the segment of the story about the old man in a priest's white robe, which Tetlanetza had emphasized as a key part of his story:

> 8 years after that he [Tetlanetza] was working in the government trail, down Sywash Creek, near Yale [practically outside of the Lower Thompson Territory]. He was sleeping one night, down there. All at once a figure of what appeared to be an old man, appeared to him in his dream. This old man was clad in white, in a long robe, something like a priest's robe. He had a white woven belt around his waist. And he sang the same song, belonging to the Bear Sisters. He said, "Do you recognize me?" He [Tetlanetza] never answered to this question. This man said, "If you don't sing this song that I am singing, at noon tomorrow you will die. You must sing my song very well for me." Tetl. started to sing in his dream, when he woke up.[43]

Barbeau had not only cut all of the above, but he had also composed a completely new version of Tetlanetza's story:

> Eight years then followed like a gap in my life, eight full years without a glimpse of my *snams*. The *snams* are forgetting us nowadays; they are leaving the country. I was working on a Government trail, working with pick and shovel. As I slept there at night, I had a dream. The Twin Sisters appeared to me, singing the song of Nature, and they asked "Do you recognize it?" I had recognized it, but there was no spirit voice left in me; I could not reply.[44]

In the original telling (as dictated to Barbeau by Teit), Tetlanetza had made no mention of "the *snams*" as "forgetting us" and "leaving the country." On the contrary, in his discussion with Teit, Tetlanetza had stressed that his "manitous" (as Teit called them in English) were alive and well in 1912 and 1916, and doing a good job of protecting him.

Barbeau's prefatory comments in *The Indian Speaks* explained some of these cuts and changes. There, he and his illustrator, Grace Melvin, stated that their goal for the book was to present "the authentic utterances and sayings" of the Indian peoples of Canada, whom they described as "native survivors of a past," and part of a world that was "well on its way to complete disappearance." In a reference to Tetlanetza's story, they noted that "the Indian nowadays can no longer hope to hear, in the bosom of Nature, 'the word that alone can save his life.'"[45] To speak of sᴇɴā'ms as alive and well, and white priest's robes as part of the contemporary tapestry of traditional oral narrative tradition, clearly disrupted their goal of portraying Indian life as in a steady state of decay.

With the CBC interview in mind, I scoured Barbeau's 1912 and 1916 Ottawa notes for more details about Tetlanetza's offer of his song to Barbeau as a special gift. I found nothing. I also searched the notes for evidence of the special instructions that Tetlanetza supposedly gave Barbeau about withholding the release of the manitou song until after his death. Again, nothing. What I did find, however, contradicted Barbeau's point that the song should be kept from public view. Tetlanetza had explained, through Teit, that members of his community knew his manitou song well and sang it regularly at public gatherings. He had noted, in the context of another vision song, that it was common practice for trainees to share the stories of their vision experience with their families and others on their return from their training.

In his pursuit of one-on-one exchanges with John Tetlanetza and Ignace Jacob about the relationships between the human and the non-human, between the individual and the group, between place and space, between cultural survival and cultural demise, Teit was on a path that the new guard in anthropology was just beginning to recognize as important: an anthropology of "belonging." Frustrated by the anonymity and sterility of anthropology's emphasis on the large-group survey, Boas's former students, Edward Sapir and his colleague Paul Radin, argued for a focus on the "primacy" of "actual individuals" as a way to gain a more "intimate picture of how a people lived, worked, ate."[46] "You must have the ability to put yourself in another man's place," Radin wrote to Sapir in 1914, "knowing nevertheless that you are not the other man – and try to feel like him."[47] By 1916, Teit was far along on this path. Barbeau, however, was fixed on his own objectives, perhaps aware he might use such "information" to his personal advantage someday.

Invisibilizing Teit

Barbeau was not alone in his effacement of Teit. After Teit's death in 1922, Boas quietly invisibilized him. Teit's reports on Nlaka'pamux basketry and basket designs, ethnobotany, and place names were more or less finished, but his reports on the US Salish groups, and his studies of clothing, horse equipment, and designs in painting and beadwork, were still incomplete.[48] Having funded the fieldwork for most of these projects, Teit's longtime benefactor, Homer Sargent, wanted to see them through to publication. Sargent also had personal reasons for this, as he and Teit had become close friends over the years.[49] Sargent sent Boas funds to finalize Teit's unpublished works.

It took six years to see the results of Sargent's funding. Between 1928 and 1930, Boas released five monographs: *The Middle Columbia Salish, Coiled Basketry in British Columbia and Surrounding Region, The Salishan Tribes of the Western Plateaus, Ethnobotany of the Thompson Indians of British Columbia,* and *Tattooing and Face and Body Painting of the Thompson Indians.* He published the first one with the University of Washington Press, and the latter four with the Smithsonian's Bureau of American Ethnology. He issued Teit's "Traditions and Information Regarding the Tona'xa" as an article in *American Anthropologist.*[50]

Of all these works, the basketry manuscript was closest to completion at the time of Teit's death, so it should have been the easiest to finalize. In fact, it was the most problematic. Boas submitted the manuscript to the Smithsonian's Bureau of Ethnology in 1919, but the Smithsonian moved so slowly on it that he withdrew it and sent it to the Chicago Field Museum. On encountering similar delays at the Chicago end, he withdrew it again and resubmitted it to the Smithsonian. Somehow, during the transition from Washington, DC, to Chicago and back, some of the manuscript's photographic plates became separated from their captions. It was a serious problem that took Boas many months to rectify.[51] In the end, Boas had to drop some of the images because he could not reconnect them to their captions.

In this publication bonanza, Boas invisibilized Teit. Instead of publishing the basketry monograph under the single authorship of Teit, as he should have done, he published it as the joint work of three authors: H.K. Haeberlin, James Teit, and Helen H. Roberts (in that order). His non-alphabetical ordering turned Haeberlin into the lead author and Teit and Roberts into secondary authors. Boas did this with full knowledge that Teit was the primary author of the work. He had spent years interviewing basket makers about their basketry construction and design; he had made endless sketches of their basket designs and complemented these with photographs; he had compiled detailed accession notes to accompany the hundreds of baskets he sent to museums across the country; and he had recorded detailed biographies of the basket makers, which he cross-referenced to the basket designs. By comparison, the two so-called co-authors were minor contributors. Haeberlin, who spent only four days at Spences Bridge with Teit, had died of diabetes shortly after embarking on the project; his replacement, Helen Roberts, had stepped in at the last minute to help Boas prepare the manuscript for publication. Unlike Haeberlin, she had had no direct contact with either Teit or the basket makers. By placing Teit's name in the middle of the three authors, Boas rendered him the least significant of the contributors.

Teit's *Ethnobotany of the Thompson Indians* suffered the same fate. Rather than issuing it under the single authorship of Teit, Boas instead issued it as "Edited by Elsie Viault Steedman ... based on Field Notes By James A. Teit." His wording placed Steedman in a lead role and Teit in a secondary, essentially non-authorial, role. The monograph thus entered the library cataloguing system under Steedman's name rather than Teit's.[52] On receiving her copy of *Ethnobotany of the Thompson Indians,* Josie Teit, who had watched her husband gather plants and compile six hundred pages of field notes on those plants, wrote an angry response to Boas: "Perhaps I was expecting too much, but I am disappointed with the *Ethnobotany of the Thompson Indians* which is indexed by 'Elsie Viault Steedman.'"[53]

Without Teit to approve his reports, Boas also took liberties that he could not have taken had Teit been alive. For example, in the preface to Teit's *Middle Columbia Salish,* Boas wrote that "Mr. Teit's perception of sounds is not very definite ... He does not distinguish clearly between velars and middle palatals, and does not always hear labialization."[54] In fact, what Boas should have explained was that the monograph was based on a short preliminary report compiled by an ethnographer who had died before finishing it and who was fully fluent in three Interior Salish languages (Nlaka'pamux, Secwépemc, and Syilx) but not in the Middle Columbia Salish languages. In his introduction to Teit's *Salishan Tribes of the Western Plateaus,* Boas wrote that "Mr. Teit's spelling of native words is not quite certain" and cautioned readers that his immersion in the Nlaka'pamux language and culture may have "guided" his insights on the southern Interior Salish peoples.[55] Again, Boas could not have made such criticisms if Teit had been alive.

Anthropologist Lila O'Neale was one of the few scholars to draw attention to Boas's manoeuvres. Having recently completed a doctoral dissertation on the basketry traditions of the American southwest, she was asked to review the *Coiled Basketry* monograph for *American Anthropologist.* In her review, she acknowledged "Mr. Teit" as the primary producer of the "notes" that had informed the monograph.[56] The "students of textile technology," she wrote, should be "grateful" for such "authentic material" on the "proficiency, variety of patterns used, [and] so-called personal designs and devices."[57] She praised Roberts for her clerical contributions: "In spite of the exceptional difficulties and the obstacles natural to working with others' notes, Miss Roberts has reduced a vast amount of detail to accessible form."[58] She reserved her critical comments for Boas. She wrote that as the director and supervisor of the project, he had missed a huge opportunity in not writing more on "his reaction to the results of an investigation so unique in aim, and of its significance as a method of procedure."[59] She expressed disappointment that the most that Boas could conclude about the "attitude of the individual artist toward his work" was, first, that "the scope of forms ... shows that the range of individual invention is strictly limited by the traditional style," and, second, on the subject of designs, that "the power of invention of the artist is obviously under the control of tradition." She concluded by stressing that this "unique" field-based project (i.e., Teit's contribution) would have benefitted greatly from a more imaginative treatment of the data (i.e., Boas's contribution).[60] In fact, Teit professed no interest in Boas's generalizing objectives, which, in the end, essentially came to naught.

Boas's handling of Teit's field notes completes this astigmatic picture. In the fall of 1930, with the bulk of Teit's manuscript material in print, Boas decided that it was time to dispose of the "big drawer full of notes collected by Mr. Teit." With funds from Sargent, he hired his research assistant, Lucy Kramer, to sift through the contents of the drawer and set aside new material, and then to "throw out" any and all materials that were published – that is, to dispose of his detailed field notes.[61] These were undoubtedly full of information of little interest to Boas, the grand unifier, but that is today the stuff of critical, other-oriented, nuanced understanding. With the deed done – and all the losses it entailed for future scholars and Indigenous community members – Boas notified Sargent that, not surprisingly, the task had not yielded "as much as it seemed in the beginning."[62] He wrote that he wished that Teit had undertaken this cleanout himself (something Boas never did with his own rough notes). "It would have made the work very much simpler."[63] The cleanout gave closure to Boas's long collaboration with Teit.

10
Farewell Coyote, Hello Jack

> *Our esteemed friend, one who has found a warm place in the heart of every Indian in this Province, has passed away ... J.A. Teit ... was not just a friend, he was a brother of the Indians of this Province. He had their utmost confidence. He had their implicit trust; he was looked to, not as a white man, not as a sojourner among the Indians in this Province, but one of them; one who could present their views perhaps better than any other man of the present generation.*
>
> – Peter Kelly, in a speech on behalf of the Allied Indian Tribes of British Columbia, Ottawa, July 25, 1923[1]

"Benefactor of the Indians," "Leading Authority on Indian Basketry," "a loss ... to the Socialist movement," "a Man of Extraordinary Gifts." Such were the newspaper headlines and leads announcing Teit's death on October 30, 1922.[2] A feature story by Snowdon Dunn Scott, writing under the pseudonym "Lucian," in the weekend section of Vancouver's *Daily Province* was more than a simple death notice. Echoing Teit's father, John Tait, who, on the eve of his son's departure for British Columbia in 1884, had worried that his boy's sweet nature might make him an easy target of manipulation, the article argued that Teit had fallen prey to a group of foreign scholars who pumped him dry for ethnographic information and then "efface[d]" him at the publication stage.[3] The key offender was

> a famous ethnologist in Columbia University, New York who would not deny that he owes to Mr. Teit more than to all his books ... Professor Boas could not, in fifty years of study as a research student, have gained directly from the Indians as much as he obtained in two or three summers with Mr. Teit. You cannot by searching find out what the Indians know. They would not ... reveal themselves to a superior stranger asking them questions.[4]

Teit was "a man with a mine of original knowledge, a linguist in native tongues, an authority in Indian work and folklore, who had no ambition to appear in print, who claimed no copyrights, [and] who was glad to tell all he knew to any man who could make use of it." Little did he realize that "quite unconsciously, he was preparing for ... the splendid assistance he was able to give to research workers from the universities and learned societies."[5]

Snowdon Dunn Scott had known Teit for six years. A seasoned newspaperman with academic credentials that included a seat on the University of British Columbia's Board of Governors, two university degrees, an honorary doctorate, and scholarly expertise in Canadian political and constitutional history, early maritime history, and Greek and Roman classics, he had a large following. A latecomer to the Vancouver newspaper scene, he arrived in 1909 to work for the city's *News-Advertiser* after twenty-five years of editing newspapers in Nova Scotia and New Brunswick.[6] His writing career spanned the country, including Ottawa's Press Gallery, where he was known as the "dean of newspaper journalism." At the time of Teit's death in 1922, he was the managing editor of the *Vancouver Daily Province.*[7]

Scott described Teit's death as a national loss. He recalled that, shortly after taking up his Vancouver post, he had been summoned to "a conference of British Columbia Indian chiefs" on "Indian rights" with the head of Indian Affairs, where he noticed a white man translating for "one after another [of the chiefs] ... in clear, cultured English." Scott was struck by the man's "simplicity, felicity, and clearness" of speech. It was as if "every sentence was ready for the press." At the end of the meeting, he asked for an introduction to the translator.[8] His request sparked a friendship that lasted until Teit's death. The two men met up whenever Teit came to town. Scott used these visits to probe his friend's past. A skilled newspaperman who could pull a story from a stone, he emerged with a troubling account of Teit's relations with the prominent New York professor, Franz Boas.

Few of even Teit's closest friends, relatives, and associates knew the details of his arrangements with Boas. Homer Sargent, Teit's hunting companion, concluded that overexertion had contributed to Teit's death.[9] Although he knew that Boas was a factor in the exertion, he skirted the issue in a letter to the latter and blamed the plight of the Indians: "I fear that he was working so hard in their behalf and on their case that he neglected the signs of his reoccurring illness until it got so strongly fastened on to him as to be hopeless."[10] A post-mortem examination suggested that Sargent may have been correct. It revealed that Teit had not died of cancer

The Teit children on the steps of the family home at Spences Bridge around the time of their father's death in 1922. From left to right: Erik, Sigurd, Thor, Magnus, and Inga. | Photographer unknown, courtesy of Sigurd Teit.

after all but of a pelvic abscess that, if diagnosed earlier, "could have been cured by an operation."[11]

Sargent worried about how Josie and her five children would now fare. In a long letter to Boas, he explained that "Jimmy" had left her with nothing but the family house and "a couple of [bank] notes." The notes did not amount to much, especially as Teit had endorsed one to the Allied Indian Tribes.[12] In May, Sargent decided to purchase Canadian stock on Josie's behalf that would give her a quarterly dividend of $105.[13] Because it would take four months for the dividend to take effect, he would use the cheques that Boas had "sent from time to time," along with some of his own money, to cover her expenses in the interim. He wrote to Boas that he would explain this interim payment to Josie as coming "from us jointly."[14]

Sargent also worried that "the Indians will be the chief sufferers from his death." "I hardly think," he wrote, "that anyone else will take up that part of his work or even attempt it and what sentiment he had stirred up in the past which was favorable, will soon die away."[15]

As mentioned in Chapter 9, Sargent offered Boas funds to bring Teit's unfinished reports to completion. Boas used the first of the funds for a trip to Spences Bridge to see what Teit had left in his home office. It was a quick visit. He arrived in the village by train in the afternoon and spent the next morning with Josie Teit, sorting through the material. He was back at the train station in the afternoon, complaining that the Vancouver-bound train was late.[16]

Had Snowdon Dunn Scott known the details of Boas's fleeting trip to Spences Bridge, he might well have worked it into his obituary. On his whirlwind visit, Boas's concern was not the loss of a friend of twenty-eight years, but the end of his steady supply of ethnographic material. To Boas, both the ethnographer and his Nlaka'pamux consultants were "informants" in the narrowest sense of the term: sources of words and phrases that he could work into his dictionaries and grammars; of stories that he could use to explain diffusion and change; of songs that he could mine for insights on "primitive" melodic and rhythmic structures; of artistic designs that could contribute to his theories of so-called primitive art. One of Boas's final requests of Teit was to seek out Nlaka'pamux basket makers and ply them with questions about their methods of basket construction and techniques of design. Some of the basket makers were within easy reach on the day of Boas's visit,[17] but he sought out not a single one of them. There was no sorrow and no sharing in their sorrow. He made no occasion to express his sympathies or his gratitude. Instead, Boas retrieved what he thought could be useful to him and then moved on to the next destination.

Boas and Teit, 1922

Teit's story can certainly not be told without Boas. Before he met Boas, Teit dabbled in ethnography, but Boas gave that work academic structure and logistical support. The two men were a study in contrasts. Ever the modernist, Boas sought to distill the diversity and multiplicity of culture to its essentials through the lens of scientific generalization. Teit was the unconscious postmodernist, alive to the grit and grandeur of cultural diversity. Boas's loyalties were to the academy – hence his early fame and continuing appeal within mainstream anthropology. Teit's was a grounded anthropology, motivated by the cultural resistance to settler colonialism. Read Boas and you get the point but not the people; read Teit and you catch a glimpse of an "other" and want to be there. Their opposition explains Boas's stardom and Teit's exclusion. It is past time for a reassessment.

Snowdon Dunn Scott's reassessment in 1922 was astute. The even ground on which the two men had stood in 1894 – as new immigrants subsisting on short-term contracts and facing uncertain futures in their new homes – was long gone. Boas was now a model of institutional success and stability. He held a prestigious professorship in anthropology at Columbia University that provided him with a steady income, a flow of brilliant graduate students, and a large network of distinguished colleagues and contacts across the continent. His academic base in New York City helped solidify his greatest contribution, his anti-racist research paradigm. Through two seminal works – *The Mind of Primitive Man* and the "Introduction" to the Smithsonian's *Handbook of American Indian Languages* – published back to back in 1911, he had argued convincingly that "the behavior of all men, regardless of race or cultural stage," was shaped by "the particular 'cultures' in which they lived" rather than by race.[18] The "protagonists of environment and of racial equality" were elated with Boas, as finally they had "science on their side."[19] Initially Boas had deployed "historical diffusionism" to make his case for cultural relativism, but by 1920 he had shifted his focus to "the psychological study of the individual."[20] His new brand of university-based anthropology – grounded in science, linguistics, and *in situ* fieldwork – was now a staple of the social sciences.[21] A family house in the upscale neighbourhood of Grantwood, New Jersey (across the Hudson River from Columbia University), and a summer home on the fashionable shores of Lake George in northern New York State completed this embodiment of institutional and academic success. As anthropologist Herbert Lewis writes, Boas was on an upward trajectory that would end well:

> By the time of his death, Boas was considered one of the most prominent scientists of his time, a member of the National Academy of Science and the American Philosophical Society, conversant with all the sciences (mathematically sophisticated, having produced a dissertation in psychophysics, a geographer, biological anthropologist, linguist, student of culture and history), and recognized as such.[22]

Meanwhile, Teit's life in 1922 had changed little since 1894. He was still based at the Bridge and subsisting on short-term contracts.[23] Despite authoring five major ethnographic monographs and multiple reports, articles, and book chapters, he had not made it into the North American anthropological establishment. This was partly a result of his self-imposed isolation and his diverse lines of work, but it was also a result of the professionalization of anthropology. For a new scientific discipline housed in the university, a high school diploma did not measure up.

Teit was a factor in his own marginalization. In 1911, Edward Sapir had offered him a permanent position in his newly established Anthropology Division in Ottawa that would have given Teit a high public and academic profile, but he turned it down because it would also have meant abandoning the rural life in British Columbia that he loved. He thrived on all dimensions of the local. In addition to his own ranch, he had married into a busy Spences Bridge farming family that depended on his help in the growing and harvest seasons. Ten years in the wilds had turned him into one of the province's "premier" hunting guides, and he relished his days in the bush. He could never have given this up. As a confirmed naturalist, he could not live in the city. He found a way to make the Ottawa job work by negotiating a contract with Sapir that allowed him to work from home, but it kept him out of the limelight. Addicted to his community and its long-term health, he became a vital member of the newly formed Indian Rights Association and the Interior Tribes of British Columbia.

On the institutional front, there was no real place for Teit, and Boas made things work. On the ethnographic front, it was the other way around. At his death, Teit had logged close to four decades of continuous, on-the-ground fieldwork in British Columbia, Washington State, Idaho, Oregon, and Montana, much of it on foot, in boats, and on horseback. It had led to eleven major monographs on the "Interior Salish" peoples of this region and a major legacy as a political activist. His travels across the province in all seasons had turned him into an authority on the region's natural and human histories. Indeed, there were few in the settler Canadian community with his depth of knowledge of British Columbia's fish, flora, and fauna and there was no one in that community with his depth of knowledge of the Indians' perspectives on that natural history.

Meanwhile, Boas had long abandoned his British Columbia fieldwork. Between 1900 and 1922, he made only one field trip to BC (three weeks in the summer of 1914).[24] He preached fieldwork, but he had trouble practising it. His student Melville Jacobs described Boas as an "austere visitor," who "mingled politely with the natives but with some discomfort and always with a feeling of pressure to get the scientific task accomplished."[25] Unlike Teit, who relished the challenge of trekking through rough terrain and camping out with his interviewees, Boas "rarely participated in the daily lives of the Indians," and, except in the case of George Hunt, he "rarely lived in an Indian household or community unless circumstances required that he do so."[26]

Anthropology as Local Praxis

Shetland was a major force in Teit's anthropology. The nostalgic nationalism and longing for a "lost" original home that he felt on leaving Shetland at age nineteen grew stronger as he witnessed the same patterns of oppression and resistance in his old and new worlds. His allegiance to the late-nineteenth-century Shetland cultural renaissance helped him see that what, in the Nlaka'pamux context, mainstream society branded "low" culture was really "high" culture, but different. This was the foundation of Teit's anthropological training.

It is telling, writes historian George Stocking, that, of the many ethnographic research options available to Boas at the turn of the century, he chose to pursue linguistics and folklore. At a practical level, compiling word lists and recording oral stories suited his rapid-fire approach to fieldwork because both could be "easily collected" on "'flying visits' to one group after another."[27] The study of linguistics and folklore also supported his historical mission of preserving, in the name of science, not a living culture, but rather its last relics. Accepting that the cultures under study were going to disappear, he sought to rescue for posterity the last accoutrements of those cultures from their oldest members before they were gone. The abstracted transcripts of orally held myths served this objective well because, in Boas's eyes, they embodied the "whole concept of the world," its "individuality" and, ultimately, its "genius."[28] The act of creating print texts of this material was equivalent to salvaging the literary classics of Western Europe that could stand on their own without their authors or their communities. In Boas's hands, Indian myths would join the ranks of Sanskrit texts and medieval codices and offer scholars endless years of study and analysis without worry of loss. In the protective embrace of libraries and museums, they no longer needed the original tellers to keep them alive.[29]

However, myth posed problems for Boas. Language was lodged in the unconscious, but through recording and transcription, it could be taken into the laboratory, broken into its constitutive parts, and analyzed as scientific data. Myth, on the other hand, was the product of storytelling and subject to reinterpretation and retelling by multiple tellers over time. To Boas, the "true" forms of culture lay in the deep layers of the human unconscious. The interpretive overlay, or "secondary rationalization" (as Boas called it), by insiders was interference that needed to be filtered out by the professional to access the essential, singular culture.[30] This problem drove Boas's anthropological research program. By teaching his students how to identify – and remove – the outer layers of secondary rationalizations, he could infuse the culture concept with new analytical insight.[31]

Teit also pursued language and myth, but for different reasons. In his anthropological sphere, there were no "informants" with tainted secondary rationalizations in need of removal; there were friends and acquaintances with high levels of self-understanding and self-reflection. In his own way, he was one of them. When he wrote about traditional hunting practices, he wrote as a hunter who spent years with Nlaka'pamux and Tahltan hunters. When he wrote about local food practices, he wrote as one who had walked the land with its local foragers. When he wrote of the sweathouse tradition, he wrote as one who used the sweathouse as his neighbours did. When he wrote of attitudes toward death and dying, he wrote as one who sat with his friends in their dying moments. When he wrote of visionary experiences, he wrote as one who had such experiences himself. When he wrote about stories, he wrote as one who told stories. All of these experiences were reflected in the languages he learned and the stories he recorded. As Snowdon Dunn Scott noted in his newspaper tribute,

> [With his Shetland education] ... and while yet a youth and almost a stranger to the country, [Teit] became interested in the Indians. He hunted and fished with them, shared their adventures, their hardships, their entertainments [and] smoked and drank with them. He became acquainted with their habits of thought, their traditions, their superstitions, their folk-lore, their craftsmanship ... [To many, it looked like he] was wasting years of valuable time for no gain. He was, in fact, going through a period of apprenticeship in Goethe's sense. It was seen afterwards that in no other way could he have obtained that intimate and sympathetic knowledge which he acquired.[32]

Teit practised a form of communal "praxis" that responded to the appeals of living peoples to help fight the forces of colonialism. In drafting their Memorial to the head of Indian Affairs in 1911, the Interior chiefs asked him to add a statement in English that endorsed his efforts: "Only those few Whites who help us uphold the honour of their race."[33] Nothing in his ethnographic writings or his political activism suggests "salvage for salvage's sake," or anthropology as an act of "speaking for" or "about" naïve peoples lacking the capacity to speak for themselves. His was never a friendship forged to extract knowledge for abstract analysis. Teit pursued knowledge in the service of the community, of particular people, places, and histories. Instead of the single, foundational story, he recounted a multiplicity of stories. Instead of depersonalization and generalization, he highlighted the personal and the particular. There are undoubtedly problems with Teit's work, but it is difficult to find them. Meanwhile, the professional designation of the "participant-observer" does not even scratch the surface of Teit's anthropology.

Whereas Boas deferred to, indeed ignored, the colonial encounter, Teit kept it front and centre. This was especially so after 1909, when he joined forces with the Indian Rights Association and the Interior Tribes of British Columbia. He embraced such work without the expectation of recompense and often at the expense of other wage-earning opportunities. As hard as it is to believe, Teit was ten years into this work before he told Boas, the ardent debunker of racism, the full story of this side of his life. And even then, it was not because he thought Boas should know details of the controversy over land; it was because he wanted to relieve the pressure that Boas had applied over delays in his manuscript production. In a letter in August 1919, he described the political campaign to Boas as if he were describing it for the first time to a novice: "I will now reveal to you the special work I have been doing for the Indians here," he wrote, "and of which I have occasionally made mention to you. The Indian Tribes of BC for years back have been trying to get a settlement of their land rights, and the hunting, fishing and other rights claimed by them. They claim an aboriginal title in the lands of their forefathers ... Here in BC ... treaties have not been made with the tribes and reserves have been laid off arbitrarily, for bands only. Former B.C. Govs. even claimed the Indians had no rights."[34]

Without trumpeting the significance of his work for the chiefs, Teit noted that a royal commission had been established to settle the problem but that the Indians had "refus[ed] to accept its findings." The hope was that the newly formed Allied Indian Tribes of BC and its work with lawyers would help them "put their case before the Privy Council in England." In another surprising disclosure, Teit explained his financial arrangement with the chiefs:

> For several years the Interior tribes (who formerly were a separate organization) have had me doing their writing, keeping accounts for them, interpreting, and acting as chairman of their meetings, tc. When the tribes became allied they appointed me their secretary-treasurer, secretary & convenor of their executive Committee, and their special agent. For a number of years I did work for the Inds. without charge. They simply pa[id] my expenses when I went to a meeting tc. As the work has kept increasing of late they have paid me wages for what time I have put in for them.[35]

A close examination of the Teit-Boas collaboration on stories and storytelling reveals how their contrasting goals and expectations played out in their writings. At Boas's request, Teit set out in search of stories by knowledgeable storytellers. Teit had undertaken such work for years prior to meeting Boas. There was a difference in approach, however. Where Teit was drawn to first-hand narratives of personal experience, Boas was drawn to old "myths" and "legends," avowedly recounted from the precontact era. Yet there were no storytellers alive in the 1890s with direct experience of that era before 1808. Pa-ah was the main contributor to Teit's 1893 collection of stories. He was in his mid-seventies, putting his first memories (from age ten) at approximately 1827, and his first clear memories at around 1833 (age fifteen). These dates were well past first contact.[36] Another problem was that such stories were like the musical improvisations that Joe Abel had sung on my second trip to the Okanagan – that is, fluid and porous responses to their audiences and the contexts of their tellings. As I discovered with my transcription project in Vancouver, they defied fixation. Teit had tried to explain some of this to Boas: "Many of the trickster stories, and several of the motives common to the tribe, are picked up, and set into stories by different storytellers in any place where they seem to fit or can be made to fit and where they can be used to lengthen a story, or round it off."[37]

The diverse line of origin stories in Teit's 1912 *Mythology of the Thompson Indians* suggests that even in a sphere where one might expect a certain degree of agreement and consistency (e.g., the story of the origin of the world as told by Nlaka'pamux narrators from the Nicola Valley), there was little agreement. There was certainly no single, foundational storyline. What was "true" did not accord with the reach of the Boasian "scientific." What Boas could have learned had he understood his own secondary rationalizations and allowed himself to see Teit for what he was. And listened. As Teit explained to him in 1902,

> Some of the Nicola stories are peculiar. I have got several creation myths, and several semi-biblical stories. The latter have Indian elements, and are interesting as showing how stories get localized, and how Indian conceptions are engrafted on Whiteness... There are as many creation myths tc or different versions of the same thing that the Indians often wonder which is true, and some are skeptical of all.[38]

According to one story in Teit's 1912 *Mythology of the Thompson Indians,* a transformer known as "Old-One" created the earth from a ball of soil, which he threw from his home in the sky into a lake below.[39] In another story, Old-One created the earth from the wife of the Sun by turning her hair into "trees and grass," her flesh into "clay," her bones into "rocks," and her blood into "the springs of water."[40] According to a third story, Old-One created the world from one of five hairs that he pulled from his head and then transformed into a woman who "fell backwards, spread out her legs, and rolled off from the cloud into the lake, where she took the form of the earth we live on."[41] In a fourth story, Old-One created the earth from a woman's body, which he made "expand, and shape itself into valleys, mountains and plains."[42]

The multiple references in these origin stories to the postcontact world (including their key protagonist, "Old-One" or "Old Man," as he was sometimes called) challenged the idea that colonization could destroy a culture and leave its "myths" and "legends" intact. The narrator of the story about the woman whose body became "the valleys, mountains and plains" told Teit that the woman's blood "congealed in the form of a large mass of gold among the mountains." "The whites know this," he added, which is why they "always search for gold in the mountains, and not on the plains." He stressed that they would "never be able to find it," because "Old-One made the mountains all so much alike that it will be impossible for them to find the spot."[43] The narrator of an Okanagan (Syilx) origin story in Teit's 1917 *Folk-Tales of Salishan and Sahaptin Tribes* ended with "the story of the Garden of Eden and the fall of man nearly in the same way as given in the Bible."[44] The narrator of another Okanagan origin story in this volume explained that the "Chief" at the centre of his story might also have been "God." He noted that "maybe the first priests of white people told us this, but some of us believe it now."[45]

I saw strains of this in Harry Robinson's origin stories. He told a long story about how Coyote became his first ancestor. The story surprised me because it also included the origin of my first ancestor. According to Harry, his first ancestor (Coyote) and my first ancestor started out as twin brothers. The difference was that the older twin (his ancestor) was both good and bad, but the younger brother was all bad. As Harry put it, "That younger one, now today, that's the white man. And the older one, that's me."[46] Among Coyote's many antics and exploits was a trip to England to meet with the King to negotiate an end to "the war" that the King's people had wrought on Indians.[47]

Boas did not like the white incursions in stories, and in his role as Teit's editor, he often deleted details that compromised precontact purity. For example, on receiving a story from Teit about Old-One's exchange of a gun as part of a negotiation with a Nlaka'pamux boy and his grandmother, Boas published it in the 1917 collection but left out the gun.[48] Boas made a similar editorial decision in Teit's 1898 *Traditions of the Thompson River Indians.* In his introduction to the monograph, he listed the Nlaka'pamux "trickster-transformers" as: 1) "Coyote," 2) Qoā'qʟqaʟ (a group of three brothers) 3) "Kokwē'la" (a powerful figure from the plant world), and 4) Old Man (whom he would later rename "Old-One").[49] Meanwhile, he excluded from his list a fifth trickster/transformer – a young man who captured a cannibal (along with his wagon and horses) by getting him drunk on whiskey – even though this character was the primary protagonist of the last story in the volume. Like the gun in the 1917 story, the young man (along with the references to whiskey, a saloon, a horse, and a wagon in the story) affected the authenticity of the collection, but, more importantly, the exercise itself. Teit would soon stress in letters to Boas that this excluded protagonist was far from an anomaly or a misfit. He was a popular trickster-transformer known variously as "Jack," "Jack the Thief," "Bear," "Bear Boy," "John," "Wonderful Boy," "Grizzly Bear Boy," "Brothers," "Jack the Traveller," "Grizzly Bear's Son," and "Jack the Trickster,"[50] and who travelled through white men's towns eliminating negative intrusions such as naïve priests, greedy landlords, and nasty policemen (often by getting them drunk), and killing monsters, abductors, and rapists.

As a cultural disruptor in the postcontact world, Jack had no standing in Boas's salvage project. Unlike his precontact counterparts, Jack spoke to the social stratification that plagued nineteenth-century British Columbia: a world controlled by wealthy, white bosses, missionaries, government officials, landowners, and merchants with fancy houses stashed with gold, jewels, money, and, on occasion, female hostages, and surrounded by armed guards ("soldiers" and "policemen"). Priests, with their newly built churches and tales of rapture, turned up in a number of stories. In the story of "Jack and the Church," Jack was "travelling along" when suddenly he encountered a "fine church which the priests had just finished."[51] Immediately he defecated beside it. When the "evil smell" reached the priests and churchgoers, they held a meeting to decide "what they should do about it." They concluded that the church must be moved away from the smell of the excrement. However, as such a move "entailed much money and labour," they offered a reward to "anyone who would enlighten them as to the best thing to do." Jack suddenly popped into view and saved the day by advising the church fathers to remove the excrement rather than the church. He then scampered off happily with his reward.[52]

In another Jack story, a group of townspeople convinced a priest that he would be raptured by God the next morning if he climbed into a burlap sack and stayed there until the roosters began to crow the next morning. When the word went out, the villagers gathered around the trapped priest the next morning, cracking up with laughter when the roosters started up and the priest in the bag began to squirm and shake in anticipation of the impending rapture.[53]

In a world rife with inequity and anger over land theft, Boas's exclusion of Jack from the cast of Nlaka'pamux trickster-transformers underscored his lack of interest in the *living* world of the Nlaka'pamux peoples. Boas wanted only Coyote, and a pivotal Coyote at that. Jack, however, offered the Nlaka'pamux narrators a comic outlet to confront the incursions and stupidities of earnest missionaries, bureaucratic government agents, policemen, and other colonial agents. Teit collected Coyote stories, but he also revelled in Jack, a character described to him by storytellers as a longtime favourite protagonist. Jack gave Teit a view of *post*contact peoples that Boas rarely entertained.

So Where Do the Two Men Sit Today?

Like Coyote, Franz Boas's name and legacy still stand strong in the twenty-first century. In the last three decades alone, he has been the subject of multiple books and articles,[54] and the focus of numerous academic conferences.[55] The momentum, however, is fuelled by debate. On one side, a group of modernist defenders, led by Regna Darnell, Herbert Lewis, and others, assert that Boas is anthropology's much-maligned founding ancestor who deserves renewed respect and recognition for his fight for "human rights and individual liberty, freedom of inquiry and speech, equality of opportunity, and the defeat of prejudice and chauvinism." On the other side, Charles Briggs, Richard Bauman, Michael Harkin, and others argue that Boas's research paradigm is irrelevant and outdated, and perhaps even dangerous.

This debate is not new. Two of Boas's graduate students raised many of the issues on the dissenting side many decades ago. Paul Radin suggested to his colleague Edward Sapir, in a 1914 letter, that it was time to drop the "hero worship" of Boas in favour of honest appraisals.[56] Boas, he argued, certainly deserved praise for his success in the 1880s and 1890s at transforming the discipline of anthropology from an "adjunct of biology" into a mainstay of the social sciences, but he was now "done" because he lacked the "genius" to carry the discipline further. Radin characterized Boas as "an anatomist" rather than "a physiologist," and noted that he was so fixed on truth-driven "analytical examinations" rooted in his belief in cultural "dissemination, convergent evolution, independent origin, etc.," that he often missed the larger questions. Radin reminded Sapir that in their university courses with Boas, they had never once heard him express "the slightest desire" to "see the wheels go around."[57]

Such criticism escalated after Boas's death in December 1942. In a special memorial volume published under the banner of the *American Anthropologist,* Alfred Kroeber, another of Boas's former graduate students, praised Boas for his "unquenchable perseverance," his "infinite capacity for work," and his efforts to introduce new "problems" and "novel approaches" to anthropology. Like Radin, however, he would not characterize Boas as a "genius":[58]

> He made no one great summating discovery; he had no one slant, no designable and therefore closed idea-system ... No label fits him. The best he could find, in groping to make his anthropological attitudes clear to others, was the epithet, "dynamic"; which is true enough in a sense but also colorlessly inadequate. It was the man that was dynamic, and his ideas; not any ideology or methodology that he invented.[59]

Kroeber linked some of Boas's shortcomings to his university education. "It must be remembered," wrote Kroeber, "that [Boas] was trained in mathematics and all his life thought like a physicist."[60] He noted that if Boas "set limits to his conclusions that sometimes seemed narrow, it was because beyond them his intellectual conscience saw doubts and invalidities," and in the world of the scientist there should be no doubt.[61] Kroeber had much to say about the influence of science on Boas. "All his writing," he stated, "possesses an inner and very genuine form," but there is little "eloquent" or "aesthetic" about it; it is the product of the style of "decision, economy, and elegance in a mathematical demonstration." If asked about this, Kroeber noted, Boas would "undoubtedly have answered that [eloquence of] style belonged in literature and he was doing science." It was, Kroeber added, the "ice in his enthusiasm."[62]

In 1960, another of Boas's former students, Melville Herskovits, fuelled the debate with his comment that "t[h]ere have been no neutrals in the controversy" over the Boasian legacy. "For some, [Boas] is the great pioneer of anthropology ... Others, however, charge him with having blocked the development of theoretical speculation."[63] Herskovits called for a more sustained appraisal of "the various aspects" of Boas's "theoretical and methodological positions as they cut across the various anthropological sub-disciplines in which he worked, and with particular reference to the analyses of his point of view that have been made since his death."[64] With a group of post-war cultural materialists and neo-evolutionists led by Leslie White and Marvin Harris criticizing Boas as an anti-theoretical chaser of empty facts, Herskovits's call was ever more urgent.[65]

A new scholar on the scene in the 1960s answered this call for more balanced appraisals of Boas. Through a series of articles and book chapters, George W. Stocking Jr. stressed that although Boas did not generate a grand theory of culture, "his critique of nineteenth century racial and cultural evolutionary assumptions, both in anthropology and popular thought, [had] ... cleared the way for a more meaningful 'anthropological' (i.e., pluralistic, holistic, non-hierarchical, relativistic, behaviorally determinist) concept of culture."[66] Anthropologist Ronald Rohner added a new perspective on Boas with the publication in 1969 of the latter's field journals and family letters from the Northwest Coast.[67] They showed the Columbia University anthropologist struggling with fieldwork, sometimes to the point of nervous breakdown and depression. The letters also highlighted Boas's reliance on a single Tlingit/English "informant," George Hunt, for much of his research on Kwakwa̱ka̱'wakw culture.[68]

The "postmodern turn" in the social sciences in the 1980s subjected Boas to yet more criticism as anthropology struggled to come to terms with the charge that its imposition of Western rules and "truths" on other cultures – its scientism – was not only wrong but destructive. As a "fundamentalist modernist," the founding father of American anthropology became the target of this movement. A string of theorists – from James Clifford to Charles Briggs, Richard Bauman, and Michel Verdon – argued that Boas had inadvertently promoted the settler-colonial agenda by "claim[ing] consciousness and rationality for [himself] ... and [his] followers while denying it to [his subjects of study]."[69] Columbia University anthropologist Audra Simpson has recently added her voice to this debate. In a new essay on Boas, she highlights the latter's "inability to see or read Indigenous sovereignty and politics in any form other than the reduced, the primitive, or the ethnographically classic, a reading that disappears Indigenous political form, is blind to it, easily hitches it to other things, or diminishes it altogether."[70]

Unfortunately, a prerequisite to understanding Teit and his anthropology is to situate him, first, in a critique of Boas and his anthropology, as it was Boas who both enabled and bracketed Teit and his contribution. So where does Teit fit in this spectrum of adulation and critique? The quick answer is "nowhere." From George Stocking and Ronald Rohner in the 1960s to Charles Briggs, Richard Bauman, Regna Darnell, and Herbert Lewis more recently, anthropologists have simply ignored him. If they mention him at all, it is as Boas's "Scottish" assistant (a national designation he disdained) or Boas's backwoods field "informant." In a new book on Boas, Regna Darnell revised her position on Teit slightly by acknowledging him as "an anthropologist in his own right." However, she also described him as an ethnographer who "continued to publish independently after Boas's death," a stunning error that simply confirms anthropology's uninformed view of Teit.[71]

To date there have been no conferences, no research projects, and little sustained published work on Teit. Were Snowdon Dunn Scott to assess the situation today, he would have to conclude that the Teit-Boas alignment has changed little since 1922. To remove Teit from Boas's shadow and underscore his stature as an anthropologist in his own right, Scott bypassed his long list of monographs produced under Boas and highlighted his submission to the 1914 multivolume series *Canada and Its Peoples.* "If anyone wishes to know whether James Teit could write," Dunn Scott stated, "let him take that monumental work." It is "singularly clear and precise, without rhetorical adornment, and far less technical than the corresponding account of the Coast Indians by Dr. E. Sapir in the same work." It is "a pity," he added, that Teit died when "he was at his best," and at a time when he could have added so much more on "the aboriginal life of this province."[72] This tribute by a prominent Vancouver newspaper journalist was a powerful endorsement of Teit's cutting-edge anthropology.

Snowdon Dunn Scott died a year after publishing the piece, and Edward Sapir left his Ottawa post three years later to take up a professorship at the University of Chicago.[73] The task of keeping Teit's name alive fell to Sapir's Anthropology Division colleagues, Marius Barbeau, Diamond Jenness, and Harlan Smith. None of this trio had any interest in doing so; Barbeau, like Boas, had more to gain by burying it.

Close to a century after Teit's death, he has yet to be acknowledged within the discipline of anthropology for his pioneering achievements: his emphasis on the interplay between the personal story and the cultural whole; his elevation of the particulars over the generalities, of raw field notes over published monographs; his efforts to connect the physical world with the social world; and his grounding of the anthropological endeavour in living praxis rather than abstract salvage. If anthropologists today are asked to distill their disciplinary mission in a sentence, most would frame it in Teit's terms: as a self-reflective enterprise grounded in the details and the commitment to a mutuality and conversation between itself and its "others." The old model of top-down interrogation by all-knowing anthropologists with their un-self-reflective ethnographic informants is gone. That Teit saw the two models in operation a century ago and rejected the latter for the former, deserves recognition today. A testament to his foresight is the extent to which his century-old work – on place names, personal names, maps, stories, songs, plants – continues to animate scholars, teachers, artists, and land-claims researchers who live and work in the Indigenous communities today.

The legacy of James Teit and "all his relations" offers rewards without measure. This book is but a beginning.

Acknowledgments

A project that has gestated as long as this one accrues many debts. I owe the first and largest debt to the many Indigenous elders and their families who welcomed me into their homes and communities and gave generously of their time: Harry Robinson, Aimee August, Adeline Willard, Mary Abel, Mary Louise Powers, Mary Paul, Eva Lawrence, Rosie Marchand, Carrie Allison, Victor Antoine, Annie and Billy Swallwell, Edward Fred, Nellie Guitterrez, Annie York, Mamie Johnson, Willy Justice, Hilda Austin, Millie Michel, Mamie Henry, Louie Phillips, Bert Seymour, Jimmy Toodlican, Rosie Joe, Antony Joe, Mabel Joe, Ruby Dunstan, Karen Dunstan, Denise Dunstan, Hilda Belanger, Mariel Belanger, Janice Antoine, Percy Joe, David Walkem, John Haugen, Mandy Jimmie, Carol Holmes, Darwin Hanna, Charon Spinks, Ruby Dunstan, Leonard Andrew, Byron Spinks, Bernadette Manuel, Lynne Jorgesen, Dorothy Ursaki, and Rose Vandrich.

I also owe a major debt to a collection of BC books that appeared exactly when I needed them in the late 1970s and 1980s. Robin Fisher's *Contact and Conflict: Indian-European Relations in British Columbia, 1774–1890* and Rolf Knight's *Indians at Work: An Informal History of Native Labour in British Columbia, 1858–1930* addressed glaring gaps in the province's Indigenous history; Hugh Brody's eloquently told story of the Dunne-za peoples of northeastern BC, *Maps and Dreams: Indians and the British Columbia Frontier*, showed by example that good historical scholarship could also be good literature. Douglas Cole's *Captured Heritage: The Scramble for Northwest Coast Artifacts* challenged historians to consider the impact of the "museum age" on the lives of the Indigenous peoples of the Pacific Northwest. Finally, George Manuel's *Fourth World: An Indian Reality* offered a rare insider perspective on twentieth-century Indigenous life.[1]

Another book was formative for different reasons. In the spring of 1979, Professor Johannes Fabian, a member of Wesleyan University's Anthropology Department, had a new book manuscript that he wanted to test on the students in his "History of Anthropological Thought" course.[2] I was fortunate to be one of those students. Fabian's thesis, bold for its time, was that anthropologists needed to confront a "fundamental contradiction" within their discipline:

> On the one hand we dogmatically insist that anthropology rests on ethnographic research involving personal, prolonged interaction with the Other. But then we pronounce upon the knowledge gained from such research a discourse which construes the Other in terms of distance, spatial and temporal. The Other's empirical presence turns into [the anthropologist's] theoretical absence, a conjuring trick which is worked with the help of an array of devices that have common intent and function to keep the Other outside the Time of Anthropology.[3]

I had entered Fabian's class skeptical of the whole enterprise of anthropology. I left it with renewed enthusiasm. Fabian was at the forefront of a major disciplinary shakeup. As he put it in his book, "If we [anthropologists] can show that our theories of [others'] societies are *our praxis* – the way in which we produce and reproduce knowledge of the Others for our societies – we may (paraphrasing Marx and Hegel) put anthropology back on its feet."[4] One of Fabian's key themes was the extent to which anthropologists had adopted an oppositional time frame that placed the researchers in the "here and now" and the researched – their subjects of study – in the "then and there." Throughout his course, he highlighted Franz Boas, the so-called father of American anthropology, as a prime example of this problem. Because Boas had used British Columbia as a test site for his academic theorizing, Fabian's analysis had direct application for some of the research questions that I was considering in the region.

My shift from graduate school in the United States in the 1980s to the academic community in British Columbia in the 1990s was well timed because it coincided with a surge of new scholarship on the region by an army of political scientists, legal scholars, Indigenous activists, historians, anthropologists, linguists, and others. It also coincided with the landmark *Delgamuukw* court case. The latter, along with an explosion of new books (for example, Cole Harris's *The Resettlement of British Columbia,* Jean Barman's *The West beyond the West,* Paul Tennant's *Aboriginal Peoples and Politics,* and Bridget Moran's *Stoney Creek Woman: The Story of Mary John*), fuelled debate on the dynamics of settler colonialism.[5] Cole Harris added his own can of fuel to the debate, not only through his writings, but also through his circle of graduate students, his home seminars, and his "academic" road and rafting trips.

To those who gave comments on individual chapters – Lynne Jorgesen, Lorna Williams, Alice Turski, Jenny Clayton, Bonnie Campbell, Dana Lepofsky, Dorothee Schreiber, Rosemary Collard, and Lynne Van Luven – I am grateful. I especially thank Elizabeth Vibert, Anne Kittredge, Bev Sellars, Cole Harris, Audra Simpson, Marjory Harper, Judith Tabb, Julie Cruikshank, Ira Jacknis, Hamar Foster, and Brian Smith for commenting on the full manuscript. I am especially grateful to Hamar for dropping everything in the middle of his busy summer to prepare detailed written feedback, especially for the chapters on politics. Three anonymous reviewers also gave excellent feedback. I accept full responsibility for any errors or omissions.

I thank Ruby Dunstan, former chief of the Lytton First Nation, for her regular mid-morning, mid-week pep talks. One pep talk during a slow period in December 2017 helped me to the finish line. "Don't you ever say you wish you didn't start this great book," she said. "My ancestors would say, 'You crazy SHA-ma!' For pete's sake, do not give up!" I also thank Julie Cruikshank for her many years of supportive phone calls and emails and for never losing faith in my ability to reach the finish line. I thank my friend and colleague Judith Berman for helping me see links between my Teit/Boas story and her George Hunt/Boas story. I also thank Judith for reminding me regularly that writing is a slow and often painful process. Dorothee Schreiber helped me through one slow period by pointing out that just as there are slow and fast food movements, there are also slow and fast scholarship movements and that I should be proud to be a member of the former. I thank my friend John Haugen for encouraging me to make the Teit story accessible to all readers. I thank my close friend Anne Kittredge for test-reading the manuscript for me. She warned me before embarking on the task that she would stop if she found it hard going. With trepidation, I dropped off the first chapter, then the second, and then the third. On delivery of the fourth chapter (the "slow" chapter), I was sure she'd stop. It was a relief when she telephoned to request the last chapter.

I owe a huge round of thanks to my colleagues at the University of Victoria, in particular to those in the History Department's "Canadian Section" – John Lutz, Eric Sager, Lynne Marks, Penny Bryden, Elizabeth Vibert, Rick Rajala, Jordan Stanger-Ross, Peter Baskerville, and Pat Roy – for supporting me and my unorthodox research and teaching interests. Their endorsement of my annual requests to teach History 358 ("Observers Observed: Anthropologists and First Nations in BC") allowed me to test various parts of my book manuscript on the department's undergraduate students. Through the History Department, I received several internal research grants, a Faculty of Humanities faculty research fellowship, and a three-year SSHRC strategic research grant to help with various parts of the research. This support allowed me to hire a talented group of research assistants. I especially thank Laura Ishiguro, Jonathan Peyton, Karen Inkster, Elina Hill, Leah Kaskinski, Laticia Chapman, Ben Clinton-Baker, and Emma Battell-Lowman.

Over the many years I worked on this project, I relied on the assistance of a long line of archivists and curators from the following institutions: the Archives at the American Museum of Natural History in New York City; the Library and Archives at the American Philosophical Society in Philadelphia, Pennsylvania; the Peabody Museum of Archaeology and Ethnology in Cambridge, Massachusetts; the Canadian Museum of History in Gatineau, Quebec; the British Columbia Archives in Victoria, BC; and the Shetland Museum and Archives in Lerwick, Shetland. Brian Smith of the Shetland Archives deserves special thanks for answering my endless questions about his island's history and pointing me to helpful sources. I especially thank him for his thorough and thoughtful comments on the Shetland chapter. I also thank Ian Tait of the Shetland Museum for his help with photographs. I am indebted to Anthony Gott, whose website "North Isles Family History" helped fill many gaps in the Tait family history. Brian Carpenter of the American Philosophical Society Library gave generously of his time during my 2016 research visit to Philadelphia and continued to offer help right to the end of the project. Judy Thompson, former subarctic curator at the Canadian Museum of History, deserves thanks for sharing her research materials with me as she worked on her 2007 book on Teit.[6] I thank Louise Dallaire, Benoit Theriault, Erin Gurski, Jonathan Wise, and Vincent Lafond of the Canadian Museum of History for their help in locating James Teit, Edward Sapir, and Marius Barbeau items in their collections.

UBC Press deserves huge thanks for its unwavering support of me and my manuscript. Darcy Cullen and Nadine Pedersen shepherded it smoothly through the acquisition process; Katrina Petrik and copy editor Audrey McClellan then gave it a good polish and carried it swiftly to the finish line. I also owe thanks to Kerry Kilmartin and Laraine Coates for their work in promoting the book. I cannot imagine a more dedicated or supportive team! I thank cartographer Eric Leinberger for his excellent work on the maps.

For their work on the photographs, I thank Annette Calvert and Nicholas Bowlin of Bowlin Photo in Sidney, and Leithen M'Gonigle.

I could not have completed this project without the assistance of James Teit's son Sigurd and his daughter Inga. Their generosity appears to be a family trait. A recent phone chat with Teit's grandson, Jim Teit of Prince George, BC, led a week later to the delivery of seven family photo albums to my doorstep. Jim then read the manuscript chapter by chapter and offered a steady stream of excellent feedback. A telephone chat with Teit's grandson Joe Perkin led to more family stories and more helpful feedback. I am grateful to Joe's wife, Georgina Perkin, and their daughter, Christina Perkin, for joining in on the family feedback. Teit's great-nephew Iain Nicholson (grandson of Teit's sister Alice) also read the full manuscript and provided continuous support and encouragement from his home in Newcastle upon Tyne in northern England. I am grateful to Kate Petrie and Larry Paul in New Zealand for filling gaps in the New Zealand side of the Teit family history.

Finally, to my family ... My sister, Sue Ann Wickwire, read and commented on the draft (often more than once) and kept tabs on my progress through long, weekly phone calls. My father, Jim Wickwire, read the full manuscript just before it went to the press in the summer of 2018 and offered excellent feedback. I thank my Aunt Joan (Wickwire) Parker for spending much of her spring 2018 visit to Victoria in an armchair in the back corner of our family room, dutifully reading the manuscript. Huge thanks go to Leithen and Patrick M'Gonigle, who endured years of stories about the "other man" in their mother's life. Both read the full manuscript in the summer of 2018, probably as a means to better understand the dynamics of this strange love affair. Their touching and enthusiastic responses gave me a major boost when I needed it.

My largest debt of gratitude goes to my partner, Michael M'Gonigle. Most acknowledgments list an army of editors. I had only one. Michael read every chapter of this book multiple times and offered detailed commentary and edits after each reading. Concerned that I had missed the forest for the trees, he dropped everything in the summer of 2011 to help me pull the whole thing apart and then put it all back together. I cannot count the number of nights that Michael poked me at 3 a.m. to announce that he had found an innovative way to fix a problem. To my best friend and devoted partner, this book is yours as it is mine.

Notes

Preface

1 Catherine Hall, *Civilising Subjects: Metropole and Colony in the English Imagination, 1830–1867* (Chicago: University of Chicago Press, 2002), 22.

2 Bob Joseph, *21 Things You May Not Know About the Indian Act: Helping Canadians Make Reconciliation with Indigenous Peoples a Reality* (Port Coquitlam, BC: Indigenous Relations Press, 2018), 12.

3 James A. Teit Papers, "Salish Ethnographic Materials," Slb. 7, American Council of Learned Societies Committee of Native American Languages (ACLS) collection, American Philosophical Society Library (APS).

4 For more on the intricacies of the Nlaka'pamux language and the challenges of phonetic transcription, see the work of Nlaka'pamux linguist Mandy Jimmie, "A Prosodic Analysis of Nłeʔkepmx Reduplication" (master's thesis, University of British Columbia, 1994). See also Laurence C. Thompson and M. Terry Thompson, *Thompson River Salish Dictionary*, University of Montana Occasional Papers in Linguistics 12 (Missoula: University of Montana, 1996); and Steven Egesdal, M. Terry Thompson, and Mandy Jimmie, *nłeʔkèpmxcín: Thompson River Salish Speech* (Bellingham: Whatcom Museum Publications, 2011).

5 In his notes on his conversations with Tetlanetza during the latter's visit to Ottawa in 1912, anthropologist Marius Barbeau noted that the chief signed his name as "Tetlanetza." See "Thompson River Songs (miscellaneous)," Marius Barbeau fonds, Box (temp.) 287.f.7, Canadian Museum of History (CMH).

Chapter 1: Missing in History

1 "'Memorial' to the Hon. Frank Oliver, Minister of the Interior," Chiefs of the Shuswap, Couteau or Thompson, Okanagan, Lillooet, Stalo or Lower Fraser, Chilcotin, Carrier, and Tahltan Tribes in the interior of British Columbia, May 10, 1911, RG10, vol. 7780, file 27150-3-1, Library and Archives Canada (LAC).

2 In 1977, the common term for this group was "Okanagan." In recent years, however, it has been replaced by the term "Syilx." For more on such name changes, see the author's prefatory remarks on terminology.

3 Randy Bouchard and Dorothy Kennedy founded the Victoria-based BC Indian Language Project in 1972 as a research centre dedicated to the documentation of Indigenous languages, cultures, and histories.

4 See, for example, Barry Lopez, *Giving Birth to Thunder, Sleeping with His Daughter: Coyote Builds North America* (New York: Avon Books, 1977); see also Mourning Dove, *Coyote Stories* (Caldwell, ID: Caxton Printers, 1933). For an in-depth study of the sanitization of Indigenous stories by outsiders, see Alanna K. Brown, "The Evolution of Mourning Dove's Coyote Stories," *Studies in American Indian Literatures* 4, 2 and 3 (1992): 161–79.

5 Wendy Wickwire and Harry Robinson, *Write It on Your Heart: The Epic World of an Okanagan Storyteller* (Vancouver: Talonbooks, 1989); Wickwire and Robinson, *Nature Power: In the Spirit of an Okanagan Storyteller,* 2nd ed. (Vancouver: Talonbooks, 2004); Wickwire and Robinson, *Living by Stories: A Journey of Landscape and Memory* (Vancouver: Talonbooks, 2005).

6 See the Preface for more on terminology. The anthropological name for the Secwépemc was the anglicized term "Shuswap."

7 This discussion is distilled from a song session with Aimee August and Adeline Willard, recorded on audiotape by Randy Bouchard and Wendy Wickwire at the home of Adeline Willard, Neskonlith reserve, Chase, BC, August 17, 1977 (Wendy Wickwire audiotape collection, #1977.2).

8 Ibid.

9 This discussion took place at Mary Abel's house, Head of the Lake, Okanagan Indian Band, near Vernon, BC, on August 31, 1977 (Wickwire audiotape collection, #1977.1).

10 Ibid.

11 Interview with Aimee August and Adeline Willard, Neskonlith reserve, Chase, BC, September 4, 1977 (Wickwire audiotape collection, #1977.2).

12 Marie-Françoise Guédon, "Canadian Indian Ethnomusicology: Selected Bibliography and Discography," *Ethnomusicology* 16, 3 (1972): 475.

13 Except when quoting directly from a text by Teit, I have used Teit's 1893 spellings for names like "Whal-eenik" because he was not yet using the diacritics that interfere with easy name recognition and pronunication. In all of his post-1894 work (and this includes his song notes), Teit used Boas's orthography. With this shift, Whal-eenik turned into X̲ᴡᴇʟī'inᴇk. According to Teit's notes for song #VI.M.57, Yiôpā'tko had another name, Tarlī'nᴇk. He used the latter name in his 1893 inventory of Nlaka'pamux names, but recorded it as "Tal-eenik." As explained in the Preface, it is important to consider that all such names at this stage were part of an internal oral tradition that did not lend itself well to English transcription.

14 Interview, Wendy Wickwire with Rosie Joe, Shackan reserve, BC, August 23, 1978 (Wendy Wickwire audiotape collection, #1978.31).

15 For a fuller description of Teit's wax-cylinder song collection and associated notes, see Wendy Wickwire, "James A. Teit: His Contribution to Canadian Ethnomusicology," *Canadian Journal of Native Studies* 8, 2 (1998): 183–204.

16 Song VI.M.79. For Teit's notes on song VI.M.79 and all of the "Thompson" (Nlaka'pamux) songs he recorded at Spences Bridge (these are VI.M.25 to VI.M.219), see "James Alexander Teit, Notes on Songs of the Indians of British Columbia," VI-Z-35M, B121, f6, Canadian

Museum of History (CMH). The sound recordings that accompany these notes follow the same system (i.e., VI.M.25 to VI.M.219) but with a slightly different title: "James A. Teit, Thompson music (sound recordings)," II-C-3T to II-C-10T, CMH. Hereafter, all references to this collection, both notes and sound recordings, will be "James Teit cylinder collection, CMH."

17 Song VI.M.163, James Teit cylinder collection, CMH.
18 Song VI.M.79, James Teit cylinder collection, CMH.
19 Song VI.M.58, James Teit cylinder collection, CMH.
20 Song VI.M.122, James Teit cylinder collection, CMH.
21 Song VI.M.121, James Teit cylinder collection, CMH.
22 Song VI.M.165, James Teit cylinder collection, CMH.
23 In his song notes, Teit spelled the name .nsElkapes'kEt. He sometimes also spelled it Nsilkapesket or Nselkapêskit.
24 John Haugen of Lytton provided the date of Tommy Lick's death.
25 Dorothy Walkem Ursaki pointed this out in a taped interview with the author at her home in New Westminster, March 23, 1991 (Wickwire audiotape collection). Note that Teit also spelled Whal-eenik's name X̲wElī'nEk.
26 Photographs 23206 and 30701 in Leslie H. Tepper, *The Interior Salish Tribes of British Columbia: A Photographic Collection,* Canadian Ethnology Service Paper no. 111 (Ottawa: National Museums of Canada, 1987).
27 This is likely the woman that Teit described as "Cha-pell" in his 1893 document titled "Indians left Cookseferry for other parts of their tribe, 1884 to 1893." He noted that she had moved to the Nicola Valley with her husband, "Charley": James A. Teit Papers, "Salish Ethnographic Materials," Slb. 7, American Council of Learned Societies Committee of Native American Languages (ACLS) collection, American Philosophical Society Library (APS).
28 Interview, Wendy Wickwire with Hilda Austin, Lytton, BC, January 10, 1979 (Wickwire audiotape collection, #1979.03).
29 Roderick Sprague of the University of Idaho published a bibliography of Teit in which he assessed Teit's written legacy as consisting of "a total of 2200 printed pages in 42 sources ... [and] 5000 manuscript pages in 34 sources": Roderick Sprague, "A Bibliography of James A. Teit," *Northwest Anthropological Research Notes* 25, 1 (1991): 103.

Of Teit's eleven monographs, the following are among the highlights: *The Thompson Indians of British Columbia,* Memoir of the American Museum of Natural History, series vol. 2: Publications of the Jesup North Pacific Expedition (JNPE), vol. 1, part 4 (New York: G.P. Putnam's Sons, 1900), http://hdl.handle.net/2246/13; *The Lillooet Indians,* Memoir of the American Museum of Natural History, series vol. 4: JNPE, vol. 2, part 5 (Leiden/New York: E.J. Brill/G.E. Stechert, 1906), http://hdl.handle.net/2246/36; *The Shuswap,* Memoir of the American Museum of Natural History, series vol. 4: JNPE, vol. 2, part 7 (Leiden/New York: E.J. Brill/G.E. Stechert, 1909), http://hdl.handle.net/2246/38; *Mythology of the Thompson Indians,* Memoir of the American Museum of Natural History, series vol. 12: JNPE, vol. 8, part 2 (Leiden/New York: E.J. Brill/G.E. Stechert, 1912), http://hdl.handle.net/2246/37.

30 In addition to compiling artifact collections for Ottawa's Victoria Memorial Museum (later renamed the National Museum of Man, then the Canadian Museum of Civilization, and most recently the Canadian Museum of History), Teit compiled collections for the American Museum of Natural History in New York City; the US National Museum and the

Smithsonian Institution in Washington, DC; Harvard University's Peabody Museum of Anthropology and Archaeology in Cambridge, MA; the Provincial Museum of Natural History and Anthropology in Victoria, BC; and the Field Columbian Museum in Chicago, IL. Teit also sent artifacts to individuals, such as Homer Sargent and George Heye. Most of Sargent's personal collection ended up at the Chicago Field Columbian Museum. Heye's collection went to his self-endowed Heye Museum in New York City. For more on Heye and other collectors who assembled artifact collections from British Columbia, see Douglas Cole, *Captured Heritage: The Scramble for Northwest Coast Artifacts* (Vancouver: Douglas and McIntyre, 1985), 216–17. See also Patricia Roy, *The Collectors: A History of the Royal British Columbian Museum and Archives* (Victoria: The Royal BC Museum, 2018).

31 See Wendy C. Wickwire, "Cultures in Contact: Music, the Plateau Indian, and the Western Encounter" (PhD diss., Wesleyan University, 1983).

32 One of the key contributions of the Vancouver-based lobby group was a Stein hiking guidebook that encouraged readers to pack up and see for themselves what was at stake: Roger Freeman and David Thompson, *Exploring the Stein River Valley* (Vancouver: Douglas and McIntyre, 1979).

33 For more on the Stein Valley campaign, see Michael M'Gonigle and Wendy Wickwire, *Stein: The Way of the River* (Vancouver: Talonbooks, 1988).

34 Christopher Arnett, "Rock Art of Nlaka'pamux: Indigenous Theory and Practice on the British Columbia Plateau" (PhD diss., University of British Columbia, 2016); see also Annie York, Richard Daly, and Chris Arnett, *They Write Their Dreams on the Rock Forever: Rock Writing in the Stein River Valley* (Vancouver: Talonbooks, 1993).

35 James Teit, Livingston Farrand, Marian K. Gould, and Herbert J. Spinden, *Folk-Tales of Salishan and Sahaptin Tribes,* ed. Franz Boas, Memoirs of the American Folk-Lore Society 11 (Lancaster, PA/New York: American Folk-Lore Society, 1917), 13–14.

36 Wendy Wickwire and Dana Lepofsky, "Stein River Heritage: Summary and Evaluation" (report prepared for the Lytton Band and the Mount Currie Band, February 1986); and Wendy Wickwire, "The Stein: Its People Speak" (report prepared for the Nlaka'pamux Tribal Council, September 1988).

37 Judith Judd Banks, "Comparative Biographies of Two British Columbia Anthropologists, Charles Hill-Tout and James A. Teit" (master's thesis, University of British Columbia, 1970), offered the first in-depth study of Teit. Several members of the Nicola Valley Historical Association added to this with the publication of a special issue of the *Nicola Valley Historical Quarterly* entitled "Commemorating: James Alexander Teit," *Nicola Valley Historical Quarterly* 2, 2 (April 1979). Two smaller publications followed: Don Bunyon, "James Teit: Pioneer Anthropologist," *Heritage West,* Fall 1981, 21–22; and Ralph Maud, "James Teit of Spences Bridge," in *Guide to B.C. Indian Myth and Legend* (Vancouver: Talonbooks, 1982), 63–77.

38 Robert Lowie referred to Teit as a "squaw man" in his *History of Ethnological Theory* (New York: Farrar and Rinehart, 1937), 132–33; Marian Smith described him as a laboratory "technician" in "Boas' 'Natural History' Approach to Field Method," in *The Anthropology of Franz Boas: Essays on the Centennial of His Birth,* ed. Walter R. Goldschmidt, American Anthropological Association Memoir 89 (San Francisco: Howard Chandler, 1959), 56. (I am indebted to Judith Berman for providing me with these references.)

In his overview of Boas's Northwest Coast fieldwork, anthropologist Ronald Rohner made little mention of Teit beyond a note in his "Index of Personal Names" describing Teit as "one of Boas's principal informants": Ronald P. Rohner, "Franz Boas: Ethnographer on the Northwest Coast," in *Pioneers of American Anthropology*, ed. Judith Helm (Seattle: University of Washington Press, 1966), 149–212. See also Ronald P. Rohner, ed., *The Ethnography of Franz Boas: Letters and Diaries of Franz Boas Written on the Northwest Coast from 1886 to 1931* (Chicago: University of Chicago Press, 1969), xiii-xxx, 325.

In his extensive work on Boas, University of Chicago historian George Stocking Jr. rarely mentioned Teit. See, for example, Stocking's *Race, Culture, Evolution: Essays in the History of Anthropology* (New York: Free Press, 1968), and *A Franz Boas Reader: The Shaping of American Anthropology, 1883–1911* (Chicago: University of Chicago Press, 1974).

39 For more on this, see Mary Louise Pratt, *Imperial Eyes: Travel Writing and Transculturation* (New York: Routledge, 1992).

40 John Van Maanen, *Tales of the Field: On Writing Ethnography* (Chicago: University of Chicago Press, 1988), 47.

41 Sigurd Teit described the details of this trip in a letter to Wendy Wickwire, May 1992.

42 Roy Grønneberg, "James Teit – Friend of the Indians," *New Shetlander* 126 (December 1978): 28–30.

43 Sigurd Teit to Wendy Wickwire, May 1992.

44 Sam Anderson to Peter Jamieson, November 27, 1930, Peter Jamieson Papers, D/95/3, Shetland Archives.

45 Anderson to Jamieson, October 26, 1942, Peter Jamieson Papers, D9/95/31, Shetland Archives.

46 Ibid.

47 Peter Jamieson, "James Teit of Spence's Bridge, B.C.: A Remarkable Shetlander," *Shetland News*, April 30, 1957, 4; Peter Jamieson, "Jimmy Teit of Spence's Bridge, British Columbia," *New Shetlander* 53 (January–March 1960): 17–20.

48 Ibid.

49 Jamieson, "Jimmy Teit of Spence's Bridge," 17.

50 Jamieson, "James Teit of Spence's Bridge, B.C.," 4.

51 Jamieson, "Jimmy Teit of Spence's Bridge," 17.

52 Jessie Williamson to Jamieson, July 28, 1946, Peter Jamieson Papers, D9/182/4, Shetland Archives.

53 William Irvine to Jamieson, April 17, 1946, Peter Jamieson Papers, D9/182/2, Shetland Archives.

54 Peter Jamieson Papers, D9/182/4, Shetland Archives.

55 Peter Jamieson to Sigurd Teit, April 21, 1954, Peter Jamieson Papers, D9/182/4, Shetland Archives.

56 Teit and his New Zealand–based uncle, Robert Tait (1831–1926) carried on a mail correspondence from 1903 until shortly before Teit's death in 1922. Unfortunately, none of Robert Tait's letters have survived, but twelve letters from Teit to his uncle, written between 1903 and 1919, have survived. They are now in the possession of Robert Tait's great-granddaughter, Elisabeth Hogg, in Wellington, NZ. Sigurd likely obtained photocopies of the original letters when he visited Elisabeth's mother, Vivienne Hogg (nee Tait), in New Zealand in the 1970s. I am grateful to Katherine Petrie (Elisabeth's first cousin) of Dunedin, NZ, for providing me with this information. I am also grateful to Larry Paul, another Robert Tait descendant, for his help in locating the original letters.

57 Interview with Joe Karaus and Inga Teit at Karaus's seniors' home in Aldergove, May 17, 1991 (Wickwire audiotape collection).

58 Interview with Inga Teit at her home in Aldergrove, BC, May 17, 1991 (Wickwire audiotape collection).

59 Interview with Joe Karaus and Inga Teit at Karaus's seniors' home in Aldergove, May 17, 1991 (Wickwire audiotape collection).

60 Interview with Tom Curnow, at his home at Spences Bridge, January 6, 1979 (Wickwire audiotape collection).

61 Katharine Howes and Pat Lean, "Robert Taylor of 2663 Quilchena Ave., Recalls the Teits," *Nicola Valley Historical Quarterly* 2, 2 (April 1979): 6.

62 Sigurd and I were a year into our work together when political scientist Paul Tennant released his book *Aboriginal Peoples and Politics: The Indian Land Question in British Columbia, 1849–1989* (Vancouver: UBC Press, 1990). We were surprised to find only a scant reference to Teit's role in the early land-rights movement. Historian Peter Campbell addressed some of Tennant's gaps in "'Not as a White Man, Not as a Sojourner': James A. Teit and the Fight for Native Rights in British Columbia, 1884–1922," *Left History* 2 (1994): 37–57. I filled in a few more gaps in 1998 with an article on Teit's activism: Wendy Wickwire, "'We Shall Drink from the Stream and So Shall You': James A. Teit and Native Resistance in British Columbia, 1908–22," *Canadian Historical Review* 79, 2 (1998): 199–236.

63 Sigurd Teit, notes on his meeting with Peter Kelly, November 1952, copy courtesy of Sigurd Teit.

64 John Tait to John Murray, December 20, 1883, John Tait Letterbook, D.17/8/16, Shetland Archives.

65 Judy Thompson, *Recording Their Story: James Teit and the Tahltan* (Vancouver/Gatineau/Seattle: Douglas and McIntyre/Canadian Museum of Civilization/University of Washington Press, 2007). For more on Teit's Tahltan research, see James Teit, "Fieldnotes on the Tahltan and Kaska Indians, 1912–15," ed. J.H. McNeish, *Anthropologica* 3 (1956): 39–171. See also Catherine Fenn, "Life History of a Collection: The Tahltan Materials Collected by James A. Teit" (master's thesis, University of British Columbia, 1993); and Robert Adlam, "The Northern Athapaskan Survey of Edward Sapir and James Teit," *Anthropological Linguistics* 49, 2 (2007): 99–117.

66 In 1987, Leslie Tepper, curator of the Canadian Museum of Civilization's southern Interior collections, published a selection of Teit's photographs in *The Interior Salish Tribes of British Columbia: A Photographic Collection* (Ottawa: National Museums of Canada, 1987). In 1995, she curated an exhibit of Teit's textile collections ("Earth Line and Morning Star: Nlaka'pamux Clothing Traditions"), which included a catalogue under the same title: Leslie Tepper, *Earth Line and Morning Star: Nlaka'pamux Clothing Traditions* (Hull, QC: Canadian Museum of Civilization, 1994). In 2010, Dan Savard, curator of photography at the Royal British Columbia Museum, highlighted Teit's photographic contributions in his book on BC photography, *Images from the Likeness House* (Victoria: Royal British Columbia Museum, 2010). In 2015, Andrea Laforet, former director of ethnology and cultural studies at the Canadian Museum of History, published a chapter on Teit's ethnography, "The Ethnographic Legacy of Franz Boas and James Teit: *The Thompson Indians of British Columbia*," in a special volume on Franz Boas: *The Franz Boas Papers*, vol. 1, *Franz Boas as Public Intellectual – Theory, Ethnography, Activism*, ed. Regna Darnell, Michelle Hamilton, Robert L.A. Hancock, and Joshua Smith (Lincoln: University of Nebraska Press, 2015), 191–212.

67 For a full inventory of Teit's published and unpublished works, see Sprague, "Bibliography of James A. Teit." See also Adlam, "Northern Athabaskan Survey of Edward Sapir and James A. Teit," and the following works by Wendy Wickwire: "James A. Teit: His Contribution to Canadian Ethnomusicology"; "Women in Ethnography: The Research of

James A. Teit," *Ethnohistory* 40, 4 (Fall 1993): 539–62; "To See Ourselves as the Other's Other: Nlaka'pamux Contact Narratives," *Canadian Historical Review* 75, 1 (1994): 1–20; "Beyond Boas? Re-assessing the Contribution of 'Informant' and 'Research Assistant': James A. Teit," in *Constructing Cultures Then and Now: Celebrating Franz Boas and the Jesup North Pacific Expedition*, ed. Laurel Kendall and Igor Krupnik (Washington, DC: Smithsonian Institution, 2003), 123–33.

68 Regna Darnell, "The Pivotal Role of the Northwest Coast in the History of Americanist Anthropology," in "Ethnographic Eyes: Essays in Memory of Douglas L. Cole," ed. Wendy Wickwire, special issue, *BC Studies* 125/126 (Spring/Summer 2000): 43.

69 Curtis has been the subject of many book-length studies. For the most recent of these, see Mick Gidley, *Edward S. Curtis and the North American Indian, Incorporated* (Cambridge: Cambridge University Press, 1998), and Timothy Egan, *Short Nights of the Shadow Catcher: The Epic Life and Immortal Photographs of Edward Curtis* (New York: Houghton Mifflin Harcourt, 2012).

70 Laurence Nowry, *Man of Mana: Marius Barbeau* (Toronto: NC Press, 1995).

71 Wilson Duff, "Contributions of Marius Barbeau to West Coast Ethnology," *Anthropologica* 6, 1 (1964): 63–96; see also Andrew Nurse, "'But Now Things Have Changed': Marius Barbeau and the Politics of Amerindian Identity," *Ethnohistory* 48, 3 (2001): 433–72.

72 See, for example, Andrew Nurse, "Marius Barbeau and the Methodology of Salvage Ethnography in Canada, 1911–51," in *Historicizing Canadian Anthropology*, ed. Julia Harrison and Regna Darnell (Vancouver: UBC Press, 2006), 52–64.

73 For a full biography of Sapir, see Regna Darnell, *Edward Sapir: Linguist, Anthropologist, Humanist* (Berkeley: University of California Press, 1990). Thomas McIlwraith was the first university-appointed anthropologist in Canada. See John Barker, "Introduction," in *The Bella Coola Indians* (Toronto: University of Toronto Press, 1992), ix–xxxvii. Members of this group shared a common culture. Most were white, male, and middle-class and, for the most part, university-educated. Along with substantial institutional support, they enjoyed comfortable city lives and embraced fieldwork as a disciplinary requirement – often a form of drudgery and a self-conscious (and self-sacrificing) test of their bodies and minds in exotic locales among exotic peoples – rather than a passion. See Henrika Kuklick, "Personal Equations: Reflections on the History of Fieldwork, with Special Reference to Sociocultural Anthropology," *Isis* 102, 1 (March 2011): 1–33. Kuklick analyzes the shift from "armchair" anthropology to field-based anthropology. Unlike Teit, who focused on the "everyday lives" of his anthropological subjects, many early anthropologists, as Kuklick shows, characterized their fieldwork in heroic terms. It could be argued, therefore, that while their work represents a shift of the "centre" of anthropology from the university to the field, the ultimate centre was European so-called civilization. Kuklick's perspective is a valuable one for illuminating the historical shifts of the centre/periphery dynamic.

74 Donald B. Smith, *Chief Buffalo Child Long Lance: The Glorious Imposter* (Markham, ON: Red Deer Press, 1999). See also Donald B. Smith, *From the Land of Shadows: The Making of Grey Owl* (Saskatoon: Western Producer Prairie Books, 1990).

75 Catherine Hall, "Introduction: Thinking the Postcolonial, Thinking the Empire," in *Cultures of Empire: Colonizers in Britain and the Empire in the Nineteenth and Twentieth Centuries*, ed. Catherine Hall (New York: Routledge, 2000), 8.

76 Ibid., 24–25.

77 Ibid., 25.

78 For a detailed account of this racism in the context of African American and Indigenous American cultures, see Domenico Losurdo, *Liberalism: A Counter-History* (London: Verso, 2011).

79 See, for example, Patrick Wolfe, *Settler Colonialism and the Transformation of Anthropology: The Politics and Poetics of an Ethnographic Event* (London: Cassell, 1999); see also Paige Raibmon, *Authentic Indians: Episodes of Encounter from the Late-Nineteenth-Century Northwest Coast* (Durham, NC: Duke University Press, 2005); Ira Jacknis, *The Storage Box of Tradition: Kwakiutl Art, Anthropologists, and Museums, 1881–1981* (Washington, DC: Smithsonian Institution Press, 2002); and Douglas Cole, *Captured Heritage: The Scramble for Northwest Coast Artifacts* (Vancouver/Seattle: Douglas and McIntyre/University of Washington Press, 1985).

80 A number of Indigenous students have drawn on Teit's ethnographic monographs and field notes. See, for example, Beatrice Marie Anderson, "*Nlakapmux* Grandmothers' Traditional Teachings and Learnings" (PhD diss., University of British Columbia, 2011), and Ronald E. Ignace, "Our Oral Histories Are Our Iron Posts: Secwépemc Stories and Historical Consciousness" (PhD diss., Simon Fraser University, 2008). See also Mandy Jimmie, "A Prosodic Analysis of Nłeʔkèpmxc Reduplication" (master's thesis, University of British Columbia, 1994).

81 Lynne Jorgesen and Bernadette Manuel, "Red Flag Analysis: Ethnohistoric/Cultural Heritage Resources Review. Report Submitted to British Columbia, First Nations Tables, Past Mitigation and Compensation with Respect to the Existing Interior to Lower Mainland Transmission Line," 2010, copy courtesy of Lynne Jorgesen. Angie Bain (Nlaka'pamux) of the Lower Nicola Band and John Haugen (Nlaka'pamux) of the Lytton First Nation are part of a team of five authors who are collaborating on a forthcoming book on Teit to be published by the University of Nebraska Press under the directorship of Regna Darnell of Western University. In their new book, *Secwépemc People, Land and Laws* (Montreal/Kingston: McGill-Queen's University Press, 2017), Marianne Ignace and Ronald Ignace of the Secwépemc Nation Tribal Council make extensive use of Teit's monographs and field notes.

82 The Nlaka'pamux Rock Art Conference took place at Lytton, BC, in May 2016. In 2009, Cree playwright Tomson Highway published a play, *Ernestine Shuswap Gets Her Trout*, based on a political document that Teit drafted on behalf of the southern Interior chiefs in 1910. The play premiered in Kamloops and Vancouver in the spring of 2009. A year later, Nlaka'pamux playwright Kevin Loring wrote another play, *Words of Our Chiefs*, based on the same political document. Loring's play premiered at the opening of the Chief Tetlenitsa Memorial Outdoor Theatre at Spences Bridge, BC, in May 2010. In August 2013, Loring organized the "Songs of the Land Symposium" at Lytton, which highlighted items from Teit's wax-cylinder song collection. In 2015, he wrote and directed a play, *Battle of the Birds*, based on a story from Teit's *Traditions of the Thompson River Indians* (Boston: American Folk-Lore Society, 1898). The play premiered in Lytton and Vancouver in the late summer and fall of that year. In September 2018, Loring organized another theatre workshop at Lytton, "The Council of Spider, Ant, and Fly," which again drew on Teit's work.

83 This project is part of the Franz Boas Papers Project headed by Regna Darnell of Western University. See http://www.franzboaspapers.uwo.ca/about_us/volumes.html.

84 Katharine Howes and Pat Lean of Merritt, BC, made a major contribution in the late 1970s by organizing, under the auspices of the Nicola Valley Museum and Archives

Association (NVAA), interviews with Teit family members and others who remembered Teit. They published their findings in a special issue of their *Nicola Valley Historical Quarterly:* "Commemorating: James Alexander Teit," *Nicola Valley Historical Quarterly* 2, 2 (April 1979). With the assistance of Sigurd, the NVAA published the *Teit Times,* "A Year in the Life of James A. Teit, 1910" in the summer of 1995. It is still one of the most important sources on Teit. In 1999, the NVAA (aided by Sigurd) published a second volume of the *Teit Times* that featured a biographical sketch and a previously unpublished Teit manuscript that Josie Teit had found buried in her husband's papers after his death: "Notes on the Early History of the Nicola Valley," *Teit Times,* Summer 1999.

Chapter 2: Boats, Trains, Horses

1 Joseph Trutch to Charlotte Trutch, June 23, 1850, quoted in Robin Fisher, "Joseph Trutch and Indian Land Policy," *BC Studies* 12 (Winter 1971–72): 5.

2 This description of Boas's two days at Spences Bridge was distilled from the letters he wrote to his parents and his wife while at Spences Bridge in September 1894. See Ronald Rohner, ed., *The Ethnography of Franz Boas: Letters and Diaries of Franz Boas Written on the Northwest Coast from 1886 to 1931* (Chicago: University of Chicago Press, 1969), 134–40.

3 Franz Boas to his parents, September 17, 1894, in Rohner, *Ethnography of Franz Boas,* 137.

4 Boas to Marie Boas, September 21, 1894, in ibid., 139.

5 Ibid.

6 Ibid.

7 Ibid.

8 According to Ardith Walkem, a lawyer and member of the Cooks Ferry Band, the reserve in the Twaal Valley was abandoned early in the twentieth century because of a lack of water. She attributes the water loss to settler farmers who moved in and killed the beavers whose dams had created and maintained a regular flow of water to the range: Ardith Walkem, "The Land is Dry: Indigenous Peoples, Water and Environmental Justice," in *Eau Canada: The Future of Canada's Water,* ed. Karen Bakker (Vancouver: UBC Press, 2007), 303–4.

9 Carl Albert Purpus, "Von Spence's Bridge in die Berge am Hat Creek in British Columbia," *Das Ausland* 64 (1891): 497–500, 504–6. English translation ("From Spences Bridge into the Mountains at Hat Creek in British Columbia") courtesy of Dorothee Schreiber. Original document provided by Christopher Arnett and Michael Klassen.

10 Douglas Cole, *Franz Boas: The Early Years, 1858–1906* (Vancouver: Douglas and McIntyre, 1999), 165.

11 Boas to Marie Boas, September 12, 1894, in Rohner, *Ethnography of Franz Boas,* 133.

12 Boas to his parents, November 17, 1882, quoted in Julia Liss, "German Culture and German Science in the *Bildung* of Franz Boas," in *Volksgeist as Method and Ethic: Essays on Boasian Ethnography and the German Anthropological Tradition,* ed. George W. Stocking Jr. (Madison: University of Wisconsin Press, 1996), 176.

13 Boas to Marie Boas, September 16, 1894, in Rohner, *Ethnography of Franz Boas,* 135.

14 Boas to Marie Boas, September 17, 1894, in ibid., 136.

15 Boas to Marie Boas, September 21, 1894, in ibid., 139.

16 Boas's 1894 research agenda included work for the British Association for the Advancement of Science (BAAS) in the British Columbia Interior and on the Upper Coast; work on anthropometry and linguistics for the Bureau of American Ethnology; a project on the Chinookan language for the American Museum of Natural History (AMNH) in New

York City; a project for the National Museum in Washington, DC, that required gathering plaster casts, photographs, and collections for the Northwest Coast life groups; and, finally, an anthropometric project for the American Association for the Advancement of Science. The goal of the last project was to correct measurements of southern California peoples taken at the World's Columbian Exposition in Chicago. See Cole, *Franz Boas,* 169. Boas also had a small contract with George Dawson of the Geological Survey of Canada. See Rohner, *Ethnography of Franz Boas,* 83.

17 Cole, *Franz Boas,* 117. For a full profile of Horatio Hale, see David A. Nock, "Horatio Hale: Forgotten Victorian Author of Positive Aboriginal Representation," in *With Good Intentions: Euro-Canadian and Aboriginal Relations in Colonial Canada,* ed. Celia Haig-Brown and David A. Nock (Vancouver: UBC Press, 2006), 132–50.

18 Horatio Hale to Boas, May 21, 1888, quoted in Rohner, *Ethnography of Franz Boas,* 81.

19 Boas to Marie Boas, September 21, 1894, in ibid., 139.

20 Ibid.

21 Chinook Jargon was a popular pidgin/creole trade language used by Indians to communicate across their own language barriers and those of the Northwest Company and Hudson's Bay Company traders. Missionaries, ethnographers, and government agents also used Chinook Jargon to communicate with resident Indians. Chinook Jargon dictionaries were readily available, allowing outsiders to learn basic words and phrases within a couple of days.

22 For a Chinook–English dictionary, see Charles Lillard with Terry Glavin, *A Voice Great within Us: The Story of Chinook* (Vancouver: New Star Books, 1998). For more on the history of Chinook Jargon, see George Lang, *Making Wawa: The Genesis of Chinook Jargon* (Vancouver: UBC Press, 2008).

23 In a letter to his children on June 29, 1900, Boas described the interior of Teit's one-room log cabin in the Twaal Valley. He wrote that the furniture consisted of a table, two chairs, a "roughly-carpentered" bed, and a handmade bookshelf containing books "about Indians" and various languages. In addition to German, Swedish, and French grammars and dictionaries, he noted "many books about the Shetland Islands which is Teit's homeland." In the far corner of the room was a case that held Teit's notebooks: Boas to his children, June 29, 1900, Mss.B.B61, Boas Family Papers, "Family Correspondence," Box 8, American Philosophical Society Library (APS). English translation courtesy of Dorothee Schreiber.

24 A.L. Kroeber, "Franz Boas: The Man," in *Franz Boas, 1858–1942,* ed. A.L. Kroeber, Ruth Benedict, Murray B. Emeneau, et al. (New York: Kraus Reprint, 1969, orig. 1943), 23.

25 In the fall of 1893, Teit had contacted Father A.G. Morice, an Oblate priest based at Stuart Lake Mission in northern BC, for information about the Carrier (Dakelh) and their territorial boundaries. In his letter, Teit explained that he had heard of the work of "Dr. Boaz" on "the mythology and sociology of the Salish tribes," but that he had not yet obtained copies of it. A fragment of the undated letter was found in James Teit's unpublished papers, "Salish Ethnographic Materials," Slb. 7, American Council of Learned Societies Committee of Native American Languages (ACLS) collection, APS.

26 Boas to Marie Boas, September 21, 1894, in Rohner, *Ethnography of Franz Boas,* 139.

27 Details of Teit's travel itinerary are taken from Jessie Smith's memoir, *Widow Smith of Spence's Bridge,* as told to J. Meryl Campbell and Audrey Ward (Merritt, BC: Sonotek, 1989), 23–30.

28 For a fuller profile of Victoria in the 1880s, see Derek Pethick, *Summer of Promise: Victoria 1864–1914* (Victoria: Sono Nis, 1980), 96–101. See also "British Columbia," *The West Shore* (Portland, OR) 10, no. 9 (September 1884): 276–77; and Cole, *Franz Boas,* 100.

29 As Hamar Foster explains, however, "Vancouver Island" at this time was "more of a hybrid" colony, "because although governance was in the Crown, title to the soil was in the HBC and, because it was classified as a settled rather than ceded colony, it was entitled to an elected representative assembly." Foster, personal communication, August 10, 2018.

30 For an excellent analysis of Victoria's transition from HBC fort to provincial capital, see Cole Harris, *The Reluctant Land: Society, Space, and Environment in Canada before Confederation* (Vancouver: UBC Press, 2008), 416–47.

31 *West Shore,* 276.

32 Ibid., 277.

33 Ibid.

34 Quoted in Pethick, *Summer of Promise,* 97.

35 Adele Perry, *On the Edge of Empire: Gender, Race, and the Making of British Columbia, 1849–1871* (Toronto: University of Toronto Press, 2001), 3.

36 Pethick, *Summer of Promise,* 106.

37 Between 1850 and 1854, Douglas negotiated fourteen such "agreements" (the Douglas "treaties" as they are known today): nine agreements in the Victoria, Sooke, and Metchosin area; two on the Saanich Peninsula; two at Fort Rupert on northern Vancouver Island; and one at Nanaimo. For a fuller account of this treaty-making process, see Wilson Duff, "The Fort Victoria Treaties," *BC Studies* 3 (Fall 1969): 3–52. See also John Sutton Lutz, *Makúk: A New History of Aboriginal-White Relations* (Vancouver: UBC Press, 2008), 49–117. For more on the treaty-making process and the railway dispute, see Grant Keddie, *Songhees Pictorial: A History of the Songhees People as Seen by Outsiders, 1790–1912* (Victoria: Royal BC Museum, 2003), 48–58, 107–8. See also Hamar Foster, "Letting Go the Bone: The Idea of Indian Title in British Columbia, 1849–1927," in *Essays in the History of Canadian Law,* vol. 6, *British Columbia and the Yukon,* ed. Hamar Foster and John McLaren (Toronto: University of Toronto Press, 1995), 39–45.

38 There is an ongoing debate about these numbers. For details, see John Belshaw, *Becoming British Columbia: A Population History* (Vancouver: UBC Press, 2009), 72–90.

39 Ibid., 24–25.

40 Cole, *Franz Boas,* 100.

41 Boas, Letter-diary, September 19, 1886, in Rohner, *Ethnography of Franz Boas,* 22.

42 Pethick, *Summer of Promise,* 101; see also Patricia Roy and John Herd Thompson, *British Columbia: Land of Promises* (Oxford: Oxford University Press, 2005), 87. According to the 1881 census, 70 percent of the non-Aboriginal population was male. For a fuller analysis of population statistics, see Cole Harris with Robert Galois, "A Population Geography of British Columbia in 1881," in *The Resettlement of British Columbia: Essays on Colonialism and Geographical Change* (Vancouver: UBC Press, 1997), 137–60.

43 Pethick, *Summer of Promise,* 96.

44 Patrick A. Dunae, "Sex, Charades and Census Records: Locating Female Sex Trade Workers in a Victorian City," *Histoire sociale/Social History* 42, 84 (2009): 280.

45 Smith, *Widow Smith,* 26.

46 Jessie Smith's memoir (*Widow Smith*) provides a full itinerary of Teit's trip from Liverpool, England, to Spences Bridge, British Columbia.

47 Ibid., 26.

48 Barry Gough, "New Caledonia," in *The Canadian Encyclopedia,* article published February 7, 2006; last modified July 3, 2015, http://www.thecanadianencyclopedia.ca/en/article/new-caledonia/.

49 Frank W. Anderson, *The Fraser River Canyon, "Valley of Death"* (Aldergrove, BC: Frontier, 1968), 5. Exploration had begun in 1774–75 when the Spanish-Mexican explorers Juan Perez and Juan Francisco de la Bodega y Quadra sailed up the outer coast of British Columbia in search of the Russians. They were followed by Captain James Cook who, under the auspices of the British Admiralty, arrived at Nootka Sound on Vancouver Island in 1778 before heading north in search of a passage to the Atlantic. See Harris, *Reluctant Land,* 416–17.

50 For an excellent and nuanced interpretation of fur trade history in this region, see Elizabeth Vibert, *Traders' Tales: Narratives of Cultural Encounters in the Columbia Plateau, 1807–1846* (Norman: University of Oklahoma Press, 1997).

51 Anderson, *Fraser River Canyon,* 21; Mark Forsythe and Greg Dickson, *The Trail of 1858: British Columbia's Gold Rush Past* (Madeira Park, BC: Harbour, 2007).

52 Anderson, *Fraser River Canyon,* 36.

53 Roy and Thompson, *British Columbia,* 32. For the full story of the gold rush, see Daniel Marshall, *Claiming the Land: British Columbia and the Making of a New El Dorado* (Vancouver: Ronsdale Press, 2018).

54 David Higgins, journalist, quoted in Forsythe and Dickson, *The Trail of 1858,* 28.

55 For more on this, see Marshall, *Claiming the Land.* See also Daniel Marshall, "Conflict in the New El Dorado: The Fraser River War," in *New Perspectives on the Gold Rush,* ed. Kathryn Bridge (Victoria: Royal British Columbia Museum, 2015), 125–39.

56 Marshall, *Claiming the Land,* 159.

57 Daniel Marshall, "Grim Legacy," in Forsythe and Dickson, *The Trail of 1858,* 32–33.

58 Ibid., 32; see also Marshall, "Conflict in the New El Dorado." Over the years, Teit gave this chief's name a number of different spellings. He spelled it "Shigh-pentlam" in "Narratives of Old Pa-ah, 1893" (Papers of James Alexander Teit, T458, Box 1, folder 4, Anthropology Division, AMNH). In 1912, he spelled it "Cexpē'ntlEm" in *Mythology of the Thompson Indians,* Memoir of the American Museum of Natural History, series vol. 12: JNPE, vol. 8, part 2 (Leiden/New York: E.J. Brill/G.E. Stechert, 1912), 411, http://hdl.handle.net/2246/37. In Lytton today, the name often appears as "Spintlum."

59 George Hills's diary, July 13, 1860, quoted in Roberta L. Bagshaw, ed., *No Better Land: The 1860 Diaries of the Anglican Colonial Bishop, George Hills* (Victoria: Sono Nis, 1996), 185.

60 Hills's diary, June 25, 1862, quoted in Brett Christophers, *Positioning the Missionary: John Booth Good and the Confluence of Cultures in Nineteenth-Century British Columbia* (Vancouver: UBC Press, 1998), 47.

61 Because there were no systematic records of the losses, this number is a rough estimate only. See Andrew Yarmie, "Smallpox and the British Columbia Indians: Epidemic of 1862," *British Columbia Library Quarterly* 31, 3 (1969): 13–21. There has been much debate among historians about the extent of the losses. John Belshaw, who has analyzed BC population statistics in depth, believes that the final total of twenty thousand errs on the low side of the losses. If George Dawson's estimates for the Haida losses (approximately five thousand) and Teit's estimates of losses of "thousands" in the south central Interior are even remotely correct, it suggests "that colonial observers captured [far from] the full picture" of the losses (Belshaw, personal communication, August 20, 2018).

62 Kiran Van Rijn, "Lo, the Poor Indian! Colonial Responses to the 1862–63 Smallpox Epidemic in British Columbia and Vancouver Island," *Canadian Bulletin of Medical History* 23, 2 (2006): 549–50; Robert Boyd, *The Coming of the Spirit of Pestilence: Introduced Infectious*

Diseases and Population Decline among Northwest Coast Indians, 1774–1874 (Vancouver: UBC Press, 1999), 172–73.

63 Boyd, *Coming of the Spirit*; see also Van Rijn, "Lo, the Poor Indian!," 541–60.

64 Boyd, *Coming of the Spirit*, 172.

65 Smith, *Widow Smith*, 27.

66 Ibid., 38.

67 Ibid., 27.

68 Ibid.

69 George Hills's diary, June 12, 1860, quoted in Roberta L. Bagshaw, *No Better Land*, 143.

70 Ibid.

71 Anderson, *Fraser River Canyon*, 14–15.

72 Ibid., 15.

73 Mark D. Walters, "Promise and Paradox: The Emergence of Indigenous Rights Law in Canada," in *Indigenous Peoples and the Law: Comparative and Critical Perspectives*, ed. Benjamin Richardson, Shin Imai, and Kent McNeil (Portland, OR: Hart, 2009), 21–50.

74 Cole Harris, "How Did Colonialism Dispossess? Comments from an Edge of Empire," *Annals of the Association of American Geographers* 94, 1 (2004): 170–71. See also Daniel W. Clayton, *Islands of Truth: The Imperial Fashioning of Vancouver Island* (Vancouver: UBC Press, 2000).

75 John Locke, *Two Treatises of Government*, ed. William S. Carpenter (London: Everyman's Library, 1924 [1690]).

76 Domenico Losurdo, *Liberalism: A Counter-History* (London: Verso, 2011).

77 Locke, *Two Treatises*, 122, 125, 212.

78 Harris, "How Did Colonialism Dispossess?" 171.

79 Hugo Grotius, *The Truths of Christianity* (1639) and *The Rights of War and Peace* (1646), quoted in Losurdo, *Liberalism*, 22.

80 Alexis de Toqueville, *Democracy in America* (1835–40), quoted in Losurdo, *Liberalism*, 232.

81 Harris, "How Did Colonialism Dispossess?" 171.

82 Ibid., 170.

83 "Lytton," *The West Shore* 10, 9 (September 1884): 286.

84 In 1859 and 1860, Bishop Hills assigned four clergymen to administer to the peoples of the south central Interior region and oversaw the construction of churches in Douglas, Hope, and Lillooet. Bagshaw, *No Better Land*, 24.

85 For a full study of Good's mission efforts at Lytton, see Christophers, *Positioning the Missionary*. See also Cyril E.H. Williams and Pixie McGeachie, *Archdeacon on Horseback, Richard Small, 1849–1909* (Merritt, BC: Sonotek, 1991), 27.

86 Williams and McGeachie, *Archdeacon on Horseback*, 29–30.

87 Christophers covers this in *Positioning the Missionary*, 121.

88 Ibid., 138–40.

89 For the fuller story of these trade company mergers, see Richard S. Mackie, *Trading Beyond the Mountains: The British Fur Trade on the Pacific, 1793–1843* (Vancouver: UBC Press, 1997); see also Mary Balf, *Kamloops: A History of the District up to 1914* (Kamloops, BC: Kamloops Museum Publication, 1969); and Mary Balf, *The Mighty Company: Kamloops and the H.B.C.* (Kamloops, BC: Kamloops Museum Publication, 1973). See also Robin Fisher, *Contact and Conflict: Indian-European Relations in British Columbia, 1774–1890* (Vancouver: UBC Press, 1977), 24–48; and Cole Harris, "The Fraser Canyon Encountered," in *Resettlement of British Columbia*.

90 Harris, "The Fraser Canyon Encountered," 124–25.
91 Smith, *Widow Smith,* 28.
92 Ibid., 32.
93 Ibid., 69.
94 Quoted in Steve Rice, "Spences Bridge: Crossing the Thompson," in *Reflections: Thompson Valley Memories,* ed. Wayne Norton and Wilf Schmidt (Kamloops, BC: Plateau Press, 1998), 9.
95 Purpus, "Von Spence's Bridge in die Berge."
96 Smith, *Widow Smith,* 30; see also Rice, "Spences Bridge," 7–8.
97 Branwen C. Patenaude, *Trails to Gold* (Victoria: Horsdal and Schubart, 1995), 89–91; see also Rice, "Spences Bridge," 7–9.
98 Anderson, *Fraser River Canyon,* 14; According to Robin Fisher, Trutch negotiated a seven-year contract to collect the bridge tolls. For more on Trutch, see Fisher, "Sir Joseph William Trutch," *Dictionary of Canadian Biography,* accessed January 10, 2019, http://www.biographi.ca/en/bio/trutch_joseph_william_13E.html.
99 Rice, "Spences Bridge," 7–10.
100 Smith, *Widow Smith,* 41.
101 Lara Kozak, "The Rise and Fall of All Hallows School in Yale, B.C." (unpublished manuscript, 1996), http://yale.cariboogoldrush.com/tour/allh1.htm. See also Jean Barman, "Separate and Unequal: Indian and White Girls at All Hallows School, 1884–1920," in *Indian Education in Canada,* vol. 1, *The Legacy,* ed. Jean Barman, Yvonne Hébert, and Don McCaskill (Vancouver: UBC Press, 1986), 110–31.
102 Walter Moberly and Noel Robinson, *Blazing the Trail through the Rockies: The Story of Walter Moberly and His Share in the Making of Vancouver* (Vancouver: News-Advertiser, 1959), 47–48.
103 R.M. Galois, "The Indian Rights Association, Native Protest Activity and the 'Land Question' in British Columbia, 1903–1916," *Native Studies Review* 8, 2 (1992), 3.
104 For the full story of how this struggle over land allotments unfolded over the next two decades, see Chapters 7 and 8.
105 According to historians Cole Harris and Robert Galois, the railway construction crews who lived in camps in the Fraser and Thompson Canyons were mainly from the United States, Ireland, Ontario, and continental Europe. Harris and Galois, "Population Geography of British Columbia," 142.
106 Smith, *Widow Smith,* 35, 38–39, 75.
107 John Murray's store ledger book (original obtained from Glen and Peg Gallagher of Kamloops, BC).
108 Smith, *Widow Smith,* 35.
109 Murray store ledger book. "Nkaitu'sus" was the Nlaka'pamux name that Teit listed for the resident Nlaka'pamux community in the Twaal Valley. He noted it was also called "Atci'tcîkEn." See James Teit, *The Thompson Indians of British Columbia,* Memoir of the American Museum of Natural History, series vol. 2: JNPE, vol. 1: 1898–1900, part 4 (New York: G.P. Putnam's Sons, 1900), 173, http://hdl.handle.net/2246/13.
110 Galois, " Indian Rights Association," 3.
111 For the full story of dispossession, see Cole Harris, *Making Native Space: Colonialism, Resistance, and Reserves in British Columbia* (Vancouver: UBC Press, 2003). See also Harris, "How Did Colonialism Dispossess?" 167.

112 E. Brian Titley, *A Narrow Vision: Duncan Campbell Scott and the Administration of Indian Affairs in Canada* (Vancouver: UBC Press, 1986), 11.

113 Ibid., 11, 14. See also Bob Joseph, *21 Things You May Not Know About the Indian Act: Helping Canadians Make Reconciliation with Indigenous Peoples a Reality* (Port Coquitlam, BC: Indigenous Relations Press, 2018).

114 Judge Sir Henri-Elzear Taschereau in *St Catherines Milling and Lumber Co v. R,* (1887), 13 SCR 577, 648–49.

115 According to legal historian Hamar Foster,

> The Supreme Court of Canada's decision in the *St. Catherine's Milling* case was appealed to the Judicial Committee of the Privy Council (JCPC), which rendered its decision in 1888. Although the JCPC agreed with the SCC that the surrendered land in question was Ontario's not Ottawa's, their reasons were different from the SCC's in two very important respects. First, they said that the SCC was wrong in interpreting the phrase, "lands reserved for the Indians" as meaning Indian reserves. The JCPC held it referred to all the traditional territories of the tribes covered by the Royal Proclamation of 1763 (a point O'Meara and Kelly tried in vain to explain to the 1927 parliamentary committee). Secondly, the court said this: the fact that Ottawa had legislative authority over Indian lands is not inconsistent with "the right of the province to a beneficial interest in these lands, available to them as a source of revenue *whenever the estate of the Crown is disencumbered of the Indian title*." These two points together mean, in my view, that provinces can't mine or log or occupy land subject to the Indian title until that title is extinguished by treaty with Ottawa. This is the point that BC completely ignored and Ottawa blew hot and cold on, eventually giving in to BC. But, legally, the SCC's decision in the case was completely superseded by the JCPC's decision, and, in my view, between 1888 and 1991 both governments were acting illegally.

Hamar Foster, personal communication, August 9, 2018; emphasis added.

116 Titley, *A Narrow Vision,* 135; Harris, *Making Native Space;* Paul Tennant, *Aboriginal Peoples and Politics: The Indian Land Question in British Columbia, 1849–1989* (Vancouver: UBC Press, 1989); Galois, "Indian Rights Association"; Hamar Foster and Alan Grove, "'Trespassers on the Soil': United States v. Tom and A New Perspective on the Short History of Treaty Making in Nineteenth-Century British Columbia," *BC Studies* 138/139 (2003): 51–84; Hamar Foster, "We Are Not O'Meara's Children: Law, Lawyers, and the First Campaign for Aboriginal Title in British Columbia, 1908–28," in *Let Right Be Done: Aboriginal Title, the Calder Case, and the Fight for Indigenous Rights,* ed. Hamar Foster, Heather Raven, and Jeremy Webber (Vancouver: UBC Press, 2007), 61–84; Hamar Foster, "Honoring the Queen's Flag: A Legal and Historical Perspective on the Nisga'a Treaty," *BC Studies* 120 (Winter 1998/99): 11–35; Foster, "Letting Go the Bone," 29–86.

117 Harris with Galois, "A Population Geography of British Columbia in 1881," 158.

118 Ibid., 167.

119 Keith D. Smith, *Liberalism, Surveillance, and Resistance: Indigenous Communities in Western Canada, 1877–1927* (Edmonton: Athabasca University Press, 2009), 8, 9. These colonial constructions were a manifestation of a more general phenomenon that the French philosopher Michel Foucault described in his theoretical work in the 1970s. Noting the rise of the bureaucratic state in the 1800s, Foucault coined the terms "governmentality" and "disciplinarity" to describe the creation of regulatory imperatives that operated at a micro level (that is, at the level of the individual person) through the application of new techniques

such as the keeping of detailed statistical records, the requirement for legal permits, and the creation of subtle codes of acceptable discourse or personal conduct. See Michel Foucault, *Security, Territory, Population: Lectures at the College de France, 1977–78* (Basingstoke, UK: Palgrave Macmillan, 2007).

120 Smith, *Liberalism, Surveillance, and Resistance,* 9.

121 Ibid.

122 Portions of this correspondence between Teit and Magnus Flaws were reprinted in the *Orkney and Shetland American* (December 1888). Flaws was editor of the newspaper.

123 For more on Teit's father's skill as a marksman, see the obituary of John Tait, *Shetland Times,* September 24, 1904. I am grateful to Dr. Ian Tait, head curator of the Shetland Museum, for providing information on the status of hunting in late-nineteenth-century Shetland; personal communication, August 22, 2018.

124 According to the BC Land Titles Office records, Teit and Antko took up residence on a piece of land (E ½ of W 1/s, section 23) in the Twaal Valley in 1891. This appears in a statement that Teit made on November 6, 1907, to the "Land Settlements Records for the Railway Belt and Peace River Block, 1885–1949," in which he noted that he had claimed this as a "homestead" in January 1891. In 1906, he made an application for a land "purchase" of "Fraction Sec. 26" as a "pre-emption." "Land Settlement Records for Railway Belt and Peace River Block, 1885–1949," GR-0436, Microfilm Reel B14639, File 11869, BC Land Titles Office.

125 James Teit–Lucy Antko marriage certificate (September 12, 1892), Lytton Indian Mission (Lytton, BC) fonds, Archives of the Anglican Diocese of New Westminster, Provincial Synod of BC and Yukon, Vancouver, BC. Special thanks to Marche Wiley and Bonnie Campbell for their help in tracking down the original marriage certificate. The names of the two witnesses on the marriage certificate highlight the problems associated with documenting Indian names at the turn of the century. Reverend Small noted on the marriage certificate that "Hiawhatlah" was one of the two witnesses. In fact, Small got this wrong: the "w" (i.e., whatlah) should have been a "p" (i.e., patlah). According to a 1908 petition that Teit drafted for the Nlaka'pamux chiefs, "Yopatla" (pronounced "Yee-oh-PAT-lah") was the chief of the Cooks Ferry Band. He noted that Yopatla had another name, Whistemnitsa. "Prayer of Indian Chiefs," from the Nlaka'pamux chiefs to the Superintendent General of Indian Affairs, signed at Spences Bridge, July 21, 1908, RG10, vol. 4038, file 329, 350, Library and Archives Canada (LAC). Small recorded Antko's uncle's name as "William Quilumjoot" which was a rough approximation of "Kulla-mas-choot." Teit later transcribed the name as "Kolomastcu't."

126 John Tait to Harry Tait, April 18, 1896, John Tait Letterbook, D.17/8/18, Shetland Archives.

127 John Tait to James Teit, April 20, 1896, John Tait Letterbook, D.17/8/18, Shetland Archives.

128 Adele Perry, *On the Edge of Empire: Gender, Race, and the Making of British Columbia* (Toronto: University of Toronto Press, 2001), 114.

129 Ibid., 51.

130 Ibid., 70.

131 Ibid., 70–71.

132 Renisa Mawani, *Colonial Proximities: Crossracial Encounters and Juridical Truths in British Columbia, 1871–1921* (Vancouver: UBC Press, 2009), 171. See also Adele Perry, *Colonial Relations: The Douglas-Connolly Family and the Nineteenth-Century Imperial World* (Cambridge: University of Cambridge Press, 2015).

133 Mawani, *Colonial Proximities,* 171.

134 Ibid., 176.
135 James Teit, "Folk-Lore in Br. Col. with Some Comparative Notes on Folk-Lore in Other Countries," manuscript prepared for the Anthropology Division, c. 1921, Marius Barbeau fonds, box B351.f.13, Canadian Museum of History (CMH).
136 Smith, *Widow Smith,* 71.
137 Katharine Howes and Pat Lean, "An Interview With Inga Teit Perkin, Daughter of Noted Ethnologist, James A. Teit," *Nicola Valley Historical Quarterly* 2, 2 (April 1979): 1, 4.
138 In his song notes, Teit spelled Tetlanetza's name TetlEnī'tsa (VI.M. 49, James Teit cylinder collection CMH). I have chosen to follow Tetlanetza's spelling. Teit listed PE'qaist as one of the villages of the Spences Bridge Band in his *Thompson Indians,* 173.
139 While Boas took the measurements, Teit recorded the names of the men, women, and children whom he measured. Harlan Smith took photographs to supplement the measurements and names. In his 1895 report to the British Association for the Advancement of Science, Boas published both the measurements and the names. See Franz Boas, "Physical Characteristics of the Tribes of the North Pacific Coast," in "Tenth Report on the North-Western Tribes of Canada," *Sixty-Fifth Meeting of the British Association for the Advancement of Science at Ipswich, September 1895* (London: John Murray, 1895), 524–51, with "Ntlakya'pamuq" measurements chart, 7–10. Boas later published a selection of Smith's 1897 photographs (without the names attached) in a special Jesup North Pacific Expedition monograph, *Ethnographical Album of the North Pacific Coasts of America and Asia* (New York: American Museum of Natural History, 1900).
140 Boas to Marie Boas, September 21, 1894, in Rohner, *Ethnography of Franz Boas,* 139.
141 Boas to his parents, September 21, 1894, in ibid., 140.
142 Boas to Marie Boas, September 23, 1894, in ibid., 142.

Chapter 3: Dear Auld Rock

1 Many Shetlanders during Teit's time referred to their island home as the "Dear Old [Auld] Rock." In a letter to his old school friend J.J. Haldane Burgess in 1902, Teit wrote that he hoped that Burgess would be "long spared to do good work on dear old Shetland"; James Teit to James Haldane Burgess, August 22, 1902, D2/a/5B, Shetland Archives. In a letter of 1888, Teit praised his brother Tom for composing poems on "the right theme (Love of the Old Rock)"; Teit to Tom Tait, November 9, 1888. Sigurd Teit obtained a copy of this letter from his cousin, Olaf Tait (son of Thomas Tait), before Olaf's death in 1994.
2 W. Fordyce Clark, *The Story of Shetland* (Edinburgh: Oliver and Boyd, 1906), 15–16.
3 J.J. Haldane Burgess, *Lowra Biglan's Mutch: A Shetland Novelette* (Kirkwall: The Leonards, 1896), 3. Clark, *The Story of Shetland,* 16.
4 Sigurd Teit provided clippings from the *Orkney and Shetland American* from 1887 to 1905. For a full history of the *Orkney and Shetland American* (OSA) newspaper, see Graeme Gibson, "We Can, If We All Will Put Their Shoulder to the Wheel: The *Orkney & Shetland American* and the Construction of Community" (honours thesis, American Studies, University of Glasgow, 2004), copy courtesy of Brian Smith, Shetland Archives.
5 OSA, October 1887.
6 OSA, October 1888, November 1888, and December 1888.
7 Magnus Flaws, "A Young Shetlander," OSA, February 1890.
8 Flaws's dates do not align with Teit's dates. In 1890, Teit was based in Nanaimo where he worked in the powderwork division of the Northfield coal mine. Flaws probably drew his

date from an earlier Teit submission (1888) in which he described his two earlier seasons (1887 and 1888) of trapping in the Nechako Lake district (the region northwest of the city of Prince George in northern British Columbia). The district was also known as Omineca Country.

9 Flaws, "A Young Shetlander."

10 Ibid.

11 See, for example, the following works by J.J. Haldane Burgess: *Rasmie's Smaa Murr* (Lerwick: J.J. Haldane Burgess, 1916); *The Treasure of Don Andres: A Shetland Romance of the Spanish Armada* (Lerwick: Thomas Mathewson, 1903); *Tang: A Shetland Story* (Lerwick: Johnson and Grieg, 1898); and *The Viking Path: A Tale of the White Ghost* (Edinburgh: William Blackwood and Sons, 1903).

12 Jessie Saxby, ed., *Broken Lights: Poems and Reminiscences of Basil R. Anderson* (Edinburgh: R. and R. Clark, 1888).

13 Jessie Saxby (1842–1940) published forty-seven books and over one hundred articles. Many were on or about Shetland; see, for example, *Rock-Bound: A Story of the Shetland Isles* (Edinburgh: Thomas Gray, 1877) and *Shetland Traditional Lore* (Edinburgh: Grant and Murray Publishers, 1932).

14 Saxby edited and wrote the introduction to Anderson's *Broken Lights.* Gilbert Goudie compiled a glossary of Shetland terms for the book.

15 George Stewart, *Shetland Fireside Tales, or The Hermit of Trosswickness* (Edinburgh: Edinburgh Publishing, 1877).

16 Saxby noted Stewart's assistance in her introduction to *Broken Lights,* xxxv.

17 On the history of the late-nineteenth-century cultural renaissance in Shetland, I am indebted to B.J. Cohen's doctoral dissertation, "Norse Imagery in Shetland: An Historical Study of Intellectuals and Their Use of the Past in the Construction of Shetland's Identity, with Particular Reference to the Period, 1800–1914" (PhD diss., University of Manchester, 1983).

18 Quoted in Cohen, "Norse Imagery in Shetland," 339.

19 Flaws, "A Young Shetlander."

20 From April 1890 on, Teit signed his OSA submissions as "J.A. Teit" (OSA, April 1890).

21 Flaws was likely the author of the anonymous letter to the editor on Shetland nationhood that appeared in the April 1888 issue of the OSA. He wrote that, if asked about his nationality, he would respond that he was "a native of the Shetland Islands," and if asked what race of people they are, he would respond that they were "of the Norse race, but subject to Scotland (or Britain)."

22 John Tait's inscription appears in Teit's copy of Jas. M. Crawford, *The Parish of Lerwick, 1701–1901* (Lerwick: T. and J. Manson, 1901).

23 J.J. Haldane Burgess, *Rasmie's Büddie* (Lerwick: T. and J. Manson, 1891), n.p.

24 Burgess, *Tang.* Brian Smith and Anita Hanako Poulsen provided the English translation of Burgess's Danish inscription.

25 Teit's inscription appears under Basil Anderson's photograph, next to the title page of *Broken Lights.*

26 Saxby, "In Memoriam: Basil Ramsay Anderson," in *Broken Lights,* xi–xxxv.

27 Cohen, "Norse Imagery in Shetland," 338–39.

28 See, for example, Jane Nadel-Klein, "Reweaving the Fringe: Localism, Tradition, and Representation in British Ethnography," *American Ethnologist* 18, 3 (1991): 502. In this piece, she writes of "localism not as paradox but as irony":

> Global processes call localities into existence, but make no commitments to their continued survival. The irony lies in the fact that local identity is an unintended result of the global division of labor ... "Localism" as I use it here, refers to the representation of group identity as defined primarily by a sense of commitment to a particular place and to a set of cultural practices that are self-consciously articulated and to some degree separated and directed away from the surrounding social world.

For more on this, see Stéphane Dufoix, *Diasporas* (Berkeley: University of California Press, 2008).

29 The Faroese-Shetland Conference on Jakob Jakobsen, Scalloway, Shetland, May 12–13, 2006.

30 For an overview of Jakobsen's Shetland research, see Roy Grønneberg, *Jakobsen and Shetland* (Lerwick: Shetland Publishing, 1981).

31 Marianna Debes Dahl, "The Jakobsen Letters and What They Reveal," in *Jakob Jakobsen in Shetland and the Faroes,* ed. Turiđ Sigurđardóttir and Brian Smith (Gremista, Lerwick: Shetland Amenity Trust and the University of the Faroe Islands, 2010), 7.

32 Grønneberg, *Jakobsen and Shetland;* see also Dahl, "The Jakobsen Letters."

33 Grønneberg, *Jakobsen and Shetland;* see also James R. Nicolson, *Traditional Life in Shetland* (London: Robert Hale, 1978), 39–40.

34 John Tait Letterbooks, D.17/8/16, D.17/8/17, and D.17/8/18, Shetland Archives. See also Grønneberg, *Jakobsen and Shetland.*

35 Grønneberg, *Jakobsen and Shetland,* 17–19, lists Jakobsen's friends and assistants in Shetland.

36 Quoted in Grønneberg, *Jakobsen and Shetland,* 16.

37 August 20, 1893, quoted in Grønneberg, *Jakobsen and Shetland,* 18.

38 In a letter to his uncle Robert Tait, Teit wrote: "Of course there is the very old tradition known to Thomas Tait of Skarpegath & John Irvine tc. and given by them to Dr. Jacobson about Jan Teit who slew the 'skat' collector with his 'bismar' but that was in Norwegian times before the islands had any political connection with Britain": Teit to Robert Tait, January 15, 1909, copy courtesy of Sigurd Teit.

39 Grønneberg, *Jakobsen and Shetland,* 47–48, includes a summary of Jakobsen's account of the story.

40 Brian Smith, *Toons and Tenants: Settlement and Society in Shetland, 1299–1899* (Lerwick: Shetland Times, 2000).

41 Ibid., 67–68.

42 Ibid., 68; see also John J. Graham, *"A Vehement Thirst after Knowledge": Four Centuries of Education in Shetland* (Lerwick: Shetland Times, 1998), 3.

43 William P.L. Thomson, "Population and Depopulation," in *Shetland and the Outside World, 1469–1969,* ed. Donald J. Withrington (Oxford: Oxford University Press, 1983), 154.

44 Graham, *"A Vehement Thirst,"* 3.

45 Smith, *Toons and Tenants,* 70.

46 Ibid., 79–85; Susan Knox, *The Making of a Shetland Landscape* (Edinburgh: John Donald, 1985), 15.

47 Sigurd Teit, "Notes on Teit family history," copy courtesy of Sigurd Teit. This is an undated document that Teit compiled over a number of years with the assistance of his New Zealand–based uncle, Robert Tait. The original document is part of Robert Tait's family papers; copy courtesy of Sigurd Teit.

48 James R. Nicolson, *Shetland* (London: David and Charles Publishers, 1972), 128–31; see also Alistair Goodlad, "Five Centuries of Shetland Fisheries," in Withrington, *Shetland and the Outside World,* 107–18.

49 Nicolson, *Shetland*, 128–29.
50 Lynn Abrams, *Myth and Materiality in a Woman's World: Shetland 1800–2000* (Manchester: University of Manchester Press, 2005).
51 Abrams's research reveals that, in Lerwick, many women were family or household heads, supporting siblings, parents, and children. Some took in lodgers or worked as servants, laundresses, knitters, and dressmakers. Unlike middle-class women on the mainland, they also maintained a strong connection to their old traditions. In 1900, she notes, every parish had a "howdie woman" who served as the community midwife. Mainlanders who visited Shetland in the late nineteenth century often expressed shock at the "unwomanly and unfeminine behaviour" of the local island women. Many noted their dirty, haggard, and wrinkled appearance, which they attributed to their participation in what they considered to be men's work: Abrams, *Myth and Materiality*, 211–17.
52 Ibid., 53.
53 Knox, *Making of a Shetland Landscape*, 18.
54 Goodlad, "Five Centuries of Shetland Fisheries," 114–15.
55 Ibid., 115.
56 Ibid., 116.
57 Callum G. Brown, *Up-helly-aa: Custom, Culture and Community in Shetland* (Manchester: University of Manchester Press, 1998), 120–21, 131–32.
58 James W. Irvine, *Lerwick: The Birth and Growth of an Island Town* (Lerwick: Lerwick Community Council, 1985), 175–78.
59 Cohen, "Norse Imagery in Shetland," 238.
60 A list of "Tait" family marriages and baptisms from the Parish of Fetlar notes that the marriage of James and Catherine Tait took place on February 19, 1814, and the baptism of their first child, Ursula, on August 14, 1814. Because their next two children were born in Lerwick in 1817 and 1821, respectively, it suggests that their move to Lerwick took place between 1814 and 1817. Thanks to Elisabeth Hogg of Wellington, New Zealand, and Katherine Petrie of Dunedin, New Zealand, for this information.
61 Knox, *Making of a Shetland Landscape*, 48.
62 Robert L. Johnson, "The Deserted Homesteads of Fetlar," *Shetland Life* 13 (1981): 26–35.
63 Smith, *Toons and Tenants*, 48.
64 John J. Graham, "Social Changes during the Quinquennium," in Withrington, *Shetland and the Outside World*, 229.
65 Graham, *"A Vehement Thirst,"* 228–29.
66 Sigurd Teit, "Notes on Teit family history." See also the James Alexander Teit genealogy on the "North Isles Family History" website (www.bayanne.info).
67 Smith, *Toons and Tenants*, 48.
68 Ibid.
69 Sigurd supplied much of the information about James Teit's family genealogy. However, I am also indebted to Anthony Gott of Yell, Shetland, and his "North Isles Family History" website (www.bayanne.info) for filling in the gaps on names, birthdates, and death dates of extended family members.
70 John Tait to Gilbert Tait, January 17, 1884, John Tait Letterbook, Shetland Archives. In a letter in January 1884 to his cousin Captain Gilbert Tait, John Tait listed the names of four former Fetlar men living in Lerwick whom Tait would have known from his youth.
71 In 1839, a group of Lerwick businessmen and merchants established a private-subscription school staffed by teachers from a German Moravian sect from Saxony, Germany, to prepare

their children for entry into Scottish universities. It is likely that some of James Tait's children attended this school (John Tait was six years old when it opened): Cohen, "Norse Imagery in Shetland," 231.

72 "Death of Mr. John Tait, Merchant, Lerwick," *Shetland Times*, September 24, 1904, 5. See also Thomas Manson, *Lerwick during the Last Half Century, 1867–1917* (Lerwick: Lerwick Community Council, 1991; first published by T. and J. Manson, Shetland News Office, 1923). Manson described John Tait as a "prominent man in Lerwick for many years" (p. 8). He described John's older brother Robert as "a man of enterprise" (p. 90).

73 John Tait to John Murray, March 1, 1881, John Tait Letterbook, D.17/8/16, Shetland Archives.

74 John Tait to Joseph Teit, June 3, 1880, John Tait Letterbook, D.17/8/16, Shetland Archives.

75 Cohen, "Norse Imagery in Shetland," 202.

76 Ibid.

77 Wendy Gear, *John Walker's Shetland* (Lerwick: Shetland Times, 2005), 20.

78 Graham, "Social Changes during the Quinquennium," 229, 231.

79 Abrams, *Myth and Materiality*, 64.

80 Cohen, "Norse Imagery in Shetland," 207.

81 Ibid., 208.

82 *Undiscovered Scotland*, s.v. "Arthur Anderson," http://www.undiscoveredscotland.co.uk/usbiography/a/arthuranderson.html. Accessed January 20, 2019.

83 Ibid.

84 Graham, *"A Vehement Thirst,"* 130–32, 164–66.

85 Ibid., 128–30; "Death of Mr. John Tait."

86 "Death of Mr. John Tait."

87 Graham, *"A Vehement Thirst,"* 130–32.

88 Cohen, "Norse Imagery in Shetland," 336.

89 Laurenson's Shetland proposal has links to those of other national and subnational groups, many of which pursued similar objectives during this historical period. It also has links to indigenous and subnational groups today, who assert the centrality of language as key to an integrated environmental/cultural/personal identity. In his doctoral research on the revitalization of the contemporary Ahtna language, Greg Holt highlights the importance of "narrative frame" to successful cultural revitalization. While language is considered by many to be at the core of cultural identity, what should not be overlooked, he explains, is the connection of language to a knowledge of territory and environment, indigenous practices, and other forms of knowledge such as history and genealogy. Thus, language learning in the context of cultural revitalization (and "national"/political movements) is always embodied; it is embodied in a landscape and in interpersonal relationships, and thus also in developing a grounded sense of oneself as Shetlandic, or Ahtna, or Nlaka'pamux. For more on this, see Greg Holt, "Strategies of Language Revitalization in Alignment with Native Pedagogical Forms: Examples from Ahtna Alaska" (BA thesis, Swarthmore College, 2004). See also Catherine Nash's nuanced and complex examination of the connections between place-name mapping, Irish language revival, and the relationship between geography and postcoloniality in contemporary Ireland. She highlights both the centrality of these projects to decolonizing an Irish identity and the sensitive knowledge that such projects are always themselves infused with power and with constructions of authenticity, gender, class, intercultural difference, etc.: Catherine Nash, "Irish Placenames: Post-Colonial Locations," *Transactions of the Institute of British Geographers, New Series* 24, 4 (1999): 457–80.

90 Cohen, "Norse Imagery in Shetland," 335–36.
91 Ibid., 336.
92 See Cohen, "Norse Imagery in Shetland," 332–40; see also a letter from Laurenson to his cousin, Rev. W. Nicolson, September 15, 1883, quoted in Catherine Stafford Spence, ed., *Arthur Laurenson: His Letters and Literary Remains, A Selection – With an Introductory Memoir* (London: T. Fisher Unwin, 1901), 82.
93 Manson, *Lerwick during the Last Half Century,* 234.
94 Laurenson to Gilbert Goudie, December 8, 1873, quoted in Spence, *Arthur Laurenson,* 41.
95 A. Laurenson, "An Unfinished Chapter in English History," *Macmillan's Magazine* 21 (February 1875): 368–70, quoted in Cohen, "Norse Imagery in Shetland," 340.
96 Laurenson to Catherine Hunter, July 7, 1879, quoted in Spence, *Arthur Laurenson,* 61.
97 John Tait to Robert Tait, November 29, 1880, John Tait Letterbook, D.17/8/16, Shetland Archives.
98 John Tait to Gilbert Tait, February 21, 1884, John Tait Letterbook, D.17/8/16, Shetland Archives.
99 Teit to Robert Tait, December 28, 1903, copy courtesy of Sigurd Teit.
100 Teit to Tom Tait, November 9, 1888, copy courtesy of Sigurd Teit.
101 John Tait to Robert Tait, November 29, 1880, John Tait Letterbook, D.17/8/6, Shetland Archives.
102 For a history of education in Shetland, see Graham, *"A Vehement Thirst."*
103 Ibid., 171–73. A report on the Anderson Educational Institute's curriculum in 1874 offers a snapshot of the upper school's curriculum during Teit's time:

> The highest English class not only read Gray's Odes but, in the analytical manner of the period, parsed, analysed, and explained them. Other English textbooks used were Dalgleish's *Grammar, Analysis and Composition* and Graham's *Etymology.* The highest Latin classes read Livy; and one Mathematics class were doing the Fifth Book of Euclid, and quadratic equations. The highest French class read *Telemaque* and used Schneider's Grammar, while the highest German class read Tiark's *Progressive Reader* together with Tiark's *Grammar.* Greek, music and drawing were also taught. (Graham, 171)

104 Ibid., 172.
105 As reported in "The Institute Upper School," *Shetland Times,* July 3, 1880. A year earlier, Teit is listed as winning second prize for English: *Shetland Times,* June 28, 1879.
106 John Tait to Robert Tait, November 29, 1880, John Tait Letterbook, D.17/8/16, Shetland Archives.
107 Grønneberg, *Jakobsen and Shetland,* 93.
108 Ibid.
109 Manson, *Lerwick during the Last Half Century,* 246.
110 "Death of Mr. John Tait."
111 Cohen, "Norse Imagery in Shetland," 190.
112 Abrams, *Myth and Materiality,* 103–4.
113 Ibid., 104.
114 Graham, "Social Changes," 231.
115 Cohen, "Norse Imagery in Shetland"; see also Brown, *Up-helly-aa,* 139–53.
116 Cohen, "Norse Imagery in Shetland," 358, 362.
117 Brian Smith, "'Something More Romantic': Origins of Up Helly Aa Revisited," *New Shetlander* 231 (2005): 30.

118 John Tait's comment in a letter to his son on June 3, 1885, was typical of such comments: "I hope you don't let a day pass without reading your Bible, however small a portion," he wrote to James. "You have never told me if there be a church near you or if you go to church." John Tait Letterbook, D.17/8/16, Shetland Archives.

119 Government of Canada 1901 Census (Spences Bridge).

120 Edward Royle, *Radicals, Secularists, and Republicans: Popular Freethought in Britain, 1866–1915* (Manchester: Manchester University Press, 1980).

121 James Teit to Robert Tait, March 31, 1905, copy courtesy of Sigurd Teit.

122 Ibid.

123 John Tait to James Teit, April 7, 1884, John Tait Letterbook, D.17/8/16, Shetland Archives.

124 Ibid.

125 John Tait to Joan Hughson, June 21, 1884, John Tait Letterbook, D.17/8/16, Shetland Archives.

126 John Tait to James Teit, September 17, 1888, John Tait Letterbook, D.17.8/17, Shetland Archives.

127 I am indebted to Brian Smith, Karen Inkster, and Judy Thompson for providing me with this information. A related story surfaced in the late 1990s, when Teit's son Sigurd received a letter from James Andrew Leask about another paternity case linked to Teit. Leask wrote that "an old man, now dead," had told him a surprising story about his mother, Margaret Laurenson. "Did you know," the man asked Leask, "that your mother was born out of wedlock and that her father was James A. Tait?" Leask explained that his mother, Margaret, was born in 1882, which would have put her at two years old at the time of Teit's departure to Canada in 1884. The child's mother was Janet "Jessie" Thompson Laurenson. She was six years older than Teit. According to Leask, Jessie was pregnant with a second child when Teit departed for British Columbia. Leask stated that "he had no proof" of this. He had asked his mother, Margaret, about it before her death, but she did not respond one way or the other. He noted that Margaret's mother, Jessie, eventually married and had five more children. Sigurd refused to believe that his "father would have left Shetland with a two year old daughter and another infant on the way, or that his father would have allowed him to do this, unless there was a lot more to the story than is now known ... I don't see how it could have been kept quiet all these years": letter from Sigurd Teit to Wendy Wickwire, n.d. During a research trip to Shetland in 2006, Judy Thompson encountered both the Hughson story (in Teit's father's letterbooks) and the Laurenson story (via a meeting with Leask): Judy Thompson, *Recording Their Story: James Teit and the Tahltan* (Vancouver/Gatineau/Seattle: Douglas and McIntyre/Canadian Museum of Civilization/University of Washington Press, 2007), 11–12, 177*n*4.

128 Manson, *Lerwick during the Last Half Century,* 43. See also J. Laughton Johnston, *A Kist of Emigrants* (Lerwick: Shetland Times, 2010).

129 Johnston, *A Kist of Emigrants*, xix.

130 Brown, *Up-helly-aa,* 148. For more on this, see William P.L. Thomson, "Population and Depopulation" in Withrington, *Shetland and the Outside World,* 150–80. According to Thomson, between 1861 and 1871, "there was a net loss ... of 3557 persons" and between 1871 and 1881, there was a further loss of 4567 persons" (p. 164).

131 Johnston, *A Kist of Emigrants*. For an excellent study of this mass migration, see Marjory Harper, *Adventurers and Exiles: The Great Scottish Exodus* (London: Profile Books, 2003). See also Marjory Harper, *Scotland No More? The Scots Who Left Scotland in the Twentieth*

Century (Edinburgh: Luath Press, 2012) and *Testimonies of Transition: Voices from the Scottish Diaspora* (Edinburgh: Luath Press, 2017).

132 James Teit to Robert Tait, December 28, 1903, copy courtesy of Sigurd Teit.

133 Susan Butterworth included a brief summary of the Robert Tait story ("The Taits of Taitville) in her book *Chips Off the Auld Rock: Shetlanders in New Zealand* (Wellington: Shetland Society, 1997), 106.

134 Notes on family history prepared by Sigurd Teit, copy courtesy of Sigurd Teit.

135 The diary of Shetland rural schoolmaster Christopher Sandison (1781–1870) provides a close look at the rootedness of the lives of rural Shetlanders in the nineteenth century. For the full diary, see Robert Sandison, ed., *Christopher Sandison of Eshaness, 1781–1870: Diarist in an Age of Social Change* (Lerwick: Shetland Times, 1997). Teit's aunt Ursula Irvine had stories of two sons (Teit's cousins William and John) whose travels took them across the globe – William to India, New Zealand, and Burma, and John to the United States, Canada, and New Zealand. One son's story ended well but the other did not. John made it back to Lerwick in 1884, where he lived out the rest of his life as a successful shipping agent, but William died in Burma in 1885. The John Cowie family in Lerwick had a line of migration stories that included Canada. The family head, John, had worked as a physician for the Hudson's Bay Company in Canada in 1849, and two of his five sons later emigrated to Canada. The Thomas Stout family had one of the most colourful migrant stories. Their son, Robert, travelled to New Zealand in 1863 at age twenty to take part in the Otago gold rush. Shortly after arriving, he enrolled at the newly established Otago University and studied law. In 1884, after serving as the country's chief justice, he was elected premier of New Zealand. In his progressive stands on religion, land rights, women's issues, and poverty, he shared much with Teit. See Johnson, *A Kist of Emigrants,* and Waldo Hilary Dunn and Ivor L.M. Richardson, *Sir Robert Stout: A Biography* (Wellington: A.H. and A.W. Reed, 1961).

136 Harper, *Adventurers and Exiles,* 3.

137 John Tait to John Murray, December 20, 1883, John Tait Letterbook, D.17/8/16, Shetland Archives.

138 For the full story of Gilbert Teit's life, see "Capt. Gilbert Tait," *Shetland News,* February 2, 1897, 5.

139 James Teit to Robert Tait, September 5, 1904, copy courtesy of Sigurd Teit. Given the tradition of memorizing *scattald* (common land) boundaries in Shetland, it could be that Gilbert was drawing on this in his reconstruction of his old island home. (On such oral tradition, see Smith, *Toons and Tenants,* 43.)

140 Teit's 1904 journal lists their names, copy obtained from Sigurd Teit.

141 James Teit to Thomas Tait, November 9, 1888, copy obtained from Sigurd Teit; emphasis in original. Teit was very interested in Shetland societies (he helped found one in Nanaimo). In a letter to his uncle Robert, he mentioned that he had been corresponding with A.W. Johnston, an Orkney man whom he had met several years earlier through their mutual interest in the "Udal League": James Teit to Robert Tait, August 1, 1906, copy courtesy of Sigurd Teit.

142 OSA, July 1887.

143 James Teit to Thomas Tait, November 9, 1888, copy courtesy of Sigurd Teit.

144 Ibid.

145 Brian Smith, "Udal Law: Salvation or Romantic Fiction," *Shetland Times,* October 3, 2003, 19. Johnston's vision of Home Rule for the islands was "self-government with dominion

status, firmly under the crown, with a legitimate son of the monarch as governor of Orkney and Shetland" (19).

146 Cohen, "Norse Imagery in Shetland," 385; see also Smith, "Udal Law."

147 Smith, "Udal Law," 19.

148 Ibid. According to Smith, Johnston's ideas initially excited many Orcadians and Shetlanders because of their promise of land reform and the conversion of farm-tenants to owner-occupiers. Faced with the daily weight of rising rents, meagre common grazing land, and insecure tenures, however, many islanders had little time to engage seriously with Johnston's initiative. On the subject of Home Rule, Smith notes that few really believed that the movement would do anything for Shetland. Rather than constitutional reform or a return to medieval forms of government, what most Shetlanders craved was a Crofters' Act similar to the one that Ireland had attained fifteen years earlier. In 1892, Johnston founded the "Viking Society" (as a wing of the "Social and Literary Branch of the Orkney, Shetland and Northern Society") as a vehicle to unify "all the Orkney and Shetland societies scattered over the globe." Although he continued to explore the potential for the implementation of ancient land-tenure systems on the northern islands, Johnston moved in a more academic direction with this new organization. He created a library and a museum to house rare books, manuscripts, and artifacts, and he launched a scholarly journal, the *Saga Book,* to disseminate research.

149 Teit referred to his correspondence with Johnston in his letters to his uncle Robert Tait: James Teit to Robert Tait, January 15, 1909, copy courtesy of Sigurd Teit.

150 Brian Smith, "Udal Law."

151 James Teit to Robert Tait, June 4, 1909, copy courtesy of Sigurd Teit.

152 James Laurenson, as told to Alan Bruford, "The Smith Family Were Cursed by a Wronged Woman," *Tobar an Dualchais,* recorded September 20, 1975, www.tobarandualchais.co.uk/en/fullrecord/78185/9.

153 Peter Guy, "Walking the Coastline of Shetland: The Island of Fetlar" (Shetland: Old Haa Trust and Nelson Smith Printers, 1992), 23.

154 Burgess, *Tang,* 137.

Chapter 4: Encounter

1 Franz Boas to Toni Boas, September 5, 1875, quoted in Rainer Hatoum, "'I Wrote All My Notes in Shorthand': A First Glance into the Treasure Chest of Franz Boas's Shorthand Field Notes," in *Local Knowledge, Global Stage,* ed. Frederic W. Gleach and Regna Darnell (Lincoln: University of Nebraska Press, 2016), 221.

2 George W. Stocking Jr., "Introduction: The Basic Assumptions of Boasian Anthropology," in *A Franz Boas Reader: The Shaping of American Anthropology, 1883–1911* (New York: Basic Books, 1974), 1.

3 For a full itinerary of Boas's field trips by date and location, see Ronald P. Rohner, "Franz Boas: Ethnographer on the Northwest Coast," in *Pioneers of American Anthropology,* ed. June Helm (Seattle and London: University of Washington Press, 1966), 149–212. For more context, see Douglas Cole, *Franz Boas: The Early Years, 1858–1906* (Vancouver/Seattle: Douglas and McIntyre/University of Washington Press, 1999).

4 Boas to his parents, December 14, 1897, in Ronald Rohner, ed., *The Ethnography of Franz Boas: Letters and Diaries of Franz Boas Written on the Northwest Coast from 1886 to 1931* (Chicago: University of Chicago Press, 1969), 195.

5 Ibid.
6 Boas to Marie Boas, December 15, 1894, in Rohner, *Ethnography of Franz Boas,* 196.
7 Ibid., 195.
8 Ibid., 196.
9 "Squaw man," as noted in Chapter 2, was a common label for a white man who cohabited with, or married an Indian woman.
10 Robert Lowie, *The History of Ethnological Theory* (New York: Farrar and Rinehart, 1937), 132–33. With Teit in view, Lowie wrote that "an intelligent nonprofessional observer familiar with the language and collaborating by correspondence with an ethnologist may learn to interpret native life 'from within' while simultaneously answering the specialist's queries." In fact, the sources on Teit do not support this. Beyond sending Teit lists of topics that he wanted him to cover and, in the case of the basketry project, sending Teit questions that he wanted Teit to take to the basket makers, there is little in the correspondence between the two men that shows Boas teaching Teit how "to interpret native life 'from within.'" Boas simply suggested the report to Teit after two days together in September 1894, mailed him a list of topics he wanted him to cover, then awaited Teit's submission of the final product. When Boas returned to Spences Bridge to check on Teit's progress in December, he found Teit close to finishing the report. He sent Boas the full report three months later. Boas had struggled with his own fieldwork in the region, often collecting stories and anthropometric measurements but little else. Moreover, the sophistication and detail of Teit's ethnographic reports were well beyond what Boas could have generated on his own. When Boas did try to intervene in Teit's ethnographic work, as when he sent questions for the basket makers, it resulted in frustration for both Teit and the basket makers (with the women charging that some of Boas's questions were "foolishness"; see Chapter 5).
11 Verne Ray, review of *Franz Boas: The Science of Man in the Making,* by Melville Herskovits, *American Anthropologist* vol. 1, part 1 (1955): 138–41.
12 Marian Smith, "Boas' 'Natural History' Approach to Field Method," in *The Anthropology of Franz Boas: Essays on the Centennial of His Birth,* ed. Walter R. Goldschmidt, American Anthropological Association Memoir 89 (San Francisco: Howard Chandler, 1959), 56.
13 For the full story, see Cole, *Franz Boas.*
14 Franz Boas, "An Anthropologist's Credo," *The Nation* 147 (1938): 201–4, reprinted in Stocking, *A Franz Boas Reader,* 41.
15 Julia Liss chronicles the story of Boas's youth in her article "German Culture and German Science in the *Bildung* of Franz Boas," in *Volksgeist as Method and Ethic: Essays on Boasian Ethnography and the German Anthropological Tradition,* ed. George W. Stocking Jr. (Madison: University of Wisconsin Press, 1996), 155–84. See also Cole, *Franz Boas.*
16 Cole, *Franz Boas,* 17.
17 This is how Boas described his graduate program in a letter to his uncle: Boas to A. Jacobi, April 10, 1882, in Stocking, *Franz Boas Reader,* 43. According to Alfred Kroeber, Boas's dissertation was "wholly theoretical and mathematical": A.L. Kroeber, "Franz Boas: The Man," in *Franz Boas, 1858–1942,* ed. A.L. Kroeber, Ruth Benedict, Murray B. Emeneau, et al. (New York: Kraus Reprint, 1969, orig. 1943), 22.
18 Cole, *Franz Boas,* 54.
19 Ibid., 59.
20 Ibid., 280–82. See also Liss, "German Culture and German Science," 169.
21 Cole, *Franz Boas,* 84.

22 For an excellent article on the Baffin Island expedition, see Rainer Baehre, "Early Anthropology Discourse on the Inuit and the Influence of Virchow on Boas," *Études/Inuit/Studies* 32, 2 (2008): 13–34.
23 Cole, *Franz Boas,* 80, 172.
24 Franz Boas, "Der Eskimo-Dialekt des Cumberland-Sundes," *Mitteilungen der Anthropologischen Gesellschaft in Wien* 24 (1894): 97, quoted in Cole, *Franz Boas,* 81.
25 Cole, *Franz Boas,* 69.
26 Ibid., 95.
27 Boas, "A Year among the Eskimo," *Bulletin of the American Geographical Society* 19 (1887): 383–402. Reprinted in Stocking, *A Franz Boas Reader,* 55.
28 Cole, *Franz Boas,* 95.
29 Ibid., 97.
30 Ibid., 100.
31 Ibid., 97.
32 Ibid., 104.
33 Herbert Lewis, "The Individual and Individuality in Franz Boas's Anthropology and Philosophy," in *The Franz Boas Papers,* vol. 1, *Franz Boas as Public Intellectual – Theory, Ethnography, Activism,* ed. Regna Darnell, Michelle Hamilton, Robert L.A. Hancock, and Joshua Smith (Lincoln: University of Nebraska Press, 2015), 20. With its links to major intellectual figures such as Kant, Herder, Goethe, Schiller, Lessing, Moses Mendelssohn, Beethoven, and the Von Humboldt brothers, the 1848 Revolution had a commanding presence in Europe.
34 Cole, *Franz Boas,* 84.
35 Stocking, "The Background of Boas' Anthropology," in Stocking, *A Franz Boas Reader,* 22.
36 Herbert Lewis, "Franz Boas: Boon or Bane?" *Reviews in Anthropology* 37, 2 (2008): 172.
37 Ibid., 172–73.
38 For a detailed discussion of how the major proponents of European and American liberalism – from John Locke to Thomas Jefferson, Alexis de Tocqueville, and George Washington – viewed slaves and Indians as "non-human," see Domenico Losurdo, *Liberalism: A Counter-History* (London: Verso, 2011). The power of one group to confer absolute *non-*status on another group has links today to the power of the "nation state" to decree a "state of exception" on whomever and whatever it chooses. The most brazen example is Nazi Germany (and its Jewish citizens), but it is also widespread today in many geopolitical contexts. See Carl Schmitt, *Political Theology: Four Chapters on the Concept of Sovereignty,* trans. George D. Schwab (Chicago: University of Chicago Press, 1985; first published in 1922); and Giorgio Agamben, *Homo Sacer: Sovereign Power and Bare Life* (Stanford, CA: Stanford University Press, 1995).
39 Herbert Lewis, "The Passion of Franz Boas," *American Anthropologist* 103, 2 (2001): 453.
40 Cole, *Franz Boas,* 127.
41 Franz Boas, "The Occurrence of Similar Inventions in Areas Widely Apart," *Science* 9 (May 20, 1887): 485–86, and "Museums of Ethnology and Their Classification," *Science* 9 (June 17, 1887): 587–89.
42 Boas, "The Occurrence of Similar Inventions," 485. Also quoted in Stocking, "Introduction," *A Franz Boas Reader,* 2.
43 Cole, *Franz Boas,* 111.
44 Stocking, *A Franz Boas Reader,* 58.

45 Rohner, *Ethnography of Franz Boas,* 82.
46 Cole, *Franz Boas,* 144–45.
47 Judith Berman, "'The Culture as It Appears to the Indian Himself': Boas, George Hunt, and the Methods of Ethnography," in Stocking, *Volksgeist as Method and Ethic,* 215–56. For a full account of Boas's experience in Chicago, see Paige Raibmon, "Theaters of Contact: The Kwakwa̱ka̱'wakw at the Fair," in *Authentic Indians: Episodes of Encounter from the Late-Nineteenth-Century Northwest Coast* (Durham, NC: Duke University Press, 2005), 50–73. See also Cole, *Franz Boas,* 156–57.
48 Raibmon, "Theaters of Contact." See also Cole, *Franz Boas,* 156.
49 Cole, *Franz Boas,* 156.
50 Ibid.
51 Ibid., 157.
52 Ibid., 165.
53 Ibid., 167.
54 Ibid., 136.
55 Franz Boas, *Die Ziele der Ethnologie* (New York: Hermann Bartsch, 1889), 24. English translation, "The Aims of Ethnology," in Stocking, *A Franz Boas Reader,* 71. Also quoted in Cole, *Franz Boas,* 132.
56 Cole, *Franz Boas,* 134–35.
57 Franz Boas, "Über Seine Reisen in Britisch-Columbien," *Verhandlungen der Gesellschaft für Erdkunde zu Berlin* 16 (1889), 257–68, quoted in Rohner, *Ethnography of Franz Boas,* 13.
58 Ibid.
59 "List of Cookesferry Indians who have died from Jan. 1884 to January 1893," in James A. Teit Papers, "Salish Ethnographic Materials," Slb. 7, American Council of Learned Societies Committee of Native American Languages (ACLS) collection, American Philosophical Society Library (APS).
60 James Teit, *The Thompson Indians of British Columbia,* Memoir of the American Museum of Natural History, series vol. 2: JNPE, vol. 1: 1898–1900, part 4 (New York: G.P. Putnam's Sons, 1900), 177, 391*n*1, http://hdl.handle.net/2246/13.
61 Teit's summary of his statistics appears in *Thompson Indians,* 177.
62 Ibid., 177.
63 Ibid., 176.
64 Ibid., 175.
65 Ibid., 176.
66 Ibid.
67 Ibid.
68 Ibid., 181, 178.
69 Ibid., 368.
70 James Teit to Boas, August 24, 1895, James Teit–Franz Boas Correspondence, Anthropology Division, American Museum of Natural History (AMNH). Hereafter, all references to AMNH in relation to correspondence between Teit and Boas refer to this collection.
71 "Narratives of Old Pa-ah, 1893," Papers of James Alexander Teit, T458, Box 1, folder 4, Anthropology Division, AMNH. I later discovered that Boas included his own edited versions of two of Teit's recordings of Pa-ah's stories in Teit's Jesup monograph, *Mythology of the Thompson Indians,* Memoir of the American Museum of Natural History, series vol. 12: JNPE, vol. 8, part 2 (Leiden/New York: E.J. Brill/G.E. Stechert, 1912), 408–14, http://

hdl.handle.net/2246/37. In the published versions, however, Boas omitted the names of the storyteller and the date of the recording. He also replaced Teit's first-person pronouns with third-person pronouns.

72 In the late fall of 1893, Teit had contacted Oblate missionary Father A.G. Morice of the Stuart Lake mission in northern British Columbia with questions about BC's Indians. In this letter, Teit described Pa-ah as an elderly storyteller, approximately seventy-five years old; he described Tsilla-gheskit as ninety years old. A fragment of this undated letter was found in the James A. Teit Papers, "Salish Ethnographic Materials," Slb. 7, ACLS, APS.

73 Tsilla-gheskit's name turns up frequently in Teit's field notes (sometimes spelled TsElEqê'sket), suggesting that he was one of Teit's key sources on Nlaka'pamux history in the 1890s. Note that in his sketch, he spelled the name "Tsila-gheskit."

74 Teit, "Narratives of Old Pa-ah, 1893."

75 Teit to Boas, June 2, 1896, AMNH.

76 Teit to Boas, April 20, 1897, AMNH.

77 For a fuller account of how late-nineteenth- and early-twentieth-century historians characterized British Columbia history, see Chad Reimer, *Writing British Columbia History, 1784–1958* (Vancouver: UBC Press, 2009), 61–62.

78 In his 1909 monograph, *The Shuswap,* Teit included a story of a similar "cruel, treacherous, selfish and bloodthirsty" man named Sowâ'xexken: James Teit, *The Shuswap,* Memoir of the American Museum of Natural History, series vol. 4: JNPE, vol. 2, part 7 (Leiden/New York: E.J. Brill/G.E. Stechert, 1909), 558–59, http://hdl.handle.net/2246/38.

79 Teit, *Thompson Indians,* 365.

80 Ibid., 365–66.

81 Ibid., 366.

82 Ibid.

83 Ibid.

84 Leslie Spier was one of the first scholars to note the importance of the prophecy movement. See Spier, "The Prophet Dance of the Northwest and its Derivatives: The Source of the Ghost Dance," in *General Series in Anthropology,* no. 1 (Menasha, WI: George Banta, 1935). See also Wayne Suttles, "The Plateau Prophet Dance among the Coast Salish," *Southwest Journal of Anthropology* 13, 4 (Winter 1957): 352–96; Christopher Miller, *Prophetic Worlds: Indians and Whites on the Columbia Plateau* (New Brunswick, NJ: Rutgers University Press, 1985). Historian Elizabeth Vibert makes a convincing case for the influence of epidemic on this religious movement: Vibert, "'The Natives Were Strong to Live': Plague, Prophecy, and the Prelude to the Encounter," in *Traders' Tales: Narratives of Cultural Encounters in the Columbia Plateau, 1807–1846* (Norman: University of Oklahoma Press, 1997), 50–83.

85 Larry Cebula, *Plateau Indians and the Quest for Spiritual Power, 1700–1850* (Lincoln: University of Nebraska Press, 2003), 53.

86 Ibid., 54.

87 Teit to Boas, April 16, 1895, AMNH.

88 Teit to Boas, November 8, 1895, AMNH.

89 Ibid.; emphasis in original.

90 Ibid.

91 Teit to Boas, December 6, 1894, AMNH.

92 Teit to Boas, October 6, 1894, AMNH.

93 Teit to Boas, January 14, 1896, AMNH.

94 Teit to Boas, June 8, 1895, AMNH.
95 Teit to Boas, May 20, 1895, AMNH.
96 Teit to Boas, November 9, 1895, AMNH. Included with this letter was Teit's financial statement to the American Museum of Natural History: "Copy of Collection a/c, J.A. Teit to American Museum of Natural History."
97 Ibid. To maintain consistency, I have used the spellings that Teit used in his 1893 inventory of Nlaka'pamux names. In his Novemver 1895 financial statement, Teit used some of the new spellings: Wax'tko, Kaxpi'tsa, Wazi'nek, Haisê'ska, Waxani'nek, Whali'nek, and Helasa'tko. (Helasa'tko was not on his 1893 list.)
98 Ibid.
99 Teit to Boas, January 14, 1896, AMNH.
100 Teit to Boas, October 6, 1894, AMNH.
101 Teit to Boas, February 1, 1897, AMNH.
102 Teit to Boas, February 20, 1897, AMNH.
103 Teit to Boas, February 1, 1897, AMNH.
104 Teit to Boas, November 9, 1895, AMNH. Teit included in this letter his first financial statement to the AMNH. He noted the following: $9.25 paid in "cash to Harvey & Bailey for Buckskins," $2.50 "paid for Doeskins at Nicola," and $3.25 "paid for Buckskins at Ashcroft."
105 The phenomenon of mixing paid labour for women's craft work (in the home) with their traditional non-monetary activities (gathering food, for example) and their wage work in the larger capitalist sector (such as hop-picking in the summer months) raises questions that transcend the usual categories of materialist analysis. On such questions, see Ann McGrath, "Modern Stone-Age Slavery: Images of Aboriginal Labour and Sexuality," *Labour History* 69 (November 1995): 30–51; Paige Raibmon, "The Practice of Everyday Colonialism: Indigenous Women at Work in the Hop Fields and Tourist Industry of Puget Sound," *Labor: Studies in Working-Class History of the Americas* 3, 3 (2006): 23–56; Niara Sudarkasa, "'The Status of Women' in Indigenous African Societies," *Feminist Studies* 12, 1 (Spring 1986): 91–103; Gerald Pocius, "Material Culture Research: Authentic Things, Authentic Values," *Material History Review* 45 (Spring 1997): 5–15; Lynn Stephen, "Culture as a Resource: Four Cases of Self-Managed Indigenous Craft Production in Latin America," *Economic Development and Cultural Change* 40, 1 (October 1991): 101–30; and Anthony Bebbington, "Reencountering Development: Livelihood Transitions and Place Transformations in the Andes," *Annals of the Association of American Geographers* 90, 3 (2000): 495–520.
106 Elizabeth Dijour to Boas, August 20, 1931, Franz Boas Papers, Mss.B.B61, Series 1: Correspondence, APS.
107 Cole, *Franz Boas,* 173.
108 Ibid.
109 Ibid., 181–84.
110 Stocking, *A Franz Boas Reader,* 1. Herbert Lewis notes that Boas produced approximately 650 books and articles and trained more than sixty PhDs: Lewis, "Franz Boas: Boon or Bane?" 176–77. For a full review of Boas's legacy, see Lewis, "The Passion of Franz Boas."
111 On the role of George Hunt in Boas's research projects, see Berman, "'The Culture as It Appears to the Indian Himself'"; Jeanne Cannizzo, "George Hunt and the Invention of Kwakiutl Culture," *Canadian Review of Sociology and Anthropology* 20, 1 (1982): 44–58. See also Ira Jacknis, *The Storage Box of Tradition: Kwakiutl Art, Anthropologists and Museums* (Washington, DC: Smithsonian Institution Press, 2002).

Chapter 5: Paper Mountain

1 George W. Stocking Jr., "Franz Boas and the Culture Concept," in *Race, Culture, and Evolution: Essays in the History of Anthropology* (New York: Free Press, 1968), 204.
2 James Teit to Franz Boas, June 8, 1895, AMNH. According to this letter, Boas had floated the idea to Teit within a few months of their first meeting.
3 Boas to Marie Boas, June 6, 1897, in Ronald P. Rohner, ed., *The Ethnography of Franz Boas: Letters and Diaries of Franz Boas Written on the Northwest Coast from 1886 to 1931* (Chicago: University of Chicago Press, 1969), 202–3.
4 "James A. Teit, 1897, Field notes on Thompson songs and language," S1b.8, American Council of Learned Societies Committee of Native American Languages (ACLS) collection, American Philosophical Society Library (APS). This document consists of Teit's rough notes on thirty of the forty songs that Boas recorded at Spences Bridge in 1897. The original recordings are housed at the Archives of Traditional Music, University of Indiana. See "Songs of Thompson River Indians," Franz Boas and James Teit, 1897, 54-129-F.
5 According to Teit's notes, Antko was one of the singers who sang for Boas in 1897. I have used Teit's 1893 spellings of these names. In his notes for Boas on the song session, Teit transcribed the names according to Boas's orthography: Kaxpī'tsa, X̱walī'inek, Kilka'lus, Haisê'ska, and Nsilkapês'kit. Harlan Smith, the Jesup photographer, took four photographs of Antko, one of which included Teit (Photograph #11686, Library and Special Collections, American Museum of Natural History).
6 Boas to Marie Boas, June 5, 1897, in Rohner, *Ethnography of Franz Boas,* 202. See also Wendy Wickwire, "The Grizzly Gave Them the Song: James Teit and Franz Boas Interpret Twin Ritual in Aboriginal British Columbia, 1897–1920," *American Indian Quarterly* 25, 3 (Summer 2001): 431–52; and Wendy Wickwire, "James A. Teit: His Contribution to Canadian Ethnomusicology," *Canadian Journal of Native Studies* 8, 2 (1988): 183–204.
7 Boas to Marie Boas, June 5, 1897, and Boas to Marie Boas, June 6, 1897, in Rohner, *Ethnography of Franz Boas,* 202.
8 Boas to his parents, June 15, 1897, in Rohner, *Ethnography of Franz Boas,* 205. Boas noted in a letter to Marie that the first day of travel was June 14: Boas to Marie Boas, June 14, 1897, in ibid., 204. According to Teit's trip log, the party left Spences Bridge on June 12. James Teit, "Trip to Bella Coola with Dr. Boas and Dr. Farrand," copy courtesy of Sigurd Teit.
9 Teit to Boas, April 29, 1897, AMNH.
10 Boas to Marie Boas, June 14, 1897, in Rohner, *Ethnography of Franz Boas,* 204.
11 Boas to Marie Boas, June 15, 1897, in ibid., 205.
12 Boas to Marie Boas, June 18, 1897, and June 21, 1897, in ibid., 206–7.
13 Boas to Marie Boas, July 6, 1897, in ibid., 208–9.
14 Boas to Marie Boas, and Boas to his parents, July 21, 1897, in ibid., 214–15.
15 Ibid., 213.
16 Boas to Marie Boas, July 6, 1897, in ibid., 208.
17 Teit to Boas, August 19, 1897, AMNH. Teit's journal gives slightly different dates. Copy of Teit's journal courtesy of Sigurd Teit.
18 This was Teit's first major guiding contract. His client was the Honourable Joseph Petri of London. Sigurd Teit notes.
19 Teit's 1897 journal, copy courtesy of Sigurd Teit.

20 Boas to Marie Boas, July 30, 1897, in Rohner, *Ethnography of Franz Boas,* 216.

21 Boas to Marie Boas, August 5, 1897, in ibid., 219. For the full story of Boas's work with Hunt in 1897, see Aaron Glass, Judith Berman, and Rainer Hatoum, "Reassembling *The Social Organization:* Collaboration and Digital Media in (Re)making Boas's 1897 Book," *Museum Worlds: Advances in Research* 5 (2017): 110–34.

22 Douglas Cole, *Franz Boas: The Early Years* (Vancouver/Seattle: Douglas and McIntyre/University of Washington Press, 1999), 189.

23 Ibid., 188.

24 Franz Boas, "The Jesup North Pacific Expedition," *Publications of the Jesup North Pacific Expedition* 1 (1898): 1–11, quoted in George W. Stocking Jr., ed., *A Franz Boas Reader: The Shaping of American Anthropology, 1883–1911* (New York: Basic Books, 1974), 108.

25 Franz Boas, "The Limitations of the Comparative Method in Anthropology," *Science* 4, 18 (1896): 901–8, quoted in Cole, *Franz Boas,* 191.

26 Ibid.

27 Boas, "The Jesup North Pacific Expedition," in Stocking, *A Franz Boas Reader,* 112.

28 Ibid.

29 Quoted in Stocking, *A Franz Boas Reader,* 113.

30 Ibid.

31 Teit to Boas, March 10, 1897, AMNH.

32 Teit to Boas, May 17, 1897, AMNH.

33 James A. Teit, *Traditions of the Thompson River Indians* (Boston: American Folk-Lore Society, 1898); Teit, *The Thompson Indians of British Columbia,* Memoir of the American Museum of Natural History, series vol. 2: JNPE, vol. 1, part 4 (New York: G.P. Putnam's Sons, 1900), http://hdl.handle.net/2246/13.

34 Cole, *Franz Boas,* 192. See also Boas's comments on Smith in his letter to his parents, August 15, 1897, in Rohner, *Ethnography of Franz Boas,* 227.

35 Boas to Marie Boas, August 19, 1897, in Rohner, *Ethnography of Franz Boas,* 227.

36 Brian Thom, "Harlan I. Smith's Jesup Fieldwork on the Northwest Coast," in *Gateways: Exploring the Legacy of the Jesup North Pacific Expedition, 1897–1902,* ed. Igor Krupnik and William W. Fitzhugh (Washington, DC: Smithsonian Institution, 2001), 139–80.

37 The Jesup would serve Smith well. In 1911, Edward Sapir hired him as the archaeologist for the newly founded Anthropology Division of the Geological Survey of Canada, Ottawa. Over the next three decades, Smith undertook archaeological projects in eastern Canada, Ontario, and British Columbia. From 1920 on, he moved into more general ethnography, including ethnobiology, film, and photography, among the Nuxalk peoples of Bella Coola on British Columbia's Central Coast. For more on Smith, see Dorothee Schreiber, "Forms of Relatedness: Harlan Smith and the Taxonomic Method," in *Corridor Talk and Culture History: Public Anthropology and Its Consequences,* ed. Regna Darnell and Frederick Gleach (Lincoln: University of Nebraska Press, 2015), 33–80.

38 Cole, *Franz Boas,* 192.

39 In the end, Farrand gained much from his participation in the Jesup. In addition to authoring two Jesup monographs (Livingston Farrand, *Traditions of the Chilcotin Indians,* Memoir of the American Museum of Natural History, series vol. 4: JNPE, vol. 2, part 1 [Leiden/New York: E.J. Brill/G.E. Stechert, 1900], http://hdl.handle.net/2246/39; Farrand, *Basketry Designs of the Salish Indians,* Memoir of the American Museum of Natural History, series vol. 2: JNPE, vol. 1, part 5 [New York/Berlin: G.P. Putnam's Sons/R. Friedlander and Sohn, 1900], http://hdl.handle.net/2246/35), he assisted Boas with the editorial work on

several other of the Jesup monographs. This work helped him secure a professorship in anthropology at Columbia University in 1903. He served as president of the University of Colorado from 1914 to 1919 and as president of Cornell University from 1921 to 1937. He appeared on the cover of *Time* magazine on June 17, 1929.

40 Teit to Boas, December 25, 1897, AMNH. In this letter Teit referred to Boas's proposal of several months of fieldwork in "Lillooet" territory.

41 Ibid.

42 He made the first trip in April and the second trip in June. See Teit to Boas, April 6, 1898, and June 3, 1898, AMNH.

43 Teit to Boas, June 3, 1898, AMNH.

44 Ibid.

45 Teit to Boas, June 13, 1898, AMNH.

46 Note that the term "Lillooet" was Boas's term-of-choice. In his introduction to his 1906 monograph, Teit noted that this was not the term the peoples in this region used to refer to themselves. It was a term that "whites" used to describe this region of the province. In fact, as Teit noted, the "Lillooet" peoples had no common name for themselves as a whole. Instead, they had two names for two divisions within their territory. They called those who lived south of the watershed between Mosquito or Pole River and Anderson River the "Li'luet" and they called those who lived north and east of this watershed the "SLā'Lemux." The two divisions were respectively the "Lower and Upper Lillooet of the Whites": James Teit, *The Lillooet Indians,* Memoir of the American Museum of Natural History, series vol. 4: JNPE, vol. 2, part 5 (Leiden/New York: E.J. Brill/G.E. Stechert, 1906), 196, http://hdl.handle.net/2246/36. Today these peoples refer to themselves as the Lower St'at'imc (Lower Lillooet or Mount Currie Lillooet), the Upper St'at'imc (the Upper Lillooet or Fraser River Lillooet, living near the town of Lillooet), and the Lakes Lillooet (those located in the Seton-Anderson Lakes region).

47 Teit to Boas, September 9, 1898, AMNH. Teit wrote of arriving in the town of Douglas on this day.

48 Teit to Boas, September 9, 1898, and October 8, 1898, AMNH.

49 Teit to Boas, October 8, 1898, AMNH.

50 Teit to Boas, March 7, 1899, AMNH.

51 Teit to Harlan Smith, March 12, 1899, AMNH.

52 Teit to Boas, July 19, 1899, AMNH.

53 Boas to Teit, June 4, 1900, AMNH.

54 Teit's journal, courtesy of Sigurd Teit.

55 Teit to Boas, September 20, 1900, AMNH.

56 Teit to Boas, August 5, 1900, AMNH; see also Teit to Boas, September 1, 1900, AMNH.

57 Teit to Boas, October 21, 1900, AMNH.

58 Teit to Boas, August 5, 1900, AMNH.

59 Teit to Boas, October 21, 1900, AMNH.

60 Ibid.

61 Teit to Boas, November 23, 1900, AMNH.

62 According to Sigurd Teit, the party consisted of Alex Neilson, Walter Neilson, W.C. Neilson, and James Miller, all from Scotland. Sigurd Teit provided a copy of Teit's trip log, along with photographs taken by his clients.

63 Teit mentioned his plans for a Shetland trip to Boas in a letter: Teit to Boas, March 29, 1901, AMNH.

64 Teit kept a journal of this trip, copy courtesy of Sigurd Teit.
65 Teit to Boas, August 3, 1902, AMNH.
66 Ibid.
67 Teit to Boas, December 24, 1902, AMNH.
68 Teit to Boas, March 16, 1903, AMNH.
69 Boas to Teit, June 5, 1903, AMNH.
70 Teit to Boas, May 29, 1903, AMNH.
71 Boas to Marie Boas, August 9, 1897, in Rohner, *Ethnography of Franz Boas,* 221.
72 Ibid., 222.
73 In fact, Teit would continue to work for Charles Newcombe off and on for the next fifteen years. Newcombe was a Victoria-based physician who collected artifacts for various museums across Canada and the United States. A founding member of the Victoria Natural History Society, Newcombe played a leading role in the founding of Victoria's Provincial Museum of Natural History and Ethnology in 1886. For more on Newcombe, see Kevin Neary, "Charles Frederic Newcombe," *Dictionary of Canadian Biography*, accessed January 10, 2019, http://www.biographi.ca/en/bio/newcombe_charles_frederic_15E.html. See also Patricia Roy, *The Collectors: A History of the Royal British Columbia Museum and Archives* (Victoria: Royal British Columbia Museum, 2018), 13–16.
74 Teit to Boas, June 14, 1903, AMNH.
75 Teit to Boas, August 24, 1903, AMNH.
76 Teit referred to this report in a letter: Teit to Boas, March 10, 1904, AMNH. The CPR Archives has no record of the original or any publication associated with it. Sigurd Teit found Teit's copy among his miscellaneous personal papers.
77 Teit to Boas, August 24, 1903, AMNH.
78 Teit to Boas, November 15, 1903, AMNH.
79 James Teit, "British Columbia and Big Game Hunting," report prepared for the Canadian Pacific Railway, copy courtesy of Sigurd Teit.
80 Teit to A. Bryan Williams, January 15, 1905, Provincial Game Warden files, GR 446, Box 12, file 2, BC Archives. See also Jonathan Peyton, "Imbricated Geographies of Conservation and Consumption in the Stikine Plateau," *Environment and History* 17 (2011): 1–27.
81 Teit to Boas, May 25, 1904, AMNH.
82 Branwen C. Patenaude, *Trails to Gold* (Victoria: Horsdal and Schubart, 1995), 92.
83 Teit journal, 1904, copy courtesy of Sigurd Teit.
84 Teit to Boas, August 5, 1905, AMNH. Teit reported similarly in a letter to his uncle Robert Tait that he had finished this long report in mid-March, and he was relieved as "it was getting a little tedious (not withstanding that I take great interest in it)": Teit to Robert Tait, March 31, 1905, copy courtesy of Sigurd Teit.
85 Teit to Boas, February 16, 1911, Mss.B.B61, Franz Boas Papers, Series 1: Correspondence, APS (hereafter, all references to APS refer to this collection).
86 For more on Homer Sargent, see Ira Jacknis, "'The Artist Himself': The Salish Basketry Monograph and the Beginnings of a Boasian Paradigm," in *The Early Years of Native American Art History: The Politics of Scholarship and Collecting,* ed. Janet Catherine Berlo (Vancouver/Seattle: UBC Press/University of Washington Press, 1992), 134–62. Teit wrote to Boas at this time to report that he was interviewing people about tattoos and tattooing, documenting lists of names of plants, birds, and fish, collecting stories, and reviewing all of his notes on language. He noted that he planned to work with the local Tahltan Indians of the Stikine at the end of his guiding trip: Teit to Boas, June 10, 1905, AMNH. In August,

he wrote to say that he had collected the names of three hundred plants and trees: Teit to Boas, August 5, 1905, AMNH.

87 Sargent had made an unscheduled visit to the AMNH in December 1906, hoping to meet with Boas. Because Boas was not there, Harlan Smith met with Sargent and reported to Boas that Sargent was interested in offering funds to cover Teit's fieldwork. On hearing this, Boas contacted Sargent to say that he would be pleased to accept Sargent's offer. He noted that an endowment of $1,000 annually for five years would take Teit's research a long way: Boas to Homer Sargent, December 18, 1906, APS.

88 Sargent to Boas, January 31, 1907, APS.

89 Boas to Teit, April 30, 1907, APS.

90 Teit to Boas, May 10, 1907, APS.

91 Teit to Boas, November 22, 1907, APS.

92 For more on this, see Jacknis, "'The Artist Himself,'" 142.

93 Ibid., 149.

94 Teit to Boas, January 1, 1908, APS.

95 Boas to Teit, May 1, 1908, APS.

96 Boas to Teit, December 22, 1908, APS.

97 Ibid.

98 Teit prepared a financial statement for his Smithsonian Institution research and sent it to Boas. See Teit to Boas, 28 July 1908, APS. It indicates eleven days spent with Whistemnitsa in February, March, and April 1908, working on language and texts. It also states that Teit paid Whistemnitsa fifteen dollars for this work. Teit had replaced his old spelling of the chief's name (Wheestim-neetsa) with this new spelling XwistEmni'tsa.

99 Teit described his itinerary in his personal journal. He also described details in a series of long letters to Boas written between May 23 and June 26, 1908. A copy of the 1908 journal is in the author's files, courtesy of Sigurd Teit. The letters are in the APS collection.

100 Teit to Boas, June 12, 1908, APS.

101 Teit explained some of the details of his work with Whistemnitsa in a letter to Boas. See Teit to Boas, July 28, 1908, APS.

102 Teit to Boas, November 20, 1908, APS.

103 Ibid.

104 Teit to A. Bryan Williams, June 25, 1908, Provincial Game Warden files, GR 446, Box 16, file 2, BC Archives.

105 Teit to Williams, January 28, 1908, Provincial Game Warden files, GR 446, Box 16, file 2, BC Archives. In this letter, Teit offered detailed corrections to the inventory of wildlife that had appeared on "page 18" of a document he referred to as "Official Bulletin No. 17."

106 For more on Revais, see James A. Teit, *The Middle Columbia Salish,* ed. Franz Boas, University of Washington Publications in Anthropology series, vol. 2, iss. 4 (Seattle: University of Washington Press, 1928), 105–6.

107 Teit to Boas, August 7, 1910, APS. Teit noted in his trip log that he returned to Spences Bridge on November 30.

108 Boas to Teit, May 3, 1910, APS.

109 Teit to Boas, February 16, 1911, APS.

110 Ibid.

111 Boas to Teit, February 24, 1911, APS.

112 Teit to Boas, March 16, 1911, APS.

113 Ibid.

114 Lincoln Wilbar, "British Columbia for the Sportsman," *Travel and Exploration* (October 1910), 279.
115 Regna Darnell, "The Sapir Years at the National Museum," *Proceedings of the Canadian Ethnological Society* (1976): 98–121. Sapir had notified Boas of his GSC appointment on June 6, 1910. Teit heard the news of Sapir's Ottawa appointment the following January; he mentioned it in a letter to Charles Newcombe, January 1, 1911, Newcombe Collection, BC Archives.
116 Boas to Teit, April 21, 1911, APS.
117 Ibid.
118 Sapir to Teit, November 14, 1911, 1-A-236M, Canadian Museum of History (CMH) Archives (hereafter, all references to CMH refer to this collection); Teit to Sapir, November 21, 1911, ibid.
119 Teit to Sapir, May 16, 1911; Sapir to Teit, November 14, 1911; Teit to Sapir, November 21, 1911, CMH.
120 Teit wrote to Boas stating that he had received a letter from Sapir asking "when the funds with which I am presently working will be furnished. I told him I did not know. They were in your hands." Teit to Boas, May 22, 1911, APS.
121 Boas to Teit, June 8, 1911, APS.
122 Teit to Boas, January 21, 1912, APS.
123 Boas to Teit, May 11, 1912, APS; see also Teit to Sapir, July 7, 1912, CMH.
124 Teit to Sapir, August 9, 1912, CMH.
125 Sapir to Teit, August 9, 1912, CMH.
126 Teit to Sapir, November 2, 1912, and December 4, 1912, CMH.
127 Teit to Sapir, December 4, 1912, CMH.
128 Sapir to Teit, January 16, 1913, CMH.
129 Teit described this administrative problem to Boas in a letter, December 26, 1912, CMH.
130 Sapir to Boas, September 3, 1912, CMH.
131 Teit to Boas, December 26, 1912, APS.
132 Ibid.
133 Teit to Sapir, February 17, 1913, CMH.
134 Boas to Teit, January 13, 1913, APS.
135 Teit to Boas, March 10, 1904, AMNH.
136 Teit to Boas, January 21, 1913, APS.
137 Ibid.
138 Ibid.
139 Teit to Boas, February 24, 1913, APS.
140 Teit to Boas, March 3, 1913, and March 20, 1913, APS.
141 Teit to Boas, April 12, 1913, APS.
142 Teit to Boas, January 21, 1913, APS; Teit to Sapir, February 17, 1913, CMH.
143 Teit to Sapir, March 11, 1913, CMH.
144 Ibid. He notified Sapir that he had recorded 102 songs and noted that he recorded many at the Indian meeting that had taken place at Spences Bridge. See also Teit to Sapir, June 3, 1913, CMH.
145 Judith Judd Banks, "Comparative Biographies of Two British Columbia Anthropologists, Charles Hill-Tout and James A. Teit" (master's thesis, University of British Columbia, 1970), 96.
146 Sapir to Teit, June 10, 1913, CMH.

147 Teit to Boas, April 12, 1913, APS.
148 Jessie Ann Smith, *Widow Smith of Spence's Bridge,* as told to J. Meryl Campbell and Audrey Ward (Merritt, BC: Sonotek, 1989), 114.
149 Teit to Sapir, June 3, 1913, CMH.
150 Teit to Sapir, July 16, 1913, CMH.
151 Teit to Sapir, August 6, 1913, CMH.
152 Teit to Boas, May 20, 1914, APS.
153 Teit to Sapir, April 6, 1914, CMH.
154 Teit to Sapir, May 20, 1914, CMH.
155 Sapir to Teit, May 30, 1914, CMH.
156 Teit to Boas, August 6, 1914, and September 27, 1914, APS.
157 Teit to Sapir, August 29, 1914, CMH.
158 Sapir to Teit, September 4, 1914, CMH.
159 Teit to Sapir, April 23, 1915, CMH.
160 Sapir to Teit, September 4, 1914, CMH.
161 Teit to Sapir, September 21, 1914, CMH.
162 Ibid.
163 Ibid.
164 Teit to Sapir, October 30, 1914, CMH.
165 Teit notified Boas on December 21 that he had finished the Coeur d'Alene report and was working on the Columbia report. He noted that he would soon turn to the "Thompson Supplementary paper & Thompson art." His expenses report (January 1, 1915) indicates exactly how much time he gave to Boas. Teit to Boas, December 21, 1914, APS.
166 Teit to Sapir, December 1, 1914, CMH.
167 Sapir to Teit, March 8, 1915, CMH.
168 Teit to Sapir, June 8, 1915, CMH.
169 Teit described this trip in his 1915 journal, copy courtesy of Sigurd Teit.
170 Details from Teit's journal. See also his letters to Sapir: September 7, 1915, and October 13, 1915, CMH, and Teit's "Summary Report on Kaska and Tahltan (Athabaskan) Work, 1915," CMH. Sapir noted receipt of the report on November 22, 1915. For a fuller account of this field experience, see Judy Thompson, *Recording Their Story: James Teit and the Tahltan* (Vancouver/Gatineau/Seattle: Douglas and McIntyre/Canadian Museum of Civilization/University of Washington Press, 2007).
171 Teit to Sapir, November 13, 1915, CMH.
172 Teit wrote up a full description of this trip in a letter to Sapir, November 13, 1915, CMH.
173 Sapir to Teit, November 22, 1915, CMH.
174 Teit to Sapir, December 16, 1915, CMH.
175 Teit to Sapir, January 9, 1916, January 20, 1916, and January 31, 1916, CMH.
176 Teit to Sapir, February 20, 1916, CMH. In the end, Teit reported good results to both Boas and Sapir in 1917. Recognizing their shared interest in bringing Teit's unfinished work to fruition, Sapir and Boas edited 104 stories that Teit had recorded on his Stikine field trips in 1912 and 1915 and published them over three issues of the *Journal of American Folklore:* James A. Teit, "Tahltan Tales," *Journal of American Folklore* 32, 124 (1919): 198–250; James A. Teit, "Tahltan Tales," *Journal of American Folklore* 34, 133 (1921): 223–53; and James Teit, "Tahltan Tales," *Journal of American Folklore* 34, 134 (1921): 335–56. They published Teit's Kaska collection in 1917: James A. Teit, "Kaska Tales," *Journal of American Folklore* 30, 118 (1917): 427–73. Boas also edited a collection of Nlaka'pamux, Okanagan, Coeur d'Alene,

Pend d'Oreille, and Stó:lō stories: James Teit, Livingston Farrand, Marian K. Gould, and Herbert J. Spinden, *Folk-Tales of Salishan and Sahaptin Tribes,* ed. Franz Boas, Memoirs of the American Folk-Lore Society 11 (Lancaster, PA/New York: American Folk-Lore Society, 1917).

177 Teit to Boas, June 12, 1916, APS.
178 Teit to Boas, November 4, 1916, APS.
179 Teit to Sapir, August 9, 1916, CMH.
180 Teit to Boas, June 12, 1916, APS.
181 Teit to Sapir, November 27, 1916, CMH.
182 Teit to Sapir, December 7, 1916, CMH.
183 Teit to Sapir, February 27, 1917, CMH; Sapir to Teit, March 5, 1917, CMH.
184 Teit to Sapir, March 20, 1917, CMH.
185 Ibid.
186 Sapir to Teit, March 26, 1917, CMH. See also letters between Teit and Boas, April to August, 1917, APS.
187 Jacknis, "'The Artist Himself,'" 145.
188 Boas to Sargent, October 24, 1917, APS.
189 Teit to Sapir, February 27, 1917, CMH.
190 Jacknis, "'The Artist Himself,'" 147.
191 Teit to Boas, October 31, 1917, APS.
192 Ibid.
193 Boas to Herman Haeberlin, January 22, 1918, APS.
194 Teit to Boas, March 4, 1918, APS.
195 Teit to Sapir, March 14, 1918, CMH.
196 Boas to Teit, March 14, 1918, APS.
197 Boas to Teit, March 30, 1918, APS.
198 Jacknis, "'The Artist Himself,'" 148.
199 Sapir to Boas, August 11, 1919, CMH.
200 Teit to Sapir, September 2, 1918, CMH.
201 Teit to Sapir, September 30, 1918, CMH; Teit to Sapir, October 30, 1918, CMH.
202 Teit to Sapir, September 30, 1918, CMH.
203 Teit to Sapir, November 16, 1918, CMH.
204 Teit to Boas, March 16, 1919, APS.
205 Teit to Boas, April 10, 1919, APS; Teit to Boas, May 23, 1919, APS.
206 Teit to Boas, April 30, 1919, APS.
207 Teit to Sapir, February 22, 1919, CMH.
208 Boas to Teit, February to May 1919, APS.
209 Teit to Boas, February 2, 1919, and April 30, 1919, APS.
210 Helen Roberts to Boas, June 16, 1919, APS.
211 Teit to Boas, June 6, 1919, APS.
212 Sapir to Teit, July 18, 1919, CMH.
213 Sapir to Teit, August 27, 1919, CMH.
214 Teit to Boas, August 15, 1919, APS.
215 Teit to Boas, July 30, 1919, APS.
216 Teit to Boas, August 15, 1919, APS. "Snare Indians" was, and is, an uncommon designation. According to anthropologist Diamond Jenness, "Snare" was the term that "early writers" applied to "some Interior Salish families" who used "the Fraser River headwaters towards

Yellowhead pass" as "a trapping ground." He noted that "a little later" the region was occupied by a mix of "Salish, Iroquois, Cree, and Europeans." Because it was home to the "Carrier" (Dakelh) peoples in the late eighteenth century, Jenness classified it as "Athapaskan" territory. Diamond Jenness, *The Indians of Canada* (Ottawa: National Museum of Canada, 1958, orig. 1932), 424.

217 Ibid.

218 Boas to Sargent, August 27, 1919, APS; Sargent to Boas, August 21, 1919, APS; Boas to Sargent, September 4, 1919, APS.

219 Sapir to Teit, September 16, 1919, CMH.

220 Teit to Sapir, August 9, 1919, CMH.

221 Teit to Sapir, September 22, 1919, CMH; see also Teit to Boas, November 20, 1919, APS.

222 Teit to Sapir, March 15, 1920, CMH; see also Teit to Boas, January 11, 1921, APS.

223 Teit to Boas, January 11, 1921, APS.

224 Teit to Sapir, February 2, 1921, CMH.

225 Teit to Boas, March 5, 1921, APS; Teit to Sapir, March 6, 1921, CMH.

226 Teit to Sapir, March 13, 1921, CMH.

227 Teit to Boas, March 11, 1921, APS.

228 Teit to Sapir, March 13, 1921, CMH.

229 Teit to Sapir, March 22, 1921, CMH.

230 Teit notified Sapir that he was leaving for the "Mayo Bros."clinic on March 27. Teit to Sapir, March 24, 1921, CMH.

231 Teit to Boas, May 9, 1921, APS.

232 Teit to Sapir, September 26, 1921, CMH.

233 Sargent to Boas, October 9, 1921, APS.

234 Teit to Boas, November 7, 1921, APS.

235 Ibid.

236 Teit to Sapir, July 31, 1922, CMH.

237 Franz Boas to Toni Boas, August 30, 1922, in Rohner, *Ethnography of Franz Boas,* 277.

Chapter 6: Dwelling

1 John Swanton, review of *The Lillooet Indians,* by James Teit, *American Anthropologist* 9, 4 (1907): 744–45.

2 Tom Hawthorn, "Celebrating the Female Pioneer Perspective," *Globe and Mail,* September 7, 2010, https://www.theglobeandmail.com/news/british-columbia/celebrating-the-female-pioneer-perspective/article4325737/.

3 Ibid.

4 Art Martens, "Allisons of the Similkameen," *Living Significantly* (blog), May 1, 2015, http://livingsignificantly.ca/2015/05/01/allisons-of-the-similkameen/.

5 Susan Allison, "Account of the Similkameen Indians of British Columbia," *British Association for the Advancement of Science,* section 2, report 60 (1891): 815, and "Account of the Similkameen Indians of British Columbia," *Journal of the Anthropological Institute of Great Britain and Ireland* 21 (1892): 305–18.

6 Allison published this book under her pen name, Stratton Moir: *In-Cow-Mas-Ket* (Chicago: Scroll Publishing, 1900). See also Margaret Ormsby's introduction to *A Pioneer Gentlewoman in British Columbia: The Recollections of Susan Allison* (Vancouver: UBC Press, 1976), ix-li.

7 Ormsby, introduction in *A Pioneer Gentlewoman,* li.
8 Parks Canada, "Government of Canada Designates Susan Louisa Moir Allison as a Person of National Historic Significance," news release, September 4, 2010, https://www.canada.ca/en/news/archive/2010/09/government-canada-designates-susan-louisa-moir-allison-person-national-historic-significance.html.
9 Allison, "Account of the Similkameen Indians of British Columbia," 305. Interest in Allison continues to grow. See, for example, Diane Sterne, *In Her Words: Selected Works by Susan Louisa Allison* (Princeton, BC: Princeton District Museum and Archives, 2010).
10 Allison, "Account of the Similkameen Indians," *Journal of the Anthropological Institute of Great Britain and Ireland,* 318.
11 Ibid., 309.
12 Ibid., 307.
13 Ibid., 317.
14 Charles Hill-Tout, "Notes on the Ntlakapamuq of British Columbia, A Branch of the Great Salish Stock of North America," *Report of the British Association for the Advancement of Science* 69 (1899): 500–584, reprinted in Ralph Maud, ed., *The Salish People: The Local Contribution of Charles Hill-Tout,* vol. 1, *The Thompson and Okanagan* (Vancouver: Talonbooks, 1978), 43.
15 Hill-Tout, "Notes on the Ntlakapamuq," in Maud, *The Salish People,* 126.
16 Charles Hill-Tout, "Report on the Ethnology of the Okanaken of British Columbia, An Interior Division of the Salish Stock," *Journal of the Royal Anthropological Institute of Great Britain and Ireland* 41 (January–June 1911): 130–61, reprinted in Maud, *The Salish People,* 132–33.
17 Chad Reimer, *Writing British Columbia History, 1784–1958* (Vancouver: UBC Press, 2009), 65.
18 F.A. Talbot, *The New Garden of Canada: By Packhorse and Canoe through Undeveloped New British Columbia* (London: Cassell, 1912), 200–1.
19 John B. Thornhill, *British Columbia in the Making* (London: Constable, 1913), 145–46.
20 Reimer, *Writing British Columbia History,* 45.
21 Teit to Father A.G. Morice, n.d. (but likely early November 1893, because Teit noted receiving a response from Morice on November 23, 1893), James A. Teit Papers, "Salish Ethnographic Materials," Slb. 7, American Council of Learned Societies Committee of Native American Languages (ACLS) collection, American Philosophical Society Library.
22 In their letters to one another, Teit, Sapir, and Boas referred frequently to Hill-Tout's sloppy scholarship. See James Teit to Franz Boas, June 8, 1899, and April 4, 1907, APS.
23 Hill-Tout had published it as "Report on the Ethnology of the Stlatlumh of British Columbia," *Journal of the Anthropological Institute of Great Britain and Ireland* 35 (January–June 1905), 126–218, reprinted in Maud, *The Salish People,* 99–156.
24 Teit to Boas, March 3, 1906, AMNH.
25 Franz Boas, "Notes," in James Teit, *The Lillooet Indians,* Memoir of the American Museum of Natural History, series vol. 4: JNPE, vol. 2, part 5 (Leiden/New York: E.J. Brill/G.E. Stechert, 1906), 292–300, http://hdl.handle.net/2246/36.
26 Ibid.
27 Ibid., 292.
28 James Teit, *The Shuswap,* Memoir of the American Museum of Natural History, series vol. 4: JNPE, vol. 2, part 7 (Leiden/New York: E.J. Brill/G.E. Stechert, 1909), 472, http://hdl.handle.net/2246/38.

29 George Woodcock, "Charles Hill-Tout," *The Canadian Encyclopedia,* article published May 19, 2008, last modified December 14, 2013, http://www.thecanadianencyclopedia.ca/en/article/charles-hill-tout/.
30 Boas to R.W. Brock, May 14, 1910, APS.
31 Swanton made this point in his review of James Teit's *The Lillooet Indians.*
32 Sapir to Brock, December 5, 1911, CMH.
33 Curtis Hinsley, "Ethnographic Charisma and Scientific Routine: Cushing and Fewkes in the American Southwest, 1879–1893," in *Observers Observed: Essays on Ethnographic Fieldwork,* ed. George W. Stocking Jr. (Madison: University of Wisconsin Press, 1983), 53–69.
34 Martin Heidegger, "Building, Dwelling, Thinking," translated by Albert Hofstadter, in *Basic Writings: Nine Key Essays, Plus the Introduction to "Being and Time"* (New York: Harper and Row, 1977), 326–27. The original German text appeared in Heidegger, *Vorträge and Aufsätze* (Pfullingen: Verlag Günther Neske, 1954).
35 Boas to Teit, October 7, 1894, AMNH.
36 Teit to Boas, February 22, 1895, AMNH.
37 Teit to Boas, February 1, 1895, AMNH.
38 Teit to Boas, February 22, 1895, AMNH.
39 Teit to Boas, February 1, 1895, AMNH.
40 Boas to Teit, February 18, 1901, AMNH.
41 James A. Teit, *The Thompson Indians of British Columbia,* Memoir of the American Museum of Natural History, series vol. 2: JNPE, vol. 1, part 4 (New York: G.P. Putnam's Sons, 1900), 172, http://hdl.handle.net/2246/13.
42 Teit included five pages of discussion of place names in *The Thompson Indians,* 169–75.
43 Ibid., 195.
44 Ibid., 196.
45 Ibid.
46 Heidegger, "Building, Dwelling, Thinking," 327.
47 *Kekuli* was the Chinook Jargon term for this house. In a document titled "Indian words taken from first manuscript on the Thompson Indians," Teit listed "si īs'tikin" as the Nlaka'pamux term for the house: James Alexander Teit, "Field notes on Thompson and neighbouring Salish languages," S1b.7 lb. 7, ACLS, APS.
48 Teit, *The Thompson Indians,* 192–95.
49 Ibid., 194–95.
50 Ibid., 194.
51 Ibid., 193–94.
52 Ibid., 181–91.
53 Ibid., 250.
54 Ibid., 248; emphasis added.
55 Ibid., 235–36; emphasis added.
56 Ibid., 267.
57 Teit noted the temporal reach of his data via elders in his *Tattooing and Face and Body Painting of the Thompson Indians of British Columbia,* edited by Franz Boas. Forty-fifth Annual Report of the Bureau of American Ethnology, 1927–1928 (Washington, DC: Government Printing Office, 1930), 403. Boas noted the ages of Pa-ah (spelled Paa) and Tsilla-gheskit (spelled TsᴇlᴇqÊ'sket) in his 1895 report on his anthropometric research among the Nlaka'pamux people at Spences Bridge. See the measurements chart in Franz Boas, "Physical Characteristics of the Tribes of the North Pacific Coast," in "Tenth Report on

the North-Western Tribes of Canada," *Sixty-Fifth Meeting of the British Association for the Advancement of Science at Ipswich, September 1895* (London: John Murray, 1895), 7–10.

58 Teit, *The Thompson Indians,* 271.

59 Teit, *The Lillooet Indians,* 236.

60 Teit's analysis of warfare in the south central Interior of British Columbia contributes to the ongoing debates on the history of conflict during the fur trade era. See, for example, Robin Fisher, "The Land-Based Fur Trade," in *Contact and Conflict: Indian-European Relations in British Columbia, 1774–1890* (Vancouver: UBC Press, 1977), 24–48; and Cole Harris, "Strategies of Power in the Cordilleran Fur Trade," in *The Resettlement of British Columbia: Essays on Colonialism and Geographical Change* (Vancouver: UBC Press, 1997), 31–67.

61 Teit, *The Thompson Indians,* 270.

62 Ibid.

63 Ibid., 267.

64 "Narratives of Old Pa-ah, 1893," Papers of James Alexander Teit, T458, Box 1, folder 4, Anthropology Division, AMNH.

65 Teit, *The Thompson Indians,* 270.

66 Ibid., 271. In a recent article on the dynamics of settler colonialism in British Columbia, historian Duane Thomson made a similar point about the early imposition of British law. "British authority, including the application of civil and criminal law," he writes, "was asserted on the mainland almost immediately after the creation of the colony of British Columbia." After 1860, "Indians would henceforth abide by and obtain protection from British rather than Indian laws": Duane Thomson, "The Ethno-Genesis of the Mixed-Ancestry Population in New Caledonia," *BC Studies* 191 (Autumn 2016): 71–72.

67 Teit, *The Thompson Indians,* 289–90.

68 Hill-Tout, "Notes on the Ntlakapamuq," quoted in Maud, *The Salish People,* 43.

69 Teit, *The Thompson Indians,* 357.

70 Hill-Tout, "Notes on the Ntlakapamuq," quoted in Maud, *The Salish People,* 47.

71 Teit, *The Thompson Indians,* 320.

72 Ibid.

73 Ibid., 311–17.

74 For more on Waght-ko's explanations of the paintings on this boulder, see Teit, "Explanation of Plate XIX," in *The Thompson Indians.* Although this account excludes her name, we know from an earlier article by Teit that she was Teit's source for the information on Plate XIX. In an 1896 article about the same site, Teit had acknowledged "Waxtko" (a different spelling of "Waght-ko") as having provided him with the information on this site: James Teit, "A Rock Painting of the Thompson River Indians, British Columbia," *Bulletin of the American Museum of Natural History* 8 (1896): 227–29. On instruction from Boas, Teit removed most of the Nlaka'pamux names and terms from his report prior to publication. For a full study of Teit's research on rock art, see Christopher Arnett, "Rock Art of Nlaka'pamux: Indigenous Theory and Practice on the British Columbia Plateau" (PhD diss., University of British Columbia, 2016).

75 Teit, "Explanation of Plate XIX," in *The Thompson Indians,* n.p.; and Teit, "A Rock Painting of the Thompson River Indians." Both sources relied on information given to Teit by Waght-ko.

76 Hill-Tout, "Notes on the Ntlakapamuq," in Maud, *The Salish People,* 48.

77 Teit, *The Thompson Indians,* 326.

78 Teit to Boas, November 9, 1895, AMNH.

79 John Tait referred to his son's description of the wake in his letter to James on April 12, 1899, John Tait Letterbook, D.17/8/18, Shetland Archives.

80 John Tait referred to the "paying" ceremony in a letter to his son on December 13, 1899, John Tait Letterbook, D.17/8/18. Teit placed a large headstone on Antko's grave in the small cemetery adjacent to St. Michael and All Angels Anglican Church at Spences Bridge. It included the inscription "Sacred to the Memory of ANTKO, the Beloved wife of J.A. Teit, Died March 2, 1899 (aged 33 years)," and a phrase in the Nlaka'pamux language that, in English, translates as "So she will suffer no more." Translation courtesy of Mandy Jimmie, Merritt, BC.

81 Franz Boas, conclusion in Teit, *The Thompson Indians,* 387–90.

82 Ibid., 390.

83 Paige Raibmon, *Authentic Indians: Episodes of Encounter from the Late-Nineteenth-Century Northwest Coast* (Durham, NC: Duke University Press, 2006). See also Rolf Knight, *Indians at Work: An Informal History of Native Indian Labour in British Columbia, 1858–1930* (Vancouver: New Star Books, 1978).

84 Teit had sent many baskets to New York City, and in letters and notes had described the significance of their designs and construction. See, for example, Teit to Boas, March 1, 1898, AMNH. Baskets would continue to dominate his collections. He returned from his first trip into the Lillooet region with 110 items, 40 of which he described as baskets. See Teit to Boas, October 8, 1898, AMNH. In a letter of November 2, 1898 (AMNH), he wrote that he was sending more Nlaka'pamux baskets to New York City.

85 For the details on the derivation of the term "Lillooet" and its application (or lack thereof) to the peoples occupying the region known as the "Upper Lillooet" and "Lower Lillooet" districts, see Chapter 5, note 46. For details on the derivation of the term "Shuswap" and its applications to the Secwépemc peoples, see Marianne Ignace and Ronald E. Ignace, *Secwépemc People, Land and Laws* (Montreal: McGill-Queen's University Press, 2017); see also Jim Cooperman, *Everything Shuswap* (Kamloops: Playfort Publishing, 2017).

86 Ronald P. Rohner and Evelyn C. Rohner, "Introduction: Franz Boas and the Development of North American Ethnology and Ethnography," in *The Ethnography of Franz Boas: Letters and Diaries of Franz Boas Written on the Northwest Coast from 1886 to 1931,* ed. Ronald P. Rohner (Chicago: University of Chicago Press, 1969), xxi.

87 Teit to Boas, April 3, 1895, AMNH.

88 Teit to Boas, August 24, 1895, AMNH.

89 Ibid.

90 Franz Boas, "The Tinneh Tribe of Nicola Valley," in "Tenth Report on the North-Western Tribes of Canada," *Sixty-Fifth Meeting of the British Association for the Advancement of Science at Ipswich, September 1895* (London: John Murray, 1895), 551–55.

91 Boas sent his 1897 recordings to Berlin to be transcribed and analyzed by two colleagues. Their published analysis appeared without the singers' names. See, for example, Otto Abraham and E.M. Von Hornbostel, "Phonographierte Indianermelodien aus Britisch-Columbia," in *Boas Anniversary Volume* (New York: Stechert, 1906), 447–74. During Boas's photography sessions at Spences Bridge in 1897, Teit recorded the names of the men, women, and children who were photographed. On publishing the photographs in 1900, however, Boas excluded the names. See, for example, Harlan Smith, *Ethnographical Album of the North Pacific Coasts of America and Asia* (New York: American Museum of Natural History, 1900).

92 Teit to Boas, November 22, 1900, AMNH.
93 Boas inserted Teit's critique of Hill-Tout's 1905 "Report on the Ethnology of the Stlatlumh of British Columbia" as the appendix under his own name. See Boas, "Notes," in Teit, *The Lillooet Indians,* 292–300.
94 Teit, *The Shuswap,* 447.
95 In his letters to Boas, Teit wrote of interviewing Sixwi'lexken ("Big Billy") at Churn Creek on the west side of the Fraser between Dog Creek and Canoe Creek: Teit to Boas, September 1, 1900, AMNH.
96 Teit, *The Lillooet Indians,* 199.
97 Teit, *The Shuswap,* 464.
98 Ibid., 466–67.
99 Ibid., 463.
100 Teit, *The Lillooet Indians,* 199.
101 Ibid.
102 Teit, *The Shuswap,* 466.
103 Teit, *The Lillooet Indians,* 236.
104 Teit, *The Shuswap,* 540.
105 Ibid.
106 Ibid., 541.
107 Ibid., 496.
108 Ibid., 508.
109 Ibid., 518.
110 Ibid., 537.
111 Ibid., 496, 612.
112 Teit to Boas, September 1, 1900, AMNH. See also Teit, *The Shuswap,* 613.
113 James Teit, "Indian Tribes of the Interior," in *Canada and Its Provinces: A History of the Canadian People and Their Institutions,* ed. Adam Shortt and Arthur Doughty, vol. 21, *The Pacific Province* (Glasgow: Brook, 1914), 283–312.
114 Ibid., 291.
115 Ibid., 310.
116 Ibid.
117 Ibid., 288.
118 Ibid., 287–88.
119 "Chief Tetlenitsa, Interprete[r], J.A. Teit [on] Land Tenure in his Tribe," May 23, 1916, Marius Barbeau fonds, Box 287.f.8, CMH.
120 Marius Barbeau was the note-taker for this session with Tetlanetza. Hence, the 1916 document features his efforts to spell Nlaka'pamux names and terms. As he used his own orthography, his renderings don't always agree with Teit's. To avoid confusion, I will use Teit's spellings throughout this discussion of the document. As noted above, I have chosen to use Tetlanetza's own spelling for his name.
121 "Cinamitsa" was Barbeau's spelling of the name of this chief. In his collection of Pa-ah's stories, "Narratives of Old Pa-ah, 1893," Teit spelled the chief's name "Shoona-mitza": Papers of James A. Teit, T458, Box 1, folder 4, AMNH.
122 Barbeau transcribed Ghleeghimkin's name as Tixamqon. Because Teit recorded his name as "Ghleeghimkin" in his 1893 list of names, I use that spelling rather than Barbeau's. In his 1895 report on Nlaka'pamux body measurements for the BAAS, Boas listed

Ghleeghimkin's name as "Tli'HEMkEn": Boas, "Physical Characteristics of the Tribes of the North Pacific Coast," BAAS.

123 Heidegger, "Building, Dwelling, Thinking," 327.

Chapter 7: Capital of Resistance

1 James Teit to Edward Sapir, August 2, 1912, I-A-236M, Edward Sapir–James Teit correspondence, Canadian Museum of History (CMH) Archives.

2 Ralph Maud, *A Guide to B.C. Indian Myth and Legend* (Vancouver: Talonbooks 1982), 77.

3 Wendy Wickwire, "'We Shall Drink from the Stream and So Shall You': James A. Teit and Native Resistance in British Columbia, 1908–22," *Canadian Historical Review* 79, 2 (1998): 199–236; Wendy Wickwire, "They Wanted ... Me to Help Them: James A. Teit and the Challenge of Ethnography in the Boasian Era," in *With Good Intentions: Euro-Canadian and Aboriginal Relations in Colonial Canada,* ed. Celia Haig-Brown and David A. Nock (Vancouver: UBC Press, 2006), 297–320.

4 According to a notice in the *Shetland Times,* the group launched the Lerwick Literary and Debating Society in the spring of 1903. Blair Bruce of the Shetland Archives provided this detail.

5 Brian Smith, "The History of Socialism to 1945" (unpublished manuscript obtained from the author); Robert Blatchford, *Merrie England* (London: Clarion Newspaper, 1895).

6 Smith, "The History of Socialism to 1945."

7 Brydon Leslie, *Borgar Jarl: J.J. Haldane Burgess and Up Helly Aa* (Lerwick: Shetland Amenity Trust, 2012), 39; see also "Haldane Burgess: Socialist," *New Shetlander* 31 (1952): 20–21.

8 "Haldane Burgess," 21.

9 Callum G. Brown, *Up-helly-aa: Custom, Culture and Community in Shetland* (Manchester: Manchester University Press, 1998), 142.

10 Ibid., 143.

11 Ibid., 150.

12 Teit to Robert Tait, December 28, 1903, copy courtesy of Sigurd Teit.

13 L. Williamson to T.G. Hunter, June 23, 1900, Shetland Archives, quoted in Bronwen J. Cohen, "Norse Imagery in Shetland: An Historical Study of Intellectuals and Their Use of the Past in the Construction of Shetland's Identity, With Particular Reference to the Period, 1800–1914" (PhD diss., University of Manchester, 1983), 347.

14 Teit to Burgess, quoted in Roy Grønneberg, "James Teit – Friend of the Indians," *New Shetlander* 126 (1978): 28.

15 Ibid.

16 Teit to Burgess, quoted in ibid.

17 Ibid. *Lowery's Claim* was named after its editor, Colonel Robert Thornton Lowery, who founded the newspaper in 1893 in Kaslo, BC, as a way to give voice to the illiterate miners and prostitutes of the region. For more on Lowery and his newspaper, see Lynne Marks, *Infidels and the Damn Churches: Irreligion and Religion in Settler British Columbia* (Vancouver: UBC Press, 2017), 58–59.

18 Teit to Burgess, August 22, 1902, D2/96, Shetland Archives.

19 Teit to Burgess, December 20, 1902, quoted in Grønneberg, "James Teit," 30.

20 Ibid.

21 Allen Seager, "Hawthornthwaite, James Hurst," *Dictionary of Canadian Biography*, accessed January 10, 2019, http://www.biographi.ca/en/bio/hawthornthwaite_james_hurst_15E.html?print=1.

22 Ibid.

23 Ross A. McCormack, *Reformers, Rebels, and Revolutionaries: The Western Canadian Radical Movement, 1899–1919* (Toronto: University of Toronto Press), 13–14. See also Gordon Hak, *The Left in British Columbia: A History of Struggle* (Vancouver: Ronsdale Press, 2013), 37–63.

24 McCormack, *Reformers, Rebels, and Revolutionaries,* 6.

25 Ibid., 27; see also Hak, *The Left,* 38.

26 Judith Judd Banks, "Comparative Biographies of Two British Columbia Anthropologists: Charles Hill-Tout and James A. Teit" (master's thesis, University of British Columbia, 1970).

27 Quoted in Banks, "Comparative Biographies," 52.

28 Banks, "Comparative Biographies," 53.

29 Ibid., 54. Teit appeared regularly in the *Western Clarion* newspaper offering donations, renewing his subscription, recruiting new members, donating to an "organizing fund"and a "maintenance fund," and ordering books. See, for example, the *Western Clarion* of February 24, 1906; May 13, 1906; November 25, 1911; April 14, 1912; April 28, 1912; June 22, 1912; July 6, 1912.

30 Sam Anderson to Peter Jamieson, May 8, 1945, D9/95/38, Shetland Archives.

31 John Tait to James Teit, January 31, 1887, John Tait Letterbook, D.17/8/16, Shetland Archives.

32 Martin Robin, *The Rush for Spoils: The Company Province, 1871–1933* (Toronto: McClelland and Stewart, 1971).

33 Ibid., 15.

34 Ibid., 19.

35 Ibid., 19, 21.

36 Keith D. Smith, *Liberalism, Surveillance, and Resistance: Indigenous Communities in Western Canada, 1877–1927* (Edmonton: Athabasca University Press, 2009), 133.

37 John Thistle, "A Vast Inland Empire and the Last Great West: Remaking Society, Space and Environment in Early British Columbia," *Journal of Historical Geography* 37, 4 (2011): 418–28.

38 Robin, *The Rush for Spoils,* 40.

39 Ibid., 26.

40 Hak, *The Left,* 46. See also Robin, *The Rush for Spoils,* 26. Some of the strikes – for example, the 1900 fishermen's strike – were long and messy affairs. A four-month CPR workers' strike in Vancouver in 1903 coincided with a long coal-miners' strike at Dunsmuir's Wellington mine.

41 For more on this, see Jeremy Mouat, "The Politics of Coal: A Study of the Wellington Miners' Strike of 1890–91," *BC Studies* 77 (Spring 1988): 3–29.

42 Hak, *The Left,* 41; McCormack, *Reformers, Rebels, and Revolutionaries,* 34.

43 McCormack, *Reformers, Rebels, and Revolutionaries,* 54.

44 Ibid., 58.

45 Quoted in ibid., 55.

46 Teit to Andrew B. Garrioch, March 31, 1908, Shetland Archives.

47 R.M. Galois, "The Indian Rights Association, Native Protest Activity and the 'Land Question' in British Columbia, 1903–1916," *Native Studies Review* 8 (1992): 2. Galois notes

that the 1911 census listed Indians as 5 percent of the total population (22,377 of the total of 542,582).

48 Hamar Foster, "'We Want a Strong Promise': The Opposition to Indian Treaties in British Columbia, 1850–1990," *Native Studies Review* 18, 1 (2009): 114.

49 According to legal historian Hamar Foster, a clause in the 1876 order-in-council setting up the Joint Indian Reserve Commission had caused major friction between the federal and provincial governments because it was

> quickly and not unreasonably interpreted by successive BC governments as implying that the Indians had no proprietary rights to their reserves, because as soon as the reserve land was surrendered or even leased, this clause could be used to argue that the effect of such transactions was simply to "perfect" the underlying title of the province. This is referred to as the province's so-called reversionary interest.

In Foster's view, Ottawa should never have agreed to the clause in the first place because successive BC governments would interpret it to their advantage. Hamar Foster, personal communication, August 13, 2018.

50 Foster, "'We Want a Strong Promise,'" 124.

51 Ibid., 124–25.

52 Hamar Foster, "Letting Go the Bone: The Idea of Indian Title in British Columbia, 1849–1927," in *Essays in the History of Canadian Law,* vol. 6, *British Columbia and the Yukon,* ed. Hamar Foster and John McLaren (Toronto: University of Toronto Press, 1995), 51; see also Patricia Roy, "McBride of McKenna-McBride: Premier Richard McBride and the Indian Question in British Columbia," *BC Studies* 172 (Winter 2011–12): 41.

53 Foster, "Letting Go the Bone," 125.

54 Galois, "The Indian Rights Association," 1992.

55 Ibid., 9.

56 Larry Jacobsen, *Walhachin: Birth of a Legend* (Shenzhen, China: Prolong Press, 2014).

57 Teit to Franz Boas, May 23, 1908, APS.

58 James Teit, "Account of the Lytton Chiefs," in *Mythology of the Thompson Indians,* Memoir of the American Museum of Natural History, series vol. 12: JNPE, vol. 8, part 2 (Leiden/New York: E.J. Brill/G.E. Stechert, 1912), 410–14, http://hdl.handle.net/2246/37.

59 Ibid., 412.

60 Ibid.

61 James Teit, et al., *Folk-Tales of Salishan and Sahaptin Tribes,* ed. Franz Boas, Memoirs of the American Folk-Lore Society 11 (Lancaster, PA/New York: American Folk-Lore Society, 1917), 50.

62 James A. Teit Papers, "Salish Ethnographic Materials," Part 1 of 2, 61, American Council of Learned Societies Committee of Native American Languages (ACLS) collection, American Philosophical Society.

63 Tina A. Loo, *Making Law, Order, and Authority in British Columbia, 1821–1871* (Toronto: University of Toronto Press, 1994), 134–56.

64 Edward Sleigh Hewlett, "The Chilcotin Uprising of 1864," *BC Studies* 19 (1973): 50–72. See also Patricia Roy and John Herd Thompson, *British Columbia: Land of Promises* (Oxford: Oxford University Press, 2005), 37–39; and John Sutton Lutz, *Makúk: A New History of Aboriginal-White Relations* (Vancouver: UBC Press, 2008), 295–96.

65 For a full list of the reserves with dates and surveyors, see Cole Harris, appendix, in *Making Native Space: Colonialism, Resistance, and Reserves in British Columbia* (Vancouver: UBC Press, 2003).

66 Brett Christophers, *Positioning the Missionary: John Booth Good and the Confluence of Cultures in Nineteenth-Century British Columbia* (Vancouver: UBC Press, 1998), 142–43. Three major reserves had been surveyed in the Nicola Valley in August 1868. See Harris, appendix, *Making Native Space.*

67 Christophers, *Positioning the Missionary,* 143.

68 Ibid., 142. Four reserves had been surveyed in and around Lytton between 1860 and 1862. Harris, appendix, *Making Native Space.*

69 Harris, *Making Native Space,* 73.

70 Ibid., 76.

71 Ibid., 84–85.

72 Ibid., 76.

73 Robin Fisher, *Contact and Conflict: Indian-European Relations in British Columbia, 1874–1890* (Vancouver: UBC Press, 1977), 192–93.

74 Christophers, *Positioning the Missionary,* 149; Harris, *Making Native Space,* 152–59; Douglas Harris, "The Nlha7kápmx Meeting at Lytton, 1879, and the Rule of Law," *BC Studies* 108 (1995–96): 5–25.

75 E. Brian Titley, *A Narrow Vision: Duncan Campbell Scott and the Administration of Indian Affairs in Canada* (Vancouver: UBC Press, 1986), 137.

76 Chief John Chilahitsa of Douglas Lake and Chief Louis Clexlixqen of Kamloops had made a trip to Europe two years earlier, in 1904, with Father LeJeune, but this did not, as Keith Carlson points out, have the political agenda of the 1906 trip: Keith Carlson, "Re-thinking Dialogue and History: The King's Promise and the 1906 Aboriginal Delegation to London," *Native Studies Review* 16, 2 (2005): 1–38. See also Galois, "The Indian Rights Association." As noted, the spellings of these early chiefs' names are problematic as they tend to vary from source to source. I thank Dan Marshall for providing me with the spelling of the Cowichan chief's name.

77 Carlson, "Re-thinking Dialogue."

78 Ibid.

79 Ibid., 3.

80 Galois, "The Indian Rights Association," 8.

81 Smith, *Liberalism, Surveillance, and Resistance,* 274*n*49.

82 Hamar Foster, "We Are Not O'Meara's Children: Law, Lawyers, and the First Campaign for Aboriginal Title in British Columbia, 1908–28," in *Let Right Be Done: Aboriginal Title, the Calder Case, and the Future of Indigenous Rights,* ed. Hamar Foster, Heather Raven, and Jeremy Webber (Vancouver: UBC Press, 2007), 264*n*23.

83 "Prayer of Indian Chiefs," from the Nlaka'pamux chiefs to the Superintendent General of Indian Affairs, signed at Spences Bridge, July 21, 1908, RG10, vol. 4038, file 329, 350, Library and Archives Canada (LAC). In their opening statement, these four chiefs explained that they were speaking on behalf of the full group: "We the above-named chiefs ... for ourselves and in behalf of the people of our respective bands (who having heard us in open council are in full consent with us) beg respectfully to bring the following requests before you, and pray that you will grant same as speedily as possible."

84 "Prayer of Indian Chiefs."
85 Ibid.
86 Teit to Duncan Campbell Scott, March 2, 1916, RG10, vol. 7781, file 27150-3-3, LAC.
87 Teit to Boas, March 10, 1904, AMNH.
88 Ibid.
89 Teit to Boas, February 16, 1911, APS.
90 Arthur O'Meara, an Anglican clergyman, was under surveillance by the Pinkerton Dectective Agency. See David Ricardo Williams, *Call in Pinkerton's: American Detectives at Work for Canada* (Toronto: Dundurn, 1998), 198–201.
91 Teit to Scott, March 2, 1916, LAC.
92 Smith, *Liberalism, Surveillance, and Resistance,* 172.
93 Ibid., 234.
94 Teit to Scott, March 2, 1916, LAC.
95 Ibid.
96 Galois, "The Indian Rights Association," 8; Mary Haig-Brown, "Arthur Eugene O'Meara: Servant, Advocate, Seeker of Justice," in *With Good Intentions: Euro-Canadian and Aboriginal Relations in Colonial Canada,* ed. Celia Haig-Brown and David A. Nock (Vancouver: UBC Press, 2006), 258–96; Foster, "We Are Not O'Meara's Children." For more on C.M. Tate, see Ben Clinton-Baker, "Reverend C.M. Tate and the Campaign for 'Indian Rights' in British Columbia, 1909–16" (major research paper, Department of History, University of Victoria, 2012).
97 For a full account of the role of the Royal Proclamation and its place in the Cowichan Petition, see Hamar Foster and Benjamin L. Berger, "From Humble Prayers to Legal Demands: The Cowichan Petition of 1909 and the British Columbia Indian Land Question," in *The Grand Experiment: Law and Legal Culture in British Columbia Settler Societies,* ed. Hamar Foster, Benjamin L. Berger, and A.R. Buck (Vancouver: UBC Press, 2008), 240–67.
98 Harris, *Making Native Space,* 225.
99 Galois, "The Indian Rights Association," 8–9.
100 Ibid.
101 Ibid., 66.
102 Foster, "We Want a Strong Promise," 127.
103 Galois, "The Indian Rights Association," 8.
104 Quoted in Smith, *Liberalism, Surveillance, and Resistance,* 167.
105 Ibid.
106 Ibid.
107 Ibid., 168.
108 Letter written by J.A. Teit on behalf of John Whistemnitsa, Chief of Spences Bridge Band, "and other Indians," April 24, 1909, RG10, vol. 4020, file 280, 470–2, LAC.
109 Smith, *Liberalism, Surveillance, and Resistance,* 167.
110 Galois, "The Indian Rights Association," 8.
111 This segment of of MacInnes's report, dated August 20, 1909, is quoted in Hamar Foster, "A Romance of the Lost: The Role of Tom MacInnes in the History of the British Columbia Indian Land Question," in *Essays in the History of Canadian Law,* vol. 8, *In Honour of R.C.B. Risk,* ed. G. Blaine Baker and Jim Phillips (Toronto: Osgoode Society for Canadian Legal History/University of Toronto Press, 1999), 177.
112 Foster, "A Romance of the Lost," 173.

113 Galois, "The Indian Rights Association," 16.
114 Foster, "We Want a Strong Promise," 129.
115 Galois says the costs were $1,000. See "Indian Rights Association," 9.
116 Galois, "Indian Rights Association," 31.
117 In his personal journal of 1910, Teit mentioned attending chiefs' meetings on January 8, 22, 23, and 30. On February 12, he mentioned a trip to Lytton with some chiefs from Spences Bridge for a meeting of sixteen chiefs on Sunday, Febuary 13. That meeting carried on all night. The following Saturday to Monday, he attended more meetings of chiefs at "Sulus" (a reserve community near Merritt). On February 26, he was in Kamloops for another meeting. He noted on the latter date that "Indian chiefs [were] all favourable." Presumably this refers to his goal to gain the support of the ITBC for the IRA and its efforts to have the land-title issue settled by the British high courts. On his return to Spences Bridge, he spent the first few days of March "writing Indian letters." For a copy of the 1910 journal, see the *Teit Times* 1 (Summer 1995): 6–12.
118 Teit to Boas, February 23, 1910, APS.
119 "Declaration of Interior Tribes," RG10, vol. 7780, file 27150-3-1, LAC. Teit sent a copy of the Indian Declaration with a list of its signatories to J.D. McLean, secretary of the Department of Indian Affairs in Ottawa, on July 27, 1910, with a request that he forward it to "Mr. Oliver," Frank Oliver, the federal Minister of the Interior and Superintendent General of Indian Affairs.
120 Ibid.
121 Teit to Scott, March 2, 1916, RG10, vol. 7781, file 27150-3-3, LAC.
122 According to Teit's 1910 journal, he worked on the Memorial between August 4 and August 6. See *Teit Times,* 1:18. Teit also noted in a letter to Father LeJeune that he had finished drafting the memorial: Teit to LeJeune, August 6, 1910 (copy), University of British Columbia Special Collections (UBCSC). Robert Galois and Keith Carlson provided me with the letter. "Couteau" was another name for Nlaka'pamux.
123 Teit to LeJeune, August 6, 1910, UBCSC.
124 For an excellent profile of LeJeune, see Emma Battell-Lowman, "Mamook Kom'tax Chinuk Pipa/Learning to Write Chinook Jargon: Indigenous Peoples and Literacy Strategies in the South Central Interior of British Columbia in the Late Nineteenth Century," *Historical Studies in Education* 29, 1 (Spring 2017): 77–98.
125 Teit to LeJeune, August 6, 1910, UBCSC.
126 "Memorial to Sir Wilfrid Laurier, Premier of the Dominion of Canada From the Chiefs of the Shuswap, Okanagan and Couteau Tribes of British Columbia," presented at Kamloops, BC, August 25, 1910, NWP 970.5, M533, BC Archives. See also Papers of James A. Teit, T458, Box 1, folder 4, AMNH. In making a link between pre-1858 whites as "real Whites" and post-1850 whites as "other Whites," Teit reiterated what old Pa-ah had told him in 1893: see "Narratives of Old Pa-ah, 1893" in ibid.
127 Newton H. Chittenden, *Travels in British Columbia* (Vancouver: Gordon Soules, 1984; first published in 1882), 43–47.
128 John Thistle, "A Vast Inland Empire and the Last Great West: Remaking Society, Space and Environment in Early British Columbia," *Journal of Historical Geography* 37, 4 (2011): 418–28.
129 Ibid., 426.
130 Teit to LeJeune, August 15, 1910, UBCSC. Teit writes that "Mr. Green" described it as "the best representation of the Indian case (from the Indian point of view) he had heard" and

that "Mr. O'Meara also says it is exceeding [sic] good." See also Teit to LeJeune, November 10, 1910, UBCSC. In this letter, he described the Memorial as "the best of the kind, and several Indians and Whites on the Coast. Tc. are anxious to have copies."

131 The Memorial circulated through communities in the south central Interior in the 1980s. See, for example, Joanne Drake-Terry, *The Lillooet Chronicle: The Theft of Their Lands and Resources* (Lillooet, BC: Lillooet Tribal Council, 1989). See also the doctoral dissertation by Secwépemc scholar Ron Ignace, "Our Histories Are Our Iron Posts: Secwépemc Stories and Historical Consciousness" (PhD diss., Simon Fraser University, 2008). In their new co-authored book *Secwépemc People, Land and Laws* (Montreal/Kingston: McGill-Queen's University Press, 2017), Marianne Ignace and Ron Ignace highlight the Memorial's historical and contemporary significance. As mentioned in note 82 in Chapter 1, Cree playwright Tomson Highway and Nlaka'pamux actor/playwright Kevin Loring have written plays based on the Memorial.

132 Harris, *Making Native Space,* 378*n*50.

133 A copy of the "Declaration of the Tahltan Tribe, 1910," appears in the *Teit Times,* 1:57.

134 Teit to LeJeune, November 10, 1910, UBCSC.

135 Reverend Charles M. Tate noted in his diary on February 13, 1911, that he "left (Vancouver) by the 9am train for Spences Bridge and Merritt. Met with Mr. Teit and some of the Thompson and Nicola Indians at Sp. Br., and arranged for a meeting on Wednesday at 2pm in the Chief's house." Tate also attended meetings at Merritt. By the 15th, he was back at Spences Bridge, where he attended more meetings: "Spent 4hrs at Sp. Br. as the train from the East was one hour late. Had a good meeting with the Indians": Charles M. Tate, Diary, MS 0303, BC Archives.

136 Teit to Boas, February 16, 1911, APS.

137 Alan Morley, *Roar of the Breakers: A Biography of Peter Kelly* (Toronto: Ryerson Press, 1967), 76–77.

138 Roy, "McBride of McKenna-McBride," 64. See also Galois, "The Indian Rights Association."

139 Quoted in Roy, "McBride of McKenna-McBride," 65.

140 Ibid.

141 Ibid. McBride's charges about white agitation are quoted verbatim in "ITBC Memorial Statement to the Honorable Frank Oliver," May 10, 1911, RG10, vol. 7780, file 271 50-3-1, LAC.

142 "ITBC Memorial Statement to the Honorable Frank Oliver," May 10, 1911, LAC.

143 On May 17, 1911, the situation looked more promising than ever as the Laurier government passed an order-in-council indicating its desire to obtain a decision on behalf of the Indians "against a provincial grantee, or license," as soon as a test case "arises in which the main points in difference can be properly or conveniently tried." See Titley, *A Narrow Vision,* 140; Harris, *Making Native Space,* 225, 227; Roy, "McBride of McKenna-McBride," 21.

144 Hamar Foster, "Honouring the Queen's Flag: A Legal and Historical Perspective on the Nisga'a Treaty," *BC Studies* 120 (Winter 1998/99): 21.

145 Borden had the support of the Unionist Party, a pro-conscription coalition of Conservatives and former Liberals.

146 Titley, *A Narrow Vision,* 140. The situation was futher complicated, as Hamar Foster explains, by the failure of the Justice Department to inform the DIA about the order-in-council authorizing legal action until a year after Arthur O'Meara persuaded the dominion Privy Council to enact it, which was after Borden was elected prime minister: Foster, personal communication, August 13, 2018.

147 "Deputation from the Indian Rights Association of British Columbia Upon the Prime Minister of Canada," January 8, 1912, NWp, 970.5, I395d, BC Archives.
148 Ibid.
149 Ibid.
150 Ibid.
151 Ibid.
152 Ibid.
153 Smith, *Liberalism, Surveillance, and Resistance,* 171.
154 "Letter of the Indian Rights Association of British Columbia to the Right Honourable R. Borden, Minister of the Dominion of Canada," drafted at Kamloops, March 15, 1912, and signed by chiefs, NWp, 970.5, I395tr, BC Archives.
155 Quoted in Roy, "McBride of McKenna-McBride," 70.
156 Quoted in ibid.
157 E. Brian Titley, "James Andrew Joseph McKenna," *Dictionary of Canadian Biography,* accessed January 10, 2019, http://www.biographi.ca/en/bio/mckenna_james_andrew_joseph_14E.html.
158 Ibid.
159 Teit to Sapir, August 2, 1912, CMH. In his letter, Teit wrote that "there was a big meeting here which broke up yesterday. Members of the Carrier, Chilcotin, Shuswap, Kootenay, Okanagan, Ntlakyapamuk, Lillooet & Stalo tribes were there to the number of about 450. Also several chiefs from the south coast, and one man each from the Spokane and Coeur d'Alene."
160 By now, DIA had a large dossier on Teit's activities. See, for example, "Stikine Agency, Agent's Diary," RG10, vol. 7780, file 27150-3-1A, LAC. On September 28, Indian Agent Scott Simpson reported from Telegraph Creek that an "Indian" named "Jackson" had collected "as much as $1100.00" from "his friends and others" and handed it "over to James Tait [sic] who told him he was working for the Government and has assured them that he will secure 160 miles square for them as a Game Preserve for their exclusive use from which they can exclude White men."
161 Teit referred to this first meeting with McKenna at a meeting in Ottawa in 1920. "Teit to Senate Committee," Ottawa, June 16, 1920. Teit's copy of this document obtained from Sigurd Teit.
162 For a full account of the McKenna-McBride Royal Commission, see Harris, *Making Native Space;* Roy, "McBride of McKenna-McBride"; Galois, "The Indian Rights Association"; Smith, *Liberalism, Surveillance, and Resistance;* Titley, *A Narrow Vision;* and Paul Tennant, *Aboriginal Peoples and Politics: The Indian Land Question in British Columbia, 1849–1989* (Vancouver: UBC Press, 1989).
163 Quoted in Roy, "McBride of McKenna-McBride," 74–75.
164 Smith, *Liberalism, Surveillance, and Resistance,* 72.
165 Scott Simpson to John D. McLean, March 31, 1913, RG10, vol. 7780, file 27150-3-1A, LAC; see also Simpson to McLean, June 6, 1913, RG10, vol. 7780, file 27150-3-1A, LAC.
166 Simpson to McLean, June 5, 1913, RG10, vol. 7780, file 27150-3-1A, LAC. On July 3, John D. McLean, Assistant Deputy Secretary of Indian Agencies, notified Simpson that he had expressed his concerns to the Commission on Indian Affairs "for such action as they may desire to take therein": McLean to Simpson, July 3, 1913, RG10, vol. 7780, file 27150-3-1A, LAC.
167 Simpson to James McKenna, May 26, 1913, RG10, vol. 11023, file 662, LAC.

168 T.J. Cummiskey to McLean, November 30, 1913, RG10, vol. 7780, file 27150-3-1A, LAC.
169 Hamar Foster, personal communication, August 13, 2018.
170 John B. Thornhill, *British Columbia in the Making* (London: Constable, 1913), 145–46.

Chapter 8: The Indians' Agent

1 Douglas Cole and Ira Chaikin, *An Iron Hand upon the People: The Law against the Potlatch on the Northwest Coast* (Seattle/Vancouver: University of Washington Press/Douglas and McIntyre, 1990), 92; Mark Abley, *Conversations with a Dead Man: The Legacy of Duncan Campbell Scott* (Vancouver: Douglas and McIntyre, 2013), 28.
2 E. Brian Titley, *A Narrow Vision: Duncan Campbell Scott and the Administration of Indian Affairs in Canada* (Vancouver: UBC Press, 1986), 24.
3 Duncan Campbell Scott, "Indian Affairs, 1867–1912," in S. Shortt and A.G. Doughty, eds., *Canada and Its Provinces,* vol, 7, section 4, *The Dominion* (Toronto: Glasgow, Brook and Co., 1914), quoted in Titley, *A Narrow Vision,* 34.
4 Duncan Campbell Scott, "Report of the Superintendent of Indian Education," in *Report of the Department of Indian Affairs for the Year Ended 31 March 1910* (Ottawa: Department of Indian Affairs), 273, quoted in Titley, *A Narrow Vision,* 34.
5 Quoted in Titley, *A Narrow Vision,* 25.
6 Stan Dragland, *Floating Voice: Duncan Campbell Scott and the Literature of Treaty 9* (Concord, ON: House of Anansi, 1994), 257; Titley, *A Narrow Vision,* 28–29.
7 Titley, *A Narrow Vision,* 29; Dragland, *Floating Voice,* 255.
8 Scott's published books include *The Magic House and Other Poems* (London: Methuen, 1893), *Labor and the Angel* (Boston: Copeland and Day, 1898), *Via Borealis* (Toronto: W. Tyrell, 1906), *New World Lyrics and Ballads* (Toronto: Morang, 1906), *In the Village of Viger* (Boston: Copeland and Day, 1896), and *John Graves Simcoe* (Toronto: Morang, 1905).
9 Cole and Chaikin, *An Iron Hand,* 92.
10 Dragland, *Floating Voice,* 258.
11 Titley, *A Narrow Vision,* 28–29.
12 Sandra Gwynn, *The Private Capital: Ambition and Love in the Age of Macdonald and Laurier* (Toronto: McClelland and Stewart, 1984), 437.
13 Abley, *Conversations with a Dead Man,* 174.
14 Titley, *A Narrow Vision,* 37.
15 Ibid. 13.
16 Cole and Chaikin, *An Iron Hand,* 137.
17 Abley, *Conversations with a Dead Man,* 126.
18 Ibid., 40.
19 Lisa Salem-Wiseman, "'Verily, the White Man's Ways Were Best': Duncan Campbell Scott, Native Culture, and Assimilation," *Studies in Canadian Literature* 21, 2 (1996): 120–42.
20 Dragland, *Floating Voice,* 14.
21 For a full account of DIA under Scott's watch, see Titley, *A Narrow Vision.*
22 The ITBC had recently sent Borden a strongly worded letter that stressed the need to settle the title issue *before* embarking on a royal commission. "We claim we have tribal ownership in all the unsurrendered lands of this country": "Statement of Chiefs of the Interior Tribes of BC," ITBC to Robert Borden, May 23, 1913, RG10, vol. 7780, vol. 27150-3-1A, Library and Archives Canada (LAC).

23 Keith D. Smith, *Liberalism, Surveillance, and Resistance: Indigenous Communities in Western Canada, 1877–1927* (Edmonton: Athabasca University Press, 2009), 172.
24 "Indians Come from All Over B.C.," *Inland Sentinel,* March 15, 1912, 1.
25 T.J. Cummiskey to J.D. McLean, November 30, 1912, RG10, vol. 7780, file 27150-3-1A, LAC.
26 Ibid.
27 Ibid.
28 Thomas Deasy to Duncan Campbell Scott, September 11, 1914, RG10, vol. 3822, file 59, 335-2, LAC.
29 Scott Simpson to McLean, May 26, 1913, LAC, RG10, vol. 7760, file 27150-3-1A; Simpson to McLean, May 23, 1913, RG10, vol. 3626, file 5680, LAC; Simpson to McLean, June 5, 1913, RG10, vol. 11023, file 662, LAC.
30 J.F. Callbreath to Simpson, December 23, 1912, GR466, Provincial Game Warden Files, Box 42, File 12, BC Archives.
31 According to legal historian Hamar Foster:

> All lawyers knew that an appeal could be had to the Judicial Committee of the Privy Council (JCPC). Most, however, probably thought that you had to have exhausted your appeals in Canada before you could do so. What O'Meara and Clark pointed out was that one section of this 1833 statute authorized a direct submission of an issue to the Judicial Committee of the Privy Council (JCPC) by the Imperial Privy Council in special circumstances, something lawyers seem either to have forgotten or never knew, because exhausting domestic appeals was the norm. And while it is true that the PC advised the Nisga'a's London solicitors that they would not consider referring their case to the JCPC while the royal commission was ongoing, they did so because Ottawa assured the imperial PC that Indian title was within the mandate of the royal commission. It clearly wasn't. It had been taken off the table in 1912 and bands who tried to raise it were told it was beyond the commission's mandate.

Hamar Foster, personal communication, August 13, 2018.
32 Cole Harris, *Making Native Space: Colonialism, Resistance, and Reserves in British Columbia* (Vancouver: UBC Press, 2003), 249.
33 R.M. Galois, "The Indian Rights Association, Native Protest Activity and the 'Land Question' in British Columbia, 1903–1916," *Native Studies Review* 8, 2 (1992), 20.
34 Harris, *Making Native Space,* 250; Titley, *A Narrow Vision,* 143; Hamar Foster, personal communication, August 31, 2018.
35 Titley, *A Narrow Vision,* 143.
36 The meeting was mentioned in A.M Megraw to McLean, March 6, 1915, RG10, vol. 7780, file 27150-3-1A. A, LAC. The meeting concluded on February 27, 1915, with a letter signed by thirty-eight chiefs, as representatives of the Indian Rights Association of British Columbia (IRA), to the Honorable Dr. Roche, Minister of the Interior, F5, Ins, c2. BC Archives. Copy obtained from Sigurd Teit.
37 IRA to Roche, February 27, 1915. See also Titley, *A Narrow Vision,* 144.
38 Megraw to Scott, February 6, 1915, RG10, vol. 7780, file 27150-3-1A, LAC.
39 Ibid.
40 Megraw to Scott, March 6, 1915, RG10, vol. 7780, file 27150-3-1A, LAC. This was not Megraw's first attack on Teit. A month earlier, he had contacted Scott about "the bad effect

of O'Meara-Teit propaganda which seems to have instilled into many Indians an unreasoning notion that they must negative [negate?] any and all proposals put up to them by the whites for taking over any of their lands, is apparent": Megraw to Scott, February 6, 1915, RG10, vol. 7780, file 27150-3-1A, LAC.

41 H. Graham to Megraw, March 2, 1915, RG10, vol. 7780, file 27150-3-1A, LAC.

42 Father Lambot to J.D. McLean, April 22, 1915, RG10, vol. 7780, file 27150-3-1A, LAC.

43 Cole and Chaikin, *An Iron Hand,* 82.

44 Ibid., 96.

45 Edward Sapir to Scott, March 19, 1914, CMH. In her biography of Sapir, Regna Darnell recounts this story along with Sapir's appeal to have eleven stolen treaty belts returned to the Six Nations reserve. Sapir had learned through Frank Speck, an anthropologist in Philadelphia, that they were part of the George Heye collection at the University of Pennsylvania. Regna Darnell, *Edward Sapir: Linguist, Anthropologist, Humanist* (Berkeley: University of California Press, 1990), 56.

46 Sapir to Franz Boas, February 19, 1915, APS.

47 Sapir to Scott, March 1, 1915, with anthropologists' letters attached, CMH.

48 Teit to Sapir, January 5, 1914, CMH. See also Cole and Chaikin, *An Iron Hand,* 101. For more on this, see Andrew Nurse, "The Ambiguities of Disciplinary Professionalization: The State and Cultural Dynamics of Canadian Inter-War Anthropology," *Scientia Canadiensis* 30, 2 (2007): 37–53.

49 Cole and Chaikin, *An Iron Hand,* 101.

50 Ibid., 101.

51 Ibid., 99. Cole and Chaikin cite several cases of judges issuing suspensions and dismissals between January and May 1915.

52 In a letter to Sapir on February 19, 1915, Teit wrote that he had enclosed a ten-page report on the potlatch (CMH). A twelve-page typed copy of Teit's report (dated February 18, 1915) ended up in the Department of Indian Affairs files, RG10, vol. 3629, file 6244-3, LAC. The latter was probably a typescript copy that Sapir made after receiving Teit's handwritten report.

53 Ibid.

54 For more on this, see Cole and Chaikin, *An Iron Hand,* 102.

55 Cole and Chaikin, *An Iron Hand,* 133–34.

56 John Tetlenitsa (per J.A. Teit) to the Royal Commission on Indian Affairs of B.C., January 27, 1916, RG10, vol. 11023, file 662, LAC.

57 Commission Secretary to Teit, February 1, 1916, RG10, vol. 1285, LAC.

58 McKenna to Scott, February 5, 1916, RG10, vol. 3822, file 59,335-2, LAC.

59 Scott to McKenna, February 10, 1916, RG10, vol. 3822, file 59,335-2, LAC .

60 Scott to Teit, February 11, 1916, RG10, vol. 7781, file 27150-3-3, LAC.

61 Teit to Scott, March 2, 1916, RG10, vol. 7781, file 27150-3-3, LAC.

62 Ibid.

63 For more on this meeting, see Mary Haig-Brown, "Arthur Eugene O'Meara: Servant, Advocate, Seeker of Justice," in *With Good Intentions: Euro-Canadian and Aboriginal Relations in Colonial Canada,* ed. Celia Haig-Brown and David A. Nock (Vancouver: UBC Press, 2006), 279–80.

64 Haig-Brown, "Arthur Eugene O'Meara," 258. See also Hamar Foster, "'We Are Not O'Meara's Children': Law, Lawyers, and the First Campaign for Aboriginal Title in British Columbia, 1908–28," in *Let Right Be Done: Aboriginal Title, the Calder Case, and the Future*

of Indigenous Rights, ed. Hamar Foster, Heather Raven, and Jeremy Webber (Vancouver: UBC Press, 2007), 81.

65 Quoted in Haig-Brown, "Arthur Eugene O'Meara," 280.

66 Scott to McKenna, March 14, 1916, RG10, vol. 3822, file 59, 335-2, LAC.

67 Peter Campbell concludes that Teit truly believed that "the Department of Indian Affairs officials shared his commitment to fair play for native people." There is "little indication," he writes, "that Teit perceived the government officials he worked with as part of the capitalist class he condemned for causing the war and suppressing the working class": Peter Campbell, "'Not as a White Man, Not as a Sojourner': James A. Teit and the Fight for Native Rights in British Columbia, 1884–1922," *Left History* 2 (1994): 47. In my research on Teit's relations with Scott, I found no corroborating evidence for this argument.

68 Teit to John Davidson, February 15, 1916, Add.-MSS 505-F-5, John Davidson Fonds, File 13, City of Vancouver Archives. John Davidson (1878–1970) was a Scottish Canadian botanist who served as BC's Provincial Botanist from 1912 until 1916 and was a professor of botany at UBC from 1916 to 1948. Teit collected specimens for Davidson and also took the latter on several botanizing trips.

69 Scott to McKenna, April 29, 1916, RG10, vol. 3822, file 59,335-2, LAC.

70 Teit to Scott, April 7, 1917, RG10, vol. 7784, file 27150-3-13, pt. 1, LAC.

71 Teit to Boas, June 12, 1916, APS.

72 Galois, "Indian Rights Association," 22. Hamar Foster, who has studied this phase of politics closely, suggests that Clark may have made this decision because he figured that the IRA were never going to get a better offer from Ottawa, "and he wanted the chance to argue the case in court. So he was probably willing to accept the other conditions and perhaps thought he had a good chance of being appointed to argue the case in court." Foster also postulates that Clark by this time was likely frustrated "with O'Meara and some of the chiefs," and decided that either he "wanted his day in court or he wanted out": Hamar Foster, personal communication, August 13, 2018.

73 J.A. Teit, "British Columbia Indian Conference Held at Vancouver, 20th to 23rd June, 1916, Statement Issued by the Committee Appointed By the Conference, 28th June, 1916," NWp, 970.53, B862, BC Archives. For more on Peter Kelly, see Alan Morley, *Roar of the Breakers: A Biography of Peter Kelly* (Toronto: Ryerson Press, 1967).

74 Galois, "Indian Rights Association," 22. The "Nootka," the "Kwakiutl," and the treaty tribes of northeastern BC were not part of this organization. For more on this, see Darcy Mitchell, "The Allied Indian Tribes of British Columbia: A Study in Pressure Group Behaviour" (master's thesis, University of British Columbia, 1977), 38–41.

75 Teit to Scott, July 3, 1916, RG10, vol. 7780, file 27150-3-1B, LAC. Note that Scott was in Vancouver at this time and met with the ATBC at the outset of the conference. Teit had tried to see him, even waiting for him at his Vancouver hotel, but they somehow missed each other. In a note to Sapir, Teit wrote that the Vancouver conference had "ended with the Indian Rights Association coming over to the position of the Interior and Naas [sic] Indians and all making up their minds to work together": Teit to Sapir, July 4, 1916, Teit–Sapir correspondence, 1-A-236M, CMH.

76 Teit to Scott, July 3, 1916, RG10, vol. 7780, file 27150-3-1B, LAC.

77 Ibid.

78 Titley, *A Narrow Vision*, 144–45.

79 Ibid., 146.

80 Teit to Scott, August 11, 1916, RG10, vol. 7780, file 27150-3-1B, LAC.

81 Ibid.

82 Ibid.

83 Teit to Scott, April 6, 1917, RG10, vol. 7784, file 27150-3-13, pt. 1, LAC.

84 Duncan McPhail to Teit, March 22, 1917, RG10, vol. 7784, file 27150-3-13, pt.1, LAC. Teit forwarded McPhail's letter to Scott on April 6, noting that several physicians in the region were of the same view as McPhail. Teit explained that the "resident doctors" paid by DIA were the source of some of these problems because "often [they did] not give the attention to the Indians that the latter require." See Teit to Scott, April 6, 1917, RG10, vol. 7784, file 27150-3-13, pt. 1, LAC.

85 McPhail to Teit, March 22, 1917, LAC.

86 Ibid.

87 Scott to Teit, March 29, 1917, RG10, vol. 7784m, file 27150-3-13, pt. 1, LAC.

88 At the request of the "Chiefs of the Interior Tribes," Teit drafted a written statement, "British Columbia Indian Land Question, Notes for Mr. Brewster," that he and O'Meara presented to Brewster on May 31, 1917. O'Meara then took this document to Ottawa, and on July 5 he presented it to Scott, who immediately circulated an interdepartmental "Memorandum" with a copy of Teit's statement attached. In his memorandum, Scott noted that "Mr. O'Meara stated that Mr. Brewster had informed him that his Government would consider first the question of Indian title in British Columbia before dealing with the report of the Royal Commission on Indian Affairs." Scott, Memorandum, July 5, 1917, RG10, vol. 3821, file 59,335, pt. 4, LAC.

89 Katharine A. McGowan, "'Until We Receive Just Treatment': The Fight against Conscription in the Nass Agency, British Columbia," *BC Studies* 167 (Autumn 2010): 47–70.

90 Scott to E.L. Newcombe, October 1, 1917, quoted in McGowan, "'Until We Receive Just Treatment,'" 57.

91 McGowan, "'Until We Receive Just Treatment,'" 62.

92 See McGowan "'Until We Receive Just Treatment,'" for a full discussion of this.

93 Teit to Sapir, September 12, 1917, CMH.

94 Teit to Sapir, September 29, 1917, CMH.

95 Teit to Scott, April 5, 1917, RG10, vol. 7784, file 27150-3-13, pt. 1, LAC.

96 Ibid.

97 Telegram from "P.R. Kelly, Chairman, J.A. Teit, Secretary," on behalf of the ATBC, to Prime Minister Robert Borden, November 17, 1917, reprinted in *Victoria Daily Colonist,* November 20, 1917.

98 Ibid.

99 "Committee of Allied Tribes Says Men Regard Enforced Service as Enslavement," *Victoria Daily Colonist,* November 20, 1917.

100 "Indians Not Against Conscription Plan," *Victoria Daily Times,* December 11, 1917.

101 J.A. Tait (sic), letter to the editor, *Victoria Daily Times,* December 20, 1917. Peter Campbell alerted me to this exchange. See Peter Campbell, "Not as a White Man, Not as a Sojourner: James A. Teit and the Fight for Native Rights in British Columbia, 1884–1922," *Left History* 2, 2 (Fall 1994): 50–51.

102 J.A. Tait (sic), letter to the editor, *Victoria Daily Times,* December 20, 1917.

103 McGowan, "'Until We Receive Just Treatment,'" 63.

104 Ibid.

105 Scott to Anaham Bob, December 14, 1917, RG10, vol. 6768, file 452-20, pt.1, LAC.

106 Scott to Teit, December 14, 1917, RG10, vol. 6768, file 452-20, pt.1, LAC.
107 Teit to Scott, December 20, 1917, RG10, vol. 6768, file 452-20, pt. 1, LAC.
108 Ibid.
109 McGowan, "'Until We Receive Just Treatment,'" 64–65.
110 See McGowan, "'Until We Receive Just Treatment,'" 65; Scott to Newcombe, November 23, 1917, RG10, vol. 6768, file 452-20, pt. 1, LAC.
111 Scott to W.E. Ditchburn, December 1, 1917, quoted in McGowan, "'Until We Receive Just Treatment,'" 66.
112 McGowan, "'Until We Receive Just Treatment,'" 67–68.
113 Order-in-Council 111 from the Governor General of Canada in Council, January 17, 1918, RG10, vol. 6768, file 452-20, p. 2, LAC.
114 Scott to Teit, January 3, 1918, RG10, vol. 6768, file 452-20, pt. 1, LAC.
115 Teit to Scott, January 12, 1918, RG10, vol. 6768, file 452-20, pt. 2, LAC.
116 Scott to Teit, January 23, 1918, RG10, vol. 6768, file 452-20, pt. 2, LAC.
117 Titley, *A Narrow Vision,* 145.
118 Ibid., 145.
119 Ibid., 141.
120 Teit to Sapir, July 25, 1919, CMH.
121 Peter R. Kelly and J.A. Teit, *Statement of the Allied Indian Tribes of British Columbia for the Government of British Columbia* (Vancouver: Cowan and Brookhouse Printers, 1919), 11.
122 Ibid.
123 Paul Tennant, *Aboriginal Peoples and Politics: The Indian Land Question in British Columbia, 1849–1989* (Vancouver: UBC Press, 1989), 99.
124 Titley, *A Narrow Vision,* 147.
125 Ibid. I am indebted to Hamar Foster for clarifying this for me: personal communication, August 13, 2018.
126 Titley, *A Narrow Vision,* 146–48; Tennant, *Aboriginal Peoples and Politics,* 99.
127 Abley, *Conversations with a Dead Man,* 182–83; Titley, *A Narrow Vision,* 102–9.
128 Teit made two stops on this trip, both of which were intended to raise funds to pay for the Ottawa visit. One was at Spences Bridge and another at Penticton. In the end, he raised $1,500 (equivalent to $18,000 today) in donations.
129 Teit to Boas, August 15, 1919, APS.
130 Ibid.
131 Canada, House of Commons, *Debates,* 13th Parl., 4th Sess., Vol. 1, March 26, 1920, 792–96.
132 Ibid.
133 Ibid.
134 Quoted in Titley, *A Narrow Vision,* 50.
135 Titley, *A Narrow Vision,* 48–49.
136 For an excellent discussion of this, see ibid., 108.
137 Ibid., 49.
138 Canada, House of Commons, *Debates,* 13th Parl., 4th Sess., Vol. 5. June 23, 1920, 4036.
139 Ibid. See also Titley, *A Narrow Vision,* 50.
140 Canada, House of Commons, *Debates,* 13th Parl., 4th Sess., Vol. 5, June 23, 1920, 4036.
141 Ibid.
142 Sapir to Barbeau, June 29, 1920, CMH.

143 Barbeau to Sapir, July 7, 1920; Sapir to Barbeau, July 16, 1920, CMH. Sapir included a transcript of the *Debates* with his letter.
144 Sapir to Barbeau, July 16, 1920, CMH.
145 Sapir to O'Meara, July 13, 1920, CMH.
146 Edward Sapir, "Notes on Canadian Indians as Likely to be Affected by Enfranchisement," a report submitted to Arthur O'Meara, July 13, 1920, CMH.
147 Titley, *A Narrow Vision,* 51.
148 Ibid., 148.
149 Ibid. Historian Peter Campbell argues that by taking this position, Teit was co-opted by Scott. See Campbell, "'Not as a White Man,'" 54. All available evidence, however, suggests that Teit had no choice but to accept Scott's offer, as Scott informed him that this would be the one and only opportunity the chiefs would be given to review the McKenna-McBride report. Teit discusssed this with the chiefs, who insisted that he accept on their behalf.
150 Scott to Sir James Lougheed, October 1, 1920, RG10, vol. 3820, file 59, 355, pt.3, LAC.
151 Teit to Sapir, November 10, 1920, CMH.
152 Ditchburn to Teit, September 20, 1921, RG10, C-11-2, vol. 11302, LAC.
153 Teit to Ditchburn, January 2, 1922, RG10 C-11-2, vol. 11302, LAC.
154 Fred Ball to McLean, January 14, 1922, RG10, vol. 7780, file 27150-3-1B, LAC.
155 Harry Graham to Scott, January 21, 1922, RG10, vol. 7780, file 27150-3-1B, LAC.
156 Scott to Ditchburn, January 25, 1922, RG10, vol. 7780, file 27150-3-1B, LAC; McLean to Teit, March 9, 1922, RG10, vol. 8064, file 901/30-1-14, LAC; and Ditchburn to Scott, February 8, 1922, RG10, vol. 7784, file 27150-3-13, LAC.
157 Ineas George et al. to Scott, December 18, 1920, RG10, vol. 7784, file 27150-3-13, pt. 1, LAC.
158 Teit to Scott, January 27, 1921, RG10, vol. 7784, file 27150-3-13, pt. 1, LAC.
159 Ibid.
160 Foster, "'We Are Not O'Meara's Children,'" 82.
161 Ditchburn to Scott, January 17, 1923, RG10, vol. 7784, file 27150-3-13, pt. 1, LAC.
162 Ibid.
163 Harris, *Making Native Space,* 253.
164 Ibid., 254; Titley, *A Narrow Vision,* 149; see also Hamar Foster, "'We Want a Strong Promise': The Opposition to Indian Treaties in British Columbia, 1850–1990," *Native Studies Review* 18, 1 (2009): 133.
165 Foster, "'We Want a Strong Promise,'" 134.
166 Titley, *A Narrow Vision,* 157.
167 Quoted in Foster, "'We Are Not O'Meara's Children,'" 90.
168 Notes by Sigurd Teit taken at a meeting with Peter Kelly in November 1953. Copy made for Wendy Wickwire.
169 Paull applied to join the BC bar, but his application was denied by the Law Society of British Columbia on grounds that, because he was an Indian, he could not vote, and to be eligible for the BC bar, one had to be able to vote. See Hamar Foster, "Letting Go the Bone: The Idea of Indian Title in British Columbia, 1849–1927," in *Essays in the History of Canadian Law,* vol. 6, *British Columbia and the Yukon,* ed. Hamar Foster and John McLaren (Toronto: University of Toronto Press, 1995), 28–86.
170 John Chilahitsa to Scott, March 10, 1925, RG10, vol. 7780, file 27150-3-1B, LAC.
171 Ibid.
172 Teit to Senate Committee, June 16, 1920, James Teit papers, copy courtesy of Sigurd Teit.

173 Alex D. McIntyre to Charles Stewart, March 28, 1925, RG10, vol. 7780, file 27150-3-1B, LAC.

174 Memo from D.C. Scott's secretary to Stewart, April 3, 1925, RG10, vol. 7780, file 27150-3-1B, LAC.

175 Titley, *A Narrow Vision,* 156.

Chapter 9: NOttawa

1 James Teit, "Water-Beings in Shetlandic Folk-Lore, as Remembered by Shetlanders in British Columbia," *Journal of American Folklore* 31, 120 (1918): 180–201.

2 James Teit to Edward Sapir, November 21, 1911, I-A-236M, Edward Sapir–Teit correspondence, Canadian Museum of History (CMH) Archives.

3 Sapir to Teit, November 27, 1911, CMH. Sapir forwarded Teit's note about the hotel to Harlan Smith, who arranged rooms at Ottawa's Grand Union Hotel: Teit to Harlan Smith, December 11, 1911, CMH.

4 Sapir to Teit, November 27, 1911, CMH.

5 Ignace Jacob to Smith, February 6, 1912, Harlan Smith fonds, B216.f.83, CMH.

6 Tetlanetza sang twenty-seven songs and narrated two speeches; Jacob sang nine songs; and Chief Francois, three songs. Barbeau initially assigned numbers to the songs and speeches (#224 to #264), but he later replaced these with a new system consisting of roman numerals/letters/numbers in order to highlight the songs' territories of origin – for example, "VI.M.1, VI.M.2" for "Thompson" songs; "VI.O.1, VI.O.2" for "Lillooet" songs; and "VI.N.1, VI.N.2" for "Shuswap" songs. On the 1916 Ottawa visit, Tetlanetza added six new songs (VI.M.49–VI.M.54) to Barbeau's cylinder project. Chief Paul David of the "Upper Kutenai tribe, Roosville," joined in on the singing this time, adding two Tona'xa songs (VI.K.1 a&b) to the collection. Barbeau's inventory of 1912 songs appears in a file titled "Thompson River & Fraser River: Songs transcribed," Marius Barbeau fonds, Box (temp.) 287.f.9, CMH. The 1916 songs and notes are part of the James Teit cylinder collection, CMH.

7 "Thompson River Manitous or Snams," Marius Barbeau fonds, Box (temp.) 287.f.14, CMH. See also Marius Barbeau, "Thompson River Songs (miscellaneous)," Marius Barbeau fonds, Box (temp.) 287.f.7, CMH. Sɛnā'm was Teit's spelling of the term that Barbeau transcribed as cnᴇ'ams. For Teit's spelling, see his notes on Tetlanetza's "cradle song" (VI.M. 49 & 50): James Teit cylinder collection, CMH.

8 "Thompson River Manitous or Snams," Marius Barbeau fonds, Box (temp.) 287.f.14, CMH.

9 "Thompson River Songs: Manuscript, Texts," Marius Barbeau fonds, Box (temp.) 287.f.10, CMH.

10 Ignace Jacob in a discussion with Barbeau, Teit, and Tetlanetza about his "Training and Manitou song" (#229 or VI.O.1), "Thompson River Songs: Manuscript, Texts," Marius Barbeau fonds, Box (temp.) 287.f.10, CMH. (Note that Barbeau labelled this file incorrectly – Jacob was from "Lower Lillooet" territory.

11 Tetlanetza in conversation with Teit and Barbeau in "Thompson River Manitous or Snams," Marius Barbeau fonds, Box (temp.) 287.f.14, CMH.

12 "Thompson River: Manitous or Snams," ibid.

13 "Thompson River Songs: Manuscript, Texts," Marius Barbeau fonds, Box (temp.) 287.f.10, CMH. For Barbeau's inventory of these songs, see "Thompson River & Fraser River: Songs transcribed," Marius Barbeau fonds, box 287.f.9, Song #224 (VI.M. 1), CMH.

14 "Thompson River Songs: Manuscript, Texts," Marius Barbeau fonds, Box (temp.) 287.f.10, CMH. In his inventory of songs, Barbeau listed this song as the "Loon Song" #226 (VI.M. 2b), "Thompson River & Fraser River: Songs transcribed," Marius Barbeau Fonds, box 287.f.9, CMH.

15 "Tetlenitsa's Own Dream of Vision Song (interpreted [by] James Teit)," Song #230, a&b (VI.M.4), in "Thompson River Songs: Medicine Songs," Marius Barbeau fonds, Box 287.f.7, CMH.

16 The full transcript of Teit's story appears in a document that Barbeau titled "Manitous or snams of the Ntlakapamux or Thompson River Salish," in "Thompson River: Manitous or Snams," Marius Barbeau fonds, box 287.f.14, CMH.

17 Somantza was Barbeau's transcription. Based on Teit's list of deaths between January 1884 and January 1893, it is likely that she was the young woman he listed as "Ha-zoom-manza" or "Mary Ann."

18 Ibid.

19 Barbeau listed these songs as #236 ("Doctor's song"), #244 ("Medicine song"), #245 ("The shaman song of Terapalst of Nicola"), and #256 ("Medicine song") in "Thompson River Songs (miscellaneous)," Marius Barbeau fonds, box 287.f.7, CMH. After transcribing the songs, he changed the titles of the songs and added new catalogue numbers to his original numbers: to #236 ("Medicine Man's Song)" he added VI.M.7; to #244 ("The Eel Medicine Song") he added VI.M.12; to #245 (Ptarmigan medicine song") he added VI.M.13, and to #256 ("The Lizard Medicine song") he added VI.M. 21: "Thompson River & Fraser River: Songs transcribed," Marius Barbeau fonds, Box (temp.) 287.f.9, CMH. The names of the singers are difficult to decipher as they are Barbeau's transcriptions.

20 Barbeau listed this as song #241 ("Sweat-song") in "Thompson River Songs (miscellaneous)," Marius Barbeau fonds, box 287.f.7, CMH.

21 Ibid. On transcribing this song, Barbeau gave it a new number (VI.M. 10) and a new title, "Sweat-house bathing song," in "Thompson River & Fraser River: Songs transcribed," Marius Barbeau fonds, box 287.f.9, CMH.

22 Barbeau's transcription of Teit's story appears in the file "Thompson River: Manitous or Snams," Marius Barbeau fonds, Box (temp.) 287.f.14, CMH.

23 Ibid.

24 Barbeau catalogued the first of Tetlanetza's two speeches as #258 (VI.M.22), "Formal Funeral address of a chief to his child." He catalogued the second speech as #259 (VI.M.23), "Chief's address to youths undergoing puberty training," in "Thompson River & Fraser River: Songs transcribed," Marius Barbeau fonds, Box (temp.) 287.f.9, CMH.

25 Ignace Jacob to Harlan Smith, February 6, 1912, Harlan Smith Fonds, B216.f83, CMH.

26 On May 4, 11, 12, and 15, the chiefs worked with Frederick Waugh on string games. Barbeau dated his work with Tetlanetza and Teit on land tenure as May 23. In his report of the chiefs' visit, Sapir explained that he had worked with them on "relationship terms." He also noted that the division's physical anthropologist, F.H.S. Knowles, had taken measurements of the chiefs and supplemented these with photographs and plaster casts of their facial features, heads, and shoulders.

27 James Teit, notes on Tetlanetza's "Cradle song" (VI.M. 49 &50), James Teit cylinder collection, CMH.

28 Song #VI.M. 51, "Religious or praying dance song," James Teit cylinder collection, CMH.

29 VI.M.52, "Shaman's song," James Teit cylinder collection, CMH.

30 Teit, "Water-Beings in Shetlandic Folk-Lore."

31 Ibid., 193.
32 Ibid., 194.
33 Ibid., 192–93.
34 Teit to Sapir, April 26, 1918, CMH.
35 Teit to Frances Knowles, May 15, 1918, CMH.
36 Teit noted in a letter to Sapir that he was "enclosing herewith notes to some of the songs sung by Tetlenitsa when in Ottawa. These are three songs I took from him there": Teit to Sapir, July 4, 1916, CMH.
37 Marius Barbeau and Grace Melvin, *The Indian Speaks* (Toronto: Macmillan, 1943), 59–74. Although Barbeau had recorded in his notes on his 1912 song sessions that the Nlaka'pamux chief wrote his name as "Tetlanetza," Barbeau and Melvin spelled it "Tetlaneetsa" in their book. See p. 62.
38 Barbeau and Melvin, preface in *The Indian Speaks,* 8–9.
39 Liner notes, Marius Barbeau, *My Life in Recording Canadian-Indian Folk-Lore,* Folkways Records, Album #FG 3502, 1957.
40 Marius Barbeau, "How the Twin Sisters' Song Saved Tetlenitsa," *Star Weekly Magazine* (Toronto), January 10, 1959, 12, 33.
41 Liner notes, Marius Barbeau, *I Was a Pioneer,* CBC interview, re-released by the National Museum of Man, Ottawa, No. 44, 1982.
42 Laurence Nowry, *Man of Mana: Marius Barbeau, A Biography* (Toronto: New Canada Publications, 1995), 398.
43 The full transcript of Tetlanetza's story is in "Thompson River Songs (miscellaneous)," Marius Barbeau fonds, Box (temp.) 287.f.7, CMH.
44 Tetlaneetaa, "The Mighty Voice," in Marius Barbeau and Grace Melvin, *The Indian Speaks* (Toronto: Macmillan Canada, 1943), 71.
45 Barbeau and Melvin, preface in *The Indian Speaks,* 8.
46 Quoted in Richard Preston, "Reflections on Sapir's Anthropology in Canada," *Canadian Review of Sociology and Anthropology* 17, 4 (1980): 369.
47 Ibid.
48 Teit seems to have had a different understanding of the status of his various reports. In a letter to a Shetland relative on June 21, 1922, he wrote that he had ten outstanding manuscripts, of which three – 1) "Salish Tribes of the United States," 2) "Basketry and Basketry Designs of the Thompson River Indians," and 3) "Folk-Lore Collected in British Columbia From Whites" – were "finished" papers and seven were "partly finished" papers: 1) "The Tahltan and Kaska Indians," 2) "Ethno-Botany of the Thomp. River Indians," 3) "Place-Names of the Thompson River Indians," 4) "Clothing of the Interior Salish Indians," 5) Horse Equipment of the Interior Salish Indians," 6) "Designs in Painting," and 7) "Designs in Beadwork." Teit to E.S.R. Tait, D6/262/12/2, Shetland Archives.
49 Boas to Marie Boas, November 13, 1923, in Ronald P. Rohner, ed., *The Ethnography of Franz Boas: Letters and Diaries of Franz Boas Written on the Northwest Coast from 1886 to 1931* (Chicago: University of Chicago Press, 1969), 277.
50 James A. Teit, *The Middle Columbia Salish,* ed. Franz Boas, University of Washington Publications in Anthropology series, vol. 2, iss. 4 (Seattle: University of Washington Press, 1928): 83–128; H.K. Haeberlin, James Teit, and Helen H. Roberts, under the direction of Franz Boas, *Coiled Basketry in British Columbia and Surrounding Region,* Forty-first Annual Report of the Bureau of American Ethnology, 1919–1924 (Washington, DC: Government Printing Office, 1928): 119–484; James A. Teit, *The Salishan Tribes of the Western Plateaus,*

edited by Franz Boas. Forty-fifth Annual Report of the Bureau of American Ethnology, 1927–1928 (Washington, DC: Government Printing Office, 1930), 23–396; Elsie Viault Steedman, based on field notes by James A. Teit, *Ethnobotany of the Thompson Indians of British Columbia.* Forty-fifth Annual Report of the Bureau of American Ethnology, 1927–28, (Washington, DC: Government Printing Office, 1930), 441–552; James A. Teit, *Tattooing and Face and Body Painting of the Thompson Indians,* edited by Franz Boas. Forty-fifth Annual Report of the Bureau of American Ethnology, 1927–1928 (Washington, DC: Government Printing Office, 1930), 397–439; James A. Teit, "Traditions and Information Regarding the Tona'xa," edited by Franz Boas, *American Anthropologist* 32, 4 (1930): 625–32.

51 Ira Jacknis, "'The Artist Himself': The Salish Basketry Monograph and the Beginnings of a Boasian Paradigm," in *The Early Years of Native American Art History: The Politics of Scholarship and Collecting,* ed. Janet Catherine Berlo (Vancouver/Seattle: UBC Press/University of Washington Press, 1992), 148.

52 Boas neglected to mention that Teit had informed him in 1918 that he had read Ralph Chamberlin's *The Ethno-Botany of the Gosiute Indians of Utah* (Lancaster, PA: New Era Printing, 1911), the definitive work on North American ethnobotany at the time, and he felt that his work had surpassed it: Teit to Boas, July 18, 1918, APS.

53 Josie Teit to Boas, November 9, 1930, APS.

54 Franz Boas, "Foreword," in Teit, *The Middle Columbia Salish,* 85.

55 Franz Boas, "Preface," in Teit, *Salishan Tribes of the Western Plateaus,* 25.

56 Lila M. O'Neale, review of *Coiled Basketry in British Columbia and Surrounding Region,* by Haeberlin, Teit, and Roberts, *American Anthropologist,* n.s., 32 (1930): 306–8.

57 Ibid., 306.

58 Ibid., 307.

59 Ibid., 307–8.

60 Ibid.

61 Boas to Homer Sargent, October 10, 1930, APS.

62 Boas to Sargent, December 22, 1932, APS.

63 Boas to Sargent, February 25, 1931, APS.

Chapter 10: Farewell Coyote, Hello Jack

1 "Speech of Mr. Kelly," to Charles Stewart, Minister of the Interior, and members of the Allied Indian Tribes of BC, Ottawa, July 25, 1923, DIA, RG10, vol. 3820, file 59,335, part 1, Library and Archives Canada (LAC).

2 "Pioneer of Spences Bridge & Benefactor of the Indians," *Merritt Herald,* November 3, 1922, 1; "Leading Authority on Indian Basketry," *Victoria Daily Times,* November 1, 1922, 5; "Obituary," *Western Clarion,* November 16, 1922, 2; "James Teit's Work Given Recognition: A Man of Extraordinary Gifts," *Merritt Herald,* March 9, 1923, 1.

3 Lucian [Snowdon Dunn Scott], "News of the Death of Mr. James A. Teit, Dominion Ethnologist," in "The Week-End," *Vancouver Daily Province,* November 4, 1922, 1.

4 Ibid. Snowdon Dunn Scott cast Edward Sapir, head of the Anthropology Division, Geological Survey of Canada, in a more positive light. "[Teit's] own countryman at last gave him official recognition as an ethnologist and made him a place on the appropriate branch of the geological survey." Sapir and his colleagues "will know that they have lost one of the most useful members of their staff."

5 Ibid.
6 Bessie Lamb, "Origin and Development of Newspapers in Vancouver" (master's thesis, University of British Columbia, 1942).
7 In 1923, the *Merritt Herald* reprinted Snowdon Dunn Scott's 1922 article on Teit under the title "James Teit's Work Given Recognition," March 9, 1923, p. 1. In his introduction to the piece, the *Herald*'s editor described Dunn Scott as "the Dean of newspaper men."
8 Lucian, "News of the Death of Mr. James A. Teit." This was likely the meeting that Teit mentioned in a letter to Sapir: "I have been [in Vancouver] for two weeks at an Indian Conference. Mr. Scott was there part of the time. Afterwards he went north to Port Simpson." Teit to Sapir, July 4, 1916, CMH.
9 Sargent to Boas, November 24, 1922, APS.
10 Ibid.
11 Sargent to Boas, January 23, 1923, APS.
12 Ibid.
13 Sargent to Boas, May 21, 1923, APS.
14 Ibid.
15 Sargent to Boas, November 24, 1922, APS.
16 Franz Boas to Marie Boas, November 13, 1923, APS, in Ronald P. Rohner, ed., *The Ethnography of Franz Boas: Letters and Diaries of Franz Boas Written on the Northwest Coast from 1886 to 1931* (Chicago: University of Chicago Press, 1969), 277.
17 In letters to Boas, Teit had listed the names of the women who participated in his basketry project (see Chapter 5).
18 George W. Stocking Jr., *Race, Culture, and Evolution: Essays in the History of Anthropology* (New York: The Free Press, 1968), 222.
19 Ibid., 194.
20 George W. Stocking Jr., "The Ethnographic Sensibility of the 1920s," in *The Ethnographers' Magic and Other Essays in the History of Anthropology* (Madison: University of Wisconsin Press, 1992), 292; see also Herbert Lewis, "The Individual and Individuality in Franz Boas's Anthropology and Philosophy," in *The Franz Boas Papers,* vol. 1, *Franz Boas as Public Intellectual – Theory, Ethnography, Activism,* ed. Regna Darnell, Michelle Hamilton, Robert L.A. Hancock, and Joshua Smith (Lincoln: University of Nebraska Press, 2015), 19–41; and Regna Darnell, "Mind, Body, and the Native Point of View: Boasian Theory at the Centennial of *The Mind of Primitive Man,*" in Darnell et al., *The Franz Boas Papers,* 1:3–17.
21 Stocking, "The Ethnographic Sensibility of the 1920s," 281–82.
22 Lewis, "The Individual and Individuality," 22.
23 Teit had moved the family in the summer of 1919 to the town of Merritt in the Nicola Valley so his children could attend school. He saw this as a temporary move and therefore held on to his Spences Bridge house, office, and property.
24 There were also long breaks between Boas's 1914 field season and his death in 1942 – for example, a four-year break (1923–27) and an eleven-year break (1931–42). For a list of Boas's field seasons, see Ronald Rohner, "Franz Boas: Ethnographer on the Northwest Coast," in *Pioneers of American Anthropology: The Uses of Biography,* ed. June Helm (Seattle: University of Washington Press, 1966), 153.
25 Quoted in Rohner, "Franz Boas: Ethnographer on the Northwest Coast," 209.
26 Ibid., 210. George Hunt worked for Boas in a similar capacity as Teit. Born at the Hudson's Bay Company post of Fort Rupert on Vancouver Island in 1854, into a mixed-ancestry

family (his father was British from Dorsetshire, England, and his mother was Tlingit from Tongass, Alaska), Hunt gained fluency in both English and Tlingit. Because Fort Rupert was surrounded by Kwakwa̲ka̲'wakw territory, he also learned to speak Kwak'wala. His advanced multilingual skills turned him into a translator early in life. Boas capitalized on this while working with Hunt and a troupe of Kwakwa̲ka̲'wakw performers at the Chicago World's Fair in 1893. Within a year, he struck up a working relationship with Hunt that lasted until the latter's death in 1933. As with Teit, Hunt opened a world of ethnographic insight to Boas that led to multiple journal articles, book chapters, and monographs. For more on this, see Judith Berman, "'The Culture as It Appears to the Indian Himself': Boas, George Hunt, and the Methods of Ethnography," in *Volksgeist as Method and Ethic: Essays on Boasian Ethnography and the German Anthropological Tradition,* ed. George W. Stocking Jr. (Madison: University of Wisconsin Press, 1996), 215–56. See also Ira Jacknis, "The Ethnographic Object and the Object of Ethnology in the Early Career of Franz Boas," in Stocking, *Volksgeist as Method and Ethic,* 185–214.

Despite the similarities between Boas's two British Columbia employees, there were major differences. As anthropologist Margaret Bruchac writes, the "partnership" between Boas and Hunt "crossed ethical boundaries," because Boas, "in a sense, invented Hunt, by enticing him to do [his] bidding without restraint [and] Hunt willingly responded to any request, from stealing icons to excavating graves to dismantling buildings, often knowingly violating cultural protocols to do so." Unlike Teit, Hunt usurped the role of "primary (if not sole) interlocutor of Northwest Coast culture." See Margaret Bruchac, "My Sisters Will Not Speak: Boas, Hunt, and the Ethnographic Silencing of First Nations Women," *Curator, The Museum Journal* 57, 2 (April 2014): 156. Boas also exerted more pressure on Hunt than on Teit. At times, his pressure verged on blackmail. A letter of 1901 was typical. In it, Boas warned Hunt that, should he be "successful in getting good old material from out of the various places where the Indians used to hide it we shall go on collecting; but if we cannot get the material, I shall not be able to get any more money for you": Boas to Hunt, May 1, 1901, quoted in Bruchac, "My Sisters," 165. Even in his most frustrating moments with Teit, Boas never interacted with him in such a manner.

27 George W. Stocking Jr., "Franz Boas and the Culture Concept," in *Race, Culture, and Evolution,* 223.
28 Ibid.
29 George W. Stocking Jr., "The Pattern of Boas' Fieldwork," in *A Franz Boas Reader: The Shaping of American Anthropology, 1883–1911* (New York: Basic Books, 1974), 86.
30 Richard Bauman and Charles Briggs, "The Foundation of All Future Researches: Franz Boas's Cosmopolitan Charter for Anthropology," in *Voices of Modernity: Language Ideologies and the Politics of Inequality* (Cambridge: Cambridge University Press, 2003), 297.
31 Regna Darnell and Judith T. Irvine, eds., "Introduction," in *The Collected Works of Edward Sapir III* (New York: Mouton de Gruyter, 1990), 689.
32 Lucian, "News of the Death of Mr. James A. Teit."
33 "Memorial to the Hon. Frank Oliver, Minister of the Interior, from the Chiefs of the Shuswap, Couteau or Thompson, et al.," May 10, 1911, RG10, vol. 7780, file 27150-3-1, LAC.
34 Teit to Boas, August 15, 1919, APS.
35 Ibid.
36 Pa-ah was one of a group of Nlaka'pamux men, women, and children that Boas measured (with Teit's assistance) in and around Spences Bridge in 1894. He published the list in his

British Association for the Advancement of Science report in 1895. It includes Pa-ah's age. Teit noted the temporal limits of oral memory in his *Tattooing and Face and Body Painting of the Thompson Indians of British Columbia,* 403.

37 Teit to Boas, March 3, 1913, APS.

38 Teit to Boas, August 2, 1902, APS.

39 "Creation of the World by Old-One," in James Teit, *Mythology of the Thompson Indians,* Memoir of the American Museum of Natural History, series vol. 12: JNPE, vol. 8, part 2 (Leiden/New York: E.J. Brill/G.E. Stechert, 1912), 320, http://hdl.handle.net/2246/37.

40 "Old-One and the Earth, Sun, and People," in Teit, *Mythology of the Thompson Indian,* 321.

41 "The Creation of the Earth by Old-One," in Teit, *Mythology of the Thompson Indians,* 322.

42 "Old-One and the Creation of the Nicola Country," in Teit, *Mythology of the Thompson Indians,* 324.

43 Ibid.

44 James Teit, Livingston Farrand, Marian K. Gould, and Herbert J. Spinden, *Folk-Tales of Salishan and Sahaptin Tribes,* ed. Franz Boas, Memoirs of the American Folk-Lore Society 11 (Lancaster, PA/New York: American Folk-Lore Society, 1917), 81.

45 Ibid., 80–84.

46 Wendy Wickwire and Harry Robinson, *Write It on Your Heart: The Epic World of an Okanagan Storyteller* (Vancouver: Talonbooks, 1989), 45–46; see also Wendy Wickwire, "Stories from the Margins: Toward a More Inclusive British Columbia Historiography," *Journal of American Folklore* 118, 470 (Fall 2005): 453–74.

47 Wendy Wickwire and Harry Robinson, *Living by Stories: A Journey of Landscape and Memory* (Vancouver: Talonbooks, 2005), 70–71.

48 For more on this, see Wickwire, "Stories from the Margins."

49 Franz Boas, introduction in James A. Teit, *Traditions of the Thompson River Indians* (Boston: American Folk-Lore Society, 1898), 4.

50 Teit explained this in detail to Boas in a letter: Teit to Boas, December 30, 1913, APS.

51 "Jack and the Church," in James A. Teit, "European Tales from the Upper Thompson Indians," *Journal of American Folk-Lore* 24 (July–September 1916): 315.

52 Ibid.

53 "The Boy and his Grandmother," in James A. Teit, "More Thompson Indian Tales," *Journal of American Folk-Lore* 50 (1937): 184.

54 For biographies of Boas, see the following: Marshall Hyatt, *Franz Boas, Social Activist: The Dynamics of Ethnicity* (New York: Greenwood Press, 1990); Douglas Cole, *Franz Boas: The Early Years, 1858–1906* (Vancouver: Douglas and McIntyre, 1999); and Norman Boas, *Franz Boas, 1858–1942: An Illustrated Biography* (Mystic, CT: Seaport Autographs Press, 2004).

For literature on Boas's research program, see the following: Regna Darnell, *And Along Came Boas: Continuity and Revolution in Americanist Anthropology* (Amsterdam: John Benjamins, 1998); Regna Darnell, *Invisible Genealogies: A History of Americanist Anthropology* (Lincoln: University of Nebraska Press, 2001); Herbert Lewis, "The Misrepresentation of Anthropology and Its Consequences," *American Anthropologist* 103, 2 (1998): 716–31; Regna Darnell, "Historiographic Conundra: The Boasian Elephant in the Middle of Anthropology's Room," in *The Franz Boas Papers,* vol. 1, *Franz Boas as Public Intellectual – Theory, Ethnography, Activism,* ed. Regna Darnell, Michelle Hamilton, Robert L.A. Hancock, and Joshua Smith (Lincoln: University of Nebraska Press, 2015), xi–xxvi; Herbert Lewis, "Boas, Darwin, Science, and Anthropology, *Current Anthropology* 42, 3 (2001): 381–406; Vernon

J. Williams Jr., *Rethinking Race: Franz Boas and his Contemporaries* (Lexington: University of Kentucky Press, 1996); Herbert Lewis, *Defense of Anthropology: An Investigation of the Critique of Anthropology* (New Brunswick, NJ: Transaction Press, 2014); Michel Espagne and Isabelle Kalinowski, eds., *Franz Boas: Le Travail du Regard* (Paris: Armand Colin, 2013); Ludger Müller-Wille, *The Franz Boas Enigma: Inuit, Arctic and the Sciences* (Montreal: Baraka Books, 2014); Ira Jacknis, *The Storage Box of Tradition: Kwakiutl Art, Anthropologists, and Museums, 1881–1981* (Washington, DC: Smithsonian Institution Press, 2002); and William Adams, *The Boasians: Founding Fathers and Mothers of Anthropology* (New York: Hamilton Books, 2016). See also Igor Krupnik and William W. Fitzhugh, eds., *Gateways: Exploring the Legacy of the Jesup North Pacific Expedition, 1897–1902* (Washington, DC: Smithsonian Institution, 2001); Ralph Maud, *The Porcupine Hunter and Other Stories: The Original Tsimshian Texts of Henry Tate* (Vancouver: Talonbooks, 1993); and Laurel Kendall and Igor Krupnik, eds., *Constructing Cultures Then and Now: Celebrating Franz Boas and the Jesup North Pacific Expedition* (Washington, DC: Smithsonian Institute, 2003).

55 In the fall of 1997, the American Museum of Natural History in New York City and the Smithsonian Institution of Washington, DC, co-hosted a large conference to commemorate the centenary of Boas's 1897 Jesup North Pacific Expedition. Boas has also been the focus of numerous sessions at the American Anthropological Association annual meetings. The papers of some of the sessions were published in a special Franz Boas issue of *American Anthropologist*. For an overview of the issue, see Ira Bashkow, Matti Bunzl, Richard Handler, Andrew Orta, and Daniel Rosenblatt, "A New Boasian Anthropology: Theory for the 21st Century," *American Anthropologist* 106, 3 (2004): 433–94.

In 2010, Regna Darnell hosted a large conference at Western University in London, Ontario, to launch a proposal for the Franz Boas Papers Project. The proposal was funded in 2013 by Canada's Social Sciences and Humanities Research Council. In 2011, two academic conferences – one at Yale University and the other at Columbia University – celebrated the centenary of the publication of Boas's *The Mind of Primitive Man*. Aaron Glass and Judith Berman (respectively of the Bard Graduate Centre, New York, and the University of Victoria) recently secured support from the National Endowment of the Humanities for a Franz Boas project titled "The Distributed Text: An Annotated Digital Edition of Franz Boas's Pioneering Ethnography."

56 Paul Radin to Edward Sapir, January 27, 1914, quoted in Richard Preston, "Reflections on Sapir's Anthropology in Canada," *Canadian Review of Sociology and Anthropology* 17, 4 (1980): 369.

57 Ibid.

58 A.L. Kroeber, "Franz Boas: The Man," in *Franz Boas, 1858–1942,* ed. A.L. Kroeber, Ruth Benedict, Murray B. Emeneau, et al. (New York: Kraus Reprint, 1969, orig. 1943), 24.

59 Ibid.

60 Ibid., 22.

61 Ibid.

62 Ibid., 25.

63 Melville Herskovits, review of *The Anthropology of Franz Boas: Essays on the Centennial of His Birth,* edited by Walter R. Goldschmidt, *American Anthropologist* 62, 6 (December 1960): 1063.

64 Ibid.

65 See Leslie White, *The Ethnography and Ethnology of Franz Boas,* Bulletin No. 6 (Austin: Texas Memorial Museum, 1963); and Marvin Harris, *The Rise of Anthropological Theory*

(New York: Thomas Y. Crowell, 1968). See also Murray Wax, "The Limitations of Boas' Anthropology," *American Anthropologist* 58 (1956): 63–74; and John Buettner-Janusch, "Boas and Mason: Particularism versus Generalization," *American Anthropologist* 59 (1957): 318–24.

66 George W. Stocking Jr., "The Basic Assumptions of Boasian Anthropology," in *A Franz Boas Reader: The Shaping of American Anthropology, 1883–1911,* ed. George W. Stocking Jr. (Chicago: University of Chicago Press, 1974), 5. See also Stocking, *Race, Culture, and Evolution,* and Stocking, *Volksgeist as Method and Ethic.*

67 Rohner, *The Ethnography of Franz Boas.* Boasian scholars, Judith Berman and Ira Jackins, added significantly to Rohner in the mid-1990s with their in-depth analyses of Boas's working relationship with Hunt. See, for example, Berman, "The Culture as It Appears to the Indian Himself," in Stocking, ed., *Volksgeist as Method and Ethic,* 215–56; and Ira Jacknis, "The Ethnographic Object and the Object of Ethnology," in Stocking, ed. *Volksgeist as Method and Ethic,* 185–214.

68 Between 1886 and 1900, Boas made eight field trips to the Pacific Northwest. After a fourteen-year gap, he returned to British Columbia for three weeks in August 1914, sixteen days in August 1922, and a month in November–December 1923. He made two final trips: one in 1927 for two months and one in 1930–31 for two and a half months. For details, see Rohner, "Franz Boas: Ethnographer on the Northwest Coast," 149–212.

69 Bauman and Briggs, "The Foundation of All Future Researches," 298. See also James Clifford, "Introduction: Partial Truths," in *Writing Culture: The Poetics and Politics of Ethnography,* ed. James Clifford and George Marcus (Berkeley: University of California Press, 1984); Michel Verdon, "Boas and Holism: A Textual Analysis," *Philosophy of the Social Sciences* 36, 3 (2006): 276–302; and Michel Verdon, "Franz Boas; Cultural History for the Present, or Obsolete Natural History?" *Journal of the Royal Anthropological Institute* 13 (2007): 433–51.

70 Audra Simpson, "Why White People Love Franz Boas; or, The Grammer of Indigenous Dispossession," in *Indigenous Visions: Rediscovering the World of Franz Boas,* ed. Ned Blackhawk and Isaiah Lorado Wilner (New Haven, CT: Yale University Press, 2018), 178.

71 Darnell, "Historiographic Conundra," xx.

72 Lucian, "News of the Death of Mr. James A. Teit."

73 Snowdon Dunn Scott died in Vancouver on December 9, 1923: Bessie Lamb, "Origin and Development of Newspapers in Vancouver."

Acknowledgments

1 Robin Fisher, *Contact and Conflict: Indian-European Relations in British Columbia, 1774–1890* (Vancouver: UBC Press, 1977); Rolf Knight, *Indians at Work: An Informal History of Native Labour in British Columbia, 1858–1930* (Vancouver: New Star Books, 1978); Hugh Brody, *Maps and Dreams: Indians and the British Columbia Frontier* (Vancouver: Douglas and McIntyre, 1981); Douglas Cole, *Captured Heritage: The Scramble for Northwest Coast Artifacts* (Vancouver: Douglas and McIntyre, 1985); George Manuel and Michael Posluns, *Fourth World: An Indian Reality* (Toronto: Collier-Macmillan, 1974). Another book deserves mention for its role in filling an important gap in the history of the Department of Indian Affairs: E. Brian Titley, *A Narrow Vision: Duncan Campbell Scott and the Administration of Indian Affairs in Canada* (Vancouver: UBC Press, 1986).

2 Johannes Fabian, *Time and the Other: How Anthropology Makes Its Object* (New York: Columbia University Press, 1983).

3 Ibid., xi.
4 Ibid., 165.
5 Cole Harris, *The Resettlement of British Columbia: Essays on Colonialism and Geographical Change* (Vancouver: UBC Press, 1997); Jean Barman, *The West beyond the West: A History of British Columbia* (Toronto: University of Toronto Press, 1991); Paul Tennant, *Aboriginal Peoples and Politics: The Indian Land Question in British Columbia, 1849–1989* (Vancouver: UBC Press, 1990); Bridget Moran, *Stoney Creek Woman: The Story of Mary John* (Vancouver: Tillacum Library, 1988).
6 Judy Thompson, *Recording Their Story: James Teit and the Tahltan* (Vancouver/Gatineau/Seattle: Douglas and McIntyre/Canadian Museum of Civilization/University of Washington Press, 2007).

Index

Note: A page number in italics indicates a photograph or map. JT stands for James Teit; FB stands for Franz Boas. Biographical entries are in chronological rather than alphabetical order.

ABOUT THE AUTHOR

WENDY WICKWIRE
is professor emerita in the Department of History at the University of Victoria. Her publications include *Stein: The Way of the River* (with Michael M'Gonigle), which won the Bill Duthie Booksellers' Choice Award at the BC Book Awards; *Nature Power: In the Spirit of an Okanagan Storyteller* (with Harry Robinson), which won the Roderick Haig-Brown Prize for best regional book at the BC Book Awards; *Write It On Your Heart: The Epic World of an Okanagan Storyteller* (with Harry Robinson), which was shortlisted for the Roderick Haig-Brown Prize; and *Living by Stories: A Journey of Landscape and Memory* (with Harry Robinson).

Printed and bound in Canada by Friesens
Set in Garamond by Artegraphica Design Co. Ltd.
Copy editor: Audrey McClellan
Proofreader: Lana Okerlund
Cartographer: Eric Leinberger
Cover designer: George Kirkpatrick